SAN MATEO
A CENTENNIAL HISTORY

"Miss Liberty" in the Fourth of July Parade, 1913
Evelyn Mae Cook, born in San Mateo in 1906

Courtesy Joy and Bob Estupinian

Facts about Beautiful Hayward Park

THIRTY minutes of pleasant, comfortable riding by the Bay Shore Cut-off takes one from the chill and fog of San Francisco to the delightful, balmy, orange-scented warmth of California's most appreciated residence section—San Francisco's most beautiful suburb—Hayward Park.

The city-wearied and business-worried man of affairs finds in this ideal spot the location he has long sought—exactly such a home as he wants.

The trend of the modern home life at its best is toward the suburbs. Every great city has one or more suburban towns made up of the residences of the most desirable class of citizens—men whose love of family and of family life lead them to seek for the wife, the children, themselves, the quiet, beauty and exclusive atmosphere of the semi-country life offered by such a suburb as Hayward Park.

What New Rochelle is to New York, what Evanston is to Chicago, Hayward Park will become to San Francisco, the home town of the class of professional men of refinement and intellect, the center of the most desirable home life about the metropolis of the Pacific Coast.

Hayward Park is a park in fact as well as name. Here nature has lavished her choicest gifts. Sheltered from the high winds and the chill and fog of the ocean, every variety of sub-tropical plant and fruit grows luxuriantly. Scattered picturesquely on every side are ages-old trees and close at hand to the east glisten the sparkling waters of the Bay. Small wonder that Alvinza Hayward selected this as the most ideal spot in California to build his home.

A REAL PARK

It was never intended that all this beauty—all this perfection of climatic advantage—should be enjoyed by one family.

The magnificent estate has been ruled into blocks and lots under the direction of a competent landscape artist. The lots are not stingy little parallelograms, but magnificent, sightly, double lots which provide ample room for a substantial home with plenty of lawn.

A wide private way pierces each block in such a manner that access to each lot from the rear makes deliveries from the front unnecessary. The grading where necessary is done, and the lots are ready for immediate building.

ALL IMPROVEMENTS MADE

Magnificent macadamized roadways—broad and smooth, front every lot—and artificial stone sidewalks in keeping with the attractiveness of the whole plan are provided.

The piping for gas, water and electric wiring are provided before the street is paved. There will be no necessity to destroy the paving and disfigure the streets later on.

In fact every possible precaution has been taken to put and keep Hayward Park upon the highest possible plane.

NO DRAWBACKS

The most desirable class of citizens have bought and are buying the property for homes and investment. Under the restrictions imposed by the owners the property is free from business menace and values cannot be destroyed or injured by unsightly or undesirable dwellings.

Splendid schools and churches are close at hand—the magnificent Peninsula Hotel, not approached in California for charm or for beauty of surroundings, is located in the very heart of the property.

From a pamphlet published by Baldwin & Howell Real Estate, 1907

SAN MATEO
A CENTENNIAL HISTORY

BY MITCHELL P. POSTEL

DIRECTOR,
SAN MATEO COUNTY HISTORICAL ASSOCIATION

SCOTTWALL ASSOCIATES, PUBLISHERS
SAN FRANCISCO
1994

Book design: James Heig and Suzie Kirrane
Cover design: James Heig
Editorial Assistant: Susan Little
Half-tones of photographs: Russ Guard, Guard Litho, San Mateo

First Edition: 5 4 3 2 1
Copyright ©1994 Mitchell Postel

Published in August 1994, for the San Mateo Centennial
Scottwall Associates, Publishers
95 Scott Street
San Francisco, CA 94117
Telephone (415) 861-1956

No part of this book may be reproduced in any form or by any electronic or mechanical means, including information storage and retrieval systems, without permission in writing from the publisher, except by a reviewer, who may quote brief passages.

Printed in the U.S.A.

ISBN 0-942087-08-9

For Kristie and Conrad

TABLE OF CONTENTS

ACKNOWLEDGMENTS	viii
FOREWORD	ix
AUTHOR'S NOTE	xi
CHAPTER I: The Natives and the First Settlers:	
The First San Mateans: 2,000 B.C. - 1793 A. D.	1
Establishment of the Mission Outpost: 1793 - 1822	9
Mexican Independence: Rancho Days, 1822 - 1849	13
Chapter II: A Stagecoach Stop: 1849 - 1865	19
Chapter III: From Whistle Stop to Village: 1865 - 1887	39
Chapter IV: From Village to Town: 1887 - 1920	91
Chapter V: The Town Becomes a City: 1920 - 1941	155
Chapter VI: San Mateo and World War II: 1941 - 1945	217
Chapter VII: Postwar Optimism and the Resulting Boom: 1947 - 1969	229
Chapter VIII: Highs and Lows in the Modern Age: 1968 - 1993	259
List of Sponsors	279
Index	287

Acknowledgments

The author wishes to acknowledge the following people, without whom this history could not have been compiled: Glenn Atkinson, Lawrence Atkinson, Lavina Atkinson, Jane Baker, David Bohannon, Janet Boyer, Gloria Brown, Norm Burke, Fran Comings, Deborah Eid, Mariko Endo, Joy and Bob Estupinian, Ron Fick, William Fowler, Norma Gomez, Carole Groom, Marion Holmes, George Ikuta, Edward Ishimaru, Yasuko Ann Ito, Yaneo Kawakita, Anne LeClair, Linda Liebes, Brian Louie, Claire Mack, John Murray, Richard Nakanishi, Frances Nelson, William Parrott, Ryan Pasag, Kristin Pfeifer, Florence Rhoads, Richard Schram, Mary Ide Secrest, Shizu Tabata, Kenge Takahashi, Arthur Tresser, Barney Tumey, Hasuko Watanuki, and Hugh Wayne.

We were lucky to form a partnership with James Heig, of Scottwall Associates, Publishers, who had earlier published a centennial history of Palo Alto. Without his experience we could never have succeeded in bringing this volume to completion.

Foreword

As the publisher of a dozen books on California history, I have been privileged to work at a good many historical museums, archives, and libraries. The San Mateo County Historical Museum is, I believe, one of the best organized and most complete museums of its kind in the state. Given the scope of its collection—materials having primarily to do with San Mateo County—it fulfills its purpose admirably. Thousands of photographs, pamphlets, books, memorabilia, and historic objects are carefully catalogued and easily accessible, thanks to an able staff.

In choosing photographs and maps for this book, we faced a monumental task. The original plan called for 150 illustrations; we ended up with almost twice that many, simply because the collection was so rich that we couldn't narrow it down any further. Yet for every picture we included, we had to omit at least a dozen others.

In the early days San Mateo was photographed by itinerant photographers who came through town hauling their equipment by horse and buggy; later they came by train, stopping for a day or two to earn a few dollars. Making a picture was no everyday occurrence. Townspeople eagerly turned out, often wearing their work clothes. Sometimes they changed into their Sunday best. Inevitably, two or three small boys—or less often, girls—turned up to be included in the picture.

For formal portraits, marking important occasions, people went to San Francisco to pose in studios with painted backdrops, leaning on ornate pedestals or sitting in uncomfortable chairs. Rich people—and there were some very rich people in San Mateo—could summon a photographer to their estates, to record a family gathering, or just to capture an image of a luxurious room as a proof of success or power.

Probably neither the photographers nor the subjects had any real idea they were becoming a part of history. Like us, they lived in the present, and their pleasure in a photograph was immediate and personal. Yet when we look at these images today they seem quintessentially historic. This is how people dressed, how they combed their hair or wore their whiskers. Here is where they worked, or just stood around, idling their time away. They are far beyond our memory, fixed in time. The pictures seem to make them comprehensible, though this may be our own illusion.

Eventually photographers opened studios in San Mateo, and pictures became a bit more commonplace. Then the Brownie box camera brought photography into the average home. Pictures from the 1920s and 1930s look quite different from older ones, less factual, more subject to revision. Their images are within the living memory of many people. Images from the 1940s and later often do not seem at all historic (consider the picture on page 11, for example). The pictures in the last two chapters look almost like recent newspaper photos (some of them are). Yet they too are historic—or will be, when enough time has passed.

Choosing the pictures for this book has taught me much about San Mateo's landscape and the people who inhabited it. If there is a single, overwhelming impression derivable from the entire array, it is the gradual coming to dominance of the automobile. A comparison of the pictures on pages 112 and 266 brings this change home. The pictures are only fifty years apart in time.

A society, like a person, must reach a certain stage of maturity before it begins to value its own history, and to see the importance of preserving it and learning from it. The San Mateo County Historical Association, itself almost sixty years old, is an absolutely indispensable resource for the community it serves. The Association was founded relatively early (1935); if this had happened twenty years later, after the upheaval of World War II and the ensuing enormous migrations of people, many of the items in the museum would have been lost forever.

Dr. Frank Stanger, historian, teacher, and founder of the San Mateo County Historical Museum, deserves much credit for its excellence. Dr. Stanger's own historical research enriched the museum; he found and translated documents from the Spanish and Mexican eras, collected old maps and drawings, and saved many objects which his contemporaries might have thought worthless. His students wrote monographs about local history, many of them complete with photos. These monographs, written in the 1930s and 1940s, were an invaluable source of information for this book. They illustrate Dr. Stanger's extraordinary foresight; apparently he looked into the future as well as the past.

The museum serves all segments of society. Every day it echoes with the excited voices of schoolchildren who come to see the exhibits and to learn how earlier generations lived and worked. Journalists, historians, architects and city planners, businessmen, students, teachers, or just people who want to research their house, their neighborhood, or their ancestors—all find the information they need. The museum brings nourishment and pleasure to all the people of the county. And it richly deserves their support.

Many members of the Historical Association are retired people who enjoy the rewards of working as docents or volunteers at the museum, enriching their own lives while they perform an invaluable service to the community. Younger members of the Association can learn to appreciate the depth of experience and insight offered by their elders, and to value the connection between the generations.

And people bring things to the museum: treasures from their attic or basement, albums of photographs, old deeds or receipts or documents. A few days before this book went to press, a local couple brought in an old family photograph, somewhat damaged from having been crammed into a trunk for many years. While the picture could hardly be described as being of major historical significance, it somehow concentrates, in the image of one small person, the spirit and the innocence of an age that is quickly passing out of memory. We chose the photograph as the frontispiece for this book.

—James Heig,
Scottwall Associates

Author's Note

To begin with, this is not an "official" history of San Mateo. The words here were not blessed by the city council nor approved by the chamber of commerce. Nevertheless the degree of cooperation from the city government and from the whole community of San Mateo was extraordinary. I found in virtually every quarter a desire to assist with this project.

Two and a half years ago, at a meeting organized by then councilwoman Florence Rhoads, I agreed to write this book. Two years seemed an ample time to research and write the history of San Mateo. The archives of the San Mateo County Historical Association provided almost all of the research material. I spent nights and weekends digging through the books, manuscripts, newspapers, pamphlets, letters, photographs, maps, transcripts, journals, memorabilia and official documents in the museum archives. I also interviewed many people.

In the end I felt I had more questions than answers. I grew up in San Mateo, went through its public schools, from Lakeshore Elementary to College of San Mateo. I've worked for the Historical Association for ten years, I serve on a variety of boards and citizens committees. I'm a good Rotarian. I spent nearly two years immersed in the creation of this book, and still I feel as if I only grazed the surface. I should have liked to spend twice the time, and written more.

In researching material for the last three chapters, from World War II to the present, I discovered that the information available has not yet solidified into history; it is still in a semi-fluid state. During the last five decades the population of San Mateo has more than quadrupled. In terms of human experience this has been the most crucial time in the city's history. Objective assessment of the period is extremely difficult, and is likely to remain so for another twenty or thirty years. I can only hope my work will be a launching pad for future historians, who will more fully interpret this era.

San Mateo's history follows some patterns, but is unique in many ways too. The San Mateo area boasted the largest population of native inhabitants on the San Francisco Peninsula. During the Spanish era, the San Mateo *Asistencia* was crucial to the success of Mission San Francisco de Asis. During Mexican times, while most of the Peninsula was divided into large land grants, the San Mateo outpost became the last home of the mission Indians, who remained here until after California was taken in war by the United States.

During the early American period, San Mateo became a crossroads linking the coastal stagecoach with the railroad. The land around this settlement was controlled by some of the wealthiest families in the West, who created lavish suburban estates. Before the turn of the century a new middle class chose San Mateo as a suburban haven, and eventually the town was incorporated. After two wars, Prohibition, and the Great Depression, San Mateo emerged in the postwar period as a rapidly expanding, progressive city. Many of the issues that most concern San Mateans today come as a result of that rapid expansion.

I apologize in advance for all the names I have left out, for all the important stories still not told. History, and especially local history, is constantly evolving. I urge all readers to take their old photographs, documents and memorabilia to our San Mateo County Historical Association archives, where they can be safely stored and made available to future historians who will more fully explore San Mateo's past.

—Mitchell P. Postel
San Mateo, 1994

India y Yndio de Monterey. Josef Cardero.

CHAPTER I

The Natives and the First Settlers

THE FIRST SAN MATEANS: 2,000 B.C. - 1793 A.D.

On a January day in 1987, a dredging crew off Coyote Point brought up a jumble of human bones that reminded San Mateans how far back the city's human history reaches. At first the crew was not sure whether the bones were old or the result a recent murderous crime. The San Mateo County Coroner's Office was called in, and confirmed them to be ancient. The bones were so numerous that further dredging was suspended for fear that a Native American burial ground had been discovered. However, after scholars went to work on the bones, they found that they all belonged to only one individual, a boy, probably between ten and twelve years of age. Radio carbon dating, conducted at Washington State University, revealed these amazingly well-preserved remains to be 4000 years old.

While most of the native people who inhabited the Peninsula before the coming of the first Europeans preferred to burn their dead, some were buried. This boy may have died in an accident. For thousands of years he lay submerged under twelve feet of bay mud, allowing for one of the best preserved burials of an Ohlone or Coastanoan (the names are used interchangeably) person on record.

The local Native American Heritage Commission contacted Alan Leventhal of San Jose State University and Rosemary Cambra and Norma Sanchez of Ohlone Families Consultant Services to deal with the skeleton properly. After the appropriate studies were finished, the Indian boy was returned to Coyote Point for reburial with all proper ritual and respect. Native representatives thanked the San Mateo County Board of Supervisors for dealing with the matter in a sensitive manner.[1]

Certainly this is not the way people have traditionally treated the natives of our area, who were commonly subjected to scorn and ridicule. The first history of San Mateo County, published in 1878 by the San Francisco firm of Moore and DePue, speaks contemptuously of the natives: "Their complexion was not of the traditional copper color, being much darker; in fact not much lighter than the Africans. The formation of their heads and the contour of their features indicate a very low rank in the intellectual scale."[2]

For ninety years thereafter, local historians abused the memory of the natives. They were supported by the findings of anthropologists, who neatly categorized our natives as "prehistoric" (without written language), "hunter-gatherers" (without agriculture) and "stone-age" (without metallurgy). These labels ignore their wonderful ability to live sensibly within their environment, their creation of a society that cared for the

Opposite: This drawing, made by Josef Cardero, shows the typical dress of the Ohlone or Costanoan people: the woman wears a grass skirt with a deerskin overskirt, a cape made of feathers, and shell necklaces and ear ornaments. She holds a basket, which was probably watertight. Behind her are a huntsman and another woman. Courtesy San Mateo County Historical Museum

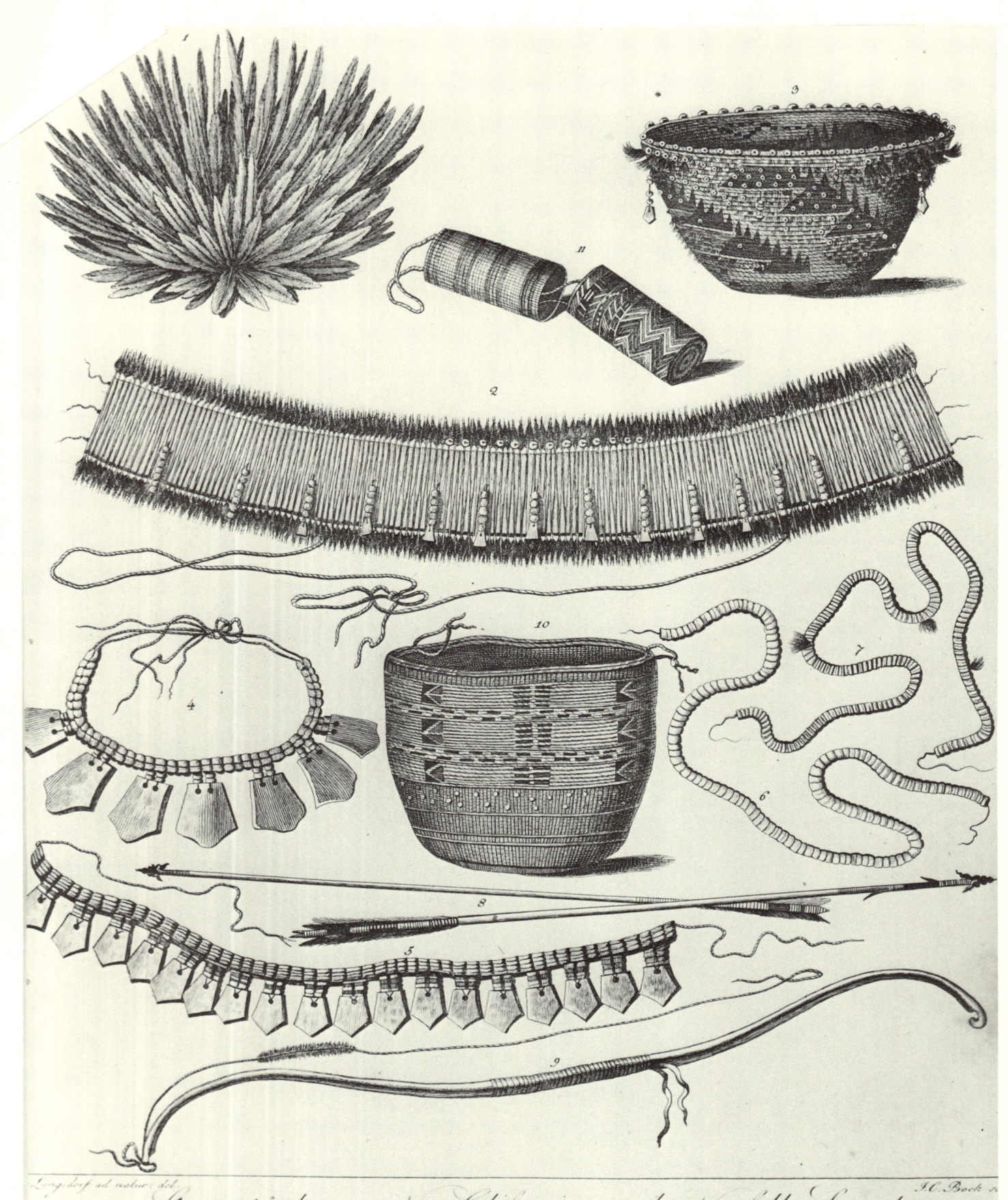

Gegenstände von Neu-Californien und Norfolk-Sound.

sick, old, crippled and orphaned in a most generous manner, and other traits which allowed them to live in what they believed to be a perfect world.

Since the early 1970s, our understanding and respect for these local native peoples have been elevated. We have studied their religious beliefs and now understand something about their great spiritual sense of the world. We have taken fresh consideration of their environment, which had everything to do with their appropriate use of technology. They used the bow and arrow, snares and traps to hunt for a wide range of animals and birds — deer, rabbits, geese, ducks, quail and others. As for the bears in the vicinity, encounters were "probably not planned."[3] The natives had tule boats for fishing salmon and sturgeon. They gathered shellfish, berries, seeds and acorns to complete a rather well-balanced diet. They kept their environment a plentiful one by not taking more than they needed, practicing ritualized birth control, and periodically burning the land to control the brush and encourage grasses. While they were not acclaimed for their technological accomplishments, these local people were great basket makers.

Today, scholars generally refer to the Native Americans of our area as the Costanoans, while their own descendants call themselves Ohlone. In fact, these original residents would not have called themselves by either term. They did not recognize any affiliation with a group of people who lived on lands from Contra Costa County to Monterey and probably numbered about 10,000 individuals. These categories were devised by later people, who tried to classify the natives of California through language and culture into neat "tribes." But the native people of this area belonged to small tribelets, numbering 100 to 250 people. On the San Francisco Peninsula, there were 10 to 12 of these tribelets, living in fixed geographical areas.

The people who lived in the San Mateo area called themselves Salson or Shalshon, the largest of all the Peninsula tribelets, ranging from South San Francisco to Belmont and from the Bay into the hills. Their greatest habitations were situated on both sides of San Mateo Creek. During the period of early Spanish exploration and settlement, the largest village was located behind today's Crystal Springs Dam, but the great shell mounds down closer to the Bay, along the Creek in today's downtown and central San Mateo areas, reveal significant activity there as well. One Salson village existed at Laurel Creek and El Camino Real.

The native people exerted a very light touch on their environment. Except for the shell mounds, we hardly would have known that they lived here for at least 4000 years. The mounds, actually garbage heaps, must have been impressive to early visitors. They could be as high as thirty feet and as wide as a city block or more. They extended from the hills down the Creek and out toward Coyote Point.[4] The greatest and most numerous mounds reached from Third Avenue on the south to Tilton Avenue on the north, and from Arroyo Court on the west to Grant Street on the east.

The Salson's strong presence in the downtown area of today was due to the natural advantages of weather, vegetation and game, and especially to the existence of San Mateo Creek. With the possible exception of San Francisquito Creek at the southern San Mateo County line, this was the largest all-year freshwater creek on the Peninsula's bayside[5]. Before the heavy agricultural developments and damming of the late nineteenth century, the creek was quite formidable, with an abundant supply of very drinkable water. In 1792, English observer George Vancouver stopped to rest at San Mateo Creek. He described the place as "a very pleasant and enchanting lawn, situated amidst a grove of trees at the foot of a small hill [Howard's Mound?], by which flowed a very fine stream of excellent water."

Vancouver also noted that on his entire trip from the San Francisco Mission to the Santa Clara Mission his party did not see "a house, hut or any place of shelter excepting such as the spreading trees presented." By this time the Salson had been taken in at the Mission in San Francisco, where they were converted to Christianity and put to work. How strange for a place like San Mateo, inhabited by natives for 4000 years, suddenly to have no human population at all.

FIRST ENCOUNTERS

THE FIRST EUROPEANS to see the land that comprises present-day San Mateo were members of California's first exploring party, led by Captain Gaspar de Portola in 1769. This group is credited with the discovery of San Francisco Bay from the hills overlooking San Bruno. They then marched down the Crystal Springs valley, eventually camping at "Palo Alto," a tall tree beside San Francisquito creek, and then returned the way they came.

In 1774, the second Spanish expedition to come through the Peninsula also stayed to the west. This time Captain Fernando Rivera and his party were exploring

---

Typical utensils and ornaments of California natives—baskets, intricate feather-trimmed headdresses, shell jewelry—show the extraordinary degree of artistry they achieved. This drawing was made by a German visitor to "New California and Norfolk Sound."

Courtesy San Mateo County Historical Museum

...sula from their newly established Presidio at ...rey. While they skirted the bay line of the ...nsula to avoid the sloughs, they did encounter ...son Indians in the upper valley. Rivera described them as numerous and friendly but dirty and flea-ridden. They went about largely naked, and the men wore beards and mustaches.

A third mission of exploration that brushed past San Mateo without actually setting foot within today's city limits was that of the crew of the *San Carlos*, the first vessel to sail through the Golden Gate in August, 1775. Under Lieutenant Juan Manuel Ayala, the ship anchored off Angel Island for about a month and a half. The crew made various forays to explore the Bay in redwood dugout boats. The South Bay, including San Mateo's bayline, was surveyed by Jaun Bautista Aquirre.

Finally, in 1776, the Spanish marched into today's San Mateo and camped here. By this time, the Spanish had decided that San Francisco should serve as the site of a mission and presidio. Lieutenant Colonel Juan Bautista de Anza had charge of bringing a colony of families to settle the northern tip of the Peninsula. Their party started in Mexico, and by March of 1776 was resting at Monterey. Anza, with Padre Pedro Font, Lieutenant José Joaquin Moraga, eleven soldiers and a pack train carrying supplies, set out in advance of the settlers to establish the sites for the mission and the presidio.

On March 26, 1776, the small band crossed San Francisquito Creek. Continuing north, around today's Redwood City, they stopped at a small village where, according to Padre Font, they met several native men and women. Anza presented them with glass beads, and a conversation of sorts took place. These Indians warned Anza and his party of hostile people to the north. Font elaborated in his diary:

> One of them was wounded in the leg by an arrow, and another stood with his bow and arrows making signs and gestures as if he were fighting, and pointing out the wounds. From this we inferred that he was telling us how they were at war with other villages ahead, and was trying to persuade us not to go there because they were warlike.

Of course Anza and company did proceed, and, according to Font: "about a league before halting, we came to a good-sized village situated on the banks of the Arroyo of San Matheo. It has many laurels and ash trees on its banks..." On the people themselves, Font commented:

> These Indians whom we saw today are very ugly, with ears and noses pierced and little sticks thrust through them, the men all naked and the women with little skirts of grass, but they are not very emaciated. Most of them are bearded and have their hair cut short, although some of them wear it rather long and tied above the head like the Yaquis. They appear to be gentle Indians, and it would seem possible to form of them a good and large mission.[6]

Indeed, Font was taken with this place, not simply because of the people, but because of the natural advantages of the fresh-water creek: "If the water is permanent this site would not be bad for a settlement, for besides a very pretty view which it enjoys, the country is level and has plentiful trees and timber, especially in the Sierra de Pinabetes (redwood), which is near here." Font could not have known it, but the creek was permanent; it drained the Spring Valley catch basin, which would in the next century be dammed to provide water to San Francisco. Font had a good sense of the place and seriously considered San Mateo as the site for another mission.

ANZA, FONT and their companions were the first Europeans to cross San Mateo Creek. Sometime during the event, Font gave the creek its name. The party moved on about half a league and camped northwest of San Mateo in today's Burlingame, at about Burlingame Avenue and El Camino Real.[7]

The next day they pushed north, eventually exploring the northern reaches of the Peninsula and marking the sites for the mission and presidio. On March 29, Anza decided to begin his return trip. He sent the bulk of his party with the pack train back to "Arroyo San Matheo" the way it had come, roughly following today's El Camino Real. Meanwhile, with Padre Font and five soldiers, he commenced further explorations. They looked for sources of wood at San Bruno Mountain, and then proceeded south along the San Andreas Valley, where Portola and Rivera had preceded him.

At about the vicinity of today's Crystal Springs Dam, Padre Font recorded: "there came out on our road a very large bear." The priest was considerably impressed with this beast. He knew that there were many grizzly bears in this section of California and that they "often attack and do damage to the Indians." He had seen for himself "many horrible examples" of wounds inflicted on the native peoples. With this particular bear, Font had a close encounter he might have done without:

> When I saw him so close and that he was looking at us in suspense I feared some disaster. But Corporal Robles fired a shot at him with aim so true that he hit him in the neck. The bear now hurled himself down the slope, crossed the Arroyo, and hid in the brush, but he was so badly wounded that after going a short distance he fell

This superb photograph, made as part of a government survey in 1865, shows San Mateo Creek as it looked before the white man's touch changed it forever.

Courtesy San Mateo County Historical Museum

dead... The commander took the hide to give as a present to the Viceroy. The bear was so old that his eye teeth were badly decayed and he lacked one tooth, but he was very fat, although his flesh smelled much like a skunk or like musk. I measured this animal and he proved to be nine spans long and four high [making the bear about seven feet long]. He was horribly fierce, large and fat, and very tough! Several bullets which they fired at him when he fled they found between his hide and his flesh, and the ball which entered his throat they found in his neck between the hide and the muscle with a little piece of bone stuck to it.[8]

Even Anza was impressed with the killing of the "monstrous bear." His journal reports that its "very fat flesh was taken advantage of by those who like it."[9]

At the appointed place at Arroyo San Matheo they met the pack train and camped. Anza wrote that he found nearly all the men of the native village "very friendly, content, and joyful, putting themselves out to serve us in every way."

Thus with the Anza expedition, we see the first European contact with the San Mateo area. We know not why Padre Font gave the creek the name San Matheo, after Saint Matthew. (The feast day for Saint Matthew is September 21; the party crossed the creek on March 26.) By 1849, the word had been altered to "San Mateo." Another geographically prominent feature of the area, Coyote Point, was for many years referred to as Point San Matheo or San Mateo. About 1890 it was given the name Coyote Point, once again for unknown reasons. It is suspected that the word coyote was used for islands in marshes during the 19th century, and that the knoll at the Point, as far back as 1850, had been referred to as Big Coyote, Coyote Hill or Coyote Knoll.[10]

A Christian People

THE COLONIZATION of the San Francisco Peninsula by the Spanish began on June 17, 1776. Setting out from Monterey on that day was a party commanded by Lieutenant Jose Moraga, consisting of three non-commissioned officers, about a dozen soldiers, their families, servants, muleteers, *vaqueros*, 200 head of cattle supplied by the king and other animals belonging to individuals. Fathers Francisco Palou and Pedro Cambon, two servants, three neophytes and 86 head of cattle went along with the special purpose of founding the mission. Along the way these pioneers noted the great fascination that the Indians had for the cattle, new creatures to a people still believing in animal gods.

The party made camp at San Mateo Creek on June 24. Because one of the soldiers was ill, and because Moraga wanted to be certain that there was plentiful fresh water at San Francisco, he remained with the main party at San Mateo for three days. On the morning of June 26, at half past six o'clock, they set out for their northern destination. By half past seven that night they arrived at the site of the mission at Dolores Creek and made camp. They immediately began work on the creation of Mission San Francisco de Asis and the San Francisco Presidio.

The native people who lived at the tip of the Peninsula were called Awastos by the Salson, meaning northerners. Wars had been waged before between the two peoples, and now that it appeared that the Awastos might have a powerful new ally in the Spanish, the Salsons may have felt threatened. The Awastos made frequent visits to the Spanish mission, and according to Padre Palou "... were apparently pleased with our arrival, although, through lack of interpreters and our ignorance of their language, we could not tell them the purpose of our coming."[11]

Then on August 12, some 40 Salson warriors appeared on the scene. They explained to the Spanish their intentions to revenge the wounding of one of their men, and fell upon the Awastos at their village. Palou tells us that the Salson burned the place:

> [They] had a fight in which there were many wounded and dead on both sides. Apparently the Indians of this vicinity were defeated and so fearful were they of the others that they made tule rafts and all moved to the shore opposite the presidio, or to the mountains on the east side of the bay. We were unable to restrain them, even though we let them know by signs that they should have no fear, as the soldiers would defend them.

After some time, the Spanish renewed contact with the Awastos, and on June 24, 1777, the first baptism of a native took place at the San Francisco Mission.

Slowly the Salson were also brought in to the Mission. Altogether the fathers listed 135 baptisms of Salson people, but there may have been more who were incorrectly identified. The largest groups became neophytes (newly converted Christians) in 1780 when a San Mateo chief was taken in, and again in 1786 when a second chief joined the flock.

By 1793 virtually all of the Indians who lived on the Peninsula had been Christianized. The San Francisco mission began making converts among the East Bay and Marin peoples by 1800, and the Peninsula souls were at this point referred to as the "Old Christians."[12] Sadly, less than half of the original Peninsula native people still survived by that time, the rest having been taken by deadly diseases (small pox, whooping cough, venereal diseases, influenza and mumps) and the demoralizing aspects of their new mission existence.

Not all of the Salson accepted their fate under the Spanish. One of the earliest converts, an eighteen-year-old named Charquin, who was baptized in 1779, became the leader of a runaway band which raided the flocks and fields of the newcomers until his capture in 1794. Charquin (or Francisco — his Christian name) was exiled to San Diego, but Spanish records are unclear about his actual fate.

Notes

[1] Steve Selby, "Ancient Bones of Indian Bay Tell a Tale," *The Times*, February 6, 1988.
[2] *Moore and De Pue's Illustrated History of San Mateo County*, San Francisco, 1878. p. 8.
[3] Alan K. Brown "Indians of San Mateo County," *La Peninsula* Vol. XVII Winter 1973-74, No. 4.
[4] Jerome Hamilton, "Indian Shell Mounds of San Mateo Creek and Vicinity," 1936. Map and Research in collection of San Mateo County Historical Museum.
[5] *History of San Mateo County, California*. B. F. Alley, Publisher, San Francisco, 1883 p. 89.
[6] Herbert Eugene Bolton, *Anza's California Expeditions*, University of California Press, Berkeley, 1930, Vol. IV, p. 329.
[7] Frank Stanger, *Peninsula Community Book*, A. H Cawston, Publisher, San Mateo, 1946, p. 17.
[8] Bolton, *Anza's*, vol. 1, p. 396.
[9] Ibid. vol. III, p. 129.
[10] Alan K. Brown, *Place Names of San Mateo County*, San Mateo County Historical Association, 1975, pp. 23 and 84.
[11] Bolton, *Anza's*, vol. III, p. 402.
[12] Brown, "Indians."

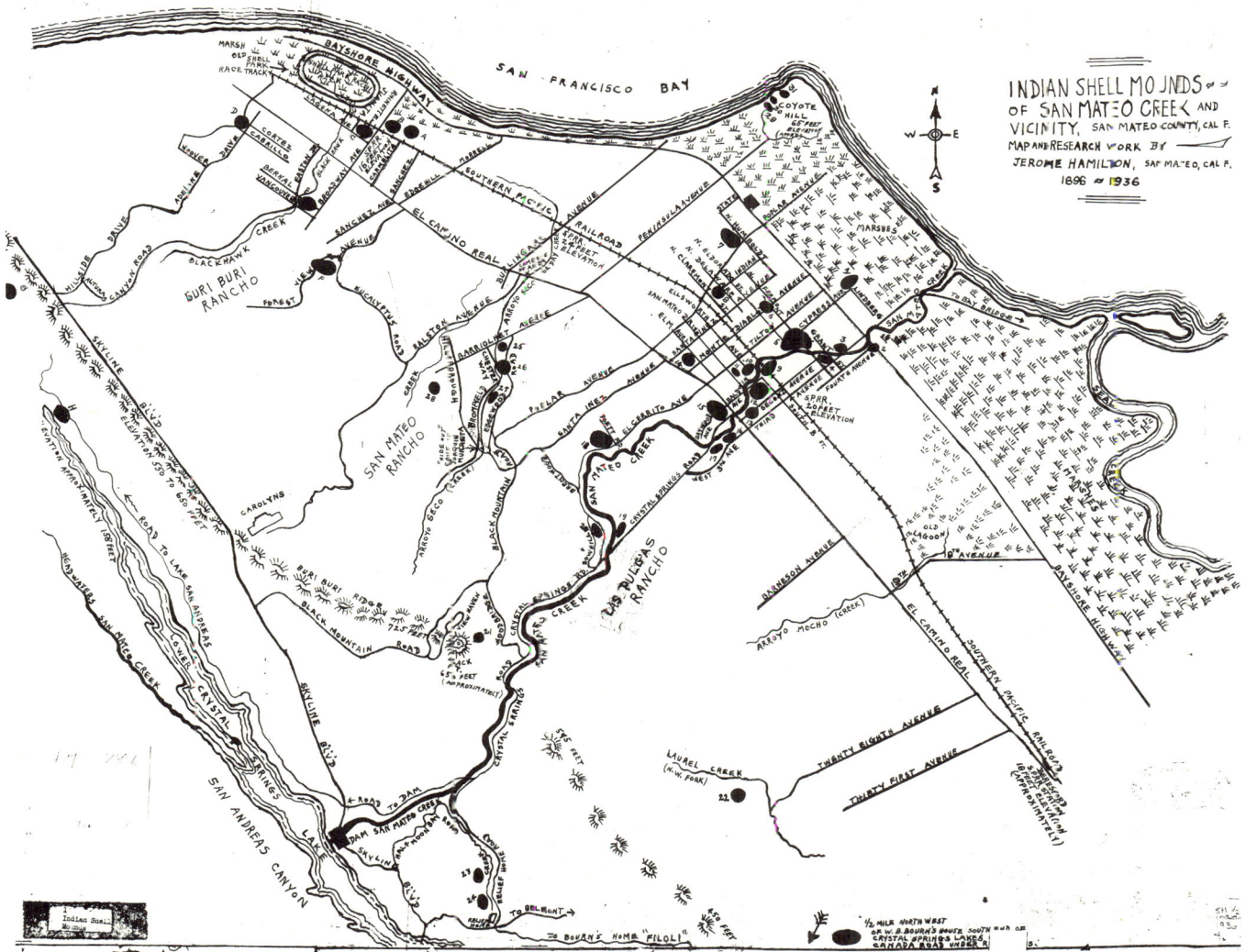

This map of shell mounds in San Mateo, drawn by Jerome Hamilton in 1936, was the first object to be accepted by the San Mateo County Historical Museum. The original is very large, which makes reproduction here somewhat less than satisfactory. The map shows the locations of middens or mounds built up by Native Americans over some 3,000 years, containing shells, bones, human remains, and other waste materials, all biodegradable.

William H. Dougal, who visited San Mateo in 1850, drew this view of the tile-roofed adobe building by the creek, titling his drawing "Mission San Mateo: Old Granary." The building has six doors, opening from interior rooms, all originally used to store grain and wool produced on the adjacent fields in support of Mission San Francisco de Asis [Mission Dolores]. At left is part of a second building, ruined by earthquake, rain and neglect. The structures were forty years old when Dougal saw them, and were being used by Nicolas de Peyster as an inn and saloon for travelers along El Camino Real.

Courtesy San Mateo County Historical Museum

Establishment of the Mission Outpost, 1793-1822

THE MISSION AND PRESIDIO were placed at the tip of the San Francisco Peninsula for strategic purposes: Spain's control of San Francisco Bay depended upon her absolute command of the Golden Gate. However, for most other reasons this was a terrible place to create a mission community. There was very little wood. Good, fresh water was in short supply. There was not much grazing land. The soil and the climate of the San Francisco area were inadequate for the type of farming necessary to keep the growing mission fed. Finally, most of the "heathen" were down the Peninsula, where environmental conditions were much better.

It was not uncommon among the missions of California to establish agricultural outposts, called *asistencias*, in order to grow enough food for survival. No mission was more dependent on such appendages than Mission San Francisco de Asis. As early as 1785, an outpost was under construction in the San Pedro Valley (today's Pacifica). It proved highly successful for a few years, but it was abandoned in the early 1790s, possibly because of an epidemic among the neophytes.

About 1793, the mission fathers established an outpost on the bayside of the Peninsula at San Mateo Creek. Its purpose was threefold. First, the rites of the Church would be practiced there. Second, it would function as a base of operations for neophytes tending herds of sheep and cattle in the area. Third, it would provide storage for wool and other agricultural products gathered in the vicinity.

The date 1793 can only be approximate, because no building was mentioned when George Vancouver stopped at the creek in November 1792 on his trip from San Francisco to Santa Clara. But mission records tell us a granary, 147 x 22 feet, with a tiled roof, was built at San Mateo in 1794, joining a structure already present.[1]

The *asistencia* (or hospice, as local historians have called it) was constructed near the Moraga campsite of the summer of 1776, in the spot which Padre Font had mentioned as showing potential for the creation of a mission. Mission records describe the first building at San Mateo as substantial, with a tile roof. It was a three-room structure, about 20 x 75 feet.

The primary activity at San Mateo in the early years was sheep raising. The herd grew quickly, and eventually numbered about 10,000 head. Just two padres directed the activities at the outpost. Christianized Indians, some Salson but including people from many tribelets of the Bay region, directed by the San Francisco Mission, did the work. They were taught how to make adobe bricks and build walls, to burn tiles for roofing, to become herdsmen and butchers, to plow and plant seed, to harvest with a sickle and thresh grain, to cure hides and render tallow, to make candles, to cook the new foodstuffs, to spin, to weave and to do other types of chores necessary to keep their outpost going, while providing important surpluses for use at San Francisco.

While disease was a problem at San Mateo, it never decimated the population, as it had at San Pedro, probably because the padres kept far fewer Indians here. Nevertheless, the thirty or so neophytes were very productive. Their bayside yields far surpassed those of the previous coastside settlement, and the asistencia became a reliable center for food production, making the success of the larger community to the north possible.[2] By 1798 the sheep herding operations were augmented by the cultivation of 175 acres of grain, probably situated on bottom land on the north side of the creek.[3]

Between 1808 and 1810 an earthquake destroyed the original hospice building, and a new, larger one, 36 x 113 feet, was constructed to replace it. The new adobe sat on the north side of the creek, at the intersection of present day El Camino Real and Baywood and Baldwin Avenues.[4] While another earthquake, this one in 1868, destroyed this adobe, its appearance was preserved in a detailed sketch drawn by an engineer, William H. Dougal, in July of 1850. The drawing reveals that as late as 1850 the ruins of the original 1793 building still stood adjacent to the newer structure. This second adobe was probably constructed in compartments and had a hip roof, not common among Spanish colonial structures of the time, making an attic possible.

SPANISH RECORDS indicate that the building had seven exterior doors and several rooms. One room probably served as a chapel, while the others provided dwelling space and storage areas for grain, wool and other agricultural products.

In the years immediately following the completion of this building, the outpost experienced peak production. The 1812 cultivation was probably the greatest, with 11,098 bushels of grain, lentils, peas and other crops harvested. At that time the herdsmen of the outpost cared for 10,000 head of sheep (still the predominant activity) while more than 10,000 head of cattle roamed in the surrounding area as well.[5]

During these bucolic days, the missionaries controlled the San Mateo area without much interference from the government or the army. Perhaps the fathers were aware of Kodiak and Aleut Indians brought from Alaska by Russian agents around 1810 to trap otter around Coyote and Little Coyote Point, but no record of any confrontation exists.

A noteworthy incident occurred in 1815, when a goodly amount of the produce gathered at San Mateo was shipped to San Francisco by boat. Mission records

This photograph shows a diorama, built for the San Mateo County Historical Museum by Cal N. Peters, of the adobe buildings at San Mateo Creek. The granary, the ruin, and the figures are based on Dougal's drawing, as well as historical records. A cart [carreta] is loaded with grain and wool for transport to San Francisco.

Courtesy San Mateo County Historical Museum

tell us a launch from the San Mateo hospice capsized at Mission Rock, and four San Mateo Indians drowned.

Even as Mexico was achieving its independence from Spain, life went on pretty much as usual at San Mateo. The writings of the fathers and official mission documents tell us that in 1822 at least two buildings existed at San Mateo, serving as granaries. At the end of the decade almost thirty Indians were still working here with the help of many more from the mission during harvest and shearing times.

NOTES

[1] Frank M. Stanger, "Hospice or Mission San Mateo," *California Historical Society Quarterly*, Vol. 23, No. 3, September, 1944.
[2] Alan Hynding, *From Frontier to Suburb: The Story of the San Mateo Peninsula*, Star Publications, 1982, p. 22.
[3] Brown, "Indians"
[4] Stanger, "Hospice"
[5] Frank M. Stanger, *South From San Francisco*, San Mateo County Historical Association, 1963, p. 24.

On February 12, 1946, the Daughters of the American Revolution placed a memorial marker on the site of the San Mateo adobe. Observing the occasion are (left to right) Councilman Carol Speers, Father Leonard W. Bose of St. Catherine's Catholic Church, Reverend John Krumm of St. Matthews Episcopal Church, Mrs. Glen Stern, Frank Stanger, founder of the San Mateo County Historical Association, Mrs. Lindley Miller, Mary Eleanor Peters, Mrs. Norman Waggoner, and Mrs. Charles Sherwood. The marker stands today in a garden, northwest of the intersection of El Camino Real and Baywood.

Courtesy San Mateo County Historical Museum

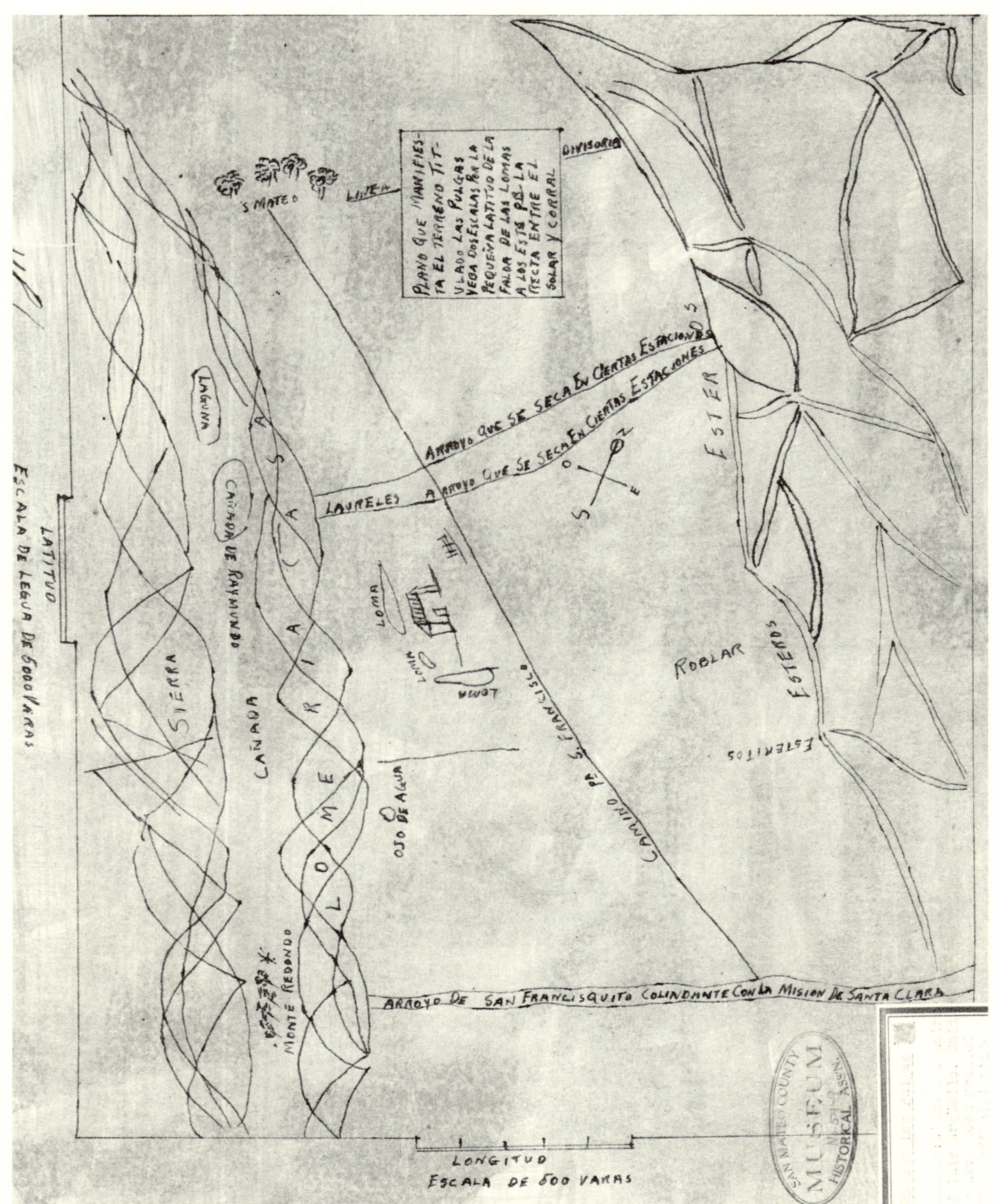

Mexican Independence: Rancho Days, 1822-1849

Revolution by the Mexican people against the Spanish crown had been going on since 1810, when in 1822 word finally reached California of Mexico's independence. California would now be a part of a new nation, but for the people at the mission outpost at San Mateo Creek, change would be very slow in coming.

For Californians the greatest reform brought by the revolution was the secularization of the missions. The state planned to take the vast lands owned by the church and distribute them to the people. The process by which this was conducted was sluggish, indeed.

For the Native Californians, secularization was supposed to bring release from the control of the priests and the eventual management of their own affairs. In the interim period the state would appoint administrators to help them organize their lives. However, not until 1834, under governor José Figueroa, was the process of secularization actually started.[1] In the meantime the fortunes of the poor Indians of California sank even lower. Support for the missions was cut drastically after 1822. At the same time, the Mexican constitution, throwing off the restrictions of the old Spanish colonial system, allowed for free trade. Suddenly merchants from around the world (and particularly the east coast of the United States) were interested in trading manufactured goods for California products such as hides and tallow, by-products of the huge cattle operations of the old mission system. The new business enterprises generated a land hunger among former Spanish soldiers, government officials and other pioneers. Instead of parceling out small tracts of land to all Californians, including the Indians, the governors following Figueroa (he died in office in the fall of 1835) doled out huge grants to political allies and other friends. Most of the former mission Indians simply went along with the land—becoming laborers in a kind of feudal system. Yet the Indian community at San Mateo Creek remained intact deep into this "rancho period" of California History. Almost until the end of the Mexican control of California the governors felt these natives, as former wards of the church and now wards of the state might have legal claim to the land occupied by the old outpost.

At the time of Mexican Independence there were about 30 native Californians at San Mateo. Of these it is hard to determine how many were of the Salson tribelet. Mission records indicate that 26 of the original neophytes from the San Mateo area were still alive in 1822, but they probably were widely dispersed up and down the Peninsula.

One of the head men at San Mateo during the Mexican period was Evencio Yocalo (who used both his native and Christian names). He had been baptized back in the 1790s, and was known to be son of Hesmon (or the Sun) of the Wirostes tribelet of the Skyline area. He built a tile-roofed house northwest of the outpost near Robler and Santa Inez in today's Hillsborough.[2]

It may well have been the home of Evencio that English observer Captain Fredrick W. Beechey described in 1826. Beechey was on a horseback trip, riding from San Francisco to Monterey. He was much impressed by the countryside. As they approached the San Mateo area he wrote of "a wide country of meadow land, with clusters of fine oak free from underwood." He paid the greatest complement in stating: "It strongly resembles a nobleman's park; herds of cattle and horses were grazing upon the rich pasture, and numerous fallow-deer, startled at the approach of strangers, bounded off to seek protection among the hills." However, the positive judgments ceased when detailing the human occupants of the place:

> Instead of a noble mansion in character with so fine a country, the party arrived at a miserable mud dwelling, before the door of which a number of half-naked Indians were basking in the sun. Several dead geese, deprived of their entrails, were fixed upon pegs around a large pole for the purpose of decoying the living game into snares which were placed for them in favorable situations. Heaps of bones also of various animals were lying about the place, and sadly disgraced the park-like scenery around. This spot is named San Matheo, and belongs to the mission of San Francisco.[3]

Indeed, after thirty years of occupation by the Spanish and Mexican regimes, little change could be discerned in the landscape. When observer Otto von Kotzebue, a Russian naval captain of German descent, visited in 1824, he never so much as caught a glimpse of human habitation. Von Kotzebue and his party were exploring the Bay by boat when they decided to land "on a pleasant little island" and have lunch. The island, of

Opposite: In 1835 Governor José Castro granted Rancho de las Pulgas (Ranch of the Fleas) to the Argüello family. This map, or deseño, *drawn in support of the family's request, shows Camino para San Francisco (El Camino) from San Francisquito to San Mateo, crossing two arroyos "which are dry in certain places," a house near three hills, a spring* (ojo de agua), *many esteros near the bay, oaks* (roblar), *laurels, a range of hills* (lomeria) *to the west, two lakes in the Cañada de Raymundo, and the mountain range* (sierra) *beyond. This deseño is unusually precise, including scales of longitude and latitude.*

Courtesy San Mateo County Historical Museum

Dona Maria de la Soledad Ortega de Argüello, widow of Luis Argüello

Courtesy San Mateo Historical Museum

course, was Coyote Point. They had a fire "... in the open air in beautiful weather, under the shade of spreading oaks." While the sailors rested, the officers explored the place:

> Its northern shore was tolerably high, and rose almost perpendicularly from the sea. Its soil consists under the upper mound of a variegated slate; probably the foot of man had never before trodden it.

Somehow from his position at Coyote Point, von Kotzebue could not see any of the buildings or activities at the outpost, for certainly he would have mentioned them, as he did describe the Mission at San Francisco and other such man-made features as they appeared.[4]

Also in 1824, the American author of travel books, Alfred Robinson, visited the outpost and found it "unoccupied." However, upon his visiting again the next year he recorded "the building occupied by the majordomo and the servants." This structure was probably the main building on El Camino Real, because Robinson described it as "spacious and covered with burnt tile."

Secularization

As SECULARIZATION loomed closer, Mexican military officers at the presidio cast their eyes down the Peninsula for possibly increasing the military's control of lands for its food reserves in the area. In 1834 Commandant José de Haro petitioned the government, asking for the mission properties at both the San Pedro and San Mateo outposts. The missionaries were able to fend off this request, but private individuals were beginning to obtain grants.

In 1835 José Sanchez received title to his rancho Buri Buri, which roughly included today's northern Burlingame, Millbrae, San Bruno, South San Francisco and a portion of San Bruno Mountain. The next year his son, José de la Cruz Sanchez, petitioned for Rancho San Mateo, or the area occupied by the Indians of the old outpost. While this request was not honored, the Sanchez clan kept a close watch on the San Mateo property, hoping to obtain it for the family some day.

Across San Mateo Creek another prominent family, the Argüellos, were more successful in acquiring properties in what we would call San Mateo today. The Argüello family had, in fact, claimed that as far back as 1795, Spanish Governor Diego Borcia had awarded his San Francisco Presidio Commandante, José Argüello, some 69,000 acres of the Peninsula south of Buri Buri (Buri Buri in those days was a rancho in the possession of the army). This was a verbal commitment, and José died without ever securing what would have been a rare Spanish land grant (even though he himself had served as one of the last Spanish governors of California). By 1820, Argüello's son, Luis, had obtained the endorsement of Pablo Sula, the last Spanish governor of California, for a smaller claim of some 35,000 acres called Rancho de las Pulgas. Luis died in 1830, still not fully realizing the family's quest to acquire the property, (although he had served as the first Mexican governor of California). Finally, in November of 1835, Governor José Castro made the binding grant to Luis' wife, Dona Maria and her children.[5]

This largest of all the Peninsula land grants stretched from San Mateo Creek to San Francisquito Creek and from the Bay into the hills, encompassing in today's terms all the land from Mills Hospital in San Mateo to the Santa Clara County line, which separates Menlo Park and Palo Alto. Its name, translated "Ranch of the Fleas," was probably derived from the earliest explorers who complained of the pesky insect especially around and within the native huts.

By 1838, Las Pulgas contained 4,000 head of cattle and 2,000 horses. At least two fixed structures existed on the property, but there was none in what we would call San Mateo today. The ranch was operated by a variety of hired hands. The Argüello family probably did not come to reside here permanently until after the American takeover in 1846.

During the early American period, the Argüello family, like many other land grant owners, had problems with squatters. At today's Menlo Park, East Palo Alto and particularly at Redwood City, whole communities of Americans materialized after the Gold Rush got underway. In order to defend their claims successfully, Dona Maria employed the services of Simón Mezes—thought to be a Puerto Rican, with a background in banking and politics—as legal counsel. In court case after court case, Mezes was able to prevail until full title was confirmed in 1856. As payment Mezes received 15% of the grant, including major portions of today's Redwood City and Belmont. In the years that immediately followed, the Argüello heirs sold off most of their Peninsula lands including the portion which makes up today's San Mateo, south of the creek.

North of the creek, despite secularization, the area remained reserved for the Native Californians. United States Federal court transcripts of 1869 include testimony indicating that as many as 300 Indians were living at the outpost around 1835. This is more than likely a number exaggerated by the passing of nearly 35 years. Other sources say the outpost was abandoned after secularization. However, an official inventory from 1835 reveals that the San Mateo outpost still had a sheep herd of 2,125 head. The inventory also lists two buildings. A run-down house of 41 x 13 varas, with adobe walls, dirt floor, tile roof, seven doorways (three still possessing doors), fourteen windows, an upper story and other improvements had a total value estimated at 2,100 pesos. The second building was described as a house in ruins, 28 x 7 varas, with three rooms, valued at 300 pesos. Also counted were 846 feet of lumber, 50 bushels of wheat, 232 bushels of barley, 16 bushels of salt, one water barrel, one crowbar, eight hitching posts, four plows, a garden within a wooden fence, and a corral.[6] According to an American observer, F. H. Teshmacher, during the 1830s, an *embarcadero*, perhaps the same used since early mission times, continued to be employed down by the bay, with ships loading grain grown at the San Mateo outpost.[7] These sources mostly agree that the San Mateo asistencia was still actively producing.

San Mateo's importance as a last place for the Native Americans was amplified in 1839, with the decision that the entire San Francisco Mission Indian community would be moved there. British-born W. E. P. Hartnell, who served as a Mexican administrator at the time, supervised the relocation. He counted 89 or 90 people at San Mateo afterwards, probably about tripling its former population. The changes are not documented, but it can be assumed some reorganization became necessary. By the 1840s, accounts of San Mateo include descriptions of Indians cultivating private plots inside a common fenced-off area. On one occasion leaders of the community, including Evencio and Tadeo, the blacksmith who has been connected with the famous native California outlaw Pomponio, visited the Mexican administrative offices in San Francisco, unannounced, and asked for farm tools and other supplies which had been promised to them since the time of secularization. No evidence exists as to whether their request was answered.[8]

By 1840, the Indians' days at San Mateo were numbered. In 1845 José de la Cruz Sanchez again tried unsuccessfully to have Rancho San Mateo granted to him. In 1846, Pío Pico, the last Mexican governor of California, awarded Rancho San Mateo to Cayetano Arenas of Los Angeles as payment for a debt. Arenas was a young clerk working in the governor's office. The award was one square league, about 6,000 acres. It occupied all the area between Rancho Buri Buri on the north (Sanchez Avenue in Burlingame) to the Argüello's property on the south (Mills Hospital). Arenas had probably never seen the land. The description used in the grant was copied directly from the original Sanchez family petition. Later that year, Arena's father, Luis, visited the property, but did not take possession for fear of possibly being harmed, for by this time the American takeover was in progress.[9]

MELLUS AND HOWARD

NOT LONG AFTER his San Mateo visit, Luis Arenas, on his son's behalf, sold Rancho San Mateo to the American mercantile firm of Mellus and Howard. We can only guess at his reason for so quick a transfer of ownership, but possibly the uncertainties of the raging Mexican-American War (concluded in 1848) had something to do with it. His son's rather recent claim to the grant might easily be challenged later. Moreover, the buyers offered a huge sum of money for those days, about $25,000. While today we would balk at selling the property we know as south Burlingame, Hillsborough and north San Mateo for about $4 an acre, this was probably a wise move on the part of Arenas. Many of the grants that had been issued late in the Mexican period (the San Mateo grant was signed May 5 or May 6, 1846) were later successfully challenged as antedated and fraudulent. It would now be up to Mellus and Howard to hire attorneys and fight the legal battles. About 1850, W. D. M. Howard bought Henry Mellus out and filed claim to the grant on February 7, 1853. The claim was

LINDERO DE BURIBURI AL N.
LAGUNA SALADA SANTOS
SANJON
ARROYO CHIQUITO
Y EMPERO QUE SE PIDE
CAMINO NACIONAL
Estero
LOMERIO
Escala de mil varas
100 200 400 600 1000
S. MATEO
ARROYO DE S. MATEO
ROBLAR

confirmed on September 18, 1855, but an appeal was attempted which was not dismissed until April 6, 1857, after Howard had died. American courts recognized the size of the grant to be 6,538.8 acres at the time.[10] Thus, Arenas not only avoided a costly and lengthy legal ordeal, but received a good price for a property little known to him, with no improvements beyond some rundown adobe buildings left over from missionary days.

Mellus and Howard were slow to do anything with their new property. The end of the Mexican-American War coincided with the discovery gold at Coloma, in the foothills of the Sierra. As businessmen, Mellus and Howard found themselves in the right place at the right time to make their fortunes. Their San Mateo land therefore lay practically abandoned. In 1847, Chester S. Lyman, an American civil engineer and later a Yale professor, was traveling on the Peninsula and reported the mission outpost unattended and in ruins. In 1849, after Mellus and Howard had taken possession, renowned traveler Bayard Taylor described not much change. He saw "a large adobe house, the ruins of a former Mission." What had happened to the Indians? Nicholas de Peyster, who came to set up a stagecoach stop at San Mateo Creek in 1849, noted that the natives were now living about a mile and a half up the creek to the southwest in the hills. Other sources corroborate this account.[11]

Eventually Howard hired an overseer, a man named Porter, who checked up on the property, and at one point had a local Indian boy look after some of the livestock. What happened to the mission outpost building? As will be detailed in the next chapter, it was used for a while by de Peyster. Then in 1868, it was badly damaged in an earthquake. W. D. M. Howard's heirs demolished it at that time.

Local legend has it that many of the roof tiles were piled near a shed on the Howard property and remained there for some years. Some were used for roofing one of the buildings at San Francisco's Midwinter Fair of 1894. After the fair they were brought back down the Peninsula and used to construct the Burlingame train station. Another 500 tiles were used still later to repair the roof of Mission San Francisco de Asis (by this time better known as Mission Dolores).[12]

William D.M. Howard
1818 - 1856

Courtesy San Mateo Historical Museum

The deseño for Rancho San Mateo, drawn hastily in pencil, shows the adobe on the north bank of Arroyo San Mateo, with oaks (roblar) and the "Camino Nacional" (El Camino Real) coming down from Rancho Buri Buri to the north. A scale showing 1,000 varas is just above the hills (lomeria). The rancho was granted to Cayetano Arenas in 1846.

Courtesy San Mateo Historical Museum

Notes

[1] Walton E. Bean, *California: An Interpretive History*, McGraw-Hill Book Co., 1968, pp. 57-68.
[2] Brown, "Indians."
[3] Stanger, *Peninsula*, p. 95.
[4] "Coyote Island," *La Peninsula*, Vol. XIV, No. 5, October, 1968.
[5] Hynding, *From Frontier*, p. 36.
[6] Stanger, "Hospice,"
[7] Margaret Beers, "History of Coyote Point," Student Monograph #316 in the archives of the San Mateo County Historical Museum, January, 1941.
[8] Brown, "Indians."
[9] Ibid.
[10] Alley, *History*, p. 213.
[11] Stanger, "Hospice."
[12] Stanger, *Community*, p. 96

The San Mateo House, originally a simple frame structure built in 1851 (at right, above), was enlarged in 1853 by Nicolas de Peyster and David Cook, by the addition of the stately Colonial Revival house at left, with an encircling porch. This house is said to have been pre-fabricated in the East and brought in nine different ships to San Francisco. It was used as an inn for travelers on the exhausting stagecoach journey from San Francisco to San Jose. Anthony G. Oakes bought the hotel in 1860, and sold it in 1863 to Captain Edward Taylor. The house was demolished in 1964 to make room for a parking lot.

Courtesy San Mateo County Historical Museum

CHAPTER II

A Stagecoach Stop: 1849 - 1865

THE AMERICANS

In 1849, Bayard Taylor, a famous author of California travelogues, decided to walk from San Francisco to Monterey to witness the creation of a constitution for California.[1] His journey took him down the San Mateo County bayside along El Camino Real. He stayed with the Sanchez family at Rancho Buri Buri, but noted no other human contact until long past San Francisquito Creek. At San Mateo Creek, all he saw was "the ruins of a former Mission," and he commented on a grove of bay trees:

> They were of a different species from the Italian bay, and the leaves gave out a most pungent odor. Some of the trees were of extraordinary size, the trunk being three feet in diameter. They grew along the bank of a dry Arroyo, and had every appearance of being indigenous.

How different the place would become over the next decade and a half. It would evolve from an old abandoned ruin to a busy stagecoach station, and then to a railroad stop. These changes had everything to do with the discovery of gold in California, statehood and the growing stature of San Francisco as the most important city in the West. The city was growing at a rate of 2,000 people a month. San Jose was slated as the new capital. Transportation between the two cities became crucial. Except for one brief endeavor out of Sacramento, the first stagecoach line in California ran in the fall of 1849 from San Francisco to San Jose along the old mission trail, right past the former outpost on San Mateo Creek.[2]

John Whistman started this stage line. His San Francisco station was located on the Plaza (now Portsmouth Square). For equipment he possessed a French Omnibus (a vehicle more rounded in appearance than a Concord Stage, but pulled by a similar number of animals), and his livestock consisted of a few mules and mustangs. The ride cost the traveler $32 or two ounces of gold dust.[3] The trip took nine hours, bumping and jolting over rough roads. During the winter, when the dirt ruts turned to mud, frequent stops were necessary.

NICOLAS DE PEYSTER

Recognizing a business opportunity in the making, on September 23, 1849, Nicolas de Peyster moved into the abandoned mission outpost building at San Mateo Creek and opened it as the first road house between San Francisco and San Jose. De Peyster, descendant of an old New York Dutch family, stocked the place with various goods and set it up as a store and public house. Since it was about half way between the two emerging cities, it soon became successful. De Peyster had established the first business enterprise, known as the San Mateo House, and thereby set the location for the original commercial strip in what was to become the city of San Mateo.

In 1850 stagecoach service improved when a competing company, Ackley and Maurison, introduced better equipment and more drivers. The running time for the trip from San Francisco to San Jose was cut to six hours, with a rest stop at San Mateo as a standard feature.

19

Looking west on Third Avenue about 1865. St. Matthew's Catholic Church is on the left, and Eugene Walker's livery stable and hotel on the right side of the dirt road.

Courtesy San Mateo County Historical Museum

During the summer of that year a 28-year-old engraver from Washington D.C., William H. Dougal, made at least two stops at the old adobe. On June 17, he wrote to a woman friend about his first horseback ride down the Peninsula from San Francisco. As he approached the "Mission of Saint Matthews," he noted that:

The face of the country is changed, we are beyond the influence of the chilling coast wind which renders San Francisco so unpleasant, the air is mild and balmy, and in place of barren hills and plains we ride through groves of beautiful and splendid oaks, the road is as level as a house floor, and as the setting sun throws the long shadows athwart our path and every turn discloses a new scene of beauty, we can imagine ourselves in fairyland. As we dash through the oak openings, the turtle doves fill the groves and countless numbers of squirrels could be seen frolicking about. Here we are at the Mission, we dismount for a few minutes to take some refreshment and let our horses breathe; the (I blush a little) Milk Punch was excellent, and now we are off again, cross a deep gulch with a fine stream of water running through it, and after a ride of three miles through the Oaks we strike out upon a level plain without tree or bush for five miles.[4]

The next month he toured the Peninsula again and made five sketches of various points of interest, one of which was of the former hospice. From the excellent drawing we can ascertain that de Peyster had been hard at work. Previous descriptions of the outpost had it a ruin. The sketch reveals no scattered debris but a well maintained building, with a fenced yard and neat and orderly grounds.[5]

By 1851, stagecoach travel became still more refined when another competitive firm, Hall and Crandell, cut fares in half and introduced daily service. De Peyster's San Mateo enterprise seemed to be more and more a permanent affair. But he was conducting his business on the property of others: the adobe building he occupied lay within the boundaries of Rancho San Mateo, which belonged to the mercantile partners William D. M. Howard and Henry Mellus. In 1849 Mellus stopped at the station as a stage passenger and ordered de Peyster off the property. But squatting was viewed differently in those days. Generally Americans felt it was their duty to use resources to their ultimate value. De Peyster did not react to the order, but he must have been uncomfortable with the prospect of continuing his increasingly important business on someone else's property.

WILLIAM D. M. HOWARD

William D. M. Howard was one of early California's great characters. The conflicting information about him truly baffles historians. He was certainly no conformist. Through all his days as a powerful San Francisco businessman, he was smooth shaven, as demonstrated by numerous photographs and drawings, in an era when almost everyone wore beards (the newspaper *The Oregonian* once wrote that only priests and actors were clean shaven in those days).

Historians agree that he was born in 1818 in Boston. But then the trouble begins. Roy Cloud, writing the County's history in 1928, says Howard was born to poor parents.[6] D. Gordon Bromfield, writing in 1957, lists Howard's father as Eleazar Howard, a banker and owner of clipper ships engaged in the China trade.[7] Both authors had plenty of access to family members, so the confusion extends even to the people closest to this historical person. Dr. Alan Hynding, a modern historian, wrote that Howard was "the unruly son of a prosperous New England merchant."[8]

All accounts agree that Howard went to sea at the age of sixteen. Frank Stanger's 1946 history, *Peninsula Community Book*, suggests his mother sent him originally as a cabin boy. Bromfield tells us that William's father wished him to go to Harvard, but the lad had just read Richard Henry Dana's *Two Years Before the Mast* and decided to go to sea instead. Hynding insists Howard was sent to sea in 1834 by his father, who hoped the experience would add discipline to the boy's character. Cloud then picks up the story by telling us Howard's first two voyages were on a trading vessel sailing to Para, Brazil. Afterwards, he was made a first officer and started off for California in 1838. Because his captain was a drunkard, most of the navigational duties fell to Howard during the voyage. Once at San Francisco (or Yerba Buena as it was known then) he left the ship to go into business for himself. All accounts agree that this took place about 1839, but Stanger has him down in Los Angeles at first.

Stanger and Hynding concur that Howard formed his famous partnership with Henry Mellus in 1845, but Cloud has Howard returning to Boston that year already a wealthy man. Cloud and Hynding agree that the partners bought out much of the stock of the Hudson Bay Company's holdings at San Francisco, which set them up as premier merchants after gold was discovered in January of 1848, and the incredible rush began.

All accounts agree that Howard became one of the great leaders of the developing town. In 1847 he was elected to the first city council. In 1848, he reportedly built the city's first brick building. His business grew beyond San Francisco, and eventually branches of the Howard and Mellus firm were established in Sacramento, San Jose and Los Angeles.

As far as affairs of the heart are concerned, Hynding reveals Howard was married twice. His first union was with Mary Warren of Honolulu. Howard married her at the islands in 1842, and then the couple came to California. Mary died in 1849. That same year Howard met and married sixteen-year-old Agnes Poett, who was en route with her family from Chile to England, where her brother Alfred was to be an apprentice civil engineer. Like many others, the family found themselves stranded at San Francisco because their crew had jumped ship for the gold diggings. According to Stanger, Agnes was helped from her boat at the still wharf-less Yerba Buena Cove by "a gallant and handsome man." It was a case of love at first sight; their whirlwind romance culminated with their marriage on July 9. Howard must have been happy to find a wife in Gold Rush California, where women were scarce. And Agnes must have been pleased to marry a rich man.

In recent years local historians have speculated about the feelings between the Howards, largely because of Agnes's rapid emotional recovery from Howard's death in 1856, as evidenced by her subsequent marriage to George Howard, William's brother. But Howard's great generosity toward his wife and her family in his will (Dr.

Among many other interests, W. D. M. Howard was in the business of importing pre-fabricated houses from the Eastern U.S. in the 1850s. He built a whole village of modest cottages in Happy Valley, along Market Street in San Francisco, where the Palace Hotel stands today. For his own country estate in San Mateo (above) he wanted something on the grand scale. This picture suggests that he brought in more than one house and then combined them. The structure on the right looks identical to Mariano Vallejo's house, Lachryma Montis, in Sonoma; Howard may have imported that one, too. The finials on the roof and the intricate barge-boards, hung like icicles along the eaves, were typical of the popular Gothic Revival style. Note the contrast with the more sober style of the San Mateo House, facing page 19.

Courtesy San Mateo County Historical Museum

Joseph Henry Poett, Agnes's father, received a major portion of the Rancho San Mateo), suggests that the couple were compatible.

In 1850, William D. M. Howard decided to own Rancho San Mateo by himself, and bought out his partner's share. From the time he dissolved his partnership with Mellus until his death six years later, Howard continued to be an important figure in San Francisco. In 1850 he helped create a militia which eventually became the National Guard of California. In 1851 he was one of the organizers of San Francisco's first Committee of Vigilance. He became a noted benefactor to the San Francisco Fire Department, school system and hospital. Cloud tells us that when a cholera epidemic struck Sacramento, Howard loaded a vessel with food, clothing and medicine and piloted the craft to Sacramento himself. This action inspired others to assist until proper aid arrived. Cloud also tells us that as the years wore on, Howard's health began to slip. He spent more time at his ranch at San Mateo Creek, where he introduced the first purebred cattle to California: bulls Orion and Harold IV, and five cows.

The building of Howard's home at San Mateo leads to more confusion. Some accounts suggest the mansion was in place as early as 1850. However, in 1852, Sir Henry Vere Huntley, an Englishman with a rather jaded view of California society, visited Howard's "country estate" and found it more characteristic of a frontier farm (as he described it in his 1856 book *California, Its Gold and Its Inhabitants*).

Perhaps this visit helped provoke action, for El Camino was soon fenced and graded, farm buildings were constructed on top of an old shell mound, and a splendid prefabricated house was ordered from Boston

The Howard family and friends celebrate July Fourth, 1884, at El Cerrito, by then known as the Bowie estate. The porch is draped in bunting, and the guests sport a marvelous variety of hats.

Courtesy San Mateo County Historical Museum

for shipment around the Horn. Cloud claims that has Howard was in bad physical shape by 1853. After a year of travel he was infected with Panama fever and retreated to his San Mateo property in 1854. Some portions of the house may have been added later than that.

All agree that the mansion was called "El Cerrito" for the little hill it was built upon, later referred to as "The Mound." This original site is on today's De Sabla Road in Hillsborough. The house sat in the midst of gardens and orchards which were in turn surrounded by the oaks, fields and imported trees that made up Rancho San Mateo. In 1857, Howard's brother, George, testified that $80,000 worth of improvements had been accomplished at El Cerrito by his brother.[9]

All historians agree that El Cerrito was the first of the great house that came to dominate the Peninsula's bayside for more than half a century. The house was eventually moved to Roehampton Road, and became Hillsborough's first town hall in 1910.

At the beginning of 1856 Howard was only 37 years old, but his body was wrecked by the devastation of the Panama fever. Hynding suggests that alcohol might have been a problem as well. Cloud tells a heroic story concerning Howard's death: Howard, already very ill, tried to break up a duel just across San Mateo Creek between Austin E. Smith, a San Francisco attorney, and Henry B. Truett, a merchant and friend. Howard, in shirt sleeves, forded the creek on foot and tried to reason with the combatants. When he could not, he rushed back across the creek so as not to have to witness the death of his friend (as it turned out, Truett survived the duel unhurt, while Smith took a pistol ball to the leg but recovered). That afternoon Howard suffered a "congestive chill" and died the following day.[10]

Howard left behind his 23-year-old wife and a young son, William H. Howard. Not long after his passing, Agnes married W. D. M.'s brother George. They lived at El Cerrito and had four children, including George, Jr., who became an architect and designed the Burlingame train station. George Sr. died in 1878, also at a relatively young age—50 years. Agnes married a third time in 1879, this time to Henry P. Bowie. After that, much of the former Rancho San Mateo, what today we would call north San Mateo and parts of Hillsborough and Burlingame, was known as the Bowie Estate.

Three daughters of David Cook (from left) Harriet, May and Elinor, who was the first American child born in San Mateo County, in 1852. Here, at age five, she looks like a small woman.

Courtesy San Mateo County Historical Museum

The David S. Cook house, though plain, was large enough to hold his family of seven children. This picture dates from 1865; the plants suggest that the house must be more than ten years old.

Courtesy San Mateo County Historical Museum

SETTLEMENT ACROSS THE CREEK AND THE BUTTERFIELD STAGE

About 1851, Nicholas de Peyster bought 75 acres on the south side of San Mateo Creek and built a new road house to continue his business. Around the same time, John B. Cooper, better known as "Sailor Jack," deserted his ship at San Francisco and married a native woman. For a while he lived at the old mission outpost; then he built a crude shack near an oak tree, and lived there. In September 1852 he purchased three acres of property south of San Mateo Creek from de Peyster, near today's downtown fire station on Ellsworth, where he constructed a house close to the creek and brought up a large family. He died in 1862.

In 1852, de Peyster took in David S. Cook as a partner. Cook had just arrived in California after starting out in Galesburg, Illinois, as a leader of a wagon train. With his wife Eliza, he went ahead of the train in their lighter wagon to scout for good resting places. Cook's granddaughter reported that Eliza was "great with child" when they arrived in San Mateo in 1852. Their baby, Elinor, is said to be the first eastern American or "white" child born in San Mateo County. Six more children followed. That first year, Cook hired David Haver to build a stage barn adjacent to the San Mateo House, at about today's Third Avenue and El Camino Real. Throughout the last century and into the present one the barn stood as a landmark. Haver hand-cut the great oak beams, and when the barn was razed many years later, its timbers were used in the construction of several existing San Mateo and Hillsborough houses. Haver remained in San Mateo and eventually opened an upholstery shop.

Tony Oakes
1830 - 1903
Courtesy San Mateo County Historical Museum

In 1853 de Peyster and Cook enlarged their San Mateo House by adding a large frame building to it. This structure was brought in from the east on board nine different ships, framed and ready for assembly. It was attached to the original establishment, making the structure a respectable hotel for that day.

Cook bought out de Peyster in 1856 and became the sole proprietor of the San Mateo House. On October 12, 1857, he was appointed San Mateo's first postmaster. For lack of use, the Post Office was discontinued in 1858, but in 1861, as the settlement grew, it was reinstituted.[12]

Not long after becoming postmaster, Cook sold the San Mateo House to the partnership of Stockton and Shafter. During their period of ownership the station became a stop for the famous Butterfield Overland Mail, a stage service initiated by the federal government to improve communications and transportation between the East and West Coasts. Entrepreneur John Butterfield successfully bid for the contract, signed September 16, 1857. He established a southern route from Missouri to Texas across New Mexico and Arizona to Los Angeles, and then through the San Joaquin Valley, over Pacheco Pass to Gilroy, San Jose and on to San Francisco through San Mateo County, with a scheduled stop at San Mateo. This 2800-mile stage line was the longest ever to exist.

The service began in September 1858. Some 140 stations linked the line. Some were already operating, such as the San Mateo House; others were a stop at someone's ranch; many had to be built for the purpose. The company eventually owned some 1500 horses and mules and 250 ranches. The original fare from St. Louis to San Francisco was $200, and from San Francisco to St. Louis $100 (It was lower on the way back east because of less demand for the service). Passengers were provided with two meals a day at forty cents to a dollar each. Many passengers could not keep up the constant day and night travel, and stayed at stations to rest.[13]

By mid 1859, improvements in the Peninsula's highway (County Road, as El Camino was known in those days) at San Bruno allowed for a faster pace through the County, and Butterfield eliminated the stop at the San Mateo House. The onset of the Civil War in 1861 ended the service of this famous line.

Tony Oakes

IN THE FALL OF 1860, Stockton and Shafter sold the San Mateo house to Tony Oakes. This created quite a sensation, as reported in the County's only newspaper, the *Gazette*, which recognized Oakes as one of the most renowned hoteliers in the state.

Although only thirty years old, Oakes had already had a life full of adventure. As a boy he acquired several talents—cooking and music making among them. When he was sixteen, he left his native Boston to join General Winfield Scott in the conquest of Mexico during the Mexican American War. When his considerable abilities were recognized, he became a personal mess boy to the General, and his troubadour as well. With his guitar and singing voice he managed to gain popularity among both American troops and the Mexican people.

At nineteen, Oakes was off to California. He arrived in San Francisco in early 1849 with a parcel of letters of introduction from friends left behind during the War. First he took a job in a restaurant, where he refined his culinary skills. Next he became the proprietor of the Elephant House on California Street. This establishment was destroyed in the great fire of 1851. Oakes then used one of his letters to gain an introduction to former California General Mariano Vallejo, who helped him start in the hotel business in Sonoma. Later in the decade he returned to San Francisco to open the Terrapin Lunch restaurant. There he combined his skills, becoming a well-known entertainer as well as chef. By 1860, he was ready for the move to San Mateo. The great California capitalist, William C. Ralston, one of Oakes's many fans, probably helped him buy the San Mateo House.[14]

The San Mateo House was sold in 1863 to Captain Edward Taylor, who moved the house and converted it from a hotel into his own residence.

<small>Courtesy San Mateo County Historical Museum</small>

San Mateo had never seen the likes of Tony Oakes. He became its first true promoter. In April and May of 1862, he ran letters in the *San Mateo County Gazette* extolling the virtues of the place and its hotel:

> The San Mateo House, twenty miles from San Francisco on the Turnpike Road, is situated on a sloping mound with spacious ground thickly studded with ancient oak and bay trees. The whole valley surrounding is protected from the cold winds and fogs from the ocean by the Coast Range. The gardens are beautifully planned and under highest state of cultivation. Nature and art have afforded to this place a climate and scenery unsurpassed in the world. Winding by the garden flows the San Mateo Creek filled with an abundance of trout, offering to the disciples of "Old Izaak" ample amusement. In the vicinity, game in season is plenty, giving the sportsman many a chance for a crack shot; while only half a mile from the house, a beautiful sandy beach of the bay entices a stroll in the quiet moonlight from the followers of Zimmerman or the worshipers of nature. The building has been further renovated for the better accommodation of the public. For families, rooms in suites have been expressly arranged. Connected with the house are fine stables and at all times guests can be accommodated with houses and carriages and saddle horses for ladies and gentlemen.

Despite the curtailment of the Butterfield service, Oakes proclaimed that "Stages to and from San Francisco and San Jose pass the house tri-daily." He had also managed to regain postal service for San Mateo, becoming its second postmaster in 1861. In fact he had gone further in linking San Mateo with the rest of the world; not only were the Post Office and Wells Fargo & Company's Express service at his establishment, but he had access to telegraph communications as well. He announced that dinner and room reservations could be made over the telegraph. After all, Oakes would "spare no pains to promote the comfort and happiness of his guests."

Oakes was clearly attempting to appeal to clientele beyond the San Francisco to San Jose stagecoach traveler. He attempted to lure wealthy city folk to San Mateo as a

Captain Edward Taylor
1820 - 1887
Courtesy San Mateo County Historical Museum

country resort. One has to use one's imagination to reconstruct San Mateo in those days. The San Mateo House sat on ten acres, from about today's Second Avenue to Third. To the east were marshes and bay. The "beautiful sandy beach" described by Oakes' advertisement must have been Coyote Point. To the west were the green rolling foothills. There was hardly evidence of man's presence, yet San Mateo was so close to booming San Francisco that from a business prospectus, the settlement's potential as a resort had tremendous promise.

Many San Franciscans who were willing to spend some money were drawn to the place. Oakes' oldest son once claimed that the man who greeted guests at the door and looked after their carriages and other rigs at the livery stable made enough in tips to retire with savings of $30,000 after only two years.[15]

Other businesses benefited from the presence of the San Mateo House. In 1859, Henry Husing opened a general store near today's Third Avenue and El Camino Real. In 1861, Charles and William Remington became the place's first white blacksmiths ("an old Indian on the hills nearby"[16] was still in business at the time).

While the hotel and adjacent businesses seemed to prosper, Tony Oakes himself did not become a rich man during his San Mateo days. Some speculate that his generous loans to others were his undoing.[17] In 1863 Oakes sold his hotel to Captain Edward Taylor. Perhaps he thought that the coming of the railroad that year meant his stagecoach and horse-and-buggy trade along the County Road would dry up. Maybe he realized that the business center of the settlement would now shift from the highway eastward to the tracks. For whatever reason, he pulled up stakes and left the area. However, his career was by no means over. He later opened a hotel in Hayward, and had many other adventures before his death in 1903.

The Taylor Family

Captain Edward Taylor was cashier for the Pacific Mail Steamship Company when he bought the San Mateo House. He had had an exciting life by the time he came to San Mateo.

According to family legend, at the age of 20, in 1840, he had set sail for a round-the-world voyage. In Malaya he was nearly murdered after a fantastic chase. Companions finally killed two of his pursuers before they could nab him. In May of 1841, he found himself in Canton while a battle was being fought with the British. While trying to escape to Whampoo in a boat, he was captured and tortured "in a frightful manner."[18] He was finally let go after showing a Chinese officer a tattoo of a star, proving him to be an American. He was then caught again, and this time was sent to prison for three days before securing another release. He lived in Canton for a while. Then in 1846 he moved to Shanghai. In 1849 he came to California, and the next year went to work for Pacific Mail Steamship Company. He and his wife Fanny were counted among the elite of San Francisco's burgeoning social community. Fanny was Ansel I. Easton's sister. Easton developed the beautiful Blackhawk Estate of today's north Burlingame area. He was married to the sister of D. O. Mills, who built a lavish estate at Millbrae.

Adeline Taylor Howard, one of the Captain's children, remembered that in 1863 the family was looking for a new home because their house on elegant Rincon Hill in San Francisco was to be torn down to make way for the infamous Second Street Cut. The Captain and his wife probably had happy memories of the San Mateo House because they had stayed there on their honeymoon in 1855. What Taylor's immediate plans were when he purchased the place are not clear. Historian Frank Stanger suggests that he waffled between using it for a dwelling or returning it to its former use as a hotel. Stanger actually places a new manager, I. N. Irwin, at the hotel after Oakes, and claims that a fire damaged the building in 1863.[19]

Whatever his purpose was, Taylor did move the structure east, back from the road, and he added a wing. It served as the Taylor family home for many years. In

1887, the Captain died. His widow passed on in 1899. The family then sold the place for use as a nurses' home in connection with the development of Mills Hospital, which moved the building back up to the roadside and made other major changes. The 113-year-old structure was finally demolished in 1964 to make room for the parking garage at El Camino Real and Second Avenue.[20]

THE DONALD FAMILY

IN 1935, the infant San Mateo County Historical Association conducted an interview with Mrs. Sarah W. Fox, who was born in 1846 and had lived in San Mateo as a girl and teenager from 1853 until 1864, a good portion of the stage coach era. Her insights into this period of the settlement's history are most interesting.

Her father, John Donald, had been born in England, her mother in Maine. The family was living in Boston when word of the Gold rush came in 1849. Like thousands of others, Donald came to California to strike it rich and return with a fortune. While he never became wealthy, he did find some gold, the first nugget of which he immediately sent back home. When Donald returned to the East, like many others, he found that he missed the warm weather of California. He came back overland and then sent for his family (a wife, a son and a daughter) to sail around the Horn and join him in San Francisco.

Sarah Fox remembered the six-month voyage of 1852 on the *Witch of the Wave* fondly: "It was like a floating palace, a lovely boat,"[21] A Captain Tay was in command and was scheduled to visit China after arriving at San Francisco. (This was only the vessel's second voyage. On her fourth voyage, she went down in the China Sea, taking Captain Tay with her.) While on board *Witch of the Wave*, Sarah nearly came to a tragic end herself. She was sitting on a rail, singing for the other passengers on board, when the ship suddenly rolled. The little girl nearly went overboard, but the heel of one of her shoes caught in some rigging and saved her life.

Once in San Francisco, the family found that John had gone into business as a florist. Their home in San Francisco was in "Happy Valley," about Market and Third Street today. In 1853, John went to work as a landscape gardener for Captain F. W. Macondray, who was building an estate on the west side of the stage road, facing the San Mateo House. John's job was to prepare the grounds of the estate while a house was being constructed. As the work went on, he had a cottage built for his family on the south side of the creek, facing the Howard properties to the north and the road to the east.

Life was fairly primitive for this pioneer family. Contact with outside people was rare. Macondray would visit on weekends to inspect the progress and direct the building of his house. The Cook family had the San Mateo House then, so there were children to play with.

Sarah Donald Fox, daughter of John Donald, in a beautiful portrait taken in 1864, after her marriage to George Fox

Courtesy San Mateo County Historical Museum

Before Henry Husing's store was built, there was no general store in the area. Sarah remembered:

> [My father] used to make out a list of things that were needed, go up to a store on Sutter Street [in San Francisco] and buy up wholesale everything like sugar, a barrel of brown sugar and a couple of barrels of white sugar and hams and everything. We had a great big storeroom where we used to hang hams and keep the stores. So when anybody came we were ready for meals at any time. Father was very hospitable.

For those smaller items that might be needed, a peddler traveled up and down the stage road. Mrs. Fox's daughter, who was also interviewed by the Historical Association, often heard about his man:

> There was a Jew who used to come from San Francisco. He used to walk. He had a great big square of ticking like bed ticking, and he used to have all his wares in that, buttons, needles, thread, pins and so on, and he carried it on his back. He

Brookside, the estate of Captain F.W. Macondray, built in 1853. This modest house, probably built by local carpenters, was later expanded by John Parrott into the magnificent Baywood estate.

Courtesy San Mateo County Historical Museum

used to stop at all of the houses and grandma would buy what she needed. Then he would go on to San Jose. He used to come about once a month. Finally he saved his money and he got a cart or covered wagon and used that.

After three or four years living at this place, which would become known as Baywood, John Donald was able to purchase 200 acres to establish a wheat farm. At twenty dollars an acre, he bought properties south of the stage stop on both sides of the stage road, from about today's Bay Meadows Track to 17th Avenue.

His daughter met her husband at San Mateo. George Fox's family had come across the plains and originally settled on the Howard property. George's father, B. F. Fox, was overseer for the ranch, and was also an attorney. He eventually became San Mateo County's first Superior Court Judge in 1858. In 1864, George Fox and Sarah Donald were married in San Francisco. They then moved to Redwood City, where George also practiced law. He eventually became County District Attorney.

SAN MATEO'S FIRST SCHOOL HOUSE

SARAH FOX remembered that San Mateo had a school house very early on. The building served the settlement for more than educational purposes. Before any churches existed in the area, religious services were held here. All denominations shared the building, worshiping in shifts. The school house was also used during elections, and "the men all went armed." Why? "Well you know what the elections are. The politicians wanted to get their friends in."

Although Sarah's recollections contradict official public school records, which show no public school in operation until 1861, we know from many other contemporary accounts that a school house at San Mateo served as a polling place and doubled as a church on Sundays, and that Mrs. S. E. Seagram, "reputed to be an excellent instructress," taught school in San Mateo at least as early as April of 1859. Some speculate that local residents funded this infant educational operation until the school district was formally organized.[22]

We also know that Captain Macondray donated one acre of land for the building of a school in 1854. Various old-timers interviewed by the San Mateo County Historical Association in 1935 placed the school house about 125 feet west of the stage road under a grove of oak trees, near today's El Camino Real and Notre Dame Avenue. The one-story building was only about 20 feet by 50 feet, and was painted tan. There was one room for classroom instruction and another, smaller room where the children could place their lunches and coats. A pile of wood in the back of the building supplied the single wood burning stove, the only source of heat. The stove was also the focus of many nostalgic memories. Long-time resident Maurice Powers recalled:

> The boys thought this stove to be of great fun for them. It was great sport for them to put bullets in it and then watch the teachers and other students

run for the door. The room would become filled with smoke and everyone would have to wait until it cleared from the room.[23]

All grades, from first to eighth, met together. Advancement to the next grade was based on an examination at the end of the year. The teacher wrote questions on the blackboards for all subjects. If the student knew the correct answer he was passed on to the next grade. There were no report cards, nor any formal graduation. After the eighth grade, public school was over; there was no public high school for San Mateo children for many years. One could go to a variety of private schools that sprouted in the area, or one could begin an adult life. Elementary education did become compulsory in California, but in the early days there were no truant officers. Most boys working on nearby farms simply could not find time to attend.

The school day ran from 9:00 a.m. to 3:30 p.m., with a recess at 10:40. The boys played shimmy sticks, a sort of hockey game, and might also have games of tag or baseball. They hung from the swings and bars, or played with tops or marbles. Old-timers remembered that, except for an occasional tomboy who was good at sports, girls did not usually participate in these activities, but normally sat, talked and watched the boys. After the railroad was completed, and private schools developed in the area, sporting contests were organized on Saturdays. Baseball games with Brewer's Military school were regular occurrences. Sometimes the routine of the school day was broken when a cattle herd was driven along the stage road up to the Miller and Lux ranch at Baden (South San Francisco). Children would watch *vaqueros* moving thousands of head up the dusty road, toward the slaughterhouses in South San Francisco.

Most children walked to school. A few had horses or ponies. Punishment was dealt out with a rawhide strap. The little school had no janitor; pupils helped to keep the building neat and clean. Summer vacation lasted from June 1 to August 1.

In 1861 the county became much more serious about its educational institutions, after the district attorney decided that the county superintendent of schools should be elected instead of appointed by the Board of Supervisors.

From that year on, better records were kept at San Mateo, and the school house formally joined the public school system. Mrs. J. H. Warren, wife of the Congregational Minister, was the teacher at that time, and the school's entire enrollment seems to have been John Donald's three children. As late as the summer of 1863, this original school house was still undergoing structural changes and receiving furnishings.[24]

The Last of the Indian Community

A CENSUS TAKEN IN 1852 reveals there were still 73 California Indians inhabiting Rancho San Mateo. But Sarah Fox, who arrived in 1853, remembered only about 12 or 13 still living there. On Sundays she and her father would take canned fruit to these people. They lived in an adobe house of about 15 feet by 15 feet (possibly the same one described by Beechey in 1826). The house was partitioned with one room following another, without hallways. The natives slept on the floor in blankets.

She remembers these people as not dangerous, but rather pathetic. They were never armed. They were heavily built, though some were small. The men and women wore blankets with holes cut through. The women also wore red skirts. The Indians ate acorn cakes and still used the stone mortar and pestle for pounding acorns according to their native custom. Sarah also remembered the natives coming to visit their cottage on the other side of the creek. She said they were "perfectly harmless," but "awful beggars," and "my mother used to be frightened to death when they came around." According to Sarah the Indians frequently walked right in the door and sat down on the floor, "the women with their papooses on their backs." There were about as many men as women. Some times they would ask for "beesket." They spoke a mixture of languages which John Donald seemed to understand. They also begged for whiskey and cold potatoes. They boiled the unskinned potatoes and then would "eat them right down." They would then go away, but would come back "in a few days for more." The Donald family regarded them as a nuisance: "They did not harm us, but they were always coming there."

After Donald had finished his landscaping for Captain Macondray, he established some walkways, using shell from Coyote Point beach for materials. Every time he went down to the beach he had company, according to Sarah: "The Indians seemed to wait to see whether he was going down to the beach; then it was just like a telegraph system, they seemed to come right out of the trees, a whole lot of them, and then my mother was afraid."

Sarah's mother was even more frightened once when Indians came to the house after Mr. Donald left for the beach. They made a circle and walked around the house. Holding her youngest baby, Mrs. Donald shut herself in a closet so the Indians would not hear the baby cry. A hired girl watched for the right opportunity, climbed out a window and went for help from a hired man.[25]

Exactly what became of this last community of Peninsula Indians is not really known. According to the 1860 census, the Indian community in San Mateo had dispersed. Only four or five dozen native Californians were listed as residing in the entire county. Sarah Fox

wondered: "Where they disappeared to is more than I can tell. After the whites settled, the Indians became fewer and fewer." Historian Allen Brown suggests that William D. M. Howard had them "removed" as part of his improvement effort after the somewhat embarrassing visit of Sir Henry Vere Huntly.[26] It is thought that as many as sixty of the natives lived in the hill country west of the stage road, herding sheep during the 1850s. Certainly Tadeo, the blacksmith, did move from the rancho into the hills, where he continued his occupation and earned a reputation as a skilled craftsman, making spurs and bridle bits. Some of the Indians found refuge with José de la Cruz Sanchez at Rancho Buri Buri to the north. Unfortunately, Sanchez was rendered almost landless himself through the American legal system.

In 1869, one of the Indians of the San Mateo Community was still living at the Sanchez Rancho. Pedro Evencio, son of Evencio Yocalo, a former leader of the small band, was called on by the Sanchez family that year to render testimony to defend the Sanchez title to Rancho Buri Buri. The words of Evencio were taken over the objections of the United States Attorney, who cited a law which forbade Indians to serve as legal witnesses. In any case, Evencio's testimony was of little help.

By 1870, only eight natives were listed as residing in San Mateo County. As the great work of the Spring Valley Water Company got underway to create the reservoirs down the middle of the County, no natives were encountered.

In 1894, Dr. Mary Sheldon Barnes of Stanford University visited Pedro Evencio, the last surviving full-blooded San Mateo Indian, at his small home in San Mateo. She described him as a laboring man, with a dignified demeanor. At first she doubted his claim to be a pure Indian because of his full beard; then she remembered Padre Palou's original 1774 description of these people as being bearded. Dr. Barnes wrote an article for the Stanford literary magazine, *Stanford Sequoia*, entitled "Pedro Evencio," a sentimental tribute to a lost people.

ROADS AND POLITICS

UNTIL 1856, there was no San Mateo County; most of the Peninsula was part of San Francisco County. And for a variety of reasons, people in the more rural southern section of the Peninsula were dissatisfied with their government center to the north. One of the main issues for the southerners was a lack of roads. San Mateo Creek residents were especially eager to link up with the agricultural promise of the coastside with a road that would go from their settlement westward over the hills. A rough road was carved out by 1855, emerging near the school house, but the better roads to the coast were at Redwood City, Belmont and San Bruno.

San Mateo County got its start not because of citizens demanding improvements and better services, but because a group of politicians and ruffians from San Francisco were being forced out of the city and wanted to have a new county organized for their benefit. In the spring of 1856 the this gang rigged the elections, and it looked like they would succeed. However, the famed San Francisco Committee of Vigilance of that year, after doing its work in the city, chased this evil element out of San Mateo County, and in November 1856 a new election took place to reorganize the infant county. The polling station at San Mateo was the school house. The three inspectors were J. B. Morton and future fathers-in-law, Judge B. F. Fox and John Donald.[27] When Sarah Fox described guns around the polling place, she was undoubtedly speaking of elections like this one, which were seriously threatened by corrupt men.

As the new County got a better start, the improvement of roads became the biggest issue. In 1857 a petition was presented, calling for creation of a better road to the base of the hills from San Mateo, roughly following today's Crystal Springs Road. The project was approved in 1859, and contractors Loveland and Bowman finished the work a year later. Funding for the work came from the Howard family and Captain Macondray (who was now calling his place Brookside). The same year the road was completed, John Parrott bought Brookside (and would call it Baywood). Macondray fell ill and died two years later. Parrott, disliking the notion that the road split his property, filed suit to prevent its use. The controversy was not completely settled until 1864, when the Howards bought 160 acres on the north side of the road from Parrott.[28] San Mateo now had use of a good road which would become the coastside's most important link with the bayside. The quarter-mile grade from the county road to the base of the hill became known as Howard Hill. After the age of automobiles made such slight inclines unnoticeable, the name fell out of use.

THE COUNTY SEAT FIGHT, PART ONE

A SECOND MAJOR ISSUE of the day was the placement of the county seat. In 1856, the gang from San Francisco had attempted to have Belmont declared the county seat to satisfy one of its leaders, John McDougal, a former governor and resident of Belmont. When the more

---

Pedro Evencio, the last survivor of the San Mateo asistencia, in a rare and beautiful portrait taken in 1894, when he was interviewed by Dr. Mary Sheldon Barnes, of Stanford.

Courtesy San Mateo County Historical Museum

John Parrott, who bought Brookside from Macondray in 1860 and renamed it Baywood.

Courtesy San Mateo County Historical Museum

legitimate leadership gained control, Redwood City, the county's largest bayside community, was made county seat. Through the years, not everyone was happy that the center of government was so far south.

In 1861 an attempt was launched to wrest the county seat away. The editors of the *San Mateo County Gazette*, a Redwood City newspaper, at first suspected that this campaign was organized by the citizens of the county's most important coastside town, Half Moon Bay. Further investigation showed that the real source of the agitation came from parties trying to locate the county seat at "a hill area" south of San Mateo Creek, on land that would one day comprise the Borel estate and the Homestead Tract (today the area west of El Camino Real at Highway 92). The murky nature of the entire campaign compelled the *Gazette* to term this as yet unborn town, "Bleackville." Actually its promoters called it "San Mateo Villa." Finally on August 31, the *Gazette* learned that the owners of San Mateo Villa, A. Herrlich and Company, offered to donate a lot to the county for the necessary public buildings.

This revelation was made known only four days before the election. The *Gazette* bitterly attacked the San Mateo Villa offer as a real estate scheme. In the election Belmont received one vote: San Mateo gathered 11; San Mateo Villa came in second place with 364, but Redwood City won easily with 650. The *Gazette* later revealed that Herrlich had bought the property only one year before the election, with speculation as his motive.

Although Redwood City was the overwhelming winner, the issue was not yet dead. Some people in San Mateo were still dissatisfied with Redwood City as the county seat. All eleven San Mateo votes came from the residents there, while only eighteen voted in favor of Redwood City. An overwhelming 131 San Mateans, along with rural residents around San Mateo, ignored the urgings of the *Gazette* and voted in favor of San Mateo Villa.[29]

More Pioneers

While San Mateo would grow much more rapidly after the building of the railroad in 1863, other pioneers were attracted to the place during the stagecoach era. Prominent among them were John Quincy Adams Tilton and family relation Samuel Goodhue, both from New England, who came to work for the Howard family. Tilton had experience with stock raising and butchering; Goodhue superintended tree planting and other improvements. The two would become important leaders within the San Mateo Creek community as it evolved from stagecoach settlement to railroad station and village.[30]

Stephen Whipple first saw San Mateo in 1851. He felt this a fine place to establish a horse farm, so he purchased parcels in stages, some of them from the original land-grant Argüello family. By 1858 he had enough acreage to establish his ranch, which became known throughout the state for its fine horses. The main house sat at the site of today's St. Matthew's Catholic School on El Camino Real.[31]

Irishman James Byrnes came to the Peninsula fresh from the gold fields in 1857. He opened a stage stop some two years later on the San Mateo - Half Moon Bay Road at the base of the hills. He invested in property at the San Mateo settlement and became involved in politics. By 1861, he was the mid-county's representative on the Board of Supervisors.[32]

Sometime in the mid 1850s, David McLellan bought some 300 acres from the Argüello family east of the County Road, now Bay Meadows and lands a little to the south. The McLellan house stood until 1930 at 36th

A STAGECOACH STOP: 1849 - 1865

The historic California Bay Laurel tree for which Baywood was named still stands in the Baywood district.

Courtesy San Mateo County Historical Museum

Avenue. David was the grandfather of Rod McLellan, who established the famous San Mateo County nurseries.[33]

Lemuel T. Murray built a dairy ranch on much of what we would call the Hillsdale residential area of today. Murray arrived in California in 1852, saw the San Mateo area, liked what he saw, returned to New England in 1856 and enlisted the aid of his younger brother Calvin. They bought sheep and cattle in Missouri and drove them across the plains in 1857. They purchased their San Mateo properties in 1862, and built their house at the site of today's Hillsdale Library.

ON THE EVE OF THE RAILROAD

DESPITE THE CURTAILMENT of the Butterfield Stagecoach service at San Mateo, by 1859 the place was quite different from what it had been in 1849, when Bayard Taylor had visited on his way to Monterey. In 1859 the renowned traveler stopped again at San Mateo, this time traveling not on foot but by stage. He commented that the "glorious trees were still standing" and that these sycamores, chestnuts and bay laurels shaded the creek as before. But now there was "a beautiful Gothic residence" (the Howard place) and a wooden bridge crossed the arroyo. On the other side, Taylor was much impressed with the "handsome hotel on the left." He noted "everywhere, neatness, comfort and a profusion of shrubs, flowers and vines." Opposite the hotel was the Brookside estate of Captain Macondray, who had accompanied Taylor on his first visit in 1849. Taylor was overjoyed with the reunion: "As

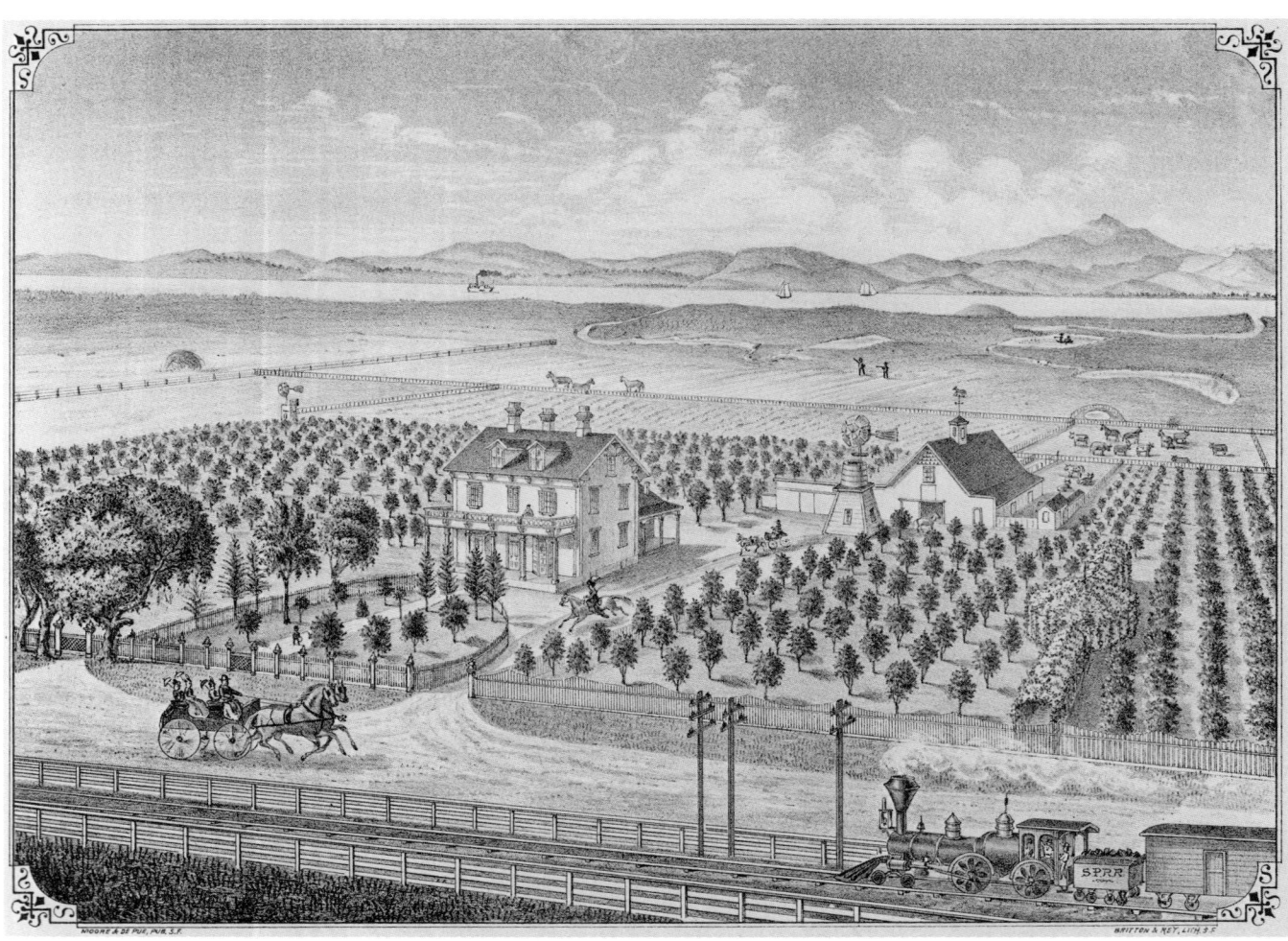

The David McLellan house, near the site of today's Bay Meadows racetrack, was demolished in 1930.

Courtesy San Mateo County Historical Museum

we reached the house, through a lawn dotted with glittering bays and live-oaks, the captain came out to welcome us; and I could not refrain my delight that San Mateo had fallen into hands which protect its beauty." Taylor was particularly taken with Macondray's garden:

> Such peaches, such pears, such apples and figs! What magic is there in this virgin soil?... Colossal, splendidly colored, overflowing with delicious juice, without a faulty specimen anywhere, it was truly the perfection of horticulture. In the glasshouse (necessary only to keep off the cool afternoon winds) we found the black Hamburg, the Muscatel, and other delicate grapes, laden from root to tip with clusters from one to two feet in length. The heaps of rich color and perfume, on the table to which we were summoned, were no less a feast to the eye than to the palate.[34]

In July of 1860, the San Francisco and San Jose Railroad was incorporated. On the eve of the railroad, the hotel and stables stood on County Road, along with Henry Husing's store. Husing lived in a house back of the store, at about the present location of the Benjamin Franklin Hotel. South of Husing's store was Charles and William Penington's blacksmith shop. Across the highway, about 1000 feet south of today's Fourth Avenue, was the school house. Close by were beautiful estates and neat farms on both sides of the El Camino. By the fall of 1863, trains were steaming between Mayfield (now Palo Alto) and San Francisco. But San Mateo was already a real destination, with an active business community.

San Mateo also had a waterfront of sorts. Down at the mouth of San Mateo Creek an embarcadero and warehouse were in operation, shipping grain and other agricultural products. A man named Thompson was in charge, but he was squatting on Howard's property; he contended that the Rancho San Mateo grant did not include all of the marshlands. In 1861, the Supreme Court of California found that the Howards did own all properties extending to the bay and forced Thompson out of business. The Howard family later operated another shipping operation off of Coyote Point.

Perhaps most important for the future of San Mateo was the presence of the road to the coast, which was substantially improved by 1863. San Mateo would become a crossroads in the coming years, linking north-south rail transportation with east-west stage service.

NOTES

[1] Bayard Taylor, *Eldorado, Or: Adventures in the Path of Empire*, G.P. Putman, New York (Eighteenth Edition), 1859, see chapter XIII, "Incidents of a Walk to Monterey."

[2] Frank Stanger, "The Stagecoach Era in San Mateo County," *La Peninsula*, October, 1970, Vol. XV No. 6, p. 3.

[3] Ernest Hills, "Stagecoach History In San Mateo County," Student monograph #150 in the archives of the San Mateo County Historical Museum, June, 1940.

[4] Letter of William H. Dougal, June 17, 1850, Archives, San Mateo County Historical Museum.

[5] Renderings of all five McDougal sketches can be found in the archives of the San Mateo County Historical Museum

[6] Roy Cloud, *History of San Mateo County*, S. J. Clarke Publishing Co., Chicago, 1928, vol. II, p. 5.

[7] D. Gordon Bromfield, *The San Mateo We Knew*, 1957, p. 39.

[8] Hynding, *From Frontier*, p. 35.

[9] Stanger, *Community*, p. 100.

[10] Cloud, *History*, vol. II, pp 11-12.

[11] Alley, *History*, p. 231.

[12] Joan Allen, "History of the Post Office, San Mateo California 1857-1916," Manuscript Collection of the San Mateo County Historical Museum, 1968.

[13] Dean Mawdsley, "The Butterfield Overland Mail," *La Peninsula*, Vol. XXII, No. 5, January, 1985, pp. 3-9.

[14] Allen, "History" pp. 5-6.

[15] Frank Stanger, "The San Mateo House in the Days of Tony Oakes" *La Peninsula*, August, 1965, Special Issue.

[16] *Moore and DePue's*, p. 26.

[17] Stanger, "San Mateo House."

[18] Cloud, *History*, Vol. II, p. 308.

[19] Stanger, *Peninsula*, p. 98.

[20] Don Ringler, Mark Still, Sandi Tateman, "The City of San Mateo: A Walking Tour," *La Peninsula*, vol. XXIII, no. 2, June, 1986, p. 12.

[21] Mrs. George W. Fox, interview contained in Manuscript #577 in the archives of the San Mateo County Historical Museum.

[22] Winifred M. Burke, *San Mateo Elementary Schools: A Hundred Year History, 1854-1957*, San Mateo School District, 1958.

[23] Max Aldrick, "San Mateo Schools" Student Monograph #136 in the archives of the San Mateo County Historical Museum, June, 1940.

[24] Burke, *San Mateo*.

[25] Fox and daughter interview, see note 21.

[26] Brown, "Indians."

[27] Alley, *History* p. 168.

[28] Leslie O. Merrill, "Crystal Springs Road," Manuscript in the archives of the San Mateo County Historical Museum, 1968.

[29] Robert Bostwick, "San Mateo Villa and the County Seat Election of September 4, 1861," Student monograph #1069 in the archives of the San Mateo County Historical Museum.

[30] Marjorie Boettcher, "Tilton Family" Student monograph #129 in the archives of the San Mateo County Historical Museum, June, 1936.

[31] Betty Plambeck, "Horse Raising in San Mateo County," Student monograph #449 in the archives of the San Mateo County Historical Museum, Fall, 1941.

[32] Hynding, *Frontier*, p. 70.

[33] John F. Boler, "South San Mateo," Student monograph in the archives of the San Mateo County Historical Museum #1483, June 1954.

[34] Bayard Taylor, "Valley of San Jose," *At Home and Abroad*, 1859. Taken from the reprint collection in the archives of the San Mateo County Historical Museum.

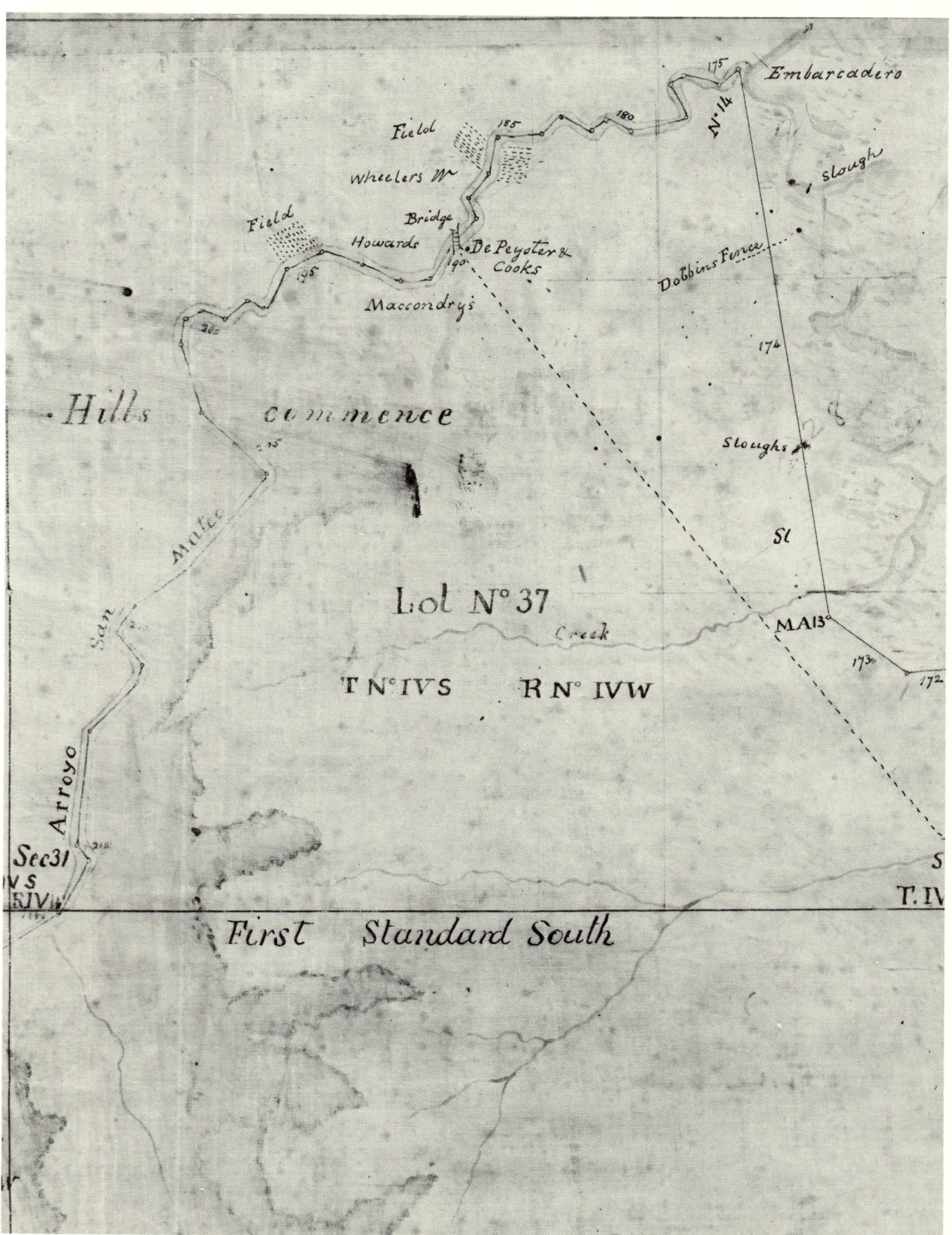

CHAPTER III

From Whistle Stop to Village: 1865 - 1887

LAYING THE TRACKS

SCHEMES TO LINK San Francisco to San Jose by rail had been seriously considered since September 1850, when the Pacific and Atlantic Railroad Company raised $100,000 from investors from the two cities to survey the 40-mile route. The company folded in 1853 for lack of capital, but in October of that year, it was reorganized, with W. D. M. Howard as one of its directors. Within a year this effort also collapsed. In 1857 a third group of investors from San Jose and San Francisco formed the San Francisco-San Jose Railroad Company. This syndicate was widely criticized by the local newspapers. They cited past failures and voiced concern for shipping lines, effectively scaring off investors. Finally in July 1860, a second San Francisco-San Jose Railroad was incorporated. One of the directors, Charles B. Polhemus, had a short time before purchased properties on the south bank of San Mateo Creek, east of the County Road. The company raised $2,000,000, partially from local governments. Bond issues of $200,000 each were passed in San Francisco and Santa Clara County. Voters in San Mateo County approved a $100,000 bond.

In May 1861, the company broke ground. While there were few engineering difficulties, work was slowed by heavy rainfall during the winter of 1861-1862, and by a shortage of construction materials because of the Civil War raging in the East. In January 1864 the track was completed. The project was accomplished without federal funds or land grants, as was the practice in other places (although Polhemus did try to lobby for help in Washington D.C.). This company's great showcase engine, "The California," was the first locomotive built in the West. Peter M. Donahue, one of the directors of the San Francisco-San Jose, fabricated the machine at his Union Iron Works in San Francisco.

For residents of the settlement at San Mateo, the great celebration occurred on October 17, 1863, when service actually commenced from San Francisco to Mayfield. A party train with 400 special passengers aboard made the first trip. It left the station at 18th and Valencia Streets in San Francisco at 10:30 am. There was no "Bayshore Cutoff" in those days. The train rounded San Bruno Mountain to the west and reached San Mateo in 37 minutes. It then headed for the end of the line across San Francisquito Creek, where a free lunch and champagne were served.

Among those who took this historic trip were the Governor of California, Leland Stanford, and San Mateo's Sara Donald. She was invited because her father's cooperation had been important to the Railroad. He had allowed a right of way to the company on the southern

---

Opposite: The first U.S. Government survey map, made in 1856, shows three fields and the Embarcadero, remnants of the days when San Mateo was an asistencia to Mission Dolores. There is a bridge across San Mateo Creek, from which El Camino leads southward. The names of De Peyster, Cook, Macondray, and Howard are recorded, along with Wheeler, who may have been a squatter. Dobbins Fence is a mystery.

Courtesy San Mateo County Historical Museum

*Charles B. Polhemus
from a portrait in the De Young Museum*

Courtesy San Mateo County Historical Museum

portion of his property. To return the courtesy, for some years the local commute trains would stop at Donald Station, "just a little place with benches" at about today's Highway 92 and the tracks. Sarah explained: "When we wanted to take the train we would go out the back door and walk down to the station."

THE ROLE OF POLHEMUS

CHARLES B. POLHEMUS, director of the San Francisco-San Jose Railroad, made San Mateo his special project. In the days when railroad development had a double profit-making edge, transportation and real estate speculation, Polhemus was one in a crowd. He was sure the property along the tracks at San Mateo Creek would increase in value after the completion of the railroad, and he intended to profit from that increase.

Polhemus was born on February 10, 1817, in New Jersey.[1] His family was from Holland. As young men he and his brother left the United States as agents of the Allsop Company, Commission Merchants, and set up offices in Ecuador and Peru. After gold was discovered in California, Polhemus left South America to organize an office for Allsop at San Francisco on California Street.

As a savvy businessman, he guessed that a railroad from San Francisco to San Jose would one day become a reality. In the 1850s he began to buy up parcels in the San Mateo Creek area, both along the stage road and further east where he reasoned the railroad might come through.

As the director of the railroad, he could influence the placement of the track, which happened to be laid right though the middle of his eastern San Mateo property. Long before construction was completed, Polhemus had a town plot drawn that encompassed his real estate, exclusively. It extended from the creek (about Baldwin Avenue) to Fifth Avenue and from A Street (today's South Ellsworth) to D Street (Delaware).

This future business district was little more than a wheat field at the time. Nevertheless Polhemus put 176 lots up for sale.[2] By 1865, only one year after the completion of the railroad, he had sold forty of these. Polhemus himself set up a country estate on his other property, near the highway, in the style of the Parrott, Howard and Taylor mansions at the present site of Central Park.

Polhemus had become the actual founder of the San Mateo downtown commercial district. The focus of the settlement now shifted east from the County Road to the tracks. The first building to go up was the railroad station, built of wood and painted red. It stood in the wheat field by itself for a while, but soon business houses joined it along both sides of the tracks, on Main Street and Railroad Avenue. B Street, one block west of the station, developed as the major thoroughfare, and remained so until the 1920s.

Within a few months after the tracks had been laid, the San Francisco-San Jose was scheduling four- and six-car passenger trains twice daily. The forty-mile trip, once a nine-hour stage ride, now took only an hour and fifteen minutes. Not only did travelers benefit, but local farmers and ranchers now had easy access to their markets in San Francisco. From the San Mateo depot, livestock, dairy products, grain, potatoes and other agricultural goods were shipped to the City.

San Mateo became much easier for tourists to visit. A favorite excursion for some San Franciscans was a trip to the nearby Crystal Springs Canyon. *New West* magazine described such an outing for easterners in 1867:

> You leave San Francisco by the San Jose Railroad, one of the few railroads yet built in the state. The cars are comfortable, and the road seems well laid. . . the passengers look like any respectable railroad

travelers on the East coast, perhaps, on the whole a tint ruddier and more robust, and fully as nicely dressed—the ladies often in quiet traveling dresses and gentlemen in good business suits and gloved... After some twenty miles and an hour's time we stop at San Mateo, a little village, not unlike any of our new villages, though with a prettier stone church [St. Matthews Episcopal] than is usual. The carriage drive now begins and carries us by some roomy, comfortable villas [Howard, Taylor, Parrott, et al.], such as one might see near Cleveland or Hartford, and then abruptly crossing a bright sparkling stream, takes us along its banks a short distance, then over rolling hills until we reach the Canyon.[3]

The attractions of San Mateo as a weekend outing were not lost on the San Francisco immigrant population. On May 20, 1866, the Fenians (a large Irish organization) held a picnic here which attracted over 15,000 members—perhaps the largest gathering of the group in California up until that time. Horse races and wagering were part of the fun. One of the promoters rented the barroom of the Walker Hotel for $150 for the day, which proved to be a pretty wise investment, for "John Barleycorn was a very popular gentleman."[4]

Despite the better freight service and more efficient transportation for residents, it is often debated how important the railroad really was to the development of Peninsula whistle stops like San Mateo. With the passing of years, local trade became less a concern for the railroad as its tracks linked up with more important commercial centers to the south. In 1868 the San Francisco-San Jose was absorbed by the original Southern Pacific. In 1870 this railroad was purchased by the Central Pacific, which decided to make Oakland, rather than San Francisco, the hub of its West Coast operations. In 1884 the Central Pacific was reorganized into the Southern Pacific. With this step the railroad became a big business on the national level. Serving people at such little-known locations as San Mateo was not a priority. Even as late as the 1890s, most of the 34 trains passing through San Mateo County daily were express carriers that made no local stops.[5] The success of the railroad in making San Francisco and San Jose so close in travel time had rendered San Mateo—once important as the halfway point between the two—less consequential as a rest stop.

The Estates

WHILE THE RAILROAD did not attract a rush of small businesses to San Mateo, it did lure another kind of community—wealthy San Franciscans who worked in the city, but wished to have weekend and summer homes in the country. Already present were the estates of the Howards, Taylors and Parrotts, and the new easy access inspired many more people to come down the Peninsula throughout the nineteenth and into the twentieth century. The families that came were among the most powerful in the West—in business and society. San Mateo evolved, in part, to serve the estates of those elite people. Observers remarked that the appearance and feel of the place was reminiscent of Europe, where villages of common people existed near the lands of the nobility and survived by catering to the needs of the aristocracy. The great estates provided jobs for the San Mateo villagers. The lavish mansions had to be maintained by servants and skilled craftsmen. A huge selection of supplies would be required in town.

In time the estates gradually hemmed in San Mateo and other Peninsula communities. Rich men bought up the best parcels of land along both sides of the railroad tracks. Many of them were reluctant to subdivide these properties, inhibiting the town's growth. The situation did seem a throwback to the feudal system. A wealthy gentry held sway over a small community of servants, villagers and tenant farmers. Throughout the nineteenth century, San Mateo was referred to as a village both by visitors and residents. Historians referring to the community during this period called it a village as well.

San Mateo's destiny seems to have been determined before the first train whistle blew. To the west of the Polhemus subdivision was the Taylor estate, the former San Mateo House, with seven acres of gardens and orchards beginning at the creek and proceeding south, sealing off most of the community from the County Road. To the south and east, Alvinza Hayward had quietly bought up all the property. The Howards, to the north, across the Creek, completed the encirclement.

Other large land holders were already in the area as well. While Stephen B. Whipple was not in the wealthy class of a John Parrott or Alvinza Hayward, he was no small-time rancher. His horse farm, which stretched south along the west side of County Road from the Parrott estate, was widely regarded as the first in California to be as "well equipped as the eastern farms."[6] This breeding ranch's most famous horse was Hambletonian; Whipple once turned down an offer of $10,000 for the animal. He employed a staff of 12 men year round. Tom McLellan was business manager, George Evans was in charge of breeding, and Tom Farrell trained the trotters. By gentleman's agreement, the racing stock was worked out on Alvinza Hayward's one-mile track across the County Road, one of the finest private tracks in the state. Whipple's grandson recalled that many private races were conducted there over the years.[7]

By 1873, Whipple had fallen into ill health. He had paralysis in his legs and was becoming blind as well. That year he decided to auction off some of his best stock. At the sale Alvinza Hayward bought Lady Blanchard for

George Bartlett's harness shop was on the east side of B Street, just north of Second Avenue.

Courtesy San Mateo County Historical Museum

Above: Third and B Streets, circa 1865. Husing's store is on the right. On the left is a butcher shop, with several carcasses hanging outside. These may be deer brought in by hunters to be dressed. People were always eager to step outside to have their picture taken.

Right: the interior of Bartlett's harness & saddlery shows a massive sewing machine for stitching leather.

Courtesy San Mateo County Historical Museum

Top: San Mateo's first train station was later moved to the corner of Second and B Streets, where it housed a real estate office, the Reindeer Saloon, a harness shop, and a vendor of candies, nuts and fruit. Bottom: The San Mateo Hotel, operated by Eugene Walker, first advertised in 1865.

Courtesy San Mateo County Historical Museum

This view of B Street looking south from First Avenue in the late 1870s shows the village looking much more substantial. The train depot has been moved to Second & B, and houses a restaurant. The wooden building with porch at right may be Wisnom's lumber & hardware.
Courtesy San Mateo County Historical Museum

$22,500. Altogether some $180,000 worth of horseflesh was sold.

In 1884 K. O'Grady took over the farm as a trotting and pacing ranch, managing it until 1890, when Walter Hobart bought the place as his country estate. Eventually Charles Clark owned the property. Today St. Matthew's Catholic School occupies the site of the main house.

THE PARROTT FAMILY

FOR MORE THAN HALF A CENTURY, perhaps the pre-eminent family in the San Mateo area were the Parrotts. By the time he purchased his San Mateo property in 1860, John Parrott was renowned in California for his success in commerce and banking. He would eventually have holdings from Hawaii to Nome, from the clipper ship *Dreadnought* to the quicksilver mines of the Sierra Nevada and Parrott City, Colorado, from his 18,000-acre ranch in Butte County, California, to Baywood, his beloved estate at San Mateo.

Parrott was born in Virginia in 1811. As a young man full of adventure, he managed to find his way to the west coast of Mexico, where he became involved in the shipping business. As hostilities between the United States and Mexico escalated in 1846, Parrott held the official title of U. S. Consul at Mazatlan. In that role, he corresponded with such national leaders as James Buchanan and Daniel Webster, and important Californian statesmen like Thomas Larkin. During this time, Parrott was partly credited for getting word to Commodore John D. Sloat and his Pacific squadron that war had commenced, resulting in the early takeover of California by American forces.

As a California businessman, Parrott built the famed granite "fire proof" building at Montgomery and California Streets in San Francisco in the early 1850s. The blocks of granite were cut to measure in China, each carefully numbered; then Chinese laborers accompanied them to San Francisco and fitted the blocks together to form a splendid building, the finest in the city. With his financial empire blossoming, Parrott returned to the East and married Abby Eastman Maher at Mobile, Alabama, in 1853. Two years later he formed his own mercantile firm, Parrott and Company.

The Parrotts' original town house was on Rincon Hill (later on they moved to Sutter Street) in San Francisco, but John wished to create a summer place for his wife, so on February 1, 1860, he formally purchased his San Mateo property from Captain Macondray for $30,000.[8]

Work on the estate began slowly. The first thing accomplished was the renaming of the place from Brookside to Baywood, after the indigenous bay trees

A stagecoach pauses on the B Street bridge in the 1880s.
Courtesy San Mateo County Historical Museum

that lined the creek. Macondray's house probably served as part of the lower floor of the mansion that was completed in 1868. It was designed with strong French influences in the Second Empire Style. The house was a wonder to the locals, with its water-powered elevators, a tunnel to the Creek, and sound proofing, made of layers of crushed sea shells packed between floors.

Summers at San Mateo for families like the Parrotts must have been elegant, indeed. Old-timers would later speak of how the afternoon commute from the city ended at the depot with a "sprinkling of important looking men" being met by "a pageant of smart vehicles," among them phaetons, pony carts, Irish jaunting carts, surreys, broughams, landaus, tandem carts, station wagons and tally-hos, "all pulled by fine horses" and "usually driven by liveried coachmen."[9]

Unlike many of their neighbors, the Parrotts were not big party givers. Theirs was a conservative life, with family and religion of paramount importance. Old-timers remembered what a sight it was to see the Parrotts and their children at the Catholic Church, the boy "in starched shirt, his Sunday best," and the girls "in their spotless frocks and huge hair bows." While they prayed with the villagers, there was a clear contrast in social status as they walked to their pews "with an air of indifference."[10]

As the children grew up (one son and six daughters), some stayed in the immediate San Mateo vicinity, establishing their own estates near Baywood, helping to box in the village's borders.

The oldest daughter, Mary Katherine, married Christian de Guigne in 1879. The aristocratic young Frenchman had come to California as an agent of a French banking firm. The couple established their estate on property purchased from the Husing Brothers, on the east side of the County Road, between today's Third and Fourth Avenues. The Husings had long before moved their store closer to the tracks at B and Third Avenue. The de Guignes built their house at about the site of the Benjamin Franklin Hotel. They called it Minne-haha after Mary's nickname—"Minnie." De Guigne did quite well in California business. He became a co-founder of the important Stauffer Chemical Company and eventually served as its president.

Another daughter, Abby Josephine or "Daisy," married Captain A. H. Payson in 1884. In 1886 they established their estate right alongside the de Guignes'—from the County Road to today's Ellsworth, and from Fourth Avenue to Fifth. Payson was born in Salem, Massachusetts, and graduated from West Point in 1868. He became an Army engineer and taught at West Point for some years until ordered to San Francisco in 1877 to work with the Lighthouse, Rivers and Harbors Department. During his tenure he oversaw construction of Point Sur and St. George's reef lighthouses. Payson resigned from the Army in 1887 and began a successful career in San Francisco business. He was a director of the Spring Valley Water Company and eventually became its president. He also served on the boards of the Santa Fe Railroad Company and San Joaquin Valley Railroad Company. He earned local celebrity as the first mayor of the newly incorporated town of San Mateo in 1894.

Son John Jr. and daughter Grace established their residences on Baywood proper. John married Mary E. Donohoe and lived in "The Bungalow." Grace married attorney Robert Young Hayne in 1881. Hayne had come to California in 1867 as a 14-year-old with his family from Charleston. He eventually became a well known judge. They lived on the southern portion of the Baywood estate, on today's West Fifth Avenue.

Youngest daughter Christine married another Donohoe, Joseph A., and lived in Menlo Park. The two remaining sisters were married in Europe and made their homes there.

John Parrott's original purchase from Macondray was 260 acres. However, over time Parrott acquired more property until the estate contained 458 acres. Besides making the place his summer home, Parrott bred Durham cattle at Baywood, and horses as well. As the years went by, John Sr. and wife Abby made longer stays at San Mateo until by the end of John's life, they spent almost all their time here. John died in San Francisco at the age of 74 in 1884.

Family legend has it that shortly before his death, John instructed Abby to remember him by being charitable to others, and to "turn no hungry man away." Abby took these words as a "sacred trust" and for more than thirty years provided meals at Baywood for poor travelers who could not afford to feed themselves. The County Road was used by thousands of vagabonds in the late 19th and early 20th centuries.

Abby's work to feed these people was formidable. She had to budget a sizable monthly allowance from her household expenses and employed staff with the specific responsibility of providing for their "guests." It is said that the quality of the food served the hobos was the same as that eaten by the hostess and her personal friends. From the back porch off the kitchen some 50 to 100 people were routinely fed each day. A special campground was established on the estate. It is reported

John Parrott
1811 - 1844
Courtesy San Mateo County Historical Museum

that Abby frequently joined the men as they gathered around their bonfires, swapping stories and singing. Before she died, Abby estimated that she had served some 300,000 of these homeless people.[11]

COMPLETING THE CIRCLE

COMPLETING THE BLOCK OF ESTATES bordering the village to the southwest was the Charles Polhemus place, the site of today's Central Park, which stretches from Fifth Avenue to Ninth. Polhemus purchased this property in 1854 from Henry Dubbers. He build a three-story, 13-room house and completed much of his strategy here for the development of the railroad and the village to the east.

After making some money selling lots in San Mateo and Los Angeles, Polhemus bought 580 acres west of town, up Crystal Springs Road, for use as a cattle ranch in 1863. He built a house for the foreman, but the Polhemus family never lived there, since they had a home close to the village. Polhemus owned this property into the 1870s. In 1876 a portion of it became the

Opposite, top: Baywood, the magnificent mansion John Parrott built in 1868, using Macondray's house as a base, shows a French Second Empire influence in its roof and window designs. Below: A rare view of the sumptuous interior of Baywood shows that the French taste prevailed here as well.

Above: John Parrott, Jr., drives a splendid matched team at "The Bungalow," his house on the Baywood estate.

Courtesy San Mateo County Historical Museum

County Poor Farm. It is now the site of the county complex on Tower Road along Highway 92.

Polhemus eventually sold all his San Mateo properties and bought real estate in Atherton and San Jose. He died in a modest house in San Jose in 1904.

Polhemus sold his property on the County Road to partner Peter Donahue in 1866. Donahue then sold it to Alexander Austin, a San Francisco city official. After Austin died his widow sold the property to William H. Kohl, about 1874.

Kohl was of Pennsylvania-Dutch ancestry. He had worked as an engineer and sea captain before making his fortune in the Alaska fur seal trade. With part of his money he created an estate at San Mateo. Still remaining is a portion of his 1874 stone and iron fence, which can be seen at Central Park on the El Camino Real side. The fence was originally 2000 feet long and cost $10,000. The house stood until 1928, and served as the Junior College for three years before its demolition. Kohl's son, Fred, built the well-known Kohl mansion in Burlingame, now used as Mercy High School.

VILLAGE LEADERS

SUPPORTING THE ACTIVITIES on the estates were various skilled and unskilled workers. Also benefiting from the presence of the elite were a variety of managers and businessmen and women who formed the nucleus of a small but enduring middle class within the village community.

Among those who can be counted in this social stratum was John Quincy Adams Tilton, who came to San Mateo sometime between 1859 and 1860. John was born in New Hampshire, one of Stephen and Julia Tilton's 13 children. In 1852, Tilton managed a dairy ranch in San Francisco. He returned east that year and married Agnes Maria Griffith of Vermont. In 1853 the couple came to California to run a ranch in Santa Clara, but a water shortage convinced them to find new employment at San Mateo. John went to work as a

Daisy Parrott and her husband, Captain A. H. Payson, built their house at Baywood in the modern style, with a porte cochere on the left side. The interior was also decidedly in the modern taste, with informal wicker and Eastlake furniture and plaid curtains below the stained-glass windows.

Courtesy San Mateo County Historical Museum

No photographs of the William Kohl house survive, but this photograph shows the gardens, which are today's Central Park. Kohl hired John McLaren to design the gardens, and surrounded them with a magnificent stone and iron fence, one of the park's chief glories today.

Courtesy San Mateo County Historical Museum

manager on the Howard's Rancho San Mateo. Tax records indicate that by 1863 the Tiltons had done quite nicely in this situation, owing $773 in property tax, based on their ownership of a considerable number of livestock (450 cattle, 300 sheep, 25 hogs and seven horses).

By 1865, the Tiltons could afford to purchase 25 acres of their own from George and Agnes Howard. Here they built a large house east of the tracks near present Tilton Avenue (a portion of the house still stands in 1993). About this time, John went into business with his brother-in-law, Samuel Goodhue. They opened a butcher shop on Main Street in the village. The Tiltons, along with the Goodhues, John's parents and another brother-in-law, A. Easton (the elder Tiltons and the Eastons lived farther north on the Peninsula), helped to form the Congregational Church in San Mateo, an early religious and social institution for San Mateo County.

Tilton died in 1868 at the age of 41. Goodhue took over most of John's business enterprises, while Agnes turned the large home into a boarding house.

Agnes was one of the primary promoters of the building of the Congregational Church, and she remained a respected member of the village community long after John's passing. Among her projects was the establishment of a 20-acre cemetery near her house in 1877. No cemetery had existed for the village before this time. She called it Evergreen, and it served the people in the San Mateo area for about eight years. Then the graveyard was moved up the hill to the newly established St. John's Cemetery, made possible by a generous gift from the Parrott family after John Sr.'s death.

John Tilton's early demise had the effect of creating a second strong woman in the family. Daughter Etta M. Tilton became a prominent teacher in San Mateo, sat on the County's first Board of Education in 1880 and eventually became County Superintendent of Schools.

Another family of this social type were the Wisnoms. Robert Wisnom, born in Ballycarry County, Northern

Above: Agnes Tilton's house in the midst of its 25 acres, near the railroad tracks. Left: The Tilton house, one of the few remaining 19th Century houses in San Mateo, retains its dormers and chimneys, but has been converted to apartments in this 1976 photo, taken by Robert Toren.

Opposite: The Wisnom family, one of the most active in building San Mateo, sat for this portrait in 1896. Standing at the rear are David, Robert Jr., William & Anna; below them are David, father Robert, sons John and Samuel, and mother Sarah. Below: The Wisnoms built a new house on B Street, with three floors of carpenters.

Courtesy San Mateo County Historical Museum

Ireland, began his apprenticeship at age 13 as a carpenter in Glasgow. He spent some time in New Zealand before coming to California, at age 21. After two years in San Francisco, Wisnom came down to San Mateo to work on the building of the Parrott family mansion in 1868. He lived in Agnes Tilton's boarding house while completing the job. Family history has it that in 1872 he planned a trip to Ireland with the expressed purpose of bringing back a bride. He promised Mrs. Tilton that if his quest proved successful, he'd buy her a new dress.[12] He did marry Sarah Donnan of Whitehead. The couple immediately sailed for California with San Mateo as their ultimate destination. Wisnom believed he had a future here. For a while the couple lived at the Tilton House. Then Robert built their first family home at Claremont and First Avenue.

Through the years Robert Wisnom became San Mateo's best known builder. One of his major early contracts was the 1874 building of Union Hall, complete with three store fronts and a large room for social gatherings. As the years went on, Wisnom invested in town properties, helped organize the community's first bank, and joined Captain Payson as an original member of the town's governing body.

Wisnom was not wealthy compared to the Parrotts or Howards, but he was a man of means, with a Chinese cook and a Portuguese gardener. His large family flourished, and played important roles in the town's development. The Wisnoms, like the Tiltons, became active in the Congregational Church. When Robert died, some fifty years after he had first seen San Mateo, in his memory Sarah donated a full pipe organ to the

The Wisnom carpentry shop, hardware store and lumber yard at Baldwin & B Streets supplied materials for building San Mateo's houses in the 1890s.

Courtesy San Mateo County Historical Museum

Church—the first for the congregation. On the day of his funeral, all stores in the community were closed, and the church overflowed with many citizens standing outside to pay their respects.

Besides the Tiltons and Wisnoms, perhaps the most prominent early businessman of the village was James E. Skidmore, the railroad agent who worked at the station house. Thanks to the importance of the railroad, in 1863, as soon as tracks reached San Mateo, Skidmore was made postmaster, replacing Tony Oakes up at the San Mateo House. By 1866, Skidmore also held the positions of justice of the peace of the Second Township of San Mateo County, notary public, agent for the two telegraph companies (State and Pacific), secretary for the San Mateo & Half Moon Bay Turnpike Road Company, magistrate, town clerk, conservator of public peace, clerk of Saint Matthew's Church and agent for all of the insurance companies operating in San Mateo County.

The single most important business in the town was Husing Brothers' General Store on the Northwest corner of Third and B. When it opened in April 1868 (after moving down from the County Road), a grand ball was organized, with gentlemen obliged to pay $1.00 for admission, while ladies were allowed in free. The new social gathering place was welcomed by residents. Previously all celebrations had taken place at the tiny school house.

Two other early village businessmen are counted among the county's first African-Americans. Tom Ricks managed the restaurant in the Railroad House, and J. J. Adams ran a barber shop in the same building. In 1874 Adams became the first African-American to serve on the San Mateo County Grand Jury.[13]

STAGE SERVICE TO THE COAST

WHILE RAIL TRANSPORTATION replaced the stagecoach for north-south service on the San Mateo County bayside, all east-west travel and transportation in

The Wisnom house, originally on B Street, was moved twice: first to the corner of Fifth & B, and then to Ellsworth Street, where it became a duplex.

Courtesy San Mateo County Historical Museum

the hill country and on the coast remained the domain of the horse-drawn vehicle until well into the twentieth century. Throughout this period, San Mateo was an important terminus for the county, linking freight, mail and passenger services from the coast with the railroad.

San Mateo County had been a county (1856) for only a few months before its leaders recognized that their most pressing problem was improvement of roads. County officials soon grew weary of the demand for their maintenance, and chose to contract the service to private companies to operate the routes as toll roads. Eventually three toll highways were established in the county, linking the coast with the bayside. In 1864, after $20,000 was expended, a vastly improved Half Moon Bay-San Mateo toll road was opened. The County Board of Supervisors set the tolls—saddle horse, ten cents, vehicle and horse, 25 cents, and sheep, hogs and goats, two cents each. Eventually this turnpike linked up with such distant habitations as San Gregorio and Pescadero. The toll gate was built about three miles up from El Camino Real, at the first place where the road could be effectively blocked off. For the companies involved, the San Mateo County toll road ventures were seldom profitable. In November 1883 the County bought back the San Mateo and Half Moon Bay Turnpike for $7,500, and again assumed responsibility for its upkeep.

Far more profitable were the stagecoach lines. Service between Half Moon Bay and San Mateo can be traced to 1860 when John Morse operated a line. The big Concord coaches were employed for the most part. They could carry sixteen passengers plus luggage.

By 1865 two firms offered service out of San Mateo, the Taft and Garretson Company and the J. C. Street Company. During this competitive period, the trip from San Mateo to Pescadero cost the traveler $2.50 and took about four and a quarter hours.

About 1872 S. L. Knight initiated service to Pescadero out of Redwood City. Since both the San Mateo and

The San Mateo & Half Moon Bay Stage stops at the train station with 13 passengers on top and more inside.

Courtesy San Mateo County Historical Museum

Redwood City lines catered to railroad passengers destined for the coast, the competition became heated. Both routes had their advantages. The San Mateo road traversed comparatively more open and less mountainous country, making for a more comfortable ride. The Redwood City stage took the passenger through beautiful scenery. The San Mateo stages had the ultimate advantage in that passengers from San Francisco stopped at San Mateo first. As the train chugged to the station, drivers would yell out "Pescadero Stage, Pescadero Stage—all aboard," and those who might have intended using Knight would purchase their round trip tickets and begin and finish their excursions from the wrong town.[14]

Taft and Garretson ran the most successful stage line out of San Mateo during the early years of this colorful era. By 1883, the partners had their Concord coaches connecting up with Santa Cruz, with daily mail and passenger service stopping at such stations as Crystal Springs, San Feliz, Byrnes' Store, Eureka Gardens, Half Moon Bay, Purissima, Lobitas, San Gregorio, Pescadero, Pigeon Point, Seaside and Davenport. Some of these are now thriving communities or quaint coastal attractions, some disappeared from the map over time, and others are now within the San Francisco watershed.

Of all the characters associated with the early stage coach days, "Buckskin Bob" Rawls is most famous. Contemporaries described "his bright smile, his hearty laugh, his ready wit, his keen repartee" as "the delight of all" who knew him. On the route from San Mateo to Pescadero he was a favorite driver with his "affability, especially with the ladies" which "gained for him many devoted friends."[15] Bob was also renowned for occasionally bringing his coach in on two wheels as he swung in at the old Occidental Hotel at Half Moon Bay.

Of course not everything was perfect about stagecoach travel. No matter what the route to the coast, the trip was bumpy and uncomfortable. There were robberies, too. The April 18, 1885, *Times Gazette* mentions what it considered to be the first hold-up when "Buckskin Bob" was accosted "in the Cañada." The newspaper explained:

> The armed robbers demanded and received the express box when they departed into the woods and pried the box with a pick. As there was no valuables in the box, the robbers had their trouble for their pains. A mask, hat and some crackers supposed to have belonged to the criminals were found, but the officers have thus far been unable to find the men.

A much more common, but no less frightening, risk of stage riding involved inebriated drivers. An old-timer from Half Moon Bay, Mrs. Mary McGintry, described such a terror-filled experience to a junior college student in 1940.[16] Although she was only a little girl at the time, McGintry remembered the stage was right on schedule

The Levy Brothers' stage, bound for Pescadero, leaves San Mateo's fine new train station.

Courtesy San Mateo County Historical Museum

until it reached the Crystal Springs Hotel. Here a longer than usual stop was made, and when the driver emerged from the Carey Saloon he seemed a bit unsteady. At the San Feliz station the same type of delay occurred. Mary recalled that when the driver finally climbed back on the coach he banged his shins on a step and swore mightily. Everyone aboard was worried about the condition of the driver by the time the coach approached Byrnes' Store. Dick "Beefsteak" Dougherty of Purissima was riding on top, and attempted to convince the driver not to stop at the store, as the stage was already behind schedule. This coaxing fell short, and, in fact, Mary suspected more than one drink was consumed at Byrnes', since "Beefsteak" had to help the driver to his seat this time.

Finally they reached the summit, where "Beefsteak" made the mistake of commenting that it would be dark before the stage would reach San Gregorio. The driver boasted he would arrive in Spanishtown (Half Moon Bay today) on time, and whipped the horses into a frenzy on the downhill road. In short order panic ensued inside the coach as passengers realized they were aboard "a runaway." A man told Mary and her mother that when the time came to jump, he would assist them. Another passenger, Henry Nichols, poked his head out the window, saw a sharp turn coming and almost fell out of

Buckskin Bob and his missus.

Courtesy San Mateo County Historical Museum

St. Matthew's, the first Roman Catholic Church, built in 1864.

Courtesy San Mateo County Historical Museum

the coach. Fortunately, up on top, "Beefsteak" wrestled the reins away from the driver, regained control of the vehicle, and drove the stage on to Spanishtown.

By the 1890s, the French-Jewish merchants of the coast, the Levy brothers, had bought the San Mateo and Half Moon Bay stage service. The pace of trips was slowed down from the more competitive early days. Instead of racing to Pescadero in less than four and a half hours, the stage left San Mateo at 10:00 in the morning, stopped for lunch and a change of horses at Half Moon Bay, and arrived at Pescadero between 3:30 and 4:00 in the afternoon. Meanwhile, the Pescadero stage left at 7:00 in the morning, stopped for lunch at Half Moon Bay and arrived at San Mateo about 3:15. The Levys eventually left the coast and became important San Mateo businessmen.

Establishment of Churches

WHILE THE MISSION OUTPOST at San Mateo had functioned in part as a house of worship, it had long since ceased serving that purpose by the time the railroad tracks were laid to the village. Now that San Mateo was becoming more than just a stage stop, people wanted permanent community institutions. The Catholics were first to establish a church at San Mateo through the efforts of Father Dennis F. Dempsey of Dublin. Dempsey had gone to Carlow College in Ireland, served his apprenticeship at Saint Mary's Cathedral in San Francisco and had worked for the Church in such places as Marysville, Sacramento and Auburn. In about 1863, Archbishop Joseph S. Alemany gave Dempsey responsibility for parish territories in San Mateo and Santa Clara Counties. His first success was establishment of Saint Dennis Chapel east of Searsville.

The church credits Charles B. Polhemus with donation of the parcel of land for the building of the first church. The property was on the southwest corner of today's Third Avenue and Ellsworth, across the street from where the second Catholic church would be built in 1900.[17] Father Dempsey and Peter Casey raised the necessary funds for construction by riding through the countryside, visiting potential donors. Peter M. Donahue cast a bell in his San Francisco iron foundry and donated it to the Church (the bell can now be seen at the County Historical Museum). A small frame building was constructed, and on February 7, 1864, Archbishop Alemany came to bless it.

Even while the San Mateo Church was being erected, Father Dempsey was busy raising money for other houses of worship. By the time of his death in 1881, he had founded six churches. Dempsey's assistant since 1871, Father William Bowman, succeeded him, but lived only a few months longer than Dempsey. The third pastor of the parish was Father Peter Birmingham, who stayed until 1884, when he was put on exchange to Saint Brigid's in San Francisco. Then came the legendary Timothy Callahan, the 40-year-old Irishman who would serve the parish for fifty-three years (1884-1937).

San Mateo's first Episcopal minister, Reverend G. A. Easton, took temporary residency here in 1864, holding services in the reception room of the newly completed San Mateo Young Ladies Institute, located southwest of the village. That fall Easton left, and was succeeded in February 1865 by Reverend A. L. Brewer of Detroit, Michigan. The Episcopal Board of Missions had sent Brewer to take control of both the San Mateo and Redwood City congregations. Brewer held services in the small school house on the County Road, sharing the building with other Protestant congregations.

In July 1865 the George Howard family donated two acres of property just north of the creek and east of the County Road as a site for an Episcopal church. A fund-raising campaign was launched, and by October a formal organization existed with some rather impressive members. George Howard himself became a Warden, as did Edward Taylor. A. H. Jordan was elected Clerk and Treasurer.

Jordan was also the church's architect. He designed what was certainly one of the most beautiful buildings on the Peninsula. Construction started in 1865, and the Church was consecrated on May 23, 1866, with clergymen from throughout California and Oregon attending. Great stones from the Crystal Springs quarry were used in the construction. It stood for many years as the only stone church in the State. Other achieve-ments of the congregation included the founding of a school (1866), the con-struction of a rectory (1867) and improvements to the school (1868 and 1872).

An account of 1878 described how the church's appearance seemed to grow more impressive with age:

> The church, since its building, has become ivy-grown, giving it a look of age and a touch of rustic beauty, refreshing amid the newness of public buildings in the State; and within it has been enriched by monumental sculpture and rich stained glass, and other accessories of a place of sacred worship, which added to association, and make it worthy of a passing visit.[18]

The Congregationalists began meeting in San Mateo in September 1862, when J. S. Zelia, acting pastor of the Congregational Church in Redwood City, visited here. A

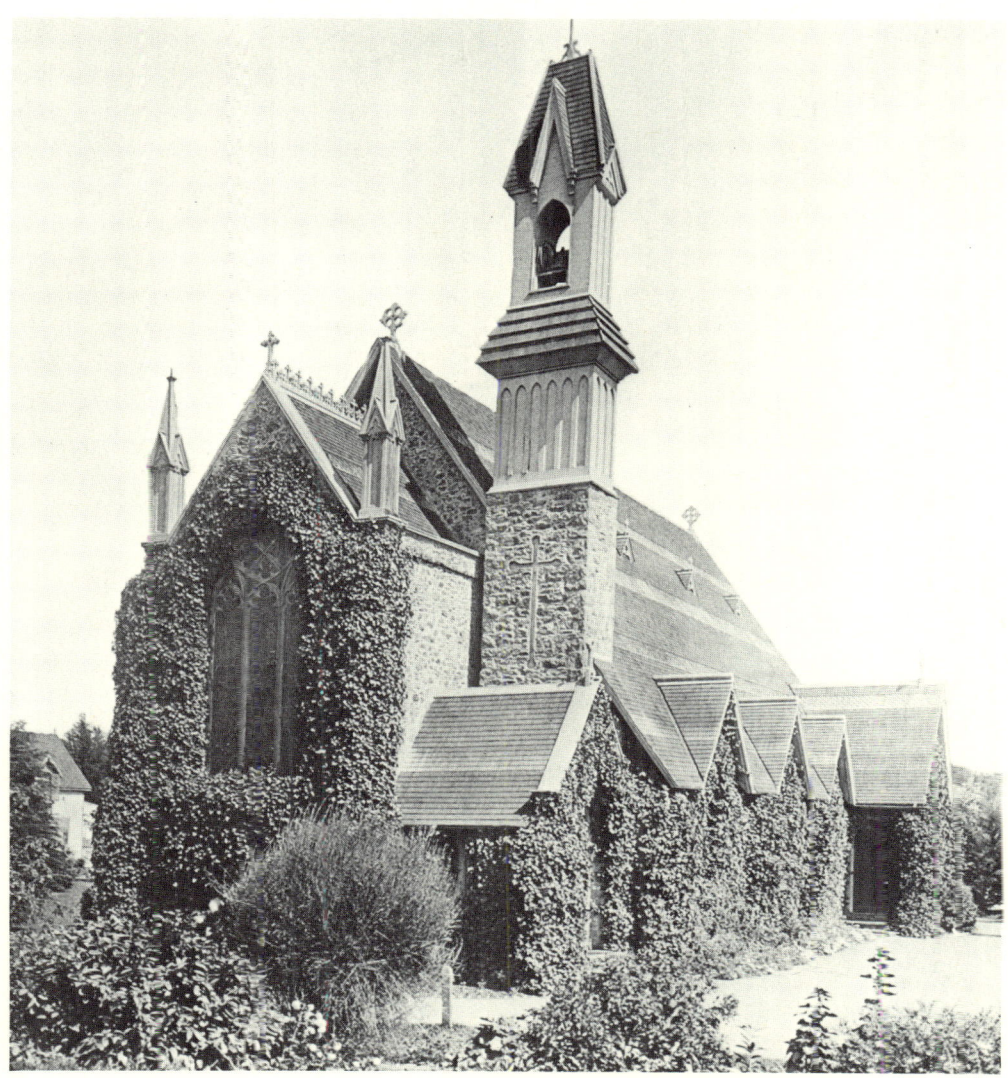

The first Episcopal church, St. Matthews, built in 1866, was the first stone church in California. It was destroyed in the 1906 earthquake.
Courtesy San Mateo County Historical Museum

month later Reverend J. H. Warren conducted the first service in the "unfurnished and uncomfortably seated school house."[19] After almost two years, in May 1864, ten members of the community decided to incorporate themselves formally as the Congregational Church of San Mateo. Its first officers were Stephen Tilton, William Dow and S. C. Goodhue. Reverend J. H. Warren served as pastor for another five months until he was succeeded by Reverend M. J. Savage.

The interior of St. Matthews Episcopal Church in a season when calla lilies were plentiful in San Mateo. Below: Reverend A. L. Brewer.

Courtesy San Mateo County Historical Museum

After his family had donated the property for the construction of the Episcopal Church, George Howard also saw to it that the Congregationalists would have a church site. He made a gift of property on the corner of today's Tilton and North Ellsworth for the purpose. By the end of 1868, the $4,535 needed to construct the building had been raised. In the mean-time, the congregation con-tinued to meet in the school house. A parsonage was completed first, then in early 1869, the church, a wood frame structure was dedicated. This building survived well into the present century. Its steeple was knocked off in the 1906 earthquake, but the building served the congregation until 1922, when it was replaced by the present church.

Two Impressive Private Schools

San Mateo's position on the San Francisco Peninsula, its access to the best possible transportation, its fine climate and its beautiful surroundings, not only brought people from the city to establish their great estates here, but also caught the attention of parents looking to place their child-ren in top-rated private schools. The San Mateo area had not one, but two such schools, a girls' institution and a boys' military academy. Both added to the growing image of San Mateo as a haven for the elite.

The girls' school was the inspiration of Miss L. A. Buckmaster, who had begun her career in her native Vermont. In that state, and later in New York, she taught in public schools and seminaries. She came to California in December 1856, and worked in the public school at Marysville from 1857 until 1860. In January of 1861, she opened her own private school in Sacramento. She started out with eleven students, and this number increased to 65. The flood of the winter of 1861 - 1862 caused the school to close. Buckmaster then moved to Oakland, taking with her a few of her students, but she could not settle on a satisfactory new location.

Sometime in 1862, Buckmaster met San Mateo's Charles B. Polhemus. He told her of the railroad that would soon tie San Mateo closer to the city. He talked her into visiting sections of San Mateo County, where she interviewed residents. She began to believe a school near the village of San Mateo could succeed. She was particularly taken with a site about a mile south of the train station and a half mile west of the County Road on "high lands" with "open views."[20] Later, to those interested in enrolling their daughters in the school, she explained:

> [The school is] a place noted for the beauty of its scenery, and delightful climate, being equally free from the cold summer winds and fogs of the coast, and the enervating heat of the interior. The place possesses many advantages for such an Institution. Situated on the line of the San Francisco and San Jose Railroad, it is easy of access from all parts of the State. Being distant but twenty miles from San Francisco, and having railroad and telegraphic communications, it commands all the educational resources of the Metropolis.[21]

Miss Buckmaster also liked the idea that the school had avoided locating itself in a city, freeing it "from those

The First Congregational Church, built in 1869 at Tilton and Ellsworth.

Courtesy San Mateo County Historical Museum

excitements so detrimental to the discipline and progress of students which are incidental to large towns."

In 1863, the young educator bought 27 acres of land from the old pioneer, David S. Cook, formerly of the San Mateo House, for $100 per acre. The exact site of the school is on today's Alameda de Las Pulgas, at the California Casualty Building property. The land was covered by oak and laurel. Architect S. C. Bugbee designed the first building, which cost $9,000 to construct. No-interest loans were offered by a group of supporters who came up with $10,525 to initiate the project. The list of names of the Trustees of this San Mateo Institute, as it was originally called, was a "who's who" of San Francisco and San Mateo County society, suggesting where the initial loans came from: George H. Howard, Alvinza Hayward, A. H. Houston, Frederick Billings, Benjamin G. Lathrop, Thomas Selby, F. F. Low, James R. Bolton, D. O. Mills, R. B. Sneath and A. I. Easton.

While the grounds were admittedly rugged, Buckmaster promised in the initial prospectus of the Institute that soon the oak and bay trees would be enhanced by "gardens, pleasure grounds, walks, etc.,"

This fine panorama looks southeast from the Howard estate. The road at center is El Camino; above it at right are St. Matthews Episcopal, with the rectory and the school at the left. Above the school is downtown San Mateo's skyline, with Walker's hotel the largest building.

Courtesy San Mateo County Historical Museum

and as for the building, it was a "new and commodious edifice, suitable, in its arrangements, for all departments of the Institute, and designed with special reference to the health and comfort of the pupils."

The school was organized into three departments: Preparatory, Academic and Collegiate. Students were to be placed according to their "age, capacity and proficiency." No specified time was "assigned to any division." Instead, students would advance "as rapidly as possible—each being required to take as many studies as she can thoroughly prepare, without overwork."

The staff, of course, was headed by Buckmaster, who assumed the title of principal. She was assisted by J. H. Warren, pastor of the Congregational Church, who specialized in Latin, "moral science," and sacred literature. His wife, E. A. Warren, was English Department head, with Miss Mary L. Ketchman as her assistant. Mlle. Adele Parrot taught French, German and gymnastics. William Schraubstadter was professor of vocal and instrumental music. Miss Mary M. Dow gave instruction on piano and music theory, and Virgil L. Williams taught drawing and painting techniques.

The school opened in early 1864 with eleven students. The basic tuition of $200 per session covered regular courses, room, board and laundering. Sessions lasted about five months; one started in the winter, and one in the summer. Optional courses in piano, singing, drawing and painting cost extra—from $10 to $50 per session.

By the school's second session, 41 girls were enrolled. Their last names included many of California's most famous—such as Starr and Selby. They came from as far away as Virginia City, Nevada. There were also quite a few local San Mateo girls on the roster, including Hattie Butler, Ellie Cook (actually born in San Mateo), Hattie Cook, Robena Lee, Carolina Polhemus, Josie Polhemus, Sara Whipple, Mary Whipple, Josie Whipple, Anna C. Warren, Mary F. Warren and Nellie Warren. While still officially recognized as the San Mateo Young Ladies' Institute, within a couple of years, many began referring to the school as Laurel Hall, after the many laurel trees on the grounds.

In 1868, several improvements were added to the property. A gymnasium, 30' x 50', was constructed, as were a barn and stables. By 1871, further improvements and the need to retire old debts required a new drive for funds. Donations were secured from a variety of prominent local people who became known as "founders" or "donors." Among them were:

George H. Howard	$500
Thomas H. Selby	$375
T. G. Phelps	$125
Mrs. A. J. Easton	$500
J. R. Bolton	$375
H. M. Newhall	$100
D. O. Mills	$375
John Parrott	$500
J. Strahle	$50
S. M. Mezes	$250
William K. Garrison	$200

The Young Ladies' Institute (Laurel Hall) was founded in 1864, when hoop skirts were in style. Miss Buckmaster's expression suggests a serene determination.
Courtesy San Mateo County Historical Museum

The prestige of the school grew during the early 1870s. The Institute placed an advertisement in the *San Francisco Daily Evening Bulletin* in January 1873, describing itself to potentially interested families:

> Laurel Hall, French, German and English Boarding School for Misses and Young Ladies. The next session will commence Saturday, January 4, 1873. The course of instruction combines the best features of the Cosmopolitan School and of the American Seminary. While pupils acquire a conversational command of French and German, the English course is thorough and complete.

In 1875 Miss Buckmaster decided to return to the east coast to visit her birthplace and talk to people there about educational "methods and means."[22] Taking her place in running the school for two years was Reverend E. Church, and then for another year, Reverend George Herbert Watson and his wife. During this period the school continued to flourish. In fact, a new cottage was constructed close to the main building, enabling the Institute to accommodate fifteen more pupils. Buckmaster returned a married woman in 1878, now known as Mrs. L. A. Buckmaster-Manson.

Unfortunately her union with A. H. Manson did not last long. In August of that year Manson attacked his wife in a drunken rage. She called on Sheriff Green in Redwood City for help. Green tracked Manson to a hotel in San Francisco. When Manson discovered he was about to be taken to jail, he shot himself.

While it is debatable how much the resulting scandal hurt the Institute, Miss Buckmaster herself certainly suffered, and her health declined. In 1886, a Laurel Hall

Laurel Hall girls enact a play, circa 1870. The winged fairies show their deep concern for a sleeping maiden.

<small>Courtesy San Mateo County Historical Museum</small>

Educational Association of San Mateo was organized by 100 former students to support the activities of the school, but it was too late. Miss Buckmaster was too ill to continue. In May 1887 the school was to be sold at auction, but no sale was made. Miss Buckmaster died on October 6 in San Francisco. Her estate then rented the property to Professor John Gamble, who operated the facility as a private school for 60 boys. The place eventually served as an orphanage before being absorbed by the Borel Estate.

The Episcopal Reverend, A. L. Brewer, founded the boys school, a military academy, which came to be known at St. Matthews Hall. In 1866, as the finishing touches were made on the Episcopal Church, the school opened in a nearby residence at what we would call 415 South Ellsworth today. The school quickly outgrew these accommodations. In 1872 a large, three-story building just east of the church was constructed.

By the 1880s, St. Matthews Hall was calling itself "A Classical and Military School" on its letterhead. The academy became famous throughout the West. Perhaps its best-known former student was journalist Lincoln Steffens, who spent his 4th, 5th and 6th grade years there, from 1881 to 1884.[23] The reputation of the school also reached far into the Pacific. In February of 1881, the King of the Sandwich Islands visited San Mateo. Among his stops was St. Matthews, where the cadets paraded in full military dress. Soon after, sons of the most influential Hawaiian families came to St. Matthews, including Anglo boys such as T. Spencer, Thomas Cummins and James Wilder, and sons of the royal families. David Piikoi, whose father was the last king of Kaui, and his wife Kekaulike Kinoiki, a princess, sent three of their sons to St. Matthews beginning in 1884. The youngest, Prince Jonah Kuhio (1871-1922), who spent four years at St. Matthews, was elected to the U. S. Congress in 1902 as delegate from Hawaii and continued to be re-elected to that office until his death.[24]

Whether their ancestry was royal or not, when parents entered their sons in the academy, they had to agree to strict terms, allowing the school to do its job. The entrance application asked for a frank disclosure of the potential student's nature:

> What are his characteristics?
> What discipline do you find best for him?
> Is he phlegmatic or disposed to idleness?
> Is he obstinate?
> Is he truthful and trustworthy?
> Has he been in the habit of swearing and if so, to what extent?
> Are his habits otherwise correct?

School fees were comparable to Laurel Hall's. In 1875 the cost for a school term of four and a half months was $168.75. This did not include incidental expenses such as books, stationary, medical attendance, chemistry and physics materials, etc. Studies that required extra charges of $10 to $75 included phonography, type-writing, drawing, musical instruments, boxing, fencing, gymnastics and dancing.25 By the 1890s the basic fee was $500 per school year.26 The school in its later years was run by Brewer's son, Dr. William Brewer, and was moved to what we call Hillsborough today.

A NEW PUBLIC SCHOOL

By 1870 SAN MATEO had made the transition from stagecoach stop to whistle stop to village. Besides having a railroad station, there were two stores, a saloon, a livery stable, a tin shop, a butcher shop, and E. H. Walker's 24-room hotel, built in 1865.

As the community grew, the population of the surrounding area did likewise. Farms abounded on both sides of the County Road and reached west to the hills. For a rather geographically expansive San Mateo School District, the small school house on the highway was clearly becoming inadequate. In 1866, the district had 81 students. It was not the largest district in San Mateo County (Redwood City had 145), but it was not the smallest either (Belmont had 28). By 1871 there were 75 students attending the San Mateo school—pupils of all grades, all taught in one room, with one teacher in charge. The citizens realized improvements had to be made. On September 6th of that year, they passed, by a close-to-unanimous vote, a bond issue to build a new $9,000 school with two classrooms, with expansion planned for two more, eventually to serve 200 pupils.

The new school was built by J. E. Butler under the supervision of Principal D. E. Hurt and County Superintendent of Schools E. W. Notting. The old school house was moved back off the Road to the west, and the new one was then built in front of it almost on the site of the first. During the 1930s, old-timers reminiscing about this school house remembered it as a two-story building with one big room downstairs and another upstairs. A library on the lower level served as a recitation room from time to time. One of the old-

Three Hawaiian Princes attended St. Matthews Academy in 1885: at center, David Laamne Kawananakoa (1868-1908), heir to the throne, who succeeded Queen Liliuokalani; at left, his brother Edward Abel Keliiahonui (1869-1887), and at right, Jonah Kuhio Kalanianaole (1871-1922).

Courtesy San Mateo County Historical Museum

timers, J. J. Casey, recalled that conditions were still primitive. For a day's supply of water, one of the children would go to a neighbor's with a bucket. Often during the school day, the bucket would be passed so the pupils could refresh themselves; all drank from the same cipper.

While instruction was free, pupils had to buy their text books. For some of the villagers and small farmers this represented a major expense. The books were well cared for, since they were often passed from older to younger siblings. Parents complained bitterly when instructors decided to change text books.

Opposite, top: Beside the new Episcopal church stand the rectory and St. Matthews Hall, a boys' academy founded in 1866. Below: Cadets pose on the grounds of the academy, where trees have grown tall and a new building was added (far left) in 1876.

Courtesy San Mateo County Historical Museum

Prince Jonah Kuhio Kalanianaole, delegate to U.S. Congress from Hawaii.

Courtesy San Mateo County Historical Museum

ALVINZA HAYWARD AND THE VILLAGERS

Unlike the other estate owners whose lands hemmed in the village, Alvinza Hayward saw economic promise in helping San Mateo develop. He therefore dabbled in civic improvements and participated in local politics to help the community grow. While his efforts did not get him the kinds of rewards he hoped for, much of what he did was extremely important to the future of the place. Perhaps his greatest accomplishment was the creation of the village's first permanent water supply.

Sometime before 1870, Hayward bought the Agostin Harasthy property up San Mateo Creek, between Byrnes' Store and Crystal Springs, for the purpose of building a watershed. By 1870 he had built a dam to form the County's first municipal reservoir. Hayward made sure he had the backing of the County Board of Supervisors. By that summer, 150 Chinese laborers had laid pipe to the doorstep of the community, allowing homes within San Mateo a constant flow of fresh water.

Regardless of his motives, Hayward had done a significant amount of good for the villagers. Later, when the Spring Valley Water Company bought up his water rights, Hayward made it a condition that the Company had to furnish without compensation 300,000 gallons of water daily to the San Mateo system in perpetuity. What was Hayward's motive? Certainly he felt real estate in the area would become more valuable, and he had bought plenty of it, adding to his considerable wealth.

Hayward had not started out a rich man. He was born in 1861 in New Hampshire. Before coming out West, he was a small-town attorney in Canton, New York. He came to California as a gold seeker and struggled at first. Legends abound about Hayward. Among them is one describing how his wife, Charity, had to take in washing in Amador County to support him as he searched for gold. It is also said that between stakes, Hayward worked the lumbering areas as an ox-driver. Finally he did strike it rich, and became fantastically wealthy as the owner of mines. It is said that he collected $25,000,000 on just one deal. Along with his wealth, his ruthless business reputation grew.

During the early 1860s, Hayward bought properties south of the village at San Mateo Creek, anticipating that the coming of the railroad would drive up property values. Hayward's lands stretched from the County Road to the bay marshlands. On the north his property bordered Polhemus' estate near the road, the village near the tracks and the creek toward the Bay. To the south his land abutted the San Mateo Homestead.

While his original intent was to make money from his San Mateo holdings, he liked the area well enough to establish a modest home near today's Hayward and Laurel Avenues. Gradually he made other improvements. Among the most spectacular was a 5000-square-foot, extraordinarily elaborate stable in 1867. The grounds themselves were transformed for traditional horse training. With the soils of the vicinity already proven by breeders like Stephen Whipple to be of the best quality for trotting tracks and race courses, Hayward made the improvements and crafted the landscape to become, as one sporting enthusiastic claimed, "without hyperbole, superb."[27] This expert felt Hayward's training track to be the "very best . . . I ever saw." He described the one mile race course as "protected on three sides by trees and a dense undergrowth, the opening being to the southward, so that while the prevailing winds are cut off, there is the vivifying sunshine to inspire the horses."

While the villagers must have been impressed with the estate Hayward was developing, they were probably awed by the man as well. When he went on business to San Francisco, locals could see him at the train station dressed in a Prince Albert coat and silk tall hat. When going to the mines he changed his headgear to a wide-brimmed slouch hat. Not many villagers ever sought to approach this rather forbidding character. It was said that

In 1871 a fine new public school, with separate entrances for girls and boys, was built to accomodate 75 pupils. The old school was moved to the rear of the lot, at left.

Courtesy San Mateo County Historical Museum

once he was in the city, at his office, he was refined, courteous and poised. Back at the estate, servants spoke of his vulgar language and coarse habits.

It was also said that Mrs. Hayward never quite got used to being rich. She remained thrifty, and was even contemptuous of the class of people they had joined, believing them wasteful. Perhaps a more accurate reason

Alvinza Hayward built his Stick-style mansion, probably the largest house ever built in San Mateo, in 1886, after two decades of family tragedy.

Courtesy San Mateo County Historical Museum

for the woman's unhappiness was a string of terrible family tragedies. Cemetery records reveal a long list of young people in the Hayward family plot: Nellie Hayward, who died of croup in 1860, at age seven; Kate Hayward, who also died of croup in 1866 at age six; Mary Hayward, who died of pneumonia in 1870 at one year and seven days; Carrie M. Hayward, who died in 1873 at age two and a half; Sammy Hayward, who died at three months and 22 days; and Alice Hayward, who died of bronchitis in 1873 at ten months and eleven days. Only one child, Emma (eventually Mrs. Andrew W. Rose) grew to adulthood.[28]

Such unending grief could certainly put strain on a marriage. In 1876, the Haywards were divorced. Charity was awarded a substantial fortune, which included the San Mateo property. But before the end of the year, they remarried; no more children preceded them in death.[29]

While the 1870s were times of family strife for Hayward, his real estate plans for San Mateo were very much on his mind too. In 1870, he subdivided a portion of his estate, formerly the Polhemus and People's tracts, and called it Oak Lawn Villa. He was sure San Mateo would soon become the county seat (and we shall see he did all he could to make it so), and that this addition to the village would become desirable real estate.

He also became increasingly involved in politics. In 1872 the Republican Party named him to one of the most powerful positions in California, chairman of its state central committee. With such influence, Hayward was able to convince Governor Newton Booth to appoint Hayward's old friend, James Bucknell, to the office of San Mateo County judge in 1873. But of all the political intrigue to which Hayward was a party, nothing compared to his efforts to have San Mateo named county seat.

The interior of Hayward's mansion was an exercise in splendor, with stained-glass skylights, ornate woodwork, fine carpets, and gilt-framed landscape paintings, all in the latest style. Who was to live in the enormous house? Hayward's children were all dead except one, and his wife had divorced him and then taken him back.
Courtesy San Mateo County Historical Museum

THE FIGHT FOR THE COUNTY SEAT, PART II

BY CREATING a reliable water system, subdividing appropriate properties and gaining political prestige, Hayward had by 1873 positioned himself to create a real estate bonanza at San Mateo. In his view, all that was needed was an extra incentive for development, and he believed that incentive could be achieved by wresting the county seat away from Redwood City and establishing it at San Mateo. Some five years before, in 1868, a great earthquake had severely damaged the county court house. Only the lower floor was usable. Obviously a new building had to go up, but no decision had been reached on its location.

On November 4, 1873, Hayward offered the County Board of Supervisors three prime lots in his Oak Lawn Villa subdivision as a donation, if the County would build its new courthouse and jail there. Besides Hayward, many other Peninsula residents thought San Mateo should be the county seat. After all, its name was the same as the county's, it was more centrally located, and there was easier access to the coastside. It was widely acknowledged at that time that people from as far south on the coast as Pescadero favored the Half Moon Bay—San Mateo Road over any other to the bayside. Even Redwood City's newspaper, the *San Mateo County Gazette*, while still favoring Redwood City, recognized the advantages of the San Mateo Road: "The road from Pescadero to San Mateo via Spanishtown or Half Moon Bay will always be a good road (and will in short time be free from toll and owned by the county, which it should be) from the fact that it will never be used as a road for heavy teams, consequently will not be cut-up and made

Alvinza Hayward (center) celebrates Christmas with his family and friends, none of whom are identified.

Courtesy San Mateo County Historical Museum

impassable, like the road from Pescadero to Redwood City." The *Gazette* also recognized that the state of the county buildings was "a disgrace," and said of the site offered by Mr. Hayward, "no finer location can be found in the county or state."

A majority of the Board of Supervisors favored the idea of removing to San Mateo. In order to settle the matter, they agreed to place the issue before the people in an election scheduled for December 9, 1873. As one contemporary historian put it during the campaign: "money was freely expended, and herculean efforts put forth by the respective partisans of the rival towns."[30] On election day, 1396 votes were cast, 703 for Redwood City and 693 for San Mateo, a difference of only ten.

This seemed to add to the controversy instead of dispelling it. On May 4, 1874, J. E. Butler of San Mateo presented a petition to the Board of Supervisors requesting a second election. The Supervisors honored the request, setting a new election for June.

Representatives of Redwood City complained that barely six months had passed since the last contest. They went to court to prevent the election. By June 13, the issue had got as far as the California Supreme Court, but no decision had yet been made. In the meantime, the Supervisors accomplished some fast work, switching voting places around so as to favor the San Mateo contingent. This time more votes were cast, and San Mateo won, with 956 votes against Redwood City's 690.

Then a new player entered into the drama: Faxon D. Atherton, a prominent California businessman of the south county with connections powerful enough to challenge Hayward's. The State Supreme Court delayed any action on the election for eight months. Finally, on February 24, 1875, under advice of their appointed referee, Colonel J. P. Hoge, the Court declared the second election null and void, finding with Atherton that the Supervisors had exceeded their authority by allowing the second election so quickly after the first.

Hayward now had to face the fact that his real estate plans for San Mateo were too ambitious. He created a San Mateo Water Works Company in 1874 to care for his water system. He sold some of his property east of the village to James Byrnes, John C. Maynard and William H. Lawrence, who built large houses for themselves, and he gradually developed his own San Mateo property into one of the grandest estates on the Peninsula.

BYRNES, MAYNARD, AND LAWRENCE

ON PROPERTY SOUTH OF THE CREEK and east of the village, Hayward peddled quite a bit of land, at a rumored $1,000 an acre, to three influential peninsulans who established substantial homes, two of which still stand today (1993). Some have reasoned that this represented San Mateo's first expansion. In reality it was simply a continuation of large residences boxing in the village, except that these houses were a bit more modest than some of their neighbors' estates.

The first to buy and build on former Hayward property in this area was James Byrnes, a native of Northern Ireland, who had previously established a store and stage stop west of town and had been one of Polhemus' early lot buyers within the village. Back in 1862, a year before the railroad reached San Mateo, Byrnes bought up ten Polhemus lots between Second Avenue and Fourth and between B and the tracks for $1200. Byrnes established a number of businesses in the vicinity, including a brickyard and a warehouse, but perhaps his best-known enterprise was the Union Saloon, which he operated in partnership with coastside businessman and county politician J. P. Ames. Byrnes eventually bought Ames out, and the place became known as the Railroad House, with a restaurant managed by Tom Ricks, probably the first African American to take up residence in the village. The building also came to include a barber shop, livery stable, rooming house, and even a treadmill for processing grain.

Byrnes continued his political career during the 1870s, moving up from his position as county supervisor to state assemblyman by 1873. In 1880, he ran successfully for state senator and remained a fixture in California politics for many years.

In 1875, Byrnes had Robert Wisnom build a house, almost a mansion, for $6,000, on several acres he had purchased from Hayward. Near today's First Avenue and Delaware (703-717 First Avenue) the structure still stands, although it has been altered considerably. Byrnes became an increasingly important real estate owner after moving into his new home. By 1878 he owned 1200 acres of farm land west of the village. In 1880 his Railroad House burned down. He replaced it with a brick building in 1883. He called the new establishment the Union Hotel, which still stands at Third Avenue and Main, much changed through the years.

South of the Byrnes residence, John C. Maynard built (or at least was an early resident there) another two-story home on former Hayward property at about Second Avenue (809 Lawrence). This house, constructed by Dick McCann, also still stands, and has been substantially restored in recent years.

Maynard is said to have come from the "Old South." During the Civil War he was keeper of Libby Prison in Richmond, Virginia. After coming west he became superintendent of the federal mint at San Francisco, and after he moved to San Mateo he received another prestigious appointment: in 1878 he became state insurance commissioner for California. In later years, Maynard was known as a real estate agent.[31]

William H. Lawrence built his place on the third Hayward parcel, south of Maynard's house. Lawrence, a New Yorker, came to San Mateo with his wife, Sarah, three daughters and two sons, to become superintendent of the Spring Valley Water Company. This privately held company owned the watershed properties that provided all of the water for San Francisco, making Lawrence quite an important person.

Years later old timers recalled that in his position he had to do substantial traveling over the lake region west of the village. The wooden flumes ran throughout the hill country and needed constant attention. During the winter there were periodic washouts. Lawrence contracted with Robert Wisnom and his team of carpenters for much of the repair work. He made his trips into the rugged country with four horses, two to pull his buggy and two in reserve.

When the king of the Sandwich Islands visited in 1881, he came to see Lawrence for a tour of the impressive Spring Valley system. It was Lawrence who arranged to show the king St. Matthew's Hall.

In his middle years, Lawrence became a well-known and respected figure. He was elected to the County Board of Supervisors, and died in office in 1888 at the age of 48. So strong was the family name that the Governor of California appointed Lawrence's brother, James M., to replace him on the Board of Supervisors. James resigned

James Byrnes built his Italianate style house in 1875; it still stands, much altered, at 703-717 First Avenue. Right: James Byrnes.

Courtesy San Mateo County Historical Museum

that same year, and the Governor then appointed Lawrence's son, William Babcock Lawrence, to fill the position. William Babcock Lawrence also followed his father's footsteps by becoming Superintendent of the Water Division of the Spring Valley Company in 1908.[32]

Village Life

During the early 1930s, Thomas Nunan of the *San Mateo Times*, operating under the pen name of "Type High," interviewed a number of the villagers who had grown up in old San Mateo. His articles gave a child's-eye view of the life of the place during the village era. The observations were nostalgic, of course, and painted a picture of simple country life almost unimaginable today.

A primary collective memory among the old boys involved the village's swimming hole, a 30' x 20' natural pool located at about the 200 block of today's Humboldt Street. In those days San Mateo Creek was still formidable, and did not dry up in the summer. Fish were plentiful, especially trout and salmon, and the view from the swimming hole was outstanding. The old-timers remembered having an unbroken outlook that swept from Hunter's Point to Redwood City, including pasture lands up to the marshlands, the marshlands to the bay, the bay to the East Bay hills and Mount Diablo.

They recalled that for many years the hole was called "Nettie Wan." The name was taken from a boy who was an excellent fisherman, but not much of an enunciator. Every time he caught a fish he called out "another one," which sounded like "nettie wan."

The boys had feared that when the Byrnes, Maynard and Lawrence houses were built in the 1870s, their access to the hole would be stopped, but the new families made no attempt to prevent the village youths from swimming. Even old man Hayward was friendly to the boys. He had orchards on his property close to the swimming hole. Understanding the inclination of young boys, Hayward invited them to come onto his property and help themselves to fruit. But he asked them not to climb trees, and to shut the gate when they were done.

The swimming hole's demise came in 1889 with the completion of the Crystal Springs Dam by the Spring Valley Water Company. A grand source of drinking water was ensured for the city and the peninsula, but the creek stopped running all year round, and the hole dried up in the summer. For the young people of the village, life was never the same.

Progress also brought the first physician to the community. Dr. B. Marshall arrived in 1867. He was replaced by Isaac R. Goodspeed, M. D., who arrived about 1872. Goodspeed was born in Maine in 1831. At the age of 20 he began studying medicine, graduating in 1854 from Bowdoin Medical College. He traveled west to Wisconsin, where he practiced for three years, returned east and then came to California in 1859, via the Isthmus of Panama. He toured the mining regions for a while and then settled at Pescadero in 1860, where he served as a doctor and taught school. In 1862 he opened a store, and stayed in Pescadero until 1872, when he decided to practice medicine at San Mateo.

Goodspeed opened his office at the southwest corner of Second and Main; the place for many years was known as "Goodspeed Corners." Here he also opened the village's first drug store, sold groceries, and formed political ambitions. He was appointed postmaster on January 25, 1875, and continued in that position until 1882, when he decided to make a bid for state senate as a Republican candidate. His campaign was unsuccessful.

In the meantime, Dr. L. D. Morse went into practice at the Walker Hotel in 1875, and then in 1878, he opened a second drug store for the village at Second and B. Thus when Goodspeed left after 1883, San Mateo was not without medical help. Dr. Morse had served as a surgeon in the Union Army during the Civil War, mostly in Missouri. He came to California in 1874. He also dabbled in politics, accepting a nomination to the state constitutional convention in the late 1870s. Morse and his son, Charles M. Morse, became important pillars of the community.

A cause of considerable excitement was the introduction of telephone service for the community. The June 1, 1878, edition of the *Times Gazette* in Redwood City reported that L. Jaszynsky of San Mateo had been appointed agent for the Bell Telephone Company in San Mateo County. The newspaper indicated that he had placed "one of the contrivances in practical operation . . . for demonstration purposes." It seems a line had been installed reaching from St. Matthews Hall to the railroad depot, "enabling two persons to converse with each other between these two points, one-eighth of a mile apart, as easily and as clearly as though standing face to face." This must have seemed miraculous. The telephone had been invented only two years before.

When in 1883 long distance lines were placed from San Francisco to San Jose, L. D. Morse's drug store on B Street was chosen as the site for San Mateo's first permanent connection. A year later, in July 1884, a telephone switchboard was placed in service at Morse's, the first on the Peninsula outside of San Francisco, and only the 26th in the state.[33] Morse thus became the first agent of the San Francisco Telephonic-Telegraphic Company.

ANOTHER MOMENTOUS incident occurred during San Mateo's village period. On April 11, 1872, the town suffered its first recorded murder. Claus Klerck, of the Klerck and Husing mercantile firm, had been a resident of the village for four years. He had married a local girl, and they had one child. On that tragic April night, Klerck closed the store as usual, but after he entered his own yard, his wife heard a gunshot. She ran for the door and met her mortally wounded husband who yelled "run for the doctor, I am shot."[34] She asked who had done it, but he did not know. He died not long after. A posse was organized among the local men, and if they had known who was responsible, the village would certainly have had its first lynching.

The County Sheriff followed a clue to the home of Joseph Herling, or "Mountain Joe," who lived over the hill on the road to Half Moon Bay. Herling was arrested, and after two trials was committed to an insane asylum for life. "Mountain Joe" escaped four times from the asylum at Stockton, and on one occasion made it all the way back to his home near Half Moon Bay before he was recaptured.

Another first for San Mateo in the 1870s was a newspaper. In 1874, P. H. McGowen, once with the *West Coast Signal*, established the original *San Mateo Times* as a weekly. However, the enterprise only lasted two years. Not until 1889 was a permanent newspaper established.

Social celebrations for the villagers were limited. There seems to have been a "grand ball" each year. In the earliest times these took place in the old school house.

Later they were held at various locations including the Walker Hotel and Wisnom's Hall. The cost rose from $1.00 to $3.00 for the gentlemen. The balls in the later years frequently included a dinner and entertainment, often consisting of a minstrel show.

The village, unlike so many others at the time, did not abound with social organizations. By 1878 only one secret society existed, the Odd Fellows, formed in October of 1877 with George H. Fisher, L. Jaszynsky, Louis Jacobson, Charles Jacobson, Fred Anderson, A. T. Bartlett and Dr. L. D. Morse as its charter members. Within a year it numbered 25 and met in the Fisher and Bartlett building at B and Second Avenue. The village did have one other organization, a young men's musical society, the Independent Cornet Band, with eleven members. William Young was the group's leader.

Some evidence exists that as early as 1869 there was forming in San Mateo an American Protection Association, essentially an anti-immigrant and anti-Catholic organization. Apparently their activities, if they existed at all, were not vigorous. San Mateo was diverse in its ethnic make up even early on. In fact, many of its foreign born assumed village and regional leadership.

The career of James Byrnes has already been mentioned, but there were quite a few other Irishmen. When the first history of San Mateo County was

Dr. I. R. Goodspeed, and Goodspeed and Son Drugstore, at the corner of Second Avenue & Main Street.

Courtesy San Mateo County Historical Museum

compiled in 1878 by the lithographers Moore and De Pue, many of the most prominent citizens on the Peninsula contributed toward its publication. Ten of the patrons came from San Mateo. Two of these, Byrnes and saloon keeper M. Kane, listed Ireland as their birth place; one, William Carl Alt (a shoe maker), claimed Germany, and the rest were east coast Americans. A. L. Brewer, I. R. Goodspeed, C. A. Murray, C. T. Murray and Agnes Tilton all hailed from New England. W. H. Lawrence came from New York, and J. C. Potter, Superintendent of the San Mateo County Hospital and Farm west of town, came from New Jersey.

In 1883 yet another history book was published, this one by B. F. Alley. It listed more San Mateo contributors, some of whom came from Ireland:

> **Hugh McDermott**, justice of the peace for the San Mateo township. He was born in Ireland in 1829, had come to the United States in 1847 and sailed to California via the Isthmus of Panama ten years later. He joined the miners in El Dorado County and actually took his prospecting to as far away as Idaho terri-tory before returning to California in 1865.
>
> **Thomas H. Perry**, boot and shoe shop keeper, was born in Ireland in 1822. He came to America in 1852, sailed to California via the Isthmus in 1863 and in 1864 settled in San Mateo.
>
> **Michael Brown**, blacksmith, was born in Ireland and came to America in 1849. He sailed to California via the Isthmus in 1854, was a miner in Nevada County and took up the second occupation of blacksmithing there. In 1870, he opened a shop in Santa Clara and later that same year moved to San Mateo.

A later history includes yet another Irishman of the village. He was William Sands, born in Ireland in 1830. He came to America as a young boy, and to California in 1857, settling in San Mateo in 1862. He was a teamster, and dealt in horses—especially driving horses. Sands served as the village's first constable, holding that position for several terms. His house still stands at 45 South Delaware and is considered the oldest standing structure in today's city.

Besides the Irish, perhaps the most numerous foreign-born residents were the Chinese. In 1870, Alvinza Hayward had used 150 Chinese laborers to lay water pipe. When they had finished the job, some stayed. A Chinatown of sorts existed at B and Second Avenue, with a rooming house, store, restaurant and at least three wash houses.

By the end of the 1870s the village's business section had changed little. There were still two hotels—the Railroad House and Edward Walker's Hotel on Third and B, as well as Agnes Tilton's boarding house north of the village. There were still just two general stores, one owned by the Husing Brothers and the other operated by James R. S. Bickford, of Maine (b. 1842), who had come to California via the Isthmus in 1864. He had worked as a carpenter before opening a store in the Railroad House.

Other establishments included two tin shops, a harness shop owned by A. T. Bartlett, Samuel Goodhue's meat market, two livery stables (each run by one of the hotels), two bakeries, one lumber yard (Wisnom's), three blacksmiths, two shoemakers, two painters and upholsterers, one carpenter and upholster (Daniel Harver), one barber shop (J. J. Adams) and two real estate offices (Hugh M. Dermott and Fisher & Bartlett). A little north of the village, between B and the tracks, was a corral with a cattle chute and sheep dip. The professional men of the town included the three religious leaders, Father Dempsey of the Roman Catholic Church, Rev. A. L. Brewer of the Episcopalians and the Congregationalist's Rev. D. F. Watkins. There were three physicians in town—Goodspeed, Morse and a Dr Rice, of whom little is known.

At the beginning of the new decade of the 1880s the village had all the essentials, yet was small. A few brick buildings replaced wooden ones, but the village certainly was no boom town. Moore and De Pue's summed it up nicely: "Though the business of the place is by no means unimportant, its distinguishing characteristic is that of a delightful place of residence."[35] In other words, the principal ingredient of San Mateo was the surrounding estates. Moore and De Pue explain: "Following the completion of the Southern Pacific Railroad the town, owing to its mag-nificent site among native oaks and to its unequaled soil and climate for healthful residence, began to attract the attention of men of fortune who had made their princely homes, and added to the charms nature has so lavishly bestowed all that wealth and refined taste could suggest."

San Mateo, despite its railroad depot and an important stage station, was not a destination. It was a place to stop before you got to where you were going. The elite stopped to shop or do business before going on to their estates. Tourists stopped on their way to the San Andreas Valley. Coastal dwellers stopped on their way to business in San Francisco or Redwood City There was little to hold the visitor in town for very long.

Overleaf: The stagecoach, several private carriages, passengers and freight handlers wait for the train in this extraordinary undated photograph.
Courtesy San Mateo County Historical Museum

The Morse house on B Street, with its neat picket fence, was typical of Gothic cottages built all over California in the 1860s and 1870s. Left: Dr. L. D. Morse.

Courtesy San Mateo County Historical Museum

Happenings Beyond the Village

Outside of the village proper, but still within the boundaries of today's San Mateo, business and real estate development was slow too, but enough was happening to make a significant impact on how the town would develop in later years.

After his defeat in the first county seat fight of 1861, August Herrlich's proposed San Mateo Villa subdivision remained as empty fields. In 1867, Herrlich sold the property for $33,000 to a man named Pringle, probably a San Francisco attorney, who built a house there in 1868[36] and transferred the property to the San Mateo City Homestead Association. This was an organization set up to sell the property. On August 28, 1869, its stockholders met and elected Jacques J. Rey, L. R. Townsend, G. Beiyor and Gustave Mahe as their representatives.[37] In early 1870 they drew up a map of some 550 lots, all of about the same size, 200' x 100,' for sale for $400 each. The Homestead Association named its own First, Second and Third Avenues. The property stretched along the west side of the Highway from Arroyo Mocho (near present highway 92) to about today's Eleventh Avenue. From the railroad tracks the property reached toward today's Alameda de las Pulgas.

The Homestead Association did not turn out to be a great real estate success. About 1872 the holdings reverted back to French banker Francois Pioche, who perhaps added onto the existing house, but did little else to the property. Pioche was hit hard by the Panic of 1873, a national financial depression. In 1874, Antoine Borel bought a great portion of the property from Pioche for $22,500, to create a country estate.

Antoine Borel was born December 29, 1840, in Switzerland. He received his education in Switzerland, Germany and England, and came to San Francisco in 1861 by way of the Isthmus of Panama, to join his brother Alfred in a shipping and banking firm. Alfred had been in California since 1855. When Alfred returned to Europe, Antoine took over the entire enterprise.[38]

By 1874, Antoine Borel was a well-known and successful businessman. Besides his own company, he had interest in a variety of the west's greatest, such as the Bank of California and the Spring Valley Water Company. He later became Swiss vice consul and from 1885 until 1913 he served as consul general. The villagers of San Mateo recognized Antoine as one of the landed elite who had a degree of concern for the proper growth of San Mateo. He became one of the town's benefactors, and later had his own real estate investments within the San Mateo Improvement Company and San Mateo Park development.

Antoine Borel and his wife Grace (Canitrot) had seven children. When one of the daughters developed bronchial troubles, the family was advised to spend some time in the warmer climate of the Peninsula. Borel made his 300-acre purchase in 1874, and moved his family into the Pringle-Pioche house, which sat on the southern end of the property. Through the years he added to the house.

Decades later, old timers remembered the Borel family greeting their "Papa" at the railroad station. The children, beribboned and dressed in their best, were accompanied by a coach and coachman, men-servants, nurses and maids. Often Borel arrived with his friend, Frenchman Henri Barroilhet, who had no children. The youngsters would rush forward to greet Barroilhet with all the enthusiasm they had for their own father, and both men responded with great affection.

Antoine never forgot his native Switzerland. He was born at Neuchatel Lake, in a setting of unparalleled vistas. He never became a citizen of the United States, and he often made visits to his native country, where he eventually died in 1915.

As the years went by, the Borel Estate grew in beauty. The property had oaks and fields of grass when Antoine purchased it, but it was his ambition to give it the charm of his native land. He planted eucalyptus as windbreaks on the western outskirts of the property, and other types of trees within the estate for ornamentation. He created a small lake, imported statuary, and laid out eight gardens, adorning them with fountains and small bridges. Mocho Creek and the lake were stocked with fish. A hay field and fruit orchard supplied the estate.

The many workers on the estate were expected to keep everything immaculate. Borel demanded that every leaf be swept off the driveway before he left for work in the morning.[39] At first the estate was used for only six months each year as a summer home, but as the family grew, it became the Borel's permanent residence. Additions were made to the property as time went by. The estate stayed intact and in the family's hands until well into the present century, and was the last of San Mateo's great estates to be broken up.

FURTHER SOUTH from Borel, until the 1940s, the Murray brothers and their heirs continued to own much of the area we call Hillsdale. Brother Calvin married David McLellan's daughter Orelda. The McLellans lived just across the county road from the Murrays.

South of the Murrays and west of the McLellans was the property of J. S. Colegrove. During the early years he used his 274 acres as a general farm, but by 1871 his place had become known as Laurel Creek Stock Farm, with considerable stature as a horse breeding ranch, mostly for trotters. Records from an 1874 auction reveal his stables holding 49 horses.[40]

South of the Laurel Creek Stock Farm, extending to today's Belmont City border and beyond, was the 211-acre Robert Mills place. Mills came to California in 1855 as a manufacturer of decorative glass. Through his acquaintance with William Ralston he received the contract to install all of the glass for the great Palace Hotel in San Francisco. In 1873, he acquired his San Mateo property close to Ralston's Belmont estate. Here he built a house about 1877 or 1878, close to today's city boundary, west of the County Road. His neighbor, Lemuel Murray, died in 1886. Mills married Murray's widow four years later. Mills himself died in 1897. His house stood until 1964, when it was torn down to make way for modern development.

East of the village, two industries thrived on the bayline by making use of the environmentally rich San Francisco Bay. The Morgan Oyster Company owned most of the baylands off San Mateo County from the 1870s until the 1920s. Oyster houses were established at various points to help the company with its cultivation process and to guard the valuable "sea fruit." One Morgan oyster house stood on piers in the bay off San Mateo.[41] Like many others, it was manned by a largely Scandinavian crew. After eastern oysters were planted off Belmont and Dumbarton, and allowed to grow for two years, they were plucked out of the Bay and replanted off San Mateo and Millbrae, where the tidal action was stronger and the shellfish could consume more food. After another two years they were ready for market.

The earliest part of Antoine Borel's house dated from 1868, but Borel added to it over the years. It was furnished in the French style, with five gas-lit chandeliers in the parlor. Right: Antoine Borel.

Courtesy San Mateo County Historical Museum

Meanwhile, Chinese shrimp fishermen established a camp close to the Morgan house, at about the site where today's San Mateo-Hayward Bridge touches Foster City. Old-timer Maurice Powers recalled that these shrimpers would come up San Mateo Creek about once a month in their redwood junks to collect fresh water and wash their nets. "China Camps" lined the San Mateo County bay line between 1869 and 1910; many of the shrimpers probably used San Mateo Creek during the early years.

During the late 1870s and into the 1880s, the estates to the north and south of the village grew in beauty to rival the Borel place. In 1878, George Howard died at the age of 50. Agnes Poett Howard waited a year, and then married Henry Pike Bowie, an old family friend, whose father, Dr. Alexander J. Bowie, had delivered George H. Howard, Jr. in 1864. Bowie hired John McLaren, the head gardener of the Howard-Poett family for fifteen years and later the famous landscaper of San Francisco's Golden Gate Park, to make various improvements, including the planting of some 20,000 trees at Coyote Point. He also diked about 650 acres of lands between the Point and the village.[42] During the village period, Bowie's and Hayward's marshland areas became locally renowned for game-bird hunting.

At Hayward's place there were tremendous improvements. Having given up on real estate speculation, Alvinza Hayward turned his farm into a great showplace, perhaps wishing to compete with the peninsula homes of rival capitalists D. O. Mills of Millbrae and James Flood in the south county. Early on, Hayward had a race track and a stables, perhaps "the most elegant and expensive"[43] on the Pacific Coast. Meanwhile, out on the bayside he built an embarcadero which came to be known as "Hayward's Landing." It had some success as a shipping point.

Less utilitarian, but far more showy, was Hayward's "park" on the infield of his track. Here he put up a fence to enclose deer and elk. A pond teemed with ducks and swans. He also kept up gardens, orchards, and ornamental trees throughout his estate.

Of all the improvements, nothing could compare to the mansion Hayward built in 1886. This massive three-story structure had a squared tower that shot up an additional two stories, making it easily the tallest building for miles. Its architectural style was of the Victorian Stick variety, reminiscent of the Carson House which stands as a landmark in Eureka, California. The mansion sat in the midst of today's Glazenwood residential district.

For all its splendor, historians have speculated that the huge house must have been a lonely place. Only Hayward, his wife and their single surviving daughter lived there. Apparently Hayward very rarely used his place for social events.[44]

Also outside of the village, in the same year Hayward built his mansion, an orphanage was founded. It originally sat at the southwest corner of Ellsworth and Tilton. The idea for its creation began with a donation of a $20 gold piece some two decades before by a woman from Boston. Episcopal Reverend A. L. Brewer's wife accepted the contribution and slowly built up the fund. In 1883, James Cunningham of San Francisco donated the land, and three years later construction was completed.

On November 13, 1886, the building was dedicated. Reverend Brewer performed the services, which were attended by a number of prominent Episcopalian clergymen, since this was the first such institution founded in the diocese. They called it the Bishop Armitage Church Orphanage of California. Its original officers were Mrs. A. L. Brewer, President, Mrs. S. M. Van Wyck, Vice President, Mrs. H. Judah, Vice President, and Mrs. J. G. Clark, Corresponding Secretary.

Originally boys and girls were accepted into the institution. In the beginning it could accommodate about twenty children. However, by the end of the first year, the directors found it necessary to add a building, the "Maria Kip Department" for girls (named for the wife of the famed Episcopal Diocesan). Crowded conditions persisted. In 1889 a house was rented in San Francisco and thirteen girls were removed to that new home, which became known as the Maria Kip Orphanage. The San Mateo institution was used strictly for boys, and had a complement of thirty on hand that year.[45]

Another private institution just outside the village was a second cemetery. Agnes Tilton's Evergreen Cemetery never totally answered the community's needs. On March 29, 1884, John Parrott died. A year and a half later his estate set aside six acres west of the village for a community burying ground. The Parrott family gave the land to the Catholic Archdiocese of San Francisco, with the understanding that one acre would be reserved for

The Borel Chapel, also known as Geneva Chapel, was built on the estate; it later became the Hillbarn Theater.

Courtesy San Mateo County Historical Museum

family plots, and two be available for non-Catholics. Mrs. Parrott also set aside some sections for the poor. Finally, the cemetery was to be called Saint John's, commemorating John Parrott's patron saint. The land would not only be given but kept up by family contributions through a separate Board of Trustees.[46] The cemetery still exists in the hills off today's Parrott Drive.

FIRE!

VIRTUALLY ALL 19th-century American communities lived in fear of fire, which destroyed huge cities like Chicago and wiped out small towns and villages as well. Some places were equipped and prepared. Other, not as much. For the people of San Mateo, no other civic need surpassed fire-fighting preparedness as a motive for community organization, eventually leading to official incorporation.

Before the 1870s there is no record of any fires in San Mateo. Even during that decade, the village itself was remarkably free of disaster, although in outlying places

Above: The Borel family enjoy a sunny day on the veranda. Left: Antoine Borel on one of his fine mounts.

Courtesy San Mateo County Historical Museum

there were blazes. Perhaps most noteworthy was the fire at the Donahue mansion (Central Park) in 1870. By and large these isolated, single-building fires had limited impact on the community. The next decade was much different.

At midnight on July 29, 1880, a locomotive whistle blew at the depot, indicating a fire had started. Byrnes' corner was ablaze.[47] The community's fire fighting equipment was negligible. The Railroad House, which included a saloon, a restaurant, J. J. Adams' barber shop and James Bickford's store, was totally destroyed.

Only three years later the village suffered an even greater catastrophe, losing its most important business block. On the morning of June 15, 1883, at a few minutes before nine o'clock, a fire started in the shed in the back yard of Hugh McKernan's saloon. By 11:00, the entire block was an inferno. A single steam fire engine and two water hydrants were simply not enough to help. No organized fire fighting force existed, but the entire village turned out to contain the blaze. Blacksmiths Dennis and William Brown spotted the fire catching Thomas Coleman's blacksmith shop and saved their competitor's business. Several bucket and wet-blanket brigades helped

Henry Bowie, third husband of Agnes Howard, at El Cerrito, the Howard estate.

Courtesy San Mateo County Historical Museum

preserve other buildings, including the new railroad station just opposite the burning block. Volunteers also rescued the goods out of Dr. I. R. Goodspeed's drug store across the tracks. Movable objects were also saved from the post office, McKernan's saloon, George Plouff's saloon and John Flynn's plumbing store. A piano was saved from the Walker Hotel. The destruction was otherwise complete. Gone was the entire block facing the depot, including the Walker Hotel, Wisnom Hall, the saloons of James Whitehead, Plouff and McKernan, the post office, Goodspeed's drug store, Flynn's plumbing store and the hotel's livery stable. The total amount of loss was estimated at between $40,000 and $50,000.

San Mateo had taken a huge step backward. Instead of having two hotels it now had one, Byrnes' Union Hotel, built after the owner had lost the Railroad House in the 1880 fire. The charred site on which the Walker Hotel stood lay vacant for two decades. The village now had one drug store instead of two, and one doctor instead of two, because Dr. Goodspeed accepted the position of surgeon with the Pacific Mail Steamship Company and left. There was now one livery stable instead of two, and, with the loss of three saloons, it became a bit harder to get a drink. Fortunately, some businesses started over, and gradually during the 1880s brick buildings replaced wooden ones.

People seemed to gain a stronger sense of community in between and after these two fires. In January 1881, a

The original orphanage, built in 1886 at the corner of Ellsworth & Tilton Streets, later moved to Laurel Hall.

Courtesy San Mateo County Historical Museum

chapter of the Ancient Order of United Workmen was organized, with officers including John McLaren, G. H. Fisher, James Byrnes, Hugh McKernan, George Plouff, William Sands and A. P. Bartlett. Three months later, locals created a lodge of the American Legion of Honor with officers C. M. Morse, E. A. Husing, Lyman Brewer, L. D. Morse, Mary E. Morse, S. G. Goodhue, John R. S. Bickford and others. And in December of 1883, after the second fire, a parlor of the Native Sons of the Golden West was created in San Mateo with county-wide representation. William Brown assumed a position as an original officer of the group.

But nothing served to galvanize the community more than the third fire of the decade—the fire of 1887, which took the village's proudest institution, Library Hall.

The story of Library Hall begins with the ladies of the St. Matthews Guild, who wished to establish a reading room and library. They organized in 1882, embracing all denominations. Their purpose was to offer more "refining influences"[48] to the young men of San Mateo. Their first fund raiser, a show put on by villagers for villagers at Wisnom Hall, cleared $200 for the cause.

The work of the Guild took on new meaning after the fire of 1883. In that conflagration, Wisnom Hall was lost. Since its construction in the mid-seventies, the hall had served the community in a variety of ways—as a place for balls and celebrations, a court for the justice of the peace, and a public meeting place. The villagers hoped to replace it, and combined efforts with those wanting to establish a library. In July 1884 a Library Association was incorporated, with George Dickie as president. The initiation fee was $5, with 25¢ monthly dues.

The activity in town inspired some of the estate owners, most notably Antoine Borel, to become involved. He donated a lot within the 1883 fire block (215 B Street today) for construction of the building, and gave money as well. Borel's old friend, Henri Barroilhet, gave two chandeliers. With this momentum established, the Association raised $7,000 and actually had the building under construction before the end of 1884.

At the northeast corner of Second and B, a handsome brick building stood next to the venerable Fisher's Hotel, which had private rooms for ladies.
Courtesy San Mateo County Historical Museum

In 1885, the fine new brick building was completed. Its value, after being furnished, was estimated to be about $12,000. While today we would give it a B Street address, the building actually fronted on Main, where a parking garage stands today. It faced the railroad depot in the very heart of the business section of the community, very close to, if not on the site of, the former Wisnom Hall. The building was 110 feet long and 50 feet wide. The January 2, 1886 *Times Gazette* described it as having "an elegant lodge room, a fine assembly hall, with stage, drop curtain, one ante-room, a library room and two small stores."

For the two years it existed, Library Hall was the social and cultural center of San Mateo. The lodge rooms of the United Order of Workmen, Odd Fellows and Native Sons all met there. A cigar factory occupied one of the store fronts. The library itself was in only one room, and that did not open right away. Books came by way of donations from a few interested families. The *Times Gazette* noted that while the Library Association was "broad and liberal" in that it admitted "all classes," it carefully weeded out from its collection "controversial ideas likely to cause discord."

The fire of 1887 destroyed this pride and joy of the community. The disaster galvanized the villagers into a cohesive populace, ready to become an organized town.

NOTES

[1] Robert B. Bolt, "C.B. Polhemus: Builder of San Mateo," Student monograph #125 in the archives of the San Mateo County Historical Museum, May, 1938.
[2] Don Ringler, *San Mateo USA: The Golden Years*, City of San Mateo, 1975, p. 9.
[3] Charles Loving Brace's 1867 *The New West* article is reprinted in the May 1956 issue of *La Peninsula* (vol. VIII, No. 5), a publication of the San Mateo County Historical Association.
[4] Cloud, *History*, vol. I, p. 355.
[5] Hynding, *From Frontier*, p. 65.
[6] Joseph Calvin Simpson, "Horses of California," *Sunset Magazine*, November, 1901.
[7] Plambeck, "Horse Raising."
[8] Barbara Donohoe Jostes, *John Parrott, Council 1811-1884, Selected Papers of a Western Pioneer*, San Francisco, 1972, p. 151.
[9] Stanger, *Community*, p. 102.

[10] Dorothy Mattis, "The Parrott Estate," Student Monograph #114, in the archives of the San Mateo County Historical Museum, June, 1939.
[11] Millie Robbins, "Hoboes for Dinner," *San Francisco Chronicle*, March 6, 1967 and confirmed by the author in an interview with great grandson William Parrott, March, 1993.
[12] Joan Valentine, "The Wisnom family of San Mateo," *La Peninsula*, vol. XXV, No. 3, December, 1989, p. 5.
[13] Ringler et al., "City" p.6.
[14] Hills, "Stagecoach."
[15] Alley, *History*, p. 281.
[16] Bob Torello, "From San Mateo to Spanishtown," Student Monograph #124 in the archives of the San Mateo County Historical Museum, January, 1940.
[17] *Saint Matthew's Church* (no author indicated) Costonbook Inc., 1966 — dedication book for the new church.
[18] *Moore and DePue's*, p.27.
[19] The original minute book of the Congregational Church in the archives of the San Mateo County Historical Museum.
[20] *Moor and DePue's* p. 27.
[21] *Propectus of the San Mateo Institute for 1864*, San Mateo California, B.F. Sterett Printer, San Francisco.
[22] Richard L. Shellens, "The Story of a Cornerstone," May 1969, manuscript collection in the archives of the San Mateo County Historical Museum.
[23] Letter from W. C. Sharpsteem to Miss Adeline W. Brewer, September 24, 1943, quoting "Catalogue of St. Matthews Hall."
[24] Letter from Agnes C. Conrad, State Archivist, Hawaii, to Frank Stanger, August 9, 1962.
[25] Receipt of W. C. Burnett of April 28, 1875 from St. Matthew's Hall — Boarding School for Boys — Under Military Discipline.
[26] "Application for Admission," St. Matthew's School, of the 1890s, in the archives of the San Mateo County Historical Museum.
[27] Simpson, "Horses."
[28] Notes from cemeteries were complied by a relative of Charity Hayward, Maxine H. Ludvigssove of Los Angeles and can be found in the archives of the San Mateo County Historical Museum.
[29] Charles Kirkbride law notes in the archives of the San Mateo County Historical Museum.
[30] Alley, *History*, p. 170.
[31] Linda Wickert, *City of San Mateo Historic Building Survey, Inventory Section*, San Mateo County Historical Association, City of San Mateo, September, 1989.
[32] Edward F. O'Day, "William Babcock Lawrence, 1866-1925," *San Francisco Water*, Publication of the Spring Valley Water Company, San Francisco, April, 1926, Vol V. No. 2.
[33] "New Light on San Mateo History," *San Mateo Times*, December 16, 1938.
[34] Cloud, *History*, Vol. I, p. 396.
[35] *Moore and DePue's*, p. 26.
[36] Judge Aylett Cotton was interviewed by *Times* reporters on June 8, 1962 in the article "Fire Razes Historic Borel Estate Mansion" and said Pringle built the original house on the property.
[37] Bostwick, "San Mateo Villa."
[38] Ronald G. Fick "The Antoine Borel Family," *La Peninsula*, Spring 1980, Vol. XX, No. 2, p. 4.
[39] From Henry Buffoni's interview with Aylett Cotton of November 1953 which is in the archives of the San Mateo County Historical Museum.
[40] Plambeck, "Horse Racing."
[41] Mitchell P. Postel, "A Lost Resource: Shellfish In San Francisco Bay," *California History*, March 1988, Vol. LXVII, No. 1, p. 30.
[42] Emily Jane Williams, "Land Use of the City of San Mateo's Shoreview District Through the Depression Era," May 15, 1991 Student Monograph in the archives of the San Mateo County Historical Museum.
[43] Ringler, "San Mateo," p. 9.
[44] Stanger, *Community*, p. 105.
[45] "Bishop Armitage Church Orphanage of California, For the Care and Training of Orphan, Half Orphan, Destitute Boys," Third Annual Report, May 30, 1890.
[46] Miguel R. Luna, "History of San Mateo County Cemeteries," May 20, 1938, Student Monograph in the archives of the San Mateo County Historical Museum.
[47] Cloud, *History*, Vol. I, p. 432.
[48] Lois J. McCue, "History of the Public Library in the City of San Mateo: 1884-1907," June 1962, student monograph in the archives of the San Mateo County Historical Museum.

Opposite, top: The Union Stable supplied a bus, driven by Tom Masterson, for customers. Mr. Russell is at the center of the door, Mr. Salter at right, and Charley McFadden holds a horse. Bottom: A banquet at the Union Hotel, undated. Mr. Chessley is named as proprietor.

Courtesy San Mateo County Historical Museum

UNION STABLE
RUSSELL & SALTER.
UNION STABLE
UNION BUS.

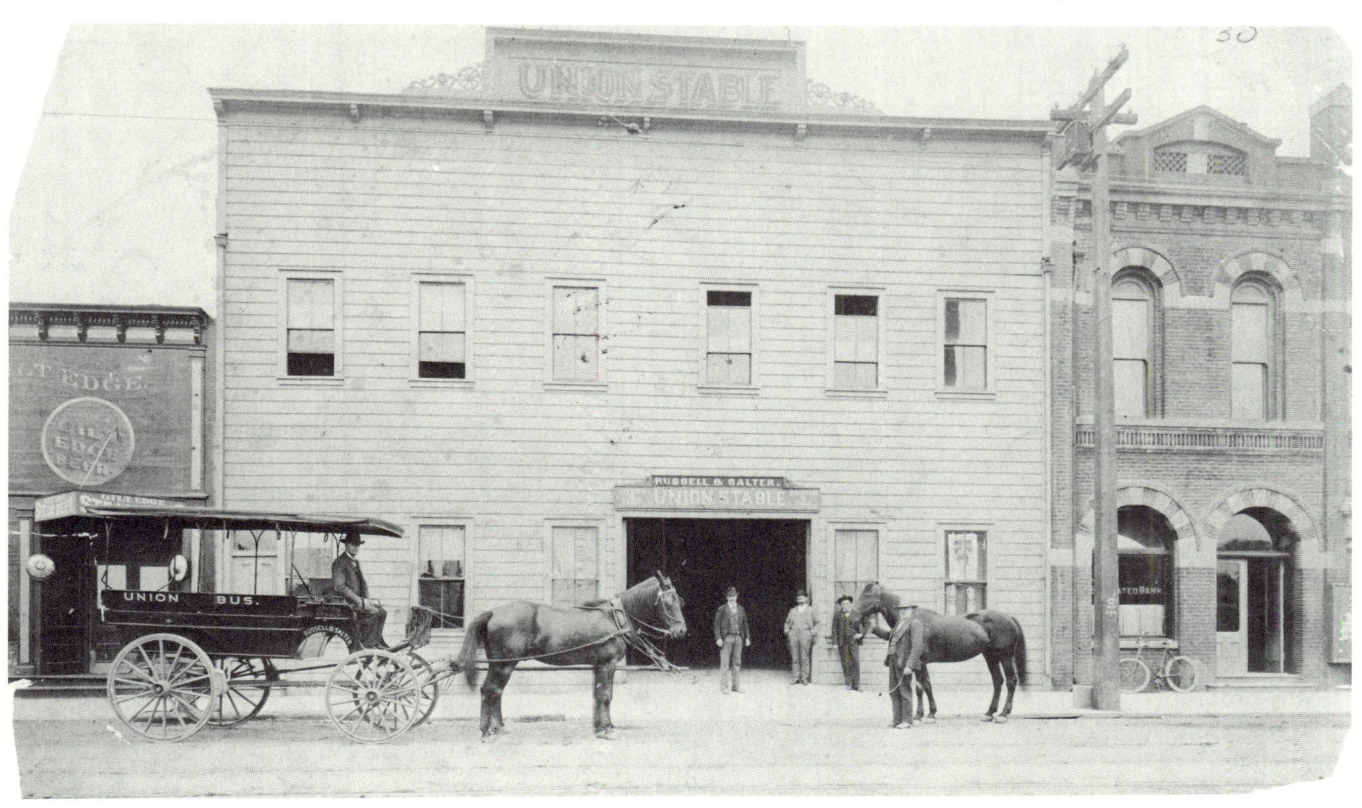

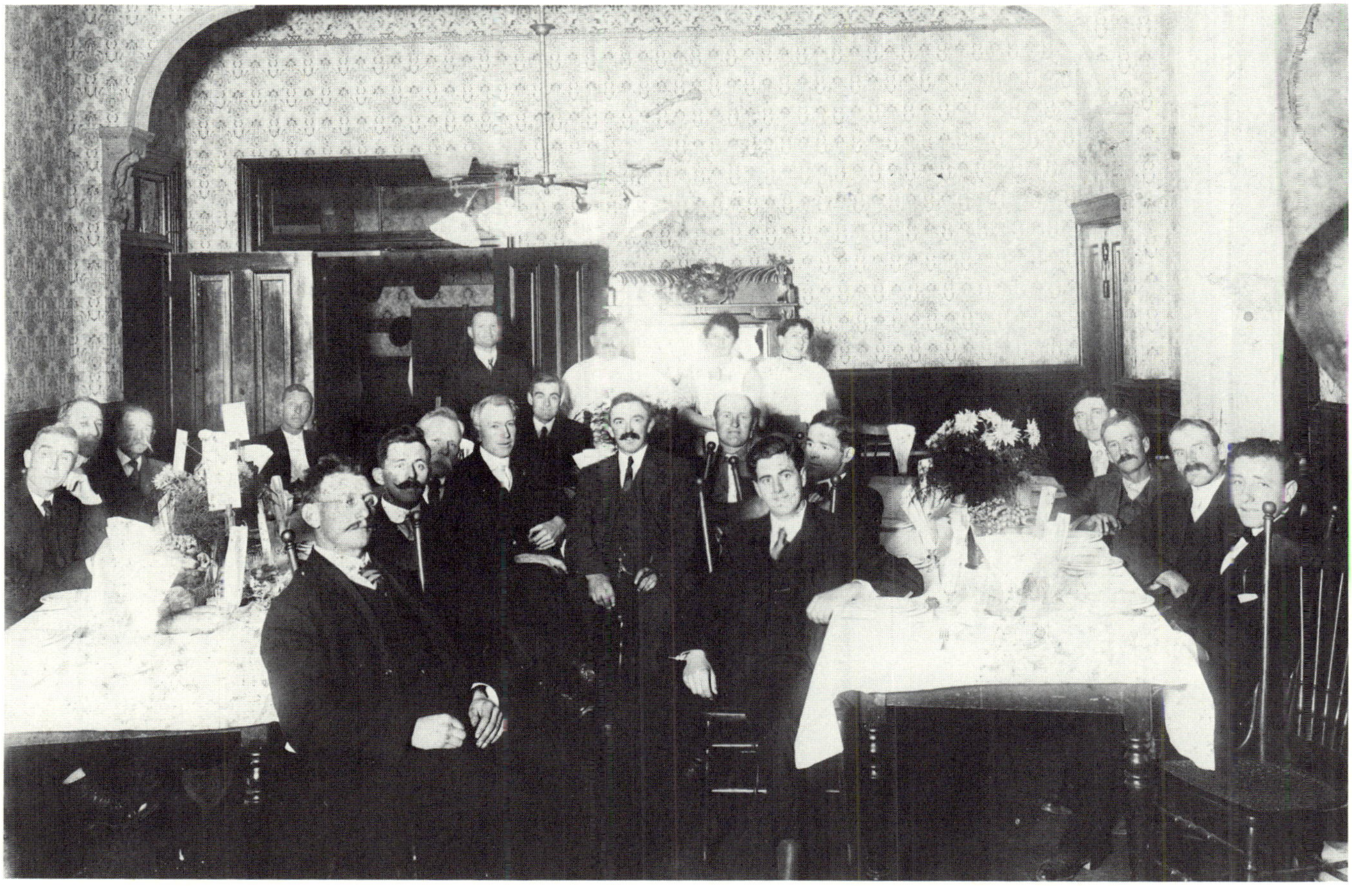

Above: Members of the San Mateo Volunteer Fire Department, Hose Company No. 1, pose proudly beside their only piece of equipment, sometime before 1890. Some of the firemen look like boys.

Left: Despite the best efforts of firemen, fires repeatedly damaged the downtown section of San Mateo. This one, in 1913, destroyed Brady's Palace Market and Saradin's restaurant. "Above was a dance hall," George Bartlett wrote on the back of the picture.

Courtesy San Mateo County Historical Museum

CHAPTER IV

From Village to Town: 1887 - 1920

Volunteer Fire Fighting

Between 1887 and 1920, San Mateo gradually grew from an unorganized village to an incorporated town. The road was a slow and bumpy one however, and began with yet another disaster.

In many small towns across America during the 19th century, community life began with the formation of a volunteer fire department. Early San Mateans recognized the need for such a body, but were slow to get it started. Within a five year period, two disastrous fires hit the heart of the village's business section. In 1885, shortly after the second blaze, H. F. Barrows, Truman Jennings, William Z. Price, John Moore, J. R. S. Bickford, A. T. Bartlett and others formed a fire fighting organization, with Barrows, manager of Byrnes' Union Livery Stable, as their foreman. Captain Kohl contributed a hand pump; Alvinza Hayward's water company had already donated three hydrants on 3rd Avenue.

This seemed to be a good start. With 600 to 700 feet of hose, the volunteers would be able to reach just about every section of the business area. But, for some reason, they couldn't obtain the hose, and the group fell apart.

Not until the spring of 1887 did five men of the community gather together again to discuss the matter. Drug store owner Charles M. Morse, blacksmith William H. Brown, harness and saddlery shop proprietor George A. Bartlett, Fisher Hotel owner Charles J. Hatch, and William Babcock Lawrence, son of William H. Lawrence of the Spring Valley Water Company, met upstairs in Library Hall. They decided to call for a public meeting on the evening of April 6 in order to create an official fire department.

At about four o'clock in the afternoon on the very day that the fire department was to be organized, Ella Moran and Kate Casey of the millinery shop near Library Hall discovered that the village's two-year-old community building was on fire. George Bartlett and Howard Tilton heard their cries for help. Many years later, Bartlett described the scene.[1] They entered the building and found the rear of the stage on fire. With just a small stream of water the blaze could have been contained, but, of course, they had no fire hose.

The bell at the Catholic Church alerted the rest of the 500 or so villagers, who gathered around Library Hall, wanting to help. But little could be done to put out the blaze. Citizens tried to save what they could: a ladder was placed against an upstairs window, and volunteers slid furniture and property down to the street.

Luckily, someone had the presence of mind to call down to Redwood City for help, because the fire continued to roar out of control, threatening the entire business section of town. Redwood City's Fire Chief, C. Beeger, and a crew of his men charged up the County Road in a two-horse spring wagon, towing a two-wheeled hose cart with 600 feet of 2 ½-inch rubber fire hose. They arrived amid cheers from the San Mateans. Beeger attached the hose to the hydrant at Third Avenue and B Street and sprayed the ruins of Library Hall until the fire was out.

By July 4, 1890, Hose Company No. 1 had grown to 23 members, plus some admirers wearing plug hats. Thomas Coleman, the foreman, is truly a giant among men. George Bartlett, one of the firemen, recorded the names on the back of the picture: Culbert, Lovie, Kelly, Byrnes Wisnom, Flaherty, Keegan, Swanson, Casey, Alt, Ward, Howard, McLean, Leavy, Halihan, Cummings, Powers, Roberts, Cronin, Schular, Nelson, Lee, Price, & Wheeler.

Courtesy San Mateo County Historical Museum

When Beeger and company went home, only brick walls remained of Library Hall. Gone were the infant library, the cigar factory, the meeting rooms, ballroom and the lodge rooms of the United Order of Workmen, Odd Fellows and Native Sons. The hall had cost $12,000 to build and furnish, but was insured for only $6,000.

With the loss of property and money providing added incentive, the meeting that had been planned for that night was held, despite the exhausted state of the people. Library Hall was gone, so they met at Morse's drug store. The villagers, wanting to create a proper fire department, decided to organize in accordance with state law.

The San Mateo County Board of Supervisors reacted quickly to San Mateo's desire to protect itself. On May 7, 1887, it appointed a fire commission consisting of William Price, E. A. Husing, and James Byrnes, chairman. The district included the village of San Mateo and the Hayward, Whipple, Parrott and Howard places. The commissioners met the same evening.

At their second meeting, a week later on May 15, William Price proposed an election in June to raise $2,000 for a hose, hose cart, a hook and ladder rig, more fire hydrants and a small storage building. The motion passed, and the election, held just two weeks later, showed the support the Commission had: 56 voted in favor; only one against. In the same election, Joseph A. Deacon, a clerk at E. A. Husing's store, received 43 votes to become assessor and tax collector. He was given a one-time service fee of $100, and managed to collect $2277, most of it from the estate owners, to buy equipment.

The new equipment was stored at the San Mateo Half Moon Bay Stage barn at the rear of the Union Hotel, on the west side of Railroad Avenue. The next step consisted of organizing the volunteers. Because the

Commission had conformed to state law, San Mateo fire fighters would be exempt from poll taxes and military service in foreign wars. Still, these were small incentives compared to the community status attached to being a volunteer fire fighter. Firemen were entitled to wear smart uniforms at social occasions. The Fire Chief and floor manager of the department displayed long, colorful ribbons attached to their badges. Fireman's balls were organized to honor the men and raise money for the department. On the Fourth of July the men showed off their equipment in a grand parade.

On June 13, 1887, the original 12 members of the department signed up. They were William Brown, S. H. Knapp, Jr., Charles H. Johnson, Charles J. Hatch,

William F. Herbst (right) was Fire Chief in 1894, a hundred years ago. Hose Company No. 2 had handsome new uniforms with brass buttons, and the traditional mascot, in 1893.

Courtesy San Mateo County Historical Museum

This familiar but captivating view of downtown San Mateo, taken just after the turn of the century, shows the roof of the train station in the lower foreground with Depot Square and the flagpole behind it; the Union Hotel at the far end of the square, and on the right, along Main Street, the Union Stable, Library Hall, the Goodspeed building, now housing a cyclery, and at the right rear the sturdy Romanesque brick St. Matthews Catholic church, built in 1900 on Third Avenue.

Courtesy San Mateo County Historical Museum

George H. Robinson, James M. Farnard, D. Brown, B. A. Peckham, George A. Bartlett, Thomas Coleman, James Deacon and William Babcock Lawrence.

On September 1, 1888, the Commission staged a second successful election. Another $1000 was raised for equipment, including more hydrants and a bell to sound the alarm. Until this time, ringing the bells at the Catholic and Episcopal Churches or firing guns summoned the volunteers. Some $150 was set aside for this expenditure, but George Bartlett remembered that back in 1885 the first volunteer unit had obtained a bell from Gustave Mahe, who owned a vineyard north of San Mateo. The bell had been cast in England in 1865 and had served on a French ship until Mahe obtained it for use as a dinner bell. The 1882 committee placed the bell in the belfry of the Congregational Church, where Bartlett and William Price found it. But it wasn't used for long: the bell developed a crack and was retired from duty. It is now on display at the County Historical Museum.

On March 18, 1889, the volunteer fire department officially organized itself and drew up a constitution and bylaws. The San Mateo Hook and Ladder and Hose Company began with 33 active and 11 contributing members. Active members paid an initiation fee of 50¢ and monthly dues of ten cents. Contributing members paid 25¢ a month. Active members also agreed to honor fines imposed by the Company, including 50¢ if a member did not come to attention after a meeting began, $1.00 if absent from roll call, and $1.00 to $5.00 for neglect of duty.

The volunteer fire department was more than a public safety organization or an excuse for happy parties and colorful parades. Its members represented the most active segment of the small community's male population, and certain business, social and political rewards came to those who belonged. By 1892 the group numbered 56 active members and several contributing members.

A new spirit of community was born out of the ashes of Library Hall. Besides the creation of a volunteer fire department, the goal of rebuilding Library Hall was also realized. The community raised money to add to the insurance refund, and builder Robert Wisnom constructed a new two-story building for $8,890.

During the 1890s, the reborn Library Hall became the focus of community life. Upstairs was the public hall where grand balls and large meetings took place. On the ground floor was a livery stable and the storage area for the fire company.

D. Gordon Bromfield, who was a child during that decade, remembered Library Hall as the place where "any melodrama, minstrel show or college glee club that played our town performed." He recalled it as rectangular and spacious, with rows of "hard-bottom, portable wooden seats." As a boy he suffered when sitting on them, "constantly squirming about, endeavoring to make my behind more comfortable, but it seemed hopeless."[2]

The toll collector's family spends a lazy summer afternoon at the toll house on Crystal Springs Road.

Courtesy San Mateo County Historical Museum

THE INCREDIBLE YEAR: 1889

IN 1889 THREE UNRELATED DEVELOPMENTS had tremendous impact on the growth of San Mateo and its surrounding region. First was completion of the Crystal Springs Dam, which further guaranteed a first-class source of drinking water for San Mateo and the entire San Francisco Peninsula. Second was the successful subdivision of a portion of one of the estates surrounding the village. Third was the founding of a newspaper which grew in various forms to become the County's most important journal to this day, The *San Mateo Times*.

Crystal Springs Dam was the crowning achievement of the Spring Valley Water Company's head engineer, Hermann Schussler. Since the 1860s, he had directed the creation of the watershed for San Francisco and the Peninsula. In 1887, he began work on the dam, which was intended to block the flow of San Mateo Creek.

Schussler's plan called for the fabrication of concrete blocks, joined together with cement. The blocks varied in size, but were 6 to 10 feet high, up to 40 feet long and 10 to 15 feet wide.

A tremendous amount of material had to be brought to the construction site. The sand required for the masonry was shipped in by barge to the landing at Coyote Point. Other items came by way of freight train. The sand, concrete, and thousands of other items had to be somehow transported up San Mateo Creek to the dam site. Hundreds of laborers had to go up every day. John Gordon Moore hauled materials from countless barges and box cars by horse drawn wagons, from Coyote Point and the rail station up Crystal Springs Road to the building site. Moore had been a San Mateo resident since 1864. He was born in New Hampshire in 1829, and came to California in 1849. In 1852 he went into the stagecoach business on the Peninsula. After selling out in the 1870s to Wooley and Taft, he took up heavy hauling, and in 1887 found himself with this, the most important project in his long career.

When Schussler completed the dam in 1889, it reached a height of 120 feet; it was (and still is) the largest interlocking concrete block dam in the world. In January of 1890, an unusually rainy winter made the dam overflow into San Mateo Creek. Locals feared San Mateo could be flooded, so a 25 foot-extension was added to

raise the dam. In 1911 another four-foot addition was piled on to give it a total height of 149 feet.³ Its greatest tributes come from historians who remind us how well Schussler's dam has held without damage, even through severe earthquakes.

The considerable activity in San Mateo brought on by the construction of the dam coincided with the opening of part the Howard estate for subdivision. In 1889, William H. Howard had Australian surveyor Davenport Bromfield (father of D. Gordon Bromfield) lay out what came to be known as the Western Addition. At first it encompassed an area between the Creek and today's Poplar Avenue, from the tracks to today's Delaware Street. Later it was expanded to reach from the Creek to today's Bellevue Avenue and the County Road to today's Humboldt Street.

The significance of this venture was not that it was the first attempt at subdivision since Polhemus' in the

Davenport Bromfield's house was modest, but he left his mark on San Mateo. He surveyed much of the land in the town, laying out boundaries that were vital to later subdivisions. One son became a partner of the Levy Brothers, and another, D. Gordon Bromfield, is quoted often in this book.   Courtesy San Mateo County Historical Museum

Crystal Springs Dam, the largest concrete-block dam in the world, was designed by Hermann Schussler, of the Spring Valley Water Company, and completed in 1889.

Courtesy San Mateo County Historical Museum

1860s. After all, Hayward tried in the 1870s, and at least two other subdivisions were carved up on maps south of the village in the 1880s, one called Beresford Park and another, the Laurel Creek Subdivision. The difference was that this time the sales pitch succeeded. People actually bought lots and built homes. This success had everything to do with an aggressive advertising campaign that became the model for future attempts to subdivide lands near the village.

The April, 1889 edition of *The California Home and Farm* kicked off the campaign. Briggs, Fergusson and Company, a San Francisco real estate firm, announced lots for sale to "the highest bidder . . . in a central part of the beautiful suburban *town* of *San Mateo*, known as the *Western Addition*." Among the features mentioned: "Streets graded: water piped: shade and ornamental trees line the Avenues and streets: magnificent country seats and beautiful suburban homes surround the property... Schools, churches and social advantages are unsurpassed."

The company boasted that this offering was *"without question the most desirable one ever made in the State,"* mentioning that by train, San Mateo was only 35 minutes from the city, and claiming that with the proposed Bayshore cutoff (which wouldn't come for another 18 years), the time was "soon to be reduced to 22 minutes." The realtors insisted that the "property must soon double and quadruple the present selling price."

Following the announcement was an extensive article that pulled out all the stops in extolling the virtues of San Mateo:

> How many of the residents of San Francisco, as they shiver in one of the summer fogs, and dig the dust from their eyes deposited by the whirlwinds that sweep the streets with almost relentless force,

know that within thirty minutes, they may, if they choose, be deposited in a spot where the sun shines brightly, the fog comes not and the air is balmy as on a May morn?

How many who go to Monterey, Santa Cruz, Santa Barbara, or any of the noted seaside resorts to enjoy the fresh sea air and the salt water bathing, know that only thirty minutes away, lies a most charming spot, embowered in trees, where the chill winds of the sea do not penetrate, where a beautiful beach of hard sand [Coyote Point] offers every facility for bathing, and where the temperature of the water is many degrees warmer than any of the places noted?

How many of the residents of San Francisco, as they read or hear of the delightful climate of the semi-tropical south, with its oranges, bananas, grapes, flowers and exotic shrubbery, know that just half an hour's ride from this city, is a region where the winter temperature is higher and the summer heat is less than in any other part of the state, and where the orange, banana, olive, magnolia, camellia and all sorts of fruits and flowers thrive as well as, if not better than, any other part of the State?

How many people, as they read of the charming scenery of the old English parks and country seats, and wish that they might be able to visit that country know that but a half an hour from their homes lies a region whose natural beauty . . . far excels anything in England . . .?

How many of the residents of San Francisco have ever seen the elegant residences and magnificent grounds of many of the oldest Californians, which may be found clustered in charming localities along the peninsula south? In a word, how many San Franciscans have ever visited San Mateo and the region round about? . . .

It may possibly seem like straining a point to say that the handsome country seats about San Mateo have no equal in the world. But, nevertheless, we make that assertion and trust to be able to present such facts in support thereof as will leave no doubt in the minds of the reader.

Then came a description of the scenery around San Mateo, commencing with a view from the "Mounds," of the Bay, East Bay, San Francisco, "the beautiful wooded eminence of the Coyote," the grand estates, the Sierra Morena (coast hills) and, of course the "charming little village" itself. San Mateo had a "'finished' aspect," the article asserted, "seen in the oldest settled region, and for that reason possesses an indescribable charm for whose eyes are aweary with the many repulsive features necessarily coincident with the building of the new towns and the settlement of unoccupied territories."

Also extolled were the recreational opportunities of country life, the advantages of Peninsula rail commuting (as compared with East Bay ferry service), and the mild climate and the healthfulness of San Mateo. Most revealing was a section of the article entitled: 'A few words to business men." In it one can see that the modern concept of the middle-class suburb had come to California:

> In every direction [from] New York City . . . the population for many miles in the interior is largely made up of men who carry on their business in the city, but maintain their families in the country, going back and forth each day by the numerous railroads . . . there is a continuous chain of settlements entirely populated by New York business men. They are thus enabled to rear their families in healthful localities, away from the noise and bustle of the city, away from its contaminating influences, and at the same time in a far less expensive manner than is required in the city.

The market for these town lots is clearly identified in this passage. San Mateo before this time was primarily a place for elite estate owners and those who served them. From this point forward new types of residents came to live here. They were not poor, but were not necessarily wealthy. They longed for the beauty, exclusiveness and privacy of the village of San Mateo, but they worked each day in the city. They bought their lots and built their wood-frame Gothic Revival, Italianate, Queen Anne and Colonial Revival houses right next door to those of the working-class carpenters, laundry workers and gardeners of the village, who also moved out into the Western Addition.[4] There were no restrictions of class, race or ethnic background; such distinctions would come later in more modern subdivisions.

The sales pitch concluded with an appealing invitation to the April 6 auction. The realtors arranged for a special railroad excursion to San Mateo: round trip at only 50 cents. The train left San Francisco at 9:15 and started back to the city at 5:30 pm. This gave agents a full day to sell the public on San Mateo and, more specifically, 250 "villa and residence lots."

Through the 19th century and into the present one, the Howards and others continued to subdivide their various properties, and the sales pitch remained basically the same. By 1895 Coyote Point beach with its bath house was proudly described as a "rendezvous for the San Francisco yachting clubs."[5] Over the years other aspects were highlighted, but the central themes of real estate ad campaigns stayed homogeneous: good weather, easy commute, country recreation, beautiful scenery and an exclusive life style reminiscent of an older era.

The same spring that Howards' Western Addition

The men who built Crystal Springs Dam look properly solemn, as if they know they have made history.

Courtesy San Mateo County Historical Museum

went up for sale, "two crazy boys" came to the village "filled with the temerity of youth"[6] to found San Mateo's first successful newspaper, the *Leader*. Some 24 years later one of the two, Richard H. Jury, who was just 21 in 1889, remembered what San Mateo was like when they arrived: "There were no cement sidewalks or paved streets . . . and one of the personal belongings of almost every resident was a lantern which he or she found very necessary in safely negotiating throughout the town after nightfall." There were no street lights.

Jury had worked for local newspapers before coming to San Mateo, as had his 21-year-old partner, Charles N. Kirkbride, who was born a preacher's son in Colorado and moved west with his family. The young men proclaimed the purpose of their newspaper in its first issue: better coverage of San Mateo, North County and Coastside happenings. Its first editorials focused on the need for gas lights in the village.

Kirkbride stayed for only one year. He went east to study law and then returned to San Mateo and became its first city attorney after the town's incorporation in 1894. He went on to become a fixture in the community, a champion of the cause of education.

Jury also assumed an important role in Peninsula history. As newspaper editor he championed the campaign for the incorporation of San Mateo and pushed for various civic improvements. He became an early clerk and assessor for the city, and eventually was elected to the state assembly.

Jury sold the newspaper in 1909 to H. W. Simpkins, editor of the *Palo Alto Times*. It went through various ownerships after that. In 1914 the *Leader* was consolidated with the *News* to become San Mateo County's first daily newspaper. In 1926 the *News Leader* merged with the *San Mateo Times*, founded in 1901 by Robert Thompson.[7]

The old stage road leading to Half Moon Bay followed the same route as today's Highway 92.
Courtesy San Mateo County Historical Museum

INCORPORATION

By 1890 THE *LEADER* was already pushing for the incorporation of San Mateo. Incorporation meant local government, which allowed more control over civic improvements and public safety. It also meant more taxes, laws and regulations—which not everyone wanted. Among those against incorporation was Judge Robert Y. Hayne of the Parrott family. He alleged the incorporation drive was a fabrication of the newspaper and "not the spontaneous movement of a majority of the citizens, but . . . the work of a few new-comers."[8]

The issue was finally resolved on September 3, 1894. The San Mateo County Board of Supervisors conducted the election, finding 150 San Mateans voted in favor of incorporation with only 25 against it.

The boundaries for San Mateo were set in the north at Peninsula Avenue, but included Coyote Point. The Bay was to the east, and 9th Avenue to the south. On the west the line was drawn about 1000 feet west of the County Road, up to, but not including, the very door steps of some of the estates. Later, in 1910, Hillsborough would be incorporated to protect the interests of estate owners west of El Camino from the burgeoning little towns of San Mateo and Burlingame. Burlingame, itself, incorporated in 1908, in order to stay independent of any annexation fever from its southern neighbor.

Elected as trustees to run the affairs of the new government (equivalent to city council members today) were two men already familiar to us, Captain A. H. Payson, who had married into the Parrott family but lived east of the County road, and Robert Wisnom, pioneer, builder and businessman. The others who served were George W. Dickie, an engineer who had designed the famous warship *Oregon*, as well as heavy equipment used for mining in the Comstock; Charles Herbst, partner in Herbst Brothers General Store on B and 1st Avenue, and Harry Hatch, hotel owner and saloon keeper. The first meeting of the Trustees concerned itself with matters of taxation, and the sprinkling of dusty B street.

Other original officers of the community included Peter Rogers, who became the first Clerk and Assessor, William Herbst (George's brother) who became

Treasurer, and James A. Wallace, who followed a long line of constables to became the first marshal.⁹ Charles Kirkbride was, of course, the first town attorney. Kirkbride assumed great responsibility in 1895 when he handled the legal work for San Mateo's first bond issue, a $40,000 measure to install sewers for the town's streets. It passed, and Kirkbride continued to serve as attorney for nearly 30 years until 1924, with a single interruption when he joined the armed forces during World War I and rose to the rank of Colonel.

Library Hall was turned over to the young town for offices, a fire station and a meeting place, making it the first city hall.

ON THE VERGE OF BECOMING A TOWN

WITH INCORPORATION, San Mateans began to think of themselves as townspeople rather than villagers. However, many legacies of the old days remained long after the official organization of the place. For example the Levy Brothers four-horse Concord Stage still met the train each day to carry passengers to the Coastside. D. Gordon Bromfield remembered "weather worn" Ed Campbell as one of the best-known of the later drivers.

> [He would help] travelers with their bags or cases for the journey and, after placing the wooden express box beneath the driver's seat, take the reins, mouth his proverbial cigar which was probably any brand offered him, and, with a wave of the hand to Henry Hull, our lanky freight agent, start off for the Crystal Springs Road.

One of the most memorable stops on the stage road was "red-faced" James Byrnes' store:

> This so-called store consisted of a few second-story hotel rooms and a musty old saloon with its lengthy bar. The windswept structure had the long veranda of the period running its entire length. One of its all-important accessories was the wooden water trough which served all dobbins, including those of the stage. Probably the owner of every passing vehicle felt that on account of free water service, there existed an obligation to visit the bar, which we did from time to time for a half-and-half of ginger ale and beer, called a shandy gaff.¹⁰

On August 17, 1905, a great drama was played out on the San Mateo-Half Moon Bay Road when the last stagecoach robbery took place. On that day a bandit, dressed in odd get-up, including a long black overcoat, blue overalls, black visor cap (similar to a railroad worker's hat), black mask, goggles and feed bags around his feet to cover any shoe prints, stopped the San Mateo bound stage near the old quarry. He had a large revolver, and demanded that stage driver Ed Campbell hand down the mail box. He also asked the passengers to pass a hat around to accumulate their money and valuables, which they did, but very slowly; some hid cash between the seats while the others stalled. Meanwhile the sound of a wagon could be heard. E. Bertilotti, its driver, was frightened off when the bandit got off some shots. The masked man then ordered Campbell on to San Mateo. At some point thereafter he must have counted his loot, which Campbell figured added up to $4.30. In San Mateo great excitement ensued as the town rallied to catch the robber. He got away.

In 1907, the newly completed Oceanshore Railroad made the north-south coast stage service obsolete. In 1910, Knight's stage from Redwood City to the coast stopped running because of competition from automobiles. By about 1913, all stagecoach service ceased operation in San Mateo County.

The business section of town in the 1890s, still mostly centered around B Street, had changed little during nearly two decades. Lining the streets in 1890 were six or seven stores, two hotels, four saloons, two drug stores, two butchers, two blacksmiths, one machinist, two plumbing shops, two barber shops, two shoemakers, a livery stable, a bakery, a jeweler, a harness shop, a tailor, a doctor, a lumber yard and the newspaper office.

But the decade did see some progress. In 1892, the San Mateo Gas Light Company was incorporated, with James Byrnes, E. A. Husing, Julius Wiesender, William Nolden and John P. Weller serving on the original board. By 1905 it had become part of the young Pacific Gas and Electric Company. On July 9, 1894, only a couple of months before the town's incorporation, San Mateo's first bank was organized. Philip M. Roedel, originally of White Cloud, Michigan, joined with long-time San Mateo business leaders such as Robert Wisnom in creating the Bank of San Mateo in a brick building on Main Street. As president of the bank, Roedel was a man of importance. He helped to establish the San Mateo Mutual Building and Loan Association in 1896.

In 1902, Roedel built a grand Tudor Revival home for himself and his wife on property west of the County Road, which came to be known as Seven Oaks. After his death in 1905, both the bank and the home were bought by A. P. Giannini.¹¹ Seven Oaks stands today, the only one of the great estate houses to survive in San Mateo.

Another lift for the business community came in 1898, when the French-Jewish Levy Brothers established a store in San Mateo. The brothers had come from the French Rhineland in 1869, fearing military conscription as the Franco-Prussian war loomed. They decided to come to California because their mother had grown up in San Francisco, in the home of Raphael Weill, founder of the White House department store. Brothers Fernand

In the 1890s the Levy Brothers took over the stagecoach service from San Mateo to Half Moon Bay and Pescadero.
Courtesy San Mateo County Historical Museum

and Joseph came first, establishing stores on the San Mateo County coastside. Later, brothers Adrien and Armand joined them. Joseph married a local girl, Hannah Maria Walker, of Half Moon Bay, while Fernand went back to France to marry in 1883. After he brought his wife to California his brothers Adrien and Armand married sisters of Fernand's wife.[12]

In 1886 the brothers purchased the stage line to San Mateo and gained familiarity with this community. They felt that ultimately the bayside of the Peninsula had a more promising future for them than the coastside. San Mateo's incorporation, the anticipated coming of the trolley line (1902), new subdivisions, and the rumblings that a San Mateo high school district might be formed motivated the family to open a small store on Main Street with the intention of eventually moving all their assets to the bayside. After a short period, the brothers moved into larger quarters on the Wisnom block on B Street.

Just before the turn of the century, the brothers sold all their holdings on the coast to concentrate on the San Mateo store. They stocked everything that people might need, from ladies' wear to farm equipment, from sugar and flour to alcoholic beverages. Their store on B Street actually included four different enterprises, a hardware division, grocery outlet, dry goods market and a clothing

Levy Bros.

SPECIAL SALES

Next Monday, Tuesday and Wednesday

October 29, 30 and 31 1906

	Regular.	Special.
Grape Nuts, pkg,	15c	2 for 25c
Kipperd Herring, tin	25c	20c
Pillsbury's Vitos, pkg	20c	2 for 35c
Ammonia, pint	15c	10c
Knox's Gelatine, pks	15c	10c
20-Mule Borax Soap, cake	5c	6 for 25c
Yellow corn meal, 10-lb sack	35c	25c
Walnuts, pound	20c	15c
Zinfandel, gal,	75c	60c
Cognac, bottle	$1	85c

Levy Bros.' Department Store

B Street, San Mateo

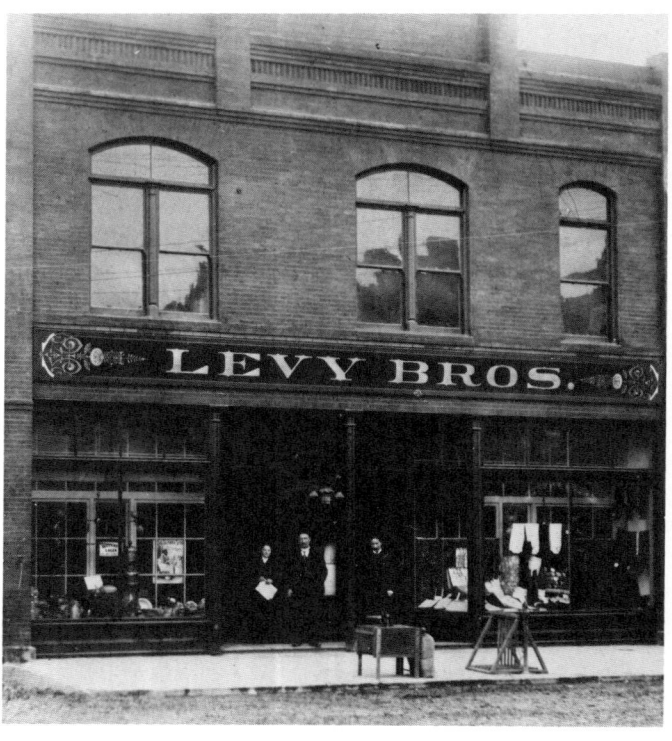

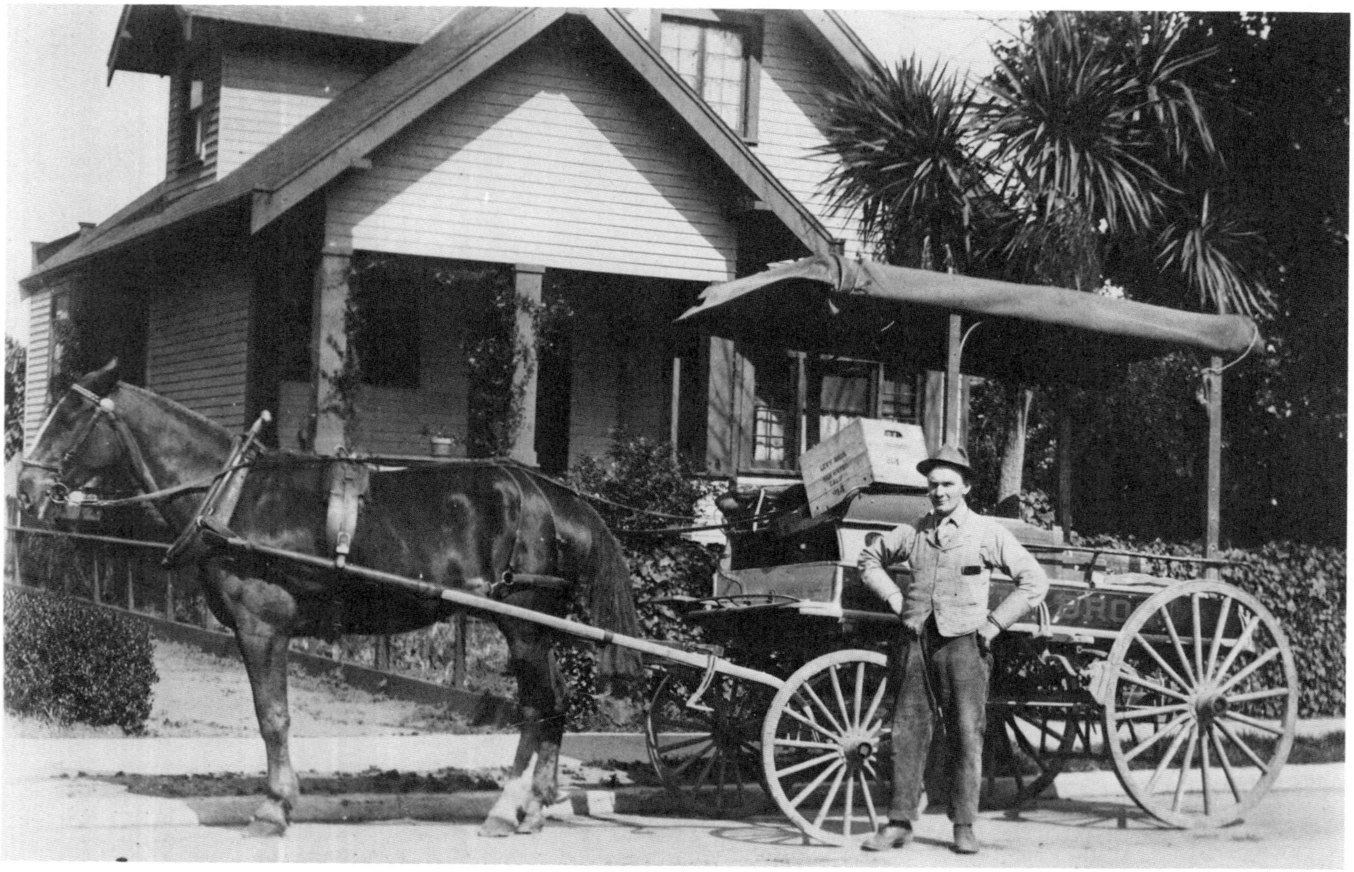

Above: Interior of the B Street store.

Right: The Levy family (from left, standing: Josephine (Mrs. Fernand Levy); Joe Levy; Emma (Mrs. Adrian Levy); Fernand Levy. Seated: Mrs. Pauline Ishare (sister); Adrian Levy; and Natalie (Mrs. Armand Levy).

Opposite, top: Levy Brothers' store on B Street, with an advertisement from 1906. Grape Nuts were an especially good buy.

Opposite below: A delivery van for Levy Brothers. The driver has his account book safely tucked in his pocket.

Courtesy San Mateo County Historical Museum

Above: Hintz's Drygoods at Second and B Street, with Doc Baldwin, Bert Lorton, Esther Terkelson, J. J. Hintz, Phyllis Baldwin, and Anna Hintz posing for the cameraman.

Left: Bicycles were all the rage in the 1890s; they were cheaper than horses, and didn't require feeding.

Opposite, top: A bicycle club stops for a rest on the B Street bridge. The sign says "Warning: This bridge is unsafe for fast driving or heavy teaming. $25 fine for driving faster than a walk."

Opposite, below: The starter fires his gun as racers leap onto their Iron Steeds.

Courtesy San Mateo County Historical Museum

From Village to Town: 1887 - 1920

emporium. The store guaranteed prompt delivery service, from San Bruno to Belmont, by horse and buggy in the early days, and by truck later on.

By 1917 a new generation of Levys was in charge. Assuming leadership of the family's business was Fernand's son Edmund. When the United States entered World War I in 1917 the 33-year-old accepted an appointment with the Red Cross. He spent two years in Paris in charge of the Commissary Department and then returned. By this time his father was 69 years old, and other members of the family had little interest in the business. He therefore brought in a boyhood friend, John D. Bromfield, another son of Davenport Bromfield, as a partner. Together they opened a store in Burlingame, and advanced the business in other ways as well.

Between the time of San Mateo's incorporation and the turn of the century, new businesses began to alter the appearance of San Mateo. For example the brick Odd Fellows Hall on B Street- still standing- had been completed by this time.

Nevertheless, D. Gordon Bromfield remembers that through the 90s the "array of old fashioned business buildings with many shabby store fronts"[13] remained. Old-timers recalled that the barber shops continued as they had for decades with their bath accommodations in the rear. The butcher shop had no refrigeration, but plenty of fly paper. The livery stable boarded splendid steeds and old nags. The sidewalks were still wooden; the town's major thoroughfares were dust or mud, depending upon the season, and the streets still had hitching posts and water troughs for horses.

The only businesses that seemed to multiply during the 1890s were the saloons, perhaps numbering as many as two dozen by 1900. Bromfield remembered their "miscellaneous array of fronts and swinging doors that opened into shabby barrooms . . . [Draft beer] was served in solid or thick glass steins from kegs that reclined on racks behind the bar." Slot machines took nickels and dimes from the customers. On the walls of these "drinking dives" were pictures "of the fair sex, race

Above: Pete Thorsen dressed as a drum major for a Fourth of July parade. Right: Slot machines at Thorsen's saloon.

Opposite: Pete Thorsen's saloon, on the corner of Third Avenue & Main Street. From left: Jim Clark, who ran a candy store; Pete and Harry Thorsen behind the bar, John van Wye, a coal & wood merchant, and William Casey, proprietor of the Linwood Hotel.

Courtesy San Mateo County Historical Museum

horses, and prize fighters of the period, such as John L. Sullivan, Bob Fitzsimmons and Jim Corbett."

Bromfield also remembered the jail—"and what a jail it was."

> [It] consisted of a small concrete shaped structure of one room having two little windows near the roof and one steel door. This lockup was in the railroad yard standing like a sore thumb just opposite the freight shed . . . and was so close to the track that a fireman of any passing train could have hit it with a lump of coal from the coal car just behind the cab. I dare say drunks and railroad hobos were the jail's most frequent guests.[14]

While the residential section of town grew during the 1890s, thanks to the Western Addition, conditions remained fairly primitive there as well. Few homes had electricity or telephone service, although they were available. Bromfield's family was one of the few to use electricity instead of oil lamps for lighting, but the service was unreliable:

> The electric lights sometimes went out at night when my elder sister Beatrice was engrossed in homework or school problems . . . For this reason, mother deemed it wise to have a few oil lamps on hand for such emergencies.[15]

After electricity at the Bromfield house came the telephone: "Our first telephone, the wall type with a buzzer handle on the side of it, was installed in my parents' bedroom, and we all looked upon this gadget as the second world wonder" (electricity being the first). San Mateo would not have the dial system until 1942.

For family outings, Bromfield wrote that Coyote Point was a much loved picnic spot "by us as well as other town residents,"[16] and it was a good place to fish for perch too. About 1890, people stopped calling the place San Mateo Point and began to call it Coyote Point. To get there, most of the townspeople took Poplar Avenue. "Here we traversed a narrow, hard surface road

Top: The San Mateo Wheelmen enjoy an outing at Coyote Point.
Below: Coyote Point offered a thirty-room bath house for those who wanted to enjoy a dip in the Bay.

Courtesy San Mateo County Historical Museum

across the marsh past an ancient shell bank or Indian mound, to the southern end of the point," Bromfield recalled.

By the 1890s, the Point was covered with Australian blue gum (eucalyptus) trees. At the northwest edge of the grove was a 30-room bath house and a bathing beach which ran west for about a third of a mile up to a pier. An 1895 description of the beach said that the water was shallow and warm, that the beach was smooth and the Bay bottom off the point was free of pebbles. At the commodious bathhouse, bathing suits could be rented. This account also noted that the beach had a special added attraction ". . . in the fact that it is never frequented by other than respectable persons."[17]

Bromfield described the wooden pier at the end of the beach as constructed of "heavy redwood planks on wooden piles." On shore was a "weather-beaten warehouse." During the late 1880s this had been a place of considerable activity as the materials for the construction of the Crystal Springs Dam were landed here and then hauled up to the construction site. Now less freight was unloaded (at $1.00 a ton) but more passengers came (at 75¢ per round-trip) to visit the beach.

South of the Point and east of the village, many of the marshlands were being diked at the turn of the century for use as dairy ranches. This included Brewer's Island (today's Foster City). Natural marshlands still extended east of the Hayward estate, along the bayline to the city limits of today's Belmont. This stretch became a well-known mecca for duck hunters, and several hunting cabins stood east of the Beresford (today's Hillsdale) train stop.

Diversions for the townspeople were simple. Children liked to watch the soldiers marching along the County Road on their way to Salinas or Monterey from the San Francisco Presidio. Bromfield remembered how artillery hauled by sleek, shiny mules accompanied by cavalry would move behind the rows of infantry. Occasionally the soldiers would camp on the outskirts of the town.

Another event that delighted the town's children as well as adults was the 1902 automobile meet. Some thirty horseless carriages started out from San Francisco. The drivers stopped in San Mateo for lunch and then proceeded up Crystal Springs Road amid great excitement. The outing has been described as the first of its kind in California history.

Although by 1900 some change had occurred at San Mateo, by and large it still was a place known primarily for the great estates around it. The landscape was dominated by mansions, beautiful gardens, tracks and polo fields. Travel writer Stanley Wood, in *From Over the Range to the Golden Gate* wrote in 1896:

> Surrounding San Mateo are a number of the most elegant country seats in California. Wealth has concentrated its forces here, and everything that money can do, when employed unstintedly [sic] and intelligently, has been done to beautify the scene. The art of the landscape gardener has been exercised to its fullest extent, and the grounds which surround these places of San Francisco millionaires are bewildering visions of arboreal and floral beauty

A large group enjoys a picnic at Coyote Point, about 1905.

Courtesy San Mateo County Historical Museum

No single person better symbolized the era of the estates than Alvinza Hayward. His gardens and grounds grew more beautiful with age. He still rode in a brougham to the railroad station. His carriage horses, remembered Bromfield, "trotted the streets with lengthy manes and tails," unusual for that time. The two splendid sorrel steeds "were certainly entitled to the interest shown them." As for Hayward himself, he remained the unchanged "dapper, slender little man, who always wore highly polished square toed boots of knee length" and "a black suit with white collar and bow tie."[18] He also carried a gold handled cane.

When Hayward died of a stroke at the age of 81 on February 14, 1904, a part of old San Mateo died too

An automobile rally at Crystal Springs in 1902, when the automobile was still thought to be a fad and a nuisance. No one could have guessed how much of San Mateo would eventually be devoted to freeways and parking lots.

Courtesy San Mateo County Historical Museum

THE CHANGING LANDSCAPE

BETWEEN THE TURN OF THE CENTURY and 1920, the landscape south of San Mateo changed dramatically. Salt harvesting dominated the baylands, nurseries covered the hillsides, and a country club was established. But perhaps the most noticeable transformation took place just to the south.

Alvinza Hayward died in 1904, and his widow, Charity, followed him one year later. Local investors gathered together to discuss what might be done with the Hayward property. They came up with a scheme to convert the old mansion into a resort hotel, along the lines of the famous Del Monte Hotel in Monterey. They would build on San Mateo's reputation as a retreat for the elite. They would make the hotel a fashionable centerpiece, one where people who wanted to participate in the outdoor activities of the upper classes could come—where people could eat, sleep and play with the wealthy people they wished to emulate.

The original directors of the hotel, which they called "The Peninsula," were all local people—Captain John Barneson, T. R. Turner, James H. Doolittle, J. H. Coleman, George C. Ross, E. A. Husing and Joseph Levy. They worked hand in hand with the real estate firm of Baldwin and Howell, which subdivided other parts of the old estate for residential sales. The portion of the Hayward place that became the hotel and its immediate grounds is known today as the Glazenwood

The San Mateo High School girls' basketball team, 1906.

Courtesy San Mateo County Historical Museum

residential area. The mansion and the surrounding 15 acres were purchased for $125,000. Another $300,000 was spent on improvements. Wings were added so that the hotel could accommodate 300 or so guests in 122 rooms.

The Peninsula Hotel opened February 22, 1908, amid great fanfare. A full page advertisement in the February 1908 *Sunset* magazine proclaimed "A TWENTIETH CENTURY HOTEL OF THE HIGHEST DEGREE OF EXCELLENCE" was only 30 minutes away by rail. It was "located in a Beautiful Park of thirty years' cultivation [offering] all the charm and delight of the country combined with the attractions and conveniences of the metropolis." One of the directors, James H. Doolittle, was the hotel's first manager.

Brochures promoting the hotel highlighted the beautiful drives for the motorist, including the trip to Crystal Springs Dam: "No where in Switzerland is there a grander view." On the grounds were a children's playground and a clubhouse complete with bowling alleys, billiard tables, card rooms and a grill, "where things both wet and dry [alcoholic and non-alcoholic] may be enjoyed to the full." On the interior of the main lobby: "With its oaken walls embellished with tasteful hand-carved ornamentation; with its grand staircase and encircling balcony; with its subdued light, mellowed by its passage through a roof of soft-hued art glass; with its gleaming polished floors and its soft, thick rugs, and the massive furniture in harmonious keeping with the restful tone of the luxurious whole, strike the key note of that hospitable efficiency in management which characterizes the hotel." The brochures also extolled the guest rooms: "Every provision has been made for safety, comfort and enjoyment of guests," including a "complete automatic fire system" and telephone service that connected "every room with any place in the whole United States."

While no one has ever adequately figured out exactly why, the Peninsula never became a financial success. It lost money for its original investors and was sold a few times. It was even closed for a while. In 1917 an

The Peninsula Hotel, created by the addition of two large wings to the already enormous Alvinza Hayward mansion, at a total cost of almost a half million dollars.

Courtesy San Mateo County Historical Museum

The Leslie Salt plant, near Sixteenth Avenue and the railroad tracks.
Courtesy San Mateo County Historical Museum

investment group headed by Samuel Newhouse of Salt Lake City reopened the hotel, but that venture failed too. Finally in April of 1920, it was re-opened under new management. Its eventual fate will be detailed at the end of this chapter.

South of the old Hayward estate, C. E. Whitney decided to try his hand at harvesting salt by means of solar evaporation. As early as 1892, he had considered the possibility of using bay marshlands for this purpose. Whitney, who worked in the dredging business for August H. Schilling, thought the west bay could render the kind of success that was being achieved on the east side. In 1903 Whitney obtained 200 acres east of the railroad tracks to begin work. His labor force was largely Japanese; he paid each man $5.40 per six-day week.

For a time he called his operation the C. E. Whitney Company, but soon changed the name to the Leslie Salt Refining Company, named after one of his uncles. Whitney built his plant just east of the railroad tracks, a little north of the present day Highway 92 overpass. This area offered the widest available marshland on the western shore, and the site was close to the tracks for convenient transportation.

C. E. died the same year the plant opened. His family then took control of operations. Arthur L. Whitney managed the company, while his wife assumed civic responsibilities in town. She is listed among the charter members of the San Mateo Women's Club.

The history of the salt industry of the Bay Area has as its central theme the process of merger and consolidation. In 1907 Whitney interests were combined with those of John Stauffer, Christian de Guigne and August H. Schilling, who formed a new firm, the Leslie Salt Company. They borrowed $1 million to upgrade the San Mateo plant, and this investment paid off. In 1910, the San Mateo works became the first on the West Coast to install the vacuum refining method essential in the production of fine table salt. Until that time, many regarded bay salt as unfit for human consumption. Leslie was also innovative in packaging and advertising. It developed the cylinder shaped container—red with tin top and cork—advising consumers that the cylinder was stronger than the boxes of the competition.

In 1913, the San Mateo plant won first prize for salt

The Beresford Country Club, around 1915. The buildings, in the Tudor Revival style, are still in use as the Peninsula Golf and Country Club.

Courtesy San Mateo County Historical Museum

production in the California Land Show and Home Industry Exhibition. In 1915, at a luncheon of the Home Industry League at the Palace Hotel in San Francisco, Leslie D. Whitney (of a new generation of Whitneys) was given top honors and asked to deliver the keynote speech, after which films of the San Mateo plant were shown. By 1919, the San Mateo refinery was harvesting 25,000 tons of salt each year, five times the 1904 yield.

Steady mergers continued to characterize the Bay Area salt industry. In 1931, the decision was made to shut down the San Mateo plant. A combination of factors probably forced this to happen. That year Arthur L. Whitney died, the company wanted to consolidate its holdings, and the City of San Mateo appeared ready to annex the Leslie property, which would mean higher taxes. Despite the steady consolidation of properties and assets within the salt industry, the company's name stayed as Leslie. This had everything to do with the well-known Leslie image of innovation and quality—a tribute to the Whitney family of San Mateo.[19]

West and south of the Leslie salt ponds and quite visible along the hills and on both sides of the County Road, wherever space could be bought or leased, people of a variety of ethnic backgrounds raised flowers during the years between the turn of the century and the Second World War. Indeed all up and down the Peninsula, the flower industry took hold, as San Mateo County growers supplied the San Francisco market and markets far beyond.

The last of the new uses of land south of San Mateo between 1900 and 1920 was the creation of a country club. By 1911, the country club concept was only nineteen years old, the first having been established at Brookline, Massachusetts. These clubs were developed for wealthy Americans who wished to emulate the British aristocracy. At the club they could participate in a variety of sports, such as tennis and golf.

In 1893 the Burlingame Country Club had been founded, the first to be established west of the Mississippi, and instantly became one of the most exclusive social institutions in California. Among the people it excluded were those of the Jewish faith.

At the turn of the century, San Francisco had a sizable Jewish population that included some of the most important businessmen in the West. These people developed a thirst for the social status and recreational activities that a country club afforded. Since they could not join the Burlingame Club, they started a club of their own. In November 1911 a group of 29 men, meeting at the Mills Building in San Francisco, decided to buy a piece of property southwest of San Mateo and to incorporate the Beresford Country Club.

Among the original organizers were some of the most famous names of San Francisco. Included among them were M. J. Brandenstein (later Bransten), who with his brothers established M. J. B. Coffee; bankers and philanthropists Herbert and Mortimer Fleishhacker; Walter Haas, of the Levi Straus family; I. W. Hellman, who became president of Wells Fargo Bank in 1913; Jess W. Lilienthal, president of United Railway of San Francisco; Morris Meyerfield, who owned the Orpheum Theater Circuit; George Roos, of Roos Brothers Clothiers; and Sigmund Stern, for whom Stern Grove in San Francisco is named.

The 150-acre Beresford Club was located west and south of the orphanage. Today it is the Peninsula Golf and Country Club, off Alameda de las Pulgas. On July 4, 1912, a celebration initiated the club's activities. A temporary clubhouse had been constructed, the golf course was completed and a membership of 200 had been recruited. It just so happened that the date of the event was the same day as the Burlingame Club's biggest party of the summer. The Beresford ceremony included a speech by Rabbi Martin A. Meyer of Temple Emanuel, patriotic band music, the raising of the American flag, and various vaudeville entertainments performed by Beresford members and friends. The climax of the program came when a caddy placed a large golf ball in front of the Club's president, William Fries. The *San Francisco Chronicle* reported that he burst it open with a swing of a golf club and two doves "carrying the club colors, blue and white, took wing." Then little candy boxes in the shape of golf balls were distributed among the crowd. Dinner was prepared on open air barbecues by Ben Diaz "and a staff of Mexicans imported for the occasion." Food and drink were served right on one of the fairways "in genuine Spanish fashion."

Exactly one year later, another celebration took place at Beresford when the large Tudor Revival clubhouse, which still stands today, was completed. Large parties could now take place year round. In the days before 1920, a special affair for the Club was the annual New Year's Eve dinner and dance. Members would board one of Jesse Lilienthal's specially chartered street cars in San Francisco for the ride to San Mateo. Because so many wished to attend the celebration, taxing the overnight accommodations at the clubhouse past their limit, many reserved rooms at the Peninsula Hotel to rest after the party.[20]

South and east of the Beresford Club, across from today's Bay Meadows, at least one portion of land was retained for traditional uses. In January 1889, K. O. O'Grady bought the 274-acre Laurel Creek Stock Farm originated by John S. Colegrove. O'Grady raced and trained horses for such equestrian enthusiasts as Alvinza Hayward. A second generation of O'Gradys held on to the property for the care of thoroughbreds, trotters and saddle horses, a good many of which came from Bay Meadows during the 1930s and 1940s. The family finally sold out to the interests of David Bohannon in 1946.

The Changing World of Culture and Society Within the Town

Between the mid-1890s and 1920, the social and cultural fabric of San Mateo began to change for the first time since the building of the railroad. Important, long-lasting community groups with a middle-class base, such as the San Mateo Woman's Club, were initiated. However, the metamorphosis was a slow one. Entering the new century, the old, privileged families still held sway over matters of society and culture.

Perhaps the Borels were the best-known family during that era. The family was large and visible, and became a real part of the community. In 1892, Antoine Borel built a chapel (sometimes called Geneva Chapel) for community use. Exactly whom he intended to occupy it is unclear. Aylett Cotton, a Borel son-in-law, remembered it being used as a nonsectarian house of worship for the family and neighbors, and as a place for young ministers to practice sermons.[21] Another source says it was a sister church for the Congregationalists for ten years.[22] Others claim that the chapel was meant for the Presbyterians.[23] All agree that by 1902 it was turned over to Saint Matthews Episcopal Church, which held services there until 1937. After that it became a community stage called the Hillbarn Theater.

While it operated as a chapel, it was also a sort of community center, especially for the farming folk of the Homestead area. Winifred M. Burke, who lived nearby during her girlhood at the turn of the century, remembered that the Borels kept a children's library there. At Christmas time, the family had a children's party, and everyone was invited regardless of denomination. At that party, the Borel girls would distribute specially selected gifts to the local youngsters.[24]

During the early twentieth century the Borel estate grew more beautiful as the trees planted by the family matured. The young and upcoming attorney, Aylett Cotton, first visited the estate in 1905. The place covered about 300 acres by that time, from the County Road to "the top of the hill," and from today's Barneson to 20th Avenue. Cotton stayed in the guest house during that first visit, about 100 yards from the main house. The trees and shrubbery confused this "city dweller," and he actually got lost trying to find his way back after an evening's visit with the family.

Cotton's memories of the estate were enhanced by his romantic involvement with Alice Borel. He remembered while courting her:

> We would spend days exploring... In the mornings, we would take long walks, crossing the 'Bridge of Sighs,' a bridge between two forks in the trees, across El Arroyo Mocho Creek... Often we had picnics in the Swiss Forest; while the ladies were resting and gossiping, we gentlemen would accompany Mr. Borel on horseback down the wooded carriage roads, or perhaps, we would go hunting on the Spring Valley property, of which he was a director.[25]

In 1906, President Theodore Roosevelt appointed Cotton Prosecuting Attorney of Manila, in the Philippines. Also that year, Alice Borel visited Switzerland. The two maintained their relationship by correspondence and determined they would be married in 1907. Alice asked in one of her letters if their wedding could take place on the estate:

> How I love that little chapel in San Mateo. I have known it always, seen it grow, and have taken an interest in all its people. Do you know, Aylett dear, I have dreamed of being married in that little chapel, of having people whom I know and love, decorate the church, for then it would be done with loving hands, and they would put their heart and soul into the work.[26]

The couple were married at the chapel. Cotton recalled that the many flowers decorating the building came from the estate's greenhouses. The choir from the nearby orphanage sang a "fine concert before the wedding march." Alice herself had trained and costumed the boys.

Around the same time, Alice's sister, Sophie, married Cotton's best friend, John Lewis. Antoine wanted to keep his family close by, so he built each a house on the estate. He also gave each a choice of an automobile or a carriage as a wedding present. Sophie chose the automobile, while Alice wanted the carriage.

Cotton resumed his prestigious law career.[27] In 1910 he became San Francisco's Chief Assistant District Attorney, serving in that capacity for a decade. During those years he continued to live at the estate at San Mateo. As we will see later, he also became involved in the political affairs of the community. After Alice died in 1936, Cotton married Sophie, who had also lost her mate.

Like the Borels, the Parrott family maintained an interest in the affairs of San Mateo, especially religious causes. In 1899, the legendary Father Timothy Callahan wished to build a new Catholic church. Widow Abby Parrott donated the property across the street from the original church, on the west side of Ellsworth between Second and Third, for the purpose. Callahan then went to work to raise the building funds. He had obtained about $6000 from the small community when Mrs. Parrott contributed $50,000 to guarantee the project would succeed. Architect Albert Pissis designed the red brick Italianate building. Its stained glass came from London. The first mass in the new church took place on September 23, 1900. It served its congregation for nearly seven decades until being replaced by the new Church on El Camino Real in 1966.

Across the County Road from the Parrotts, the Kohl estate saw significant changes. In 1904, the pioneer Alaskan fur trader William H. Kohl died after living some thirty years at San Mateo. His son, twenty-one-year old C. Frederick Kohl, inherited the mansion and lived there with his new wife, May Elizabeth Godey Kohl. Frederick was said to be a well-known society figure; he even became President of the exclusive Pacific Union Club in San Francisco. The Kohls lived at San Mateo until 1914, giving many lavish parties. They moved to Burlingame and then built a new estate, "The Oaks." Today it is known as Mercy High School.

While the affairs of the elite were regarded as most important, the growing middle-class community of San Mateo began in the 1890s to create its own social and cultural institutions. Perhaps the first was the Fortnightly Club, established in 1896, which met every other week in the home of one of its members. Various cultural programs were arranged, including musical presentations, poetry readings and lectures on a wide variety of subjects. By January of 1898 the programs of the Club were deemed topical enough to be covered in the *San Francisco Examiner*. At the meeting of January 29, Captain S. Sakurai of the Japanese navy, representing his government while the warship *Chitose* was being constructed here, discussed "Japan—Past and Present," detailing the "cause of the Japanese awakening and the aims of those who are now directing his country's destinies." Sakurai also answered questions about Japanese customs and manners.

The meetings routinely attracted about 75 people, but some drew more, as at the March 1898 get-together, when Rabbi Jacob Voorsanger discussed "The Paganism of Modern Society" at the George W. Dickie home.

Some of the evenings included a range of presentations. On February 2, 1899, Mrs. Philip Roedel and Mr. Albert L. Hall performed vocal solos, Mr. W. D. Reed read Mark Twain passages, and Mr. Charles N. Kirkbride delivered a paper entitled "Wanted Books" in which he pleaded for the establishment of a new public library in San Mateo. In presenting his case, Kirkbride described a trip he had taken to the library at Alameda. After his speech, the Club passed a resolution to petition the town's trustees about the matter.

The spirit of community within the middle class seemed particularly strong among women. In 1896, a Women's Suffrage Club was organized, with Mrs. Davenport Bromfield as its first president. More active and permanent was the San Mateo Woman's Club, founded in 1903. This club actually originated from a men's group. In 1903, local community leaders organized the Civic Club, to create and maintain pride in San Mateo, promote the welfare of the community and support the town's administration of public affairs.

Several good things came out of the Civic Club. It paved the County Road out of its treasury. It successfully dealt with a severe mosquito problem by draining or oiling standing pools of water. It posted the town's first street signs: wooden placards, painted green with white letters, placed on corner fence posts. Each cost the club $2.00. Other progressive projects were undertaken. But after a little more than a year, the group ceased to function.

In the meantime, the wives of the members of the

Civic Club formed their own Auxiliary Civic Club in 1903. With 28 charter members, they declared their objectives: "to improve and beautify the city of San Mateo, to seek the cooperation of all citizens in a persistent effort to promote the welfare of the community, and develop public sentiment along all lines of improvement."[28]

The club's first president, Mrs. A. B. Ford, focused the group's early attention on litter. The women organized school children into companies, with each responsible for a certain part of town. Rewards were promised to the youngsters maintaining the best-kept part of the community. The club also purchased 26 metal trash receptacles, placed them in key locations, and hired a scavenger to empty them three times each week. The women also attempted to put in each citizen's mind the concept that throwing debris on the street ran contrary to the well-being of the entire population of San Mateo.

Because the town did not have a public dump or a garbage company responsible for hauling away trash, many people dumped refuse in empty lots. The Auxiliary wrote letters to the owners of such properties, especially those along the street car lines, asking that they clean up these rubbish heaps. Also, as a part of their beautification program, the women had ivy planted to cover the sides of public buildings. All these projects were initiated in 1903, and if that were not enough, the women also started a sewing school for girls.

In the small reading room at Library Hall they exerted a strong influence. They had various works, especially those of the French novelist Emile Zola, taken off the shelves, believing these books to be unsuitable for reading by young people. They supported activities at the library by buying magazine subscriptions. They also played an important role in gaining community support and raising funds for a new library building, completed in 1910. In 1903 the women recognized that the Fire Department needed a chemical engine, raised the funds necessary, and in November 1905 presented one to the town.

That same year, realizing that their group was no longer an auxiliary to any other, the members voted to change the name of the organization to the San Mateo Woman's Club.

Through the early years of its existence, the Woman's Club continuously found new causes. They helped run a daily newspaper for the County Poor Farm. They provided clothing for the orphanage. By 1907, with a membership of nearly 70, literary, music and garden sections were added to the interests of the club. Art and needle work subgroups were created a little later. The women organized flower shows, lecture series and other cultural activities—all to benefit San Mateo and its citizens.

Along with these positive aspects of a growing community, negative ones began to appear as well. About the turn of the century, San Mateans began making more distinctions about themselves as townspeople. Rigid ethnic districts had not taken shape, but a certain part of town was reserved for the Chinese. An "Irishtown" existed east of the tracks, where actually some important family names were established—Byrnes, Casey, Sheehan, Flarity, Dolan, Burke, and Fitzgerald among others. There was no caste system, but a sense of difference was evident.

D. Gordon Bromfield could hear it in the church bells:

> How the bells of Episcopal and Catholic churches tolled and were distinctly heard resounding throughout the neighborhood! . . . At times when they were clanging simultaneously, it occurred to me that the sextons were definitely vying with each other.[29]

Librarian Inez Mabel Crawford, about 1915.

Courtesy San Mateo County Historical Museum

On the bottom of the social ladder was lanky Nick Walsh, the town's "moron messenger."[30] Bromfield remembered the poor man for his "ungainly shabby appearance." Walsh lived in a homemade shack two blocks east of the railroad depot. "It was a combination of sheet-tin, old boards, and canvas all fastened together in a most haphazard manner," explained Bromfield. Apparently Walsh earned a living by making daily trips to San Francisco on the train to pick up items for the residents and merchants of San Mateo.

GOODBYE TO SOME OLD INSTITUTIONS

CHANGE IN SAN MATEO was evident not only in what was new between 1887 and 1920, but in what disappeared during those years.

Since the 1860s, St. Matthew's Hall had thrived by concentrating on military discipline, enhanced by a focus on traditional education and the arts. During the 1890s closing exercises for the year usually included readings, musical solos and speeches by the boys, along with military marches and competitive drills. By the early 1890s the Brewer family felt a larger campus was necessary. The Gustave Mahe vineyard in today's Hillsborough was acquired by the school, and in 1892 it moved to the new location, where it operated until 1915.

Reverend George Wallace took over Saint Matthew's Hall and opened St. Margaret's School for Girls in 1892. D. Gordon Bromfield remembered the "buxom" headmistress, Ida Tibbetts, and her love of music.[31] The school lasted only until 1903, when it was sold to the emerging San Mateo Union High School District.

Another long-time institution to disappear before 1920 was the Armitage Orphanage. Back in 1886 the orphanage was dedicated, at Ellsworth and Tilton, as a Saint Matthew's Episcopal Church charity, with the purpose of bringing up orphaned and destitute children with the church's help. In 1889 the girls of the institution were removed to new accommodations in San Francisco, leaving thirty boys in San Mateo.

Recognizing that there were many more boys in need of shelter at the orphanage, in October 1891 George W. Gibbs bought the former Laurel Institute properties. Gibbs, a dealer in iron, steel and heavy hardware in San Francisco, acquired the place from John Gamble, who had purchased the former girls' school for $20,000 in 1890 and had established a boys' school there called Laurel Hall Academy. He sold it to Gibbs for $40,000 and moved his 50 boys to San Rafael. In November 1891, Gibbs and his wife Augusta contributed the land and improvements thereon to the orphanage. The building constructed by Miss L. A. Buckmaster once again resonated with the sounds of children. The former orphanage building became a seminary for the Episcopal Church.

By January of 1893, the orphanage was in full operation. A reporter from the Redwood City *Democrat* was most impressed. The boys were organized so well that ". . . with the exception of one servant, the cook, the boys do all the work of the house, including bread making and butter making, dish washing and general cleaning, and a more manly set of little fellows it would be hard to find. . . The boys have the best of religious training" with a chapel on the premises, and they attended Saint Matthew's on Sundays. However, the *Democrat* also added that: ". . . all orphans are gladly aided and all denominations and creeds are represented."

By 1903, 187 boys were being cared for at the orphanage, 88 from San Francisco and the others from all over California, and as far away as New York, Canada and Mexico. Boys from two to thirteen were accepted. Those over the age of six were sent to the public school down on the Homestead. The annual report for that year pointed out that these boys were always accompanied by an officer of the institution "whose duty it is to pay strict attention to their deportment." The purpose of the institution was firmly stated to secure for the boys "suitable trades and occupations" after they reached the age of thirteen, and to retain "direct supervision" of the boys from the orphanage's office in San Francisco. A sad note in that year's report was the mention that four of the boys had been lost to illness during the year, the first time such tragedy had occurred there.

By 1904, with about 200 boys in residence, new and larger quarters were needed. Answering the philanthropic call was Charles Templeton Crocker. He and his sister Jennie had been orphaned themselves in 1897, when their father, Charles Frederick Crocker (eldest son of Charles Crocker, one of the "Big Four"), died at Uplands, in today's Hillsborough. Feeling affinity for the children of the orphanage, Crocker pledged enough money to build a new three-story house. On September 2, 1905—on the day he came of age and inherited $5 million—Charles, with his sister Jennie, dedicated the cornerstone of the building. He contributed $150,000 to the project as a gift to the Episcopal Diocese of California "in perpetuity."

Frank S. Van Trees designed the new building, to be made of red brick with a Mission revival style tile roof. By the spring of 1906, construction had reached the third story. In her annual report for that year, Orphanage Superintendent Hallie Le Warne said everyone looked forward to eating Christmas dinner in the spacious new dining room. But on April 18, the great earthquake struck. Le Warne lamented: "The walls of the newly laid brick were practically razed to the ground." Luckily, no one was hurt in the catastrophe, and the four remaining buildings came through in good fashion, except for a number of chimneys being lost. During the year fewer boys were taken into the orphanage, reducing the population to about 170.

The young Crockers came to the aid of the orphanage again, and construction began anew. The revised plans called for a scaled-down version; it is unclear how much of this building was completed.

In the meantime, life got back to normal for the orphans. After the earthquake, a favorite tradition became the summer camp at Pebble Beach on the San Mateo County south coast. Local children of the Homestead remember that the boys brought back bottles and boxes full of colorful smooth rocks for showing off and trading each fall.

At Christmas time, various families of the elite circle in San Mateo would show their generosity. For the holiday of 1907, they donated 24 turkeys for Christmas dinner (of which Mrs. Kohl donated 10). Meanwhile Antoine Borel gave the institution's administration "carte blanche" for purchasing presents for the children, according to the orphanage's 1908 annual report.

Despite such generosity by the elite of San Mateo, other accounts suggest that all was not perfect for the orphans. Down at the Homestead School many of the children felt compelled to choose an "orphan pal" to share their lunch. It seems all the boys had to eat at mid-day was a "hunk of corndodger" or "rubber gunger" smeared with syrup, delivered by horse and wagon. Occasionally, fruit from the Borel estate supplemented this pitiful meal. Winifred Burke went to school with the boys and remembered them as "very pathetic." She recalled that they would be marched down today's 20th Avenue to the school. On rainy days, when the mud would be so gooey that the boys would have to stay at the home, "we would rattle around in this big four room school."

Toward the end, instead of going to camp at Pebble Beach during the summer, the boys were sent to Sebastopol, where they were hired out to pick berries. In 1911, the season lasted until September. This created problems for the Homestead School, where state funding depended on average daily attendance. San Mateo school chief George Hall sent three instructors to Sebastopol in 1912 to give lessons to the boys after their work days. By laboring during the summers, the boys earned the approximately $1600 necessary to keep all of them in clothing.

Despite their hardships, the boys of the orphanage, by and large, established productive lives for themselves. Burke recalled that the people of the Homestead followed their progress after they left: "It was amazing what they did with their education and background, and how successful they were."

In 1913, the State of California passed the Widow Pension Law which allowed many orphans to be cared for in foster homes. The orphanage in San Mateo disbanded on October 25 that same year. Antoine Borel bought the property to establish a new 1.25-mile riding course.

Pansy Jewett Abbott, who taught at the Homestead School

Courtesy San Mateo County Historical Museum

THE CHANGING FACE OF PUBLIC EDUCATION

SAN MATEO'S NEW MIDDLE CLASS championed many causes to improve the town. Perhaps their greatest success came in the field of education. During the years before 1920, the elementary school system was vastly improved, and a high school district was formed. But, as often happened in San Mateo's history, things seemed to happen only after a disastrous fire.

On July 30, 1891, while school was in session, a fire broke out at the San Mateo public school on the County Road. The rumor was that one of the boys, angry over some grievance, tossed a burning cigarette into the woodshed; he had the small town buzzing about him for many years thereafter. The blaze was 1500 feet from the nearest fire hydrant—too far. The school staff trained a garden hose from the Parrott place on the blaze, but that proved inadequate.

Principal Etta M. Tilton had never even conducted a fire drill before, but every one of the nearly 300 children were evacuated in orderly fashion. The teachers commanded the students to pick up their books, supplies and other possessions and walk quietly from the building. Older boys were sent to town to get help, and two volunteer fire fighters responded, but were fairly helpless. The older boys were then organized into a team to save what they could. The 900-volume library, various apparatus and teachers' tables were all recovered. The six room building itself was entirely destroyed, at an estimated loss of $12,000. Only $7,000 worth of insurance covered the disaster.

Immediately after the fire, school resumed at various locations, including the orphanage, a house out at the Homestead, Library Hall and other places. Planning for a new school began without delay.

On March 19, 1892, a strategy was adopted to create two new schools for San Mateo and its outlying areas. A new building would be constructed near the center of town for $20,000, and a school would be created out in the Homestead for $5000. Financing would come from the sale of the property on the County Road, insurance money and other sources. A three-acre site was selected between today's Second Avenue to the south and Baldwin to the north, and between San Mateo Drive to the west and B Street to the east. The building, completed in 1893, sat in the middle of the property, facing east.

Since it was in the center of town, the school was aptly named Central School. Children from all over the community could easily walk to school, except for those south of town, but they would have their own school.

Central School was a two-story wooden structure with eight classrooms and two other rooms. On top of the building sat an imposing tower. In those days the site was bordered by San Mateo Creek on the west and north. Oak, laurel and buckeye trees fringed the creek banks. A footbridge across the Creek led to the western part of town. Oak trees on the campus provided luxuriant shade during the warmer months. Redwood trees stood at the entrance at B and First Avenue. A gravel pathway led up to main entrance, which was for teachers and visitors only. The students used two side entrances, one for younger and one for older pupils.

A stairway with elegant banisters took students to the second floor, where large windows looked out over a panorama of hills to the west and bay to the east. From the tower, of course, an even greater vista opened up. Just after the building's completion in 1893, the *San Mateo Leader* claimed that from the tower "the observer can look into at least five counties, and the ferry boats plying between Oakland and San Francisco can be plainly seen." Only under special circumstances were the children allowed up to the tower, perhaps as a treat or reward.

The building was heated by a wood or coal-burning furnace in the basement. This system was modern for its day, and was a great improvement over the old hand-fed pot-bellied stoves of previous San Mateo schools.

When Central School opened in April of 1893, Etta Tilton continued as principal. In 1895 she was appointed Superintendent of the San Mateo County School System; she served in that capacity for twelve years.

Taking her place was George Hall, another walking institution. Hall was born in Merced County, California, in 1861. His family moved to San Mateo County early in his life. At eighteen he became principal and teacher of the Searsville School in south San Mateo County. Later he took a variety of jobs while living in Half Moon Bay, until he was called to San Mateo in 1895. Named for George Washington, he remained intensely patriotic for all of his life. His 1890s-style beard inspired kids to nickname him "Billie Whiskers."

Hall believed in physical fitness and led the children in calisthenics every day before school. He then rang a bell, indicating the school day had begun. A drummer boy beat out a march, and students were expected to keep pace in columns of two as they walked in precision into the building. Class sergeants watched closely and maintained order among the ranks. Conversation, pushing, pinching, elbowing or marching out of step were punished. Hall's favorite punishment was to require memorization of lengthy passages of poetry. Any complaining student might get a double dose of "Hiawatha" if he argued too long.

Hall had a system of speaking tubes with which to keep in touch with his teachers during the day. He most enjoyed visiting the classrooms himself, during which time he would talk to the children about the importance of Americanism, or challenge them to solve a mathematical problem. In 1907, Hall became San Mateo's first district superintendent, in charge of three schools, Central, Homestead and Peninsula.

Homestead School opened the same year as Central School, 1893. The Homestead School stood at today's Gum Street, across the County Road from Borel's chapel on the Arroyo Mocho, and faced east, giving an "enchanting view of the Bay," remembered Winifred Burke.

The Homestead School was attended by the few youngsters in the rural south San Mateo area and the boys from the orphanage. One of its teachers, Pansy Jewett Abbott, recalled having always about 50 children in her class.[32] The facilities were primitive. There was no plumbing. The old unsanitary bucket and dipper supplied water for thirsty children. They washed their hands before coming to school and when they came home. But the school stood next to a grocery store run by "a darling German lady called Mrs. Jancke," who had

Laying the tracks for the electric railway in San Mateo, at the corner of Baldwin and B Streets, circa 1902.

Courtesy San Mateo County Historical Museum

"great big jars of candy—licorice, gum-drops, cannonballs and all of those things" lining her shelves, according to Winifred Burke.[33]

The school's best-known instructor, Pansy Jewett Abbott, began her teaching career there in 1905 at the age of 18. At the same time she worked as a reporter—sometimes for the *San Mateo Times* and sometimes for the *Leader*. She was born in Nebraska in 1881, a descendant of John Adams. Her parents moved to San Jose when she was a child. Abbott taught first through fifth grade at Homestead and then moved on to teach at Central, becoming one of the most respected educators in San Mateo County History. In 1925, the Board of Supervisors unanimously appointed her County Superintendent of Schools, a position she held for more than 25 years before retiring in 1951. One of her many accomplishments was the establishment of the first county-wide school in California for children suffering from cerebral palsy.

Perhaps the most dramatic incident at Homestead occurred just before it closed in 1914. A rabid dog invaded the school grounds and terrorized the children. The call for help went to Superintendent George Hall, who quickly arrived on the scene and shot and killed the animal with his revolver.

Homestead School was obsolete and overcrowded the day that it was built. Finally, in 1914, the voters of San Mateo approved a $17,488 bond issue to build a new school in the Hayward Park subdivision, north of the Homestead. Construction was completed by August 1914, and Homestead School was closed.

Even before Homestead School was replaced, two other new schools were opened. In 1905, Peninsula Avenue School began serving the families of the northern sections of town. In 1908, Lawrence School opened. Lawrence was the first school to be named after a person, the popular County Supervisor and water company manager, William H. Lawrence, who had died of pneumonia back in 1888 at the age of 48. The school's children mostly came from east of the railroad tracks and included many from Italian and Japanese families, as well as children of transient Mexican railroad workers.

Perhaps the most important move forward in the field of education after the turn of the century was the establishment of a high school in 1902. This was largely the doing of San Mateo's town attorney, Charles N. Kirkbride. Kirkbride, still a bachelor (he remained so

The earliest United Railroads trolley cars looked very much like the cable cars in San Francisco. This one went to Baden, now South San Francisco. The crewmen on this car look ready for anything.

Courtesy San Mateo County Historical Museum

until after returning from World War I, when he married Miss Mabel Goode in 1919), roamed the countryside in 1902, gathering signatures on a petition asking for the organization of a high school district.

Superintendent Etta Tilton placed a bond issue on the ballot to create a high school district that would include the San Mateo, Laguna and Millbrae School Districts, thus offering public high school education for young people from San Mateo to San Bruno.

The election of July 26, 1902 succeeded, and A. W. Ebright, Charles N. Kirkbride and D. W. Donnelly were named to the first Board of Trustees.[34] They soon rented a small house on Ellsworth Avenue, known as the Dixon Cottage, for a school. They also hired A. G. Van Gorder of San Jose as the first principal and Marie Borough and Florence Kimball as the first teachers. San Mateo High School opened in September with 24 students enrolled.

Recognizing that the cottage could only be a temporary accommodation, in May of 1903, the trustees moved to purchase St. Margaret's School for Girls, formerly St. Matthew's Hall, which was still owned by Mrs. Francis C. Brewer. They put $1000 down and then placed another $23,000 bond issue before the citizens of the district, who approved it. The 27 students who moved into the second site thus occupied a building which already had a strong educational heritage.

RUMBLINGS OF GROWTH

IN 1895, THE HOWARD FAMILY allowed still more subdivisions of their property. They sold lots north of the Western Addition in an area realtors called San Mateo Heights. This expansion again drew a middle-class clientele. The houses tended to be more fashionable than those of the Western Addition, and attracted a number of professionals from San Francisco, as well as community and business leaders of San Mateo.

While the residential area of San Mateo was greatly expanded by the turn of the century, the business portion of town still seemed to be growing at a snail's pace. The increase in businesses between 1890 and 1900 was almost negligible. But some old companies were still going strong. D. Gordon Bromfield remembered the Brown Brothers' blacksmith shop as a center of great activity. Although they could do any kind of iron work, the brothers spent most of their ten-hour days shoeing horses. With the O'Grady stock farm and many horses still in the area, the Browns were always busy, which might account for their "frank, open expression and pleasant way of greeting customers."35

Nevertheless, there were signs that the twentieth century was on its way. At the J. T. Jennings Livery Stable on B and First Avenue, an addition completed in 1896 included an elevator capable of lifting carriages up to a second floor. Also that year saloonkeeper Bart Sheehan opened a new hotel, the Vendome, on Claremont and Second Avenue. In 1905 Robert J. Wisnom, a son of the famed pioneer, opened a hardware store with his brother William and Robert Bonner at Second and Ellsworth. They called their business Wisnom-Bonner Hardware. When the partnership was dissolved in 1924, it became known simply as Wisnom's, and remains a well-known store to the present day.

Another sign of progress could be seen in the increasing number of telephones around town. In 1894 there were only 14 telephones. In 1896 there were 31, and by the turn of the century 129. When the San Mateo and Burlingame Exchange replaced the magneto or crank-type equipment in 1907, there were 511 subscribers.

By 1900, San Mateo had 1,832 residents, as compared with about 500 at the time of the Library Hall fire just 13 years earlier. This surpassed the population of Redwood City (1,653), making San Mateo the largest town in San Mateo County.36 Of course with a population of only 12,000 people, San Mateo County itself was the smallest in the Bay Area in 1900.

This growth was quite impressive, considering that San Mateo had lost the battle for county seat, had no industry except the salt works south of town, and had no port. Besides some flower growing, it had no great agricultural significance, and it certainly did not pretend to be the logging outlet that Redwood City was from time to time. A few landholders still contained it, although not on all sides. In particular, the Parrott family to the west of town seemed unlikely to allow the town limits to reach the County Road.

San Mateo had a fine location, at the end of the highway to the coast, and it had a service-oriented economy that proved immune to the economic downturns of the turbulent 1890s. Redwood City, on the other hand, suffered from drops in exports and manufacturing.

In 1903, San Mateo received a huge boost by being linked to San Francisco by trolley service. In August 1891, the San Francisco and San Mateo Railroad Company had gained approval by state charter to operate an electric railway between the city and points in San Mateo County, from the Colma cemeteries to San Mateo and eventually Redwood City. The company planned eventually to link up with San Jose. By 1893 it had laid track as far as Baden (South San Francisco today), but a general financial downturn affected the company, and it went into receivership.

These four ladies clearly enjoy the older forms of transportation for a ride along El Camino Real. The donkey poses like a professional.

Courtesy San Mateo County Historical Museum

A newly organized San Francisco and San Mateo Electric Railway went into operation in May 1896. The new owners spent $1 million for forty new cars, and in 1900 the county granted a franchise for operating the line. San Mateo, determined to become the terminus, received a guarantee of two per cent of the company's gross revenue in exchange for various rights-of-way. The railway company also agreed to pave some streets.37

In May 1901 the company was sold to a Baltimore syndicate which planned to circle the Bay with the line, from San Francisco, to San Jose, to Oakland. Then a New Jersey corporation, United Railroads of San Francisco, bought the franchise in March 1902. United also purchased other street car lines in the city, allowing service that could link many parts of San Francisco with its southern neighbors.

United immediately put 600 laborers to work, extending the track from the north county to San Mateo. By October 1902 construction gangs were digging trenches and laying tracks on the outskirts of town. The line entered the town on San Mateo Drive (the southern part of which was called Griffith Street in those days) and ended up at Main Street, near the railroad station. On its way out of town the line turned north at Ellsworth, and at Poplar it turned west and then linked

Subdivision at Hayward Park began well before the mansion was enlarged as a hotel. For $900 per lot, buyers could claim a very grand neighbor indeed. And trolley service to the city made commuting a piece of cake.

Courtesy San Mateo County Historical Museum.

up with San Mateo Drive to complete a rather complicated loop.

The line was officially completed on December 31, 1902, and on New Year's Day, 1903, some 700 passengers rode the trolley up to Holy Cross Cemetery in record time—35 to 40 minutes—to celebrate.

In its first year of service, United could carry 900 passengers to San Francisco from its peninsula stops each hour, at 25¢ per fare. By 1910, 54 cars left San Mateo each week day, from 5:30 a.m. until 11:00 p.m. The trolleys left every 15 to 30 minutes, and ran on weekends as well.

For a dozen years there seemed to be no stopping United's success. The ultimate goal of extending service to San Jose and even Oakland was again spoken about. Then came the internal-combustion engine. In May 1915 the Peninsula Rapid Transit Company began operating a bus line to San Francisco, competing with the electric service. It had some advantages over United, including the fact that it did not have to pay out two percent of its gross income to the town of San Mateo. In 1919, United went out of business. The Market Street Railway Company then operated the electric line. Although electric service to San Mateo continued for another 30 years, autosand buses gradually replaced it.

The streetcar's ultimate fate should not blur our vision of what it meant to San Mateo in 1903. The town's continued quest to attract middle-class commuters was significantly boosted by this convenient, reliable and economical means of transportation. Just one year after trolley service began, two new subdivisions opened up.

Realtors Baldwin and Howell (with financing from Antoine Borel) were agents for both the newly subdivided San Mateo Park and the Hayward Addition in 1904. In a publication sponsored by them and published by the *San Mateo Leader*, the familiar qualities of old-world charm ("beautiful country estates"), great climate ("winter is but a name"), wondrous gardens and vegetation ("fields and forests in bloom every month in the year") were bolstered by "the extension of the United Railroads . . . which afford unexcelled transportation facilities for the businessmen of San Francisco going back and forth every day."[38]

Baldwin and Howell had begun their San Mateo adventure by buying up 400 acres of the former Clark estate, northwest of town. They hired Davenport Bromfield to lay out the subdivision. Because this tract

A new kind of house was all the rage in the Hayward Tract: the cozy bungalow, a wide, one-story, hip-roofed house with a porch, very different from the lofty, formal styles of the Victorian era. The style and the name came from India. This bungalow stood on Ninth Avenue.

Courtesy San Mateo County Historical Museum

would be created on undulating terrain, from El Camino Real (maps and references began replacing the name County Road with El Camino Real at about this time) to the hills, Bromfield's plan called for a winding system of streets which would preserve the country estate atmosphere. From El Camino on the east to Occidental on the west, from Poplar on the south to Barroilhet on the north, Bromfield arranged for a variety of beautiful trees and shrubs to be planted to enhance the beauty of San Mateo Park. Among the original buyers was Bromfield himself, who bought a lot on Occidental Avenue and built a home there in 1904 for $18,000.

Baldwin and Howell's other foray into San Mateo real estate development was made possible by the death of Alvinza Hayward in 1904. His estate was now ready to sell off the property. Baldwin and Howell were agents for residential sales and the purchase of the mansion for the Peninsula Hotel.

They laid out the flat Hayward Park subdivision in square blocks from the railroad tracks to El Camino, and from Fifth Avenue to 15th. A large block was reserved for the hotel and its grounds, from Tenth to Fifth, and Palm to B. Another San Mateo trolley stop was proposed at the east end of 12th and the railroad tracks. Owners of lots began to build modest California bungalows here beginning about 1905. The San Francisco Fire and Earthquake of 1906 greatly accelerated construction of houses, as refugees relocated outside of the city.

The completion of the Peninsula Hotel in 1903 also helped home sales. The venture's heavy promotion made the hotel seem to be the center of San Francisco society. San Mateo's beauty and reliable transportation did not save the hotel from eventual failure, but those same features brought people down from San Francisco to inspect lots, buy them and build their suburban houses.

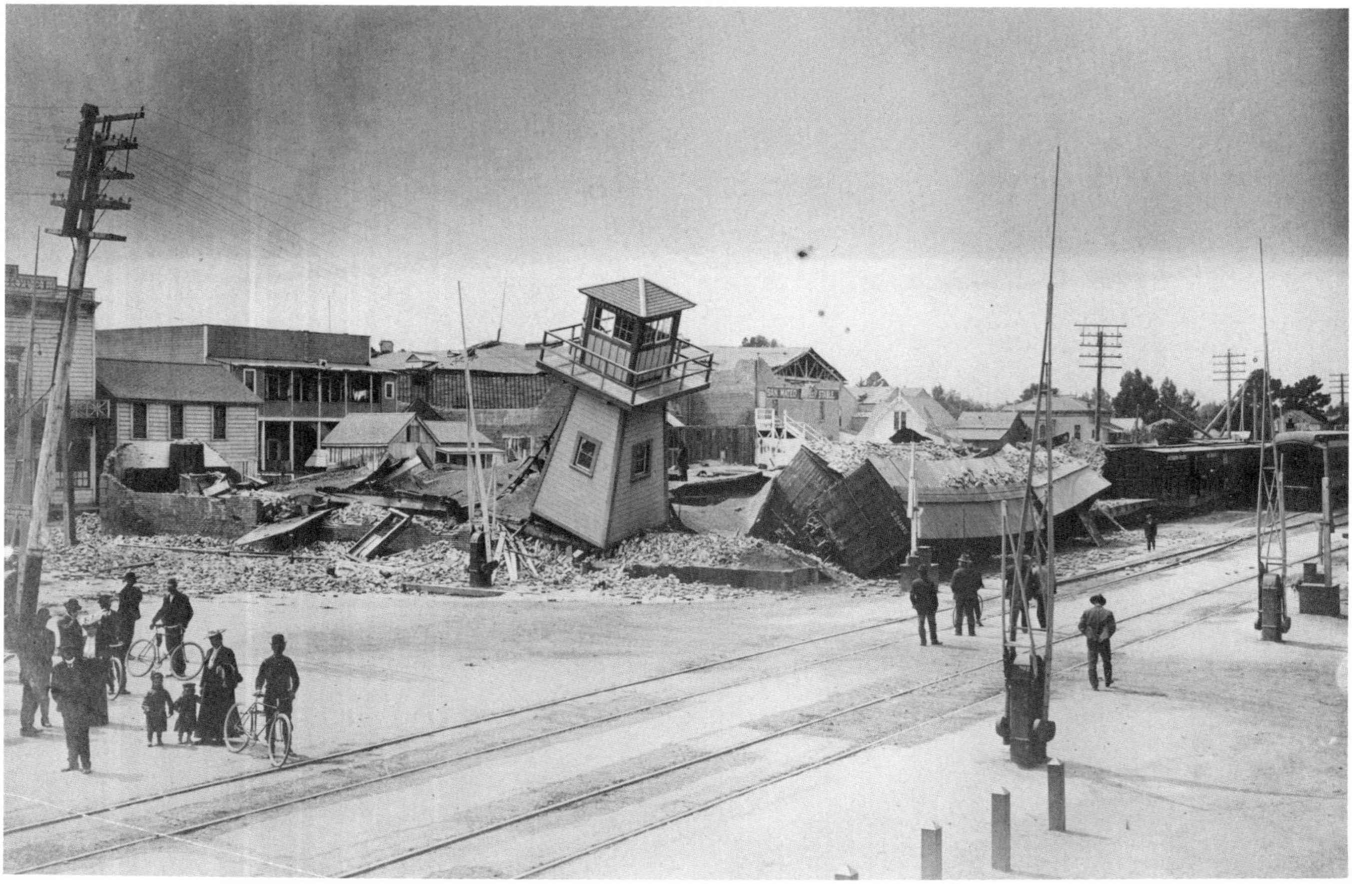

Morse's
PHARMACY
PHONE. MAIN 771.

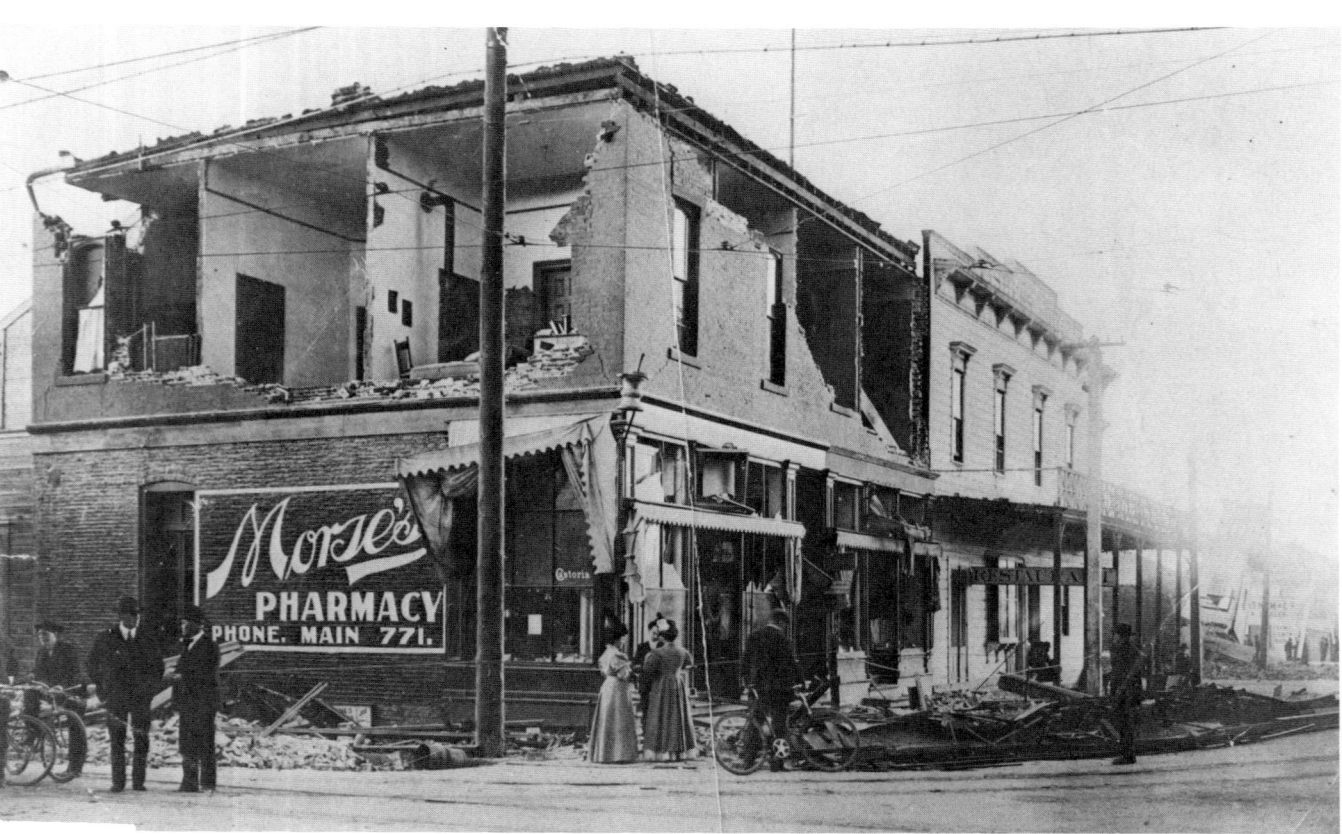

San Mateo was hard hit by the 1906 Quake. Opposite: The Southern Pacific freight shops tumbled down, leaving only the wooden tower intact, while the rooms above Morse's drugstore were opened to view. Above: a collapsed commercial building was later rebuilt to house Wisnom's Hardware. These pictures clearly show the builder's dilemma: wooden structures fare better in an earthquake, but brick is better protection against fire.

Courtesy San Mateo County Historical Museum

EARTHQUAKE!

ON WEDNESDAY MORNING, April 18, 1906 at 5:13 in the morning, D. Gordon Bromfield was sound asleep when suddenly his bed was tossed two feet away from its proper location. As the young man realized he was witnessing a severe earthquake, one of the first things he noticed "was the startled cackling of alarm emanating"[39] from the family hen house. While the the shaking continued, he staggered into his brother's bedroom and yelled, yanking at the still sleeping boy. Meanwhile, he could hear the house's chimney crumbling, with bricks rolling off the roof and crashing to the ground. Dishes fell off shelves, taller pieces of furniture toppled.

Over at the Kertell house, young George Kertell had about the same experience. He remembered the shaking and how the chimney of his house "flopped off."[40] Kertell's boyhood job was to turn on the gas-powered engine that pumped water up to the tank supplying San Mateo Park with its water. That morning he hopped on his bicycle to check if the pipes had been broken. They were all right, but on his ride back he suddenly felt as if he were cruising over "ocean waves." The land was rolling with a huge aftershock.

Young Bromfield remembered it as being a beautiful, calm spring morning; the whole week had been that way. Wild flowers had begun to bloom in the fields around San Mateo. Then he went into town:

> When we crossed the old wooden bridge and caught the first glimpse of B Street, I was shocked beyond words... piles of bricks could be seen on the sidewalks and some in the street all the way to Third Avenue where the principal stores then terminated. Twisted wire, glass and plaster lay here and there, and a few walls of the smaller aged wooden structures were out of plumb . . . The most startling [sights] were the second-story

This imposing building at Third Avenue & B Street, its elegant tower featuring bulls-eye windows, lost most of its brick wall, revealing a fine brass bed in the upstairs living quarters.   Courtesy San Mateo County Historical Museum

bedrooms exposed to view. A few would have made good bedroom settings or scenes for a play, although, if used, the sometimes necessary "pot de chambre" probably could have been dispensed with.

Bromfield was not alone as he surveyed the wreckage.

According to the *San Mateo Times* of April 21, "great crowds thronged the street, gazing at the havoc and exchanging experiences." Perhaps the most frightened person in town was telephone operator Pauline Sullivan. She was on duty in the telephone company's small office, across from the railroad station, when the shaking began. She stood in the doorway as bricks came tumbling down, and then she remained trapped there for six hours. Fearing looters would find her before rescuers, she armed herself with a Colt 45 kept in the office. But the townspeople remembered her, and she emerged from the office without a scratch.[41]

In fact no person in San Mateo or in the area surrounding San Mateo was killed, or even hurt, a remarkably lucky record considering the tons of bricks hurled about. Almost every residence in and around San Mateo had some kind of damage—mostly lost chimneys, broken glass and falling plaster—but none were destroyed.

The larger homes of the elite seemed to suffer more. At the Parrott's old Baywood Mansion, a chimney fell through the roof and through the second floor. Christian de Guigne II commented that from the dining room one could "see right up through the house to the sky."[42]

Most of the damage was done to the town's business and institutional buildings. The railroad freight depot was completely destroyed. According to the *San Mateo Leader* of April 25, a near tragedy occurred when the 50-foot gate tower came crashing down with its attendant inside. Fortunately, he too was unscratched.

The Jennings livery stable lost its roof. At Shrewsbury and Smith, makers of handsome carriage and automobile bodies, part of the building came down, dumping several carriage and auto bodies from the second floor into the street. Among the vehicles lost was the volunteer fire department's new chemical engine. This building was soon determined to be a total loss.

Also a total loss was the second Library Hall, which had been used as the town hall, complete with city offices, a public meeting hall and the fire station. Fortunately the town's books and records were recovered. Not until 1914 was a new city hall built in its place.

At the Levy's store, the upper front of the building fell, but the wall supports held. At Wisnom and Bonner's hardware store, the entire second floor slid into the street. Next door to the store, a man who manufactured water pumps and tanks was at work on the second floor when the shaking began. He was painting a tank at the time, and when the quake hit the tank broke loose, crashed through the floor and ended up in the basement. The man walked away and never returned.[43]

San Mateo's schools did not fare too badly. Central School was partially wrecked. At the high school there was a lot of broken plaster, but of most concern was the smashed chemistry lab, where tubes of smelly chemicals had splattered all over the floors and demanded immediate attention.

The churches did not make it through as well. The beautiful Episcopal Church was totally destroyed. The new Catholic Church suffered much damage. The top of the bell tower and the cross on the roof were knocked off. A portion of the overhang above the main entrance and bricks over a large circular window lay in piles of debris. Inside, the roof over the main altar had collapsed, burying the altar under rubble. A side altar was also ruined. Plaster from the ceiling lay everywhere. At the Methodist Church which had been built only the year before, there was some

Levy Brothers' store on B Street lost heaps of bricks when its cornice fell, but the lower floor was only slightly damaged.

Courtesy San Mateo County Historical Museum

damage. The Congregationalists seemed to come through best; their church only lost its steeple.

One of the most frightening aspects of the post-earthquake trauma was the lack of communication. Poles carrying telephone and telegraph wires had fallen, cutting San Mateo off from the rest of the world.

Transportation was severely disrupted as well.

Library Hall, with Hook & Ladder Company No. 1 downstairs, was badly damaged, while the frame building next door seems to be untouched.

Courtesy San Mateo County Historical Museum

Stagecoach service to Half Moon Bay was discontinued for three days because boulders blocked the road. The tracks of the trolley line were thrown out of alignment, stopping its service. Only the Southern Pacific stayed in operation, but its trains were unscheduled and sporadic.

Both of the town's newspapers were jolted, but the *San Mateo Times* came out with an edition three days later. The *Leader* had to change its type and appearance because its plant was "buried in an avalanche of plaster and debris," but it went to press on April 25. With reliable sources of information impaired, word of mouth was the only way people could find out what was happening to them and the world around San Mateo.

Walter Hobart brought the first word to the locals that San Francisco was on fire. He had rushed down from the St. Francis Hotel by automobile to check on his children. He found them safe, but his house badly damaged.

By noon every San Matean seemed to know that the great city to the north was burning, and that the Spring Valley Water Company mains were broken, meaning the worst might not be over. Making matters worse were wild rumors of total catastrophe, mostly fueled by eastern wireless accounts that grossly exaggerated the actual situation. Under such circumstances, San Mateans prepared for the worst. Fearing looters, the Parrott family armed their servants with guns.

However, San Mateo did not have much trouble with looters, or with fire, which was especially lucky, since the new chemical fire engine had been destroyed and the fire department's headquarters was in ruins. Two or three blazes that did break out were quickly contained.

The town's trustees proved most responsive. During the emergency they met twice each day to survey the situation and respond when necessary. Their first action was to close the saloons to discourage lawlessness.

More sobering was the smell of smoke and the massive glow after dark to the north, proving San

Jennings' Livery Stable at First Avenue & B Street lost most of its façade. The second floor miraculously stayed in place, despite its heavy load of hay. The laundry stayed on the clothesline.   Courtesy San Mateo County Historical Museum

Francisco was being consumed by fire. George Kertell remembered watching it for days. Ash and burned paper fragments, some with print still legible, blew into San Mateo and covered parts of the town. After dark the glow was especially awesome because San Mateo street lights were out.

At first a trickle, and then, as the hours and days went on, a flood of refugees began pouring down from the city. Some arrived via Southern Pacific. A great many simply walked, pushing wheelbarrows, carts and baby buggies filled with their last possessions. Some stopped along the roadside at the outskirts of town and camped. The Wisnom family allowed people to rest in their garden. Other refugees built shacks for temporary shelter south of town, on the site of today's County Hospital.

When San Francisco's St. Francis Hospital was threatened by fire, Southern Pacific helped transfer patients down to the old Hayward place, which had not yet become the Peninsula Hotel. George Kertell recalled that his friend Al Fitzgerald (brother of baseball great Justin Fitzgerald) asked him to help install temporary electric wiring to the buildings on the estate. A special train then came down and parked on a siding at Ninth Avenue. First the cots and equipment were unloaded, and then the patients were brought in. The *San Mateo Times* noted that among these people were those injured by the earthquake and fire, and those sick with typhoid as well. A baby was born there on April 20. "An Italian boy about three years, whose parents are unknown," was also being cared for by the hospital. The *Times* explained: "He was found in the city and cannot tell his name. He is unhurt but wants his mamma."

Although many San Mateans could tell interesting stories about their earthquake experiences, perhaps none had a more dramatic escapade than A. P. Giannini. When Giannini ascertained that his Bank of Italy in San Francisco was directly in the path of the fire, he took $80,000 in gold plus valuable bank documents from his

Beautiful St. Matthews Episcopal Church was so badly damaged it had to be replaced.

Courtesy San Mateo County Historical Museum

St. Matthew's Catholic Church, only six years old, lost the top of its tower and a big chunk of its façade, but was carefully restored and used for many years.

Courtesy San Mateo County Historical Museum

vault and placed these items under crates in a horse-drawn wagon. With three employees he drove the wagon to the home of his brother-in-law, Clarence Cuneo, in the North Beach district. That night, he and his men joined the multitude of refugees trudging down the Peninsula. They arrived at San Mateo at dawn and hid the gold and papers in an ash heap in the fire place of his home on El Cerrito Avenue. With these funds and records, Giannini was able to reopen his San Francisco banking service after only seven days, assisting a most needy city to rebuild itself.

George Kertell remembered another dramatic moment, when San Mateo officials learned that a train carrying dynamite was resting at the San Mateo station. Dynamite was being used, with varying degrees of success, to stop the fire in San Francisco. Town leaders warned Southern Pacific of the dangers of a trainload of dynamite in the event of a large aftershock. The train was moved.

On April 23, the town's Trustees organized a building inspection commission to assess damage to structures in San Mateo. Davenport Bromfield was named president, and John Morton was made secretary. The commission noted that the Shrewsbury and Smith Building had already been mostly taken down by its owners. They condemned Library Hall and the Episcopal Church. They made repair recommendations on the Union Hotel and the Coleman, "old" Jensen, Morse, San Mateo Land Association, Wisnom, Leader, "north" Levy, Odd Fellows, Jennings and Early Buildings. They judged the Catholic Church and the Hintz, south Levy, and new Jensen Buildings as being in better condition than expected.[44]

As the days wore on, everyone seem to play a role in

The interior of St. Matthews Episcopal was smashed, but the fine stained-glass window survived.

Courtesy San Mateo County Historical Museum

bringing life back to normal. The *San Mateo Leader* mentioned how pleased the Trustees were with the town's merchants for not inflating prices during the emergency. San Mateo had begun to recover very quickly compared

A new St. Matthews Episcopal Church rose on the site of the old one; many thought it was even more beautiful than the original.

Courtesy San Mateo County Historical Museum

to its great urban neighbor to the north. By noon on Thursday, the day after the shake, local telephone service had been restored. That night the street lights came back on. Central School was repaired in three days. Clean-up and temporary repairs were also rapidly accomplished at the high school, although throughout that summer further reconstruction took place.

The heavily damaged churches took longer to bring back to normal. The Catholic congregation met in the large stable on the de Guigne estate until the church could be cleared of debris. Because Father Callahan was on a pilgrimage to the Holy Land, Assistant Pastor John Duggan took responsibility for the repairs.

The Episcopal congregation had the greatest challenge. Their beautiful 1866 Church was a total loss. Reverend Neptune Blood William Gallaway had charge of rebuilding it. The great architect Willis Polk was called in to design the new structure. He incorporated steel framing and reinforced concrete into his plans, but respected the original Gothic-style stone edifice. The result of Gallaway's and Polk's work was one of the most beautiful houses of worship in the state. Sadly, Reverend Gallaway passed away only eleven days after its consecration in 1910.

Of all the amazing things to happen during the earthquake, perhaps most crucial was the one thing that did not occur. Crystal Springs Dam held, as the *Times* reported "without so much a crack." Herman Schussler's concrete-block structure and his weaker earthen dams withstood the quake and saved the town. If they had been destroyed, some 20 billion gallons of water would have flooded down San Mateo Creek and washed San Mateo away, along with a sizable portion of its population. Two years after the quake, a state earthquake investigation commission published their findings about Crystal Springs Dam; they reported it had emerged from the great shake "uninjured, . . . a careful examination having failed to reveal even a crack."

Rapid Growth Begins

In the history of San Mateo County, 1906 was a watershed year. Thousands of homeless San Franciscans decided to move to the suburbs. While the migration was uneven—certainly Daly City and Burlingame experienced more changes than Redwood City—most of the Peninsula's towns grew rapidly after the earthquake.

San Mateo was ready. New subdivisions were on the map and being promoted; water, electricity and other utilities were on line, and the trolley allowed connection to any part of San Francisco for 25 cents. There were other important improvements in transportation—both by rail and by road.

Back in 1904, Southern Pacific had finally begun work on the long anticipated "Bayshore Cutoff." The project meant cutting away the bayside hills north of South San Francisco and laying track directly from the city, instead of circling San Bruno Mountain to the west. It significantly shortened and cheapened travel to the peninsula. The cutoff was completed on December 8, 1907, speeding up the economic and residential expansion of all the bayside towns. In 1908, the San Mateo commuter could buy a pass for 30 round trips to

A big crowd waited to cheer President Theodore Roosevelt, who came through town in 1909; in only three years the damaged buildings had been repaired or replaced.

Courtesy San Mateo County Historical Museum

San Francisco for $6.00.[45] The trip took only thirty minutes each way.

At about the same time, road building for automobiles had become a priority throughout San Mateo County. The *Times* heralded such public projects as crucial to the breaking of the transportation monopolies held by the railroads. By 1911 there were already two garages in San Mateo, one on B and the other on El Camino Real.

Bus transportation came to San Mateo in May of 1915. Peninsula Rapid Transit ran a line to San Francisco, and by 1916 was catering to local San Mateo-to-Burlingame travelers as well. Peninsula Rapid Transit eventually became part of Pacific Greyhound Lines.

For George Kertell and other natives of the town, after the earthquake "San Mateo was never quite the same." Between 1900 and 1910 the population more than doubled, to 4,384. Most of this increase occurred after the quake. Between 1900 and 1905 the County Assessor's office listed 128 new structures built in San Mateo, while between 1906 and 1910, 333 new buildings were built.[46] From 1910 to 1920 the rate of growth stabilized a bit; by 1920, 5,979 people lived here. Nearly all came from the ranks of a new type of suburbanite—the steadily emerging middle class.

In a promotional piece Southern Pacific described San Mateo in 1907 as a town with "many beautiful homes of people of moderate means, who have businesses in San Francisco." The elite and their "magnificent country homes" are still mentioned, but the emphasis now is on San Mateo as a residential suburb whose popularity was rapidly increasing.[47]

Ethnic Communities

By the time these new residents began arriving in San Mateo, the town already had long-established ethnic communities, which grew along with the middle-class segment of the population. Among the foreign-born

A.P. Giannini, founder of the Bank of America, and his wife, Clorinda, on their wedding day, 1892.

Courtesy San Mateo County Historical Museum

groups, the Irish had been here in great numbers since the coming of the railroad. By 1900 a few Italian families had come to live in and around San Mateo. One of the most prominent of the early immigrants was John Maggi, who owned a hotel in town. Also well known were the truck gardening Di Martini family, and the Guidos.

Francisco Guido was typical of the Italian immigrants in the area in those days. He had come to the United States a decade or so before, worked in the mines of Nevada, made some money and returned to Italy. He married there and brought his bride back to California in 1892. They settled at about today's Poplar Avenue and the tracks in 1899. They grew celery, corn, cabbage, carrots, blackberries, string beans, and artichokes. Their farm was a fairly sophisticated operation, with a house for the family and fifteen workers. The farm had fifteen horses and several peddling and delivery wagons. Later, Guido's sons opened a successful grocery store on B Street.

Of course, of all the Italians in the San Mateo area, the most famous was A. P. Giannini. Although he was not foreign born (he was a native of San Jose), his parents brought him up to believe in the traditions of the old country, emphasizing family above all else. He raised his children with the same values.[48] Giannini married Clorinda Cuneo in 1892. Her family introduced A. P. to the world of banking. He established his own Bank of Italy in 1904. The couple lived in San Mateo, renting a home on Elm, until they purchased Seven Oaks in 1905. Giannini became known among the immigrant Italian people and other small investors as the man who catered to the "little guy." In the world of banking, he became known as the man who established the branch banking system. In 1930, he changed the name of his institution to Bank of America. By 1945, it was the largest private bank in the world.

As a boy, "romping around our neighborhood," D. Gordon Bromfield remembered the "great banking wizard" walking to and from the rail station: "Three of Mr. Giannini's noticeable characteristics were, he was always on foot, gave evidence of constant deep meditation, inclining to seriousness at all times, and seemed content with his own company."[49]

Besides European foreign born, there were also Asian immigrants in San Mateo. For these people of another race, with vastly different cultural backgrounds,

Seven Oaks, the great English Tudor style house where A. P. Giannini and his family lived, is the only one of the large estate houses still standing in San Mateo.

Courtesy San Mateo County Historical Museum

assimilation was harder. There was even conflict among the races.

The Chinese were the first Asians to come to San Mateo, arriving in 1870 to help Alvinza Hayward with his water system. Some stayed and settled at B and Second, starting a little Chinatown there. By the turn of the century, a second Chinatown had developed around the Hop Yick Company, a store at First and Claremont.[50] Outside of town, Chinese were servants on the estates and laborers on the farms.

Misunderstandings resulted in violent acts in the San Mateo area. The June 1, 1889 *San Mateo Leader* reported that "the Laurel Creek boys," William and Edgar McLellan and Thomas Fraser, had been charged with felony assault on Ant Lee. It appears they "hung the Chinaman to a rafter [probably by his queue] on the barn in order to compel him to disclose the hiding place of certain jewelry they accused him of having stolen."

Many of the Chinese living in San Mateo around 1900 worked as cooks in the homes of others. D. Gordon Bromfield remembered that their servants were visited every day by a Chinese fruit vendor from San Francisco. This peddler boarded an early train each day and made the rounds of "the better homes" with two baskets, each on one end of a pole he balanced across his shoulders.

One Chinese New Year, Bromfield with his father and brother attended dinner at Ching Lee's laundry on B Street. Ching Lee was the brother of their family's cook. The front of "the shabby old building . . . was brightly lighted by two hanging lamps covered with metal shades." His father was the guest of honor and sat next to Ching, "whose oriental politeness was decidedly in evidence on this occasion." The boys sat opposite their father, while the other Chinese diners, about eight, sat at random around the table. The Bromfields were much relieved when given knives and forks instead of chopsticks to eat their chicken, boiled rice, lichee nuts and white strip candy. At the time, Bromfield had a "peculiar feeling," for he knew the three of them were "the object of their attention and discussion," but of course they could not understand a word. "I would have liked to know what they were saying about the Bromfields," he later wrote.[51]

Tetsuo Yamanouchi established the Imperial Laundry (today's Blu-White Laundry) in 1909. Customers asked Central to ring number 485 for pickup and delivery.

Courtesy Japanese American Citizens' League

After dinner, the three were ushered into a small room in the rear of the building, which was "quite devoid of appointments, the only table and a few wooden chairs being pushed to the wall." The Bromfields then watched for two hours as their Chinese hosts played a highly entertaining drinking game. Losers were required to drink a cup of brown gin. As they passed out, they were put in beds in a third room.

Of all the immigrant groups to come to San Mateo, none had a more dramatic up-and-down kind of experience than the Japanese. Originally they came as domestic servants. Some worked and lived in the homes of their employers. Others were paid hourly or daily for general house cleaning and cooking, and lived in their own homes. Commonly they took language courses to become more effective at their work. Sometimes too, husband and wife teams worked for certain households, establishing life-long relationships. In 1900, such servants were usually paid about $1.20 a day.[52]

Probably the first Japanese who actually made San Mateo his home was Tomisuke Ito. He was born in 1866, in Yamaguchi, Japan. Despite having an education in his native country, he settled for working as a domestic in the San Mateo area in 1891, after having lived in San Francisco for three years. In 1903 he purchased three lots, from Grant to Fremont Streets. Friends of his built a rather crude four-unit apartment building with planks of redwood, with no heating or insulation, to house other immigrants when they came from Japan. The community called it Nagaya (longhouse) and it served many of San Mateo's founding Japanese families.

In later years, Nagaya became a sort of gathering place for families and friends. Meetings, parties and annual celebrations took place there. It eventually included a tea house and a bath house on the site. The bath house was especially popular, among new arrivals and old timers alike. It had a three-foot by four-foot tub, perfect for Saturday-night, Japanese-style furo or hot-tub parties.

Another early Japanese resident was Tomezo Yoshida, who arrived in 1895 and also worked as a domestic. He was employed by several wealthy families in the Hillsborough area and was treated generously at times. He also purchased property. Using $300 in gold, he bought lots adjacent to Ito's property.

Many single Japanese men went to work for the Whitney family at the Leslie salt plant. Working in the plant was at times dangerous; electrocutions and other injuries sometimes happened. Originally the workers earned less than a dollar a day. However, by the time Sayohei Kawakita went to work there in 1909, they were making 35¢ an hour.

Kawakita remembered that about 30 Japanese men worked there. During off-hours they socialized together as well. Some nights they got together and visited the Chinese gambling houses and bordellos in San Mateo. About the gambling Kawakita recalled: "I don't remember anyone ever coming back to the salt works with winnings."[53]

Many of the new San Mateans had run their own businesses back in Japan. They wanted to do likewise in their new country. S. Soto and T. Kataoka opened the first Japanese-owned business in 1900—the Yokohama Laundry, at Tilton and North Eldorado Street.

Tokumatsu Hata opened the second business, the Hata Merchant Tailor Shop at 122 B Street. Hata first came to the United States in 1896. He then went back to Japan to be married. After returning with his wife, Toku

Hamada, he settled in San Mateo. Hata took in an apprentice, Shiro Kashiwagi in 1903, who eventually became a partner in the business. Kashiwagi had been born in Fukushisma, Japan. He arrived in Seattle in 1902 before coming to San Mateo. He was taught English by Pansy Jewett Abbott.

Hata and Kashiwagi became quite successful, catering especially to Japanese men, who found only a limited supply of clothing in San Mateo stores that could fit them. Substantial alteration to ready-made clothes did not leave the apparel presentable. Since many of the men were bachelors, they needed to look their best in the pictures they sent back to Japan. Their families would present the pictures to the families of prospective brides, requiring the most dignified appearance possible.

By 1906, San Mateo had easily the largest Japanese community in the county. This inspired Tokutaro Takahashi to open an oriental grocery and merchandise store. Takahashi had come to the United States in 1898 at the age of 18, hailing from Wakayama. He first went to work at the Alvarado salt works in the east bay, becoming a supervisor. In San Mateo he set up his store on B Street between a blacksmith shop and a Chinese laundry, selling hard-to-find eastern commodities such as soy sauce and bean curd paste, fishing gear and clothing. In the early years, he would load a wagon and visit campsites of workers and homes of Japanese residents.

The same year he opened his San Mateo business, Takahashi took a bride, Ishiye Baba, also of Wakayama. The marriage had been arranged by the families; it is doubtful Ishiye had any say about it at all. She sailed to Seattle alone. The passage took two weeks. When she arrived she stayed on board the ship until Takahashi arrived. The couple honeymooned in Seattle, where Ishiye bought her first western clothes. Returning to San Mateo, Takahashi continued his successful business, which has lasted until this day, and became an important leader in the Japanese community.

In 1908, Tetsuo Yamanouchi rented space from the Wisnom family and opened a second Japanese laundry, the Imperial Laundry. For Yamaguchi, the laundry business was secondary in importance to his religion. He had been trained in Zen Buddhism back in Japan and led the founding of the Buddhist church in San Mateo.

Flower-growing brought great success to the Egashira and Eto families, who drove a really splendid touring car with two running boards (actual boards) on each side.

Courtesy Japanese American Citizens' League

Unfortunately, these early Japanese business owners were targets of some of the most shameful racial harassment in San Mateo history. The laundries were especially targeted by such organizations as the San Francisco-based Anti-Japanese Laundry League. Members of the League, some from San Mateo, followed the delivery routes of the Japanese laundries to determine who the white customers were. The "trailers" then tried to persuade these customers not to patronize the Japanese.

This scheme failed to put the laundries out of business. More successful was a local campaign in 1911 that forced tailors Hata and Kashiwagi to move from their central B Street location to a less favorable location at 301 Ellsworth. Ironically, later, in 1918, Kashiwagi became a certified agent to sell war stamps and liberty bonds as part of the patriotic effort to support the United States during World War I. Despite this, by law, he could not become a citizen because of his race. Although he was required to pay poll taxes, because he was not a citizen he could not vote.

Discrimination was a way of life in California. Most Japanese immigrants learned to tolerate it. Other aspects of the new land made survival harder. The strange

Miss Kunie Eto at age 17 and her niece, Kikuko Egashira, circa 1911.

Courtesy Japanese American Citizens' League

customs and language and the sense of loneliness in this foreign place intensified the need to relate to others of similar backgrounds. In 1906 a local branch of the Japanese Association of America was formed in San Mateo as a sort of mutual aid society, bringing a sense of community to the Japanese immigrants here. The first meeting of fifty people was conducted by Sekko Shimada, a friend of Henry Bowie (Bowie had studied art in Japan, met Shimada and persuaded him to come to San Mateo as his guest).

Another institution which brought stability and community feeling to these people was the Buddhist Church. Tetsuo Yamanouchi, of the Imperial Laundry, had been trained in a monastery at Fukuyama Hiroshima, but left short of being ordained.[54] In 1909 he organized a small group under Bishop Koyo Uchida in San Francisco. Among the founders of the church were Tomisuke Ito and Tokutaro Takahashi. At first, services were conducted in Yamanouchi's home on 1st Avenue and Ellsworth. When the congregation outgrew his living room, Yamanouchi moved the meeting place to his laundry, next door. In 1910, the San Mateans formally applied for affiliation with the San Francisco Buddhist Church.

The Japanese working community organized itself as the Rodo Kumiai (circa 1908), a laborers' association designed to assist domestic servants and gardeners. It gave employment referrals, standardized jobs, acted to settle disputes with employers and gave generally useful information to these workers.

By 1910, many of the Japanese gardeners had begun to branch out into enterprises of their own. The expanding flower industry of the Peninsula offered them an opportunity. They mostly specialized in growing chrysanthemums, in rented fields at the Beresford and Homestead areas. Renting of property was the only choice for these people by 1913, because of the passage of the Heney-Webb Alien Land Law prohibiting people ineligible for citizenship to own land.

For most Japanese in California such laws had an irritating effect, but their ultimate goal was to make their fortune in America and return to Japan anyway. This was a plan largely unfulfilled. Year after year passed, and the immigrants remained. For those Japanese men who had not yet taken a wife, this proved to be a problem. An immigration exclusion law called for cutting off the flow of Japanese coming to California by 1924. A flurry of "picture marriages," or arranged unions, took place simultaneously in Japan and in San Mateo.

Soon after the new wives arrived, a second generation (Nisei) was being born to their first generation (Issei) parents. Local midwife Kamechiyo Takahashi became one of the busiest women in San Mateo County. She had studied midwifery back in Japan, before she came to San Mateo in February of 1917. By June she had received her California license. She was on call day and night. Because many of the Issei women preferred her to white doctors, she found herself racing about San Mateo and Santa Clara Counties in her old car, which she had to crank to start. She eventually opened a care facility in her home on Second Avenue. At $20.00 per delivery, and $14.00 a day for room and board, it is said that she brought most of the Peninsula's Nisei into this world between 1917 and 1930, all normal deliveries, and with only two hospitalizations.[55]

Although the Issei were marrying and having children in America, this did not change their plans to return to Japan one day. They wanted the Nisei to know the Japanese language and customs, and so in 1916, they created a language school, the first in the county, in a

Above: Japanese employees at the Leslie Salt Refining Company, 1910.

Right: The Egashira and Eto families, pioneers in the flower business, arrived in San Mateo after 1906.

Courtesy Japanese American Citizens' League

building off Fremont Street. In 1919 the school moved to new quarters at North Delaware and Second Avenue.

There were no real segregated neighborhoods for San Mateo's ethnic communities in those days before 1920, but the Japanese and Italians tended to live east and north of the center of town. They were joined by the few African American families in town. Most of the black men were laborers—wood choppers, for example.[56] Some worked for the railroad. (More about African Americans in Chapter V).

ENHANCED PUBLIC INSTITUTIONS

WITH THE POPULATION of San Mateo suddenly swelling, there was an increased demand for quality public institutions. During the period succeeding the 1906 earthquake, San Mateo gained new library and high school buildings. A Parks commission was appointed. A parent-teacher's association was organized. A hospital was built. These improvements resulted from growth, but in turn made San Mateo a more desirable place to live and inspired further expansion.

Back in 1898, the rebuilt Library Hall seemed to function as everything but a library. The Library Association did maintain a small collection of books, but the community began to lobby the town trustees for the creation of a formal public library. In 1899, City Attorney Charles Kirkbride, a strong library advocate, drew up enabling papers allowing the town to take over the property of the Library Association, assume its debts, and create a four-cent tax on every $100 of taxable

Fire Chief George Bartlett (seated) and Assistant Chief Jim Duffy look ready for anything in this portrait; unfortunately, they weren't, as the town was to learn on June 25, 1920.

Courtesy San Mateo County Historical Museum

property in the town to generate revenue. By 1900 some $472 was collected.

In 1899, town trustees authorized the expenditure of $500 to buy the Knights of Pythias Library Collection in San Francisco. These 4160 volumes were added to the 451 from the San Mateo Library Association to form the initial stock of the San Mateo Public Library. A portion of Library Hall was reorganized to accept these books.

Within three years, San Mateans wanted to expand their library into a building of its own. Letters from the town's leaders and the San Mateo Woman's Club were sent to Andrew Carnegie, asking for a contribution to establish a new library. In 1905, City Attorney Kirkbride received the wonderful news that the Carnegie Foundation would contribute $10,000 for the project. A site on San Mateo Drive and Second Avenue was selected. Because the Carnegie grant did not provide for furniture or shelving, the San Mateo Woman's Club organized a fund-raising event at the still-closed Hayward estate. In fact, their September 1906 affair was the first time the estate had been opened to the public for a social purpose. Some $500 was raised. Letters about the town's enthusiastic progress reached Carnegie, and he granted another $2500 to reward all of the activity. The new library opened in April 1907. By the end of the next year it contained 12,389 books.

After the library's success, San Mateans turned to help their high school. By 1909, enrollment at San Mateo High School had swollen to 136 students. Town leaders such as Charles Kirkbride now began to agitate for a new high school building at the old Baldwin Avenue site. By the end of November that year a $100,000 bond issue was passed to begin the work. Architects Havens and Toepke were contracted to design the new building. Their plans called for various additions, including a gymnasium. A second bond issue passed in November of 1910 to finish the project.

On May 5, 1911, a grand celebration marked the opening of the new high school. The invitation to the event described the three-story building as being 35,000 square feet in size, with 25 classrooms and labs. Its assembly hall could seat 500. The building was constructed with reinforced concrete outer walls, metal lath and hard wall plaster on the inside, wood floors and partitions and Oregon pine moldings. At the time of its opening, 173 students (representing most of San Mateo's diverse communities) were enrolled at the school, with 10 teachers on staff. By 1914 enrollment at the school reached 323.

The next object of public interest was the town's landscaping. While San Mateo would not get its first park until ten years later, the town trustees formed a Park and Boulevard Commission in 1912 to provide for tree plantings and care of vegetation along streets, highways and public places.

In 1914, renewed civic energy was applied to the elementary school system. At Peninsula School, the first Parent Teacher Association (PTA) in the county was formed, with Miss Florence Musto of San Francisco acting as organizer. The group adopted the PTA's state constitution, "the object being the promotion of child welfare and the harmonious cooperation of teacher and parent."[57] The 48 charter members elected Mrs. H.P. Hermance president, and set dues at 10¢ per month.

In its very first year, this PTA established a kindergarten. Soon after, it arranged the installation of gas heating for the school. In 1916, Peninsula's PTA initiated a Tennis Court Fund. World War I interrupted money raising, but in 1919 the campaign was renewed. In December 1923 a check for $600 was presented to William Turnbull of the school board to take care of the cost.

While the creation of a hospital in San Mateo was not a government-driven achievement, it certainly was widely held as being necessary. This story begins with the birth of Elizabeth Mills in New York in 1858. The only daughter of Darius Ogden Mills and Jane Templeton Mills, she was brought up on the Mills estate, encompassing much of the city of Millbrae today. Her father was one of nation's great capitalists of that time. He had been one of the founders of the Bank of California, and served as its president for over 30 years. Darius Mills also believed in philanthropy; he was a heavy contributor to causes in New York.

The Mills family had many attachments to the Peninsula, and split their time between here and the East. By marriage they were related to the Eastons, Taylors and Crockers. Darius had served as a vestryman at St. Matthews Episcopal Church for some years. During the family's long stays at Millbrae, they often came to San Mateo to visit the estates of friends and attend parties and other activities. When back in New York, Darius encouraged his teenaged daughter to help with his charitable work. In 1881, at the age of 23, she organized the New York chapter of the Red Cross.

That same year she married Whitelaw Reid, editor of the *New York Tribune*. In 1892, he ran for Vice President of the United States but was defeated. In 1905, he was appointed ambassador to Great Britain. On a trip to Millbrae in 1906 Elizabeth's idea to create a health center at San Mateo was born. No hospital existed between San Francisco and Palo Alto. For Elizabeth's friend, Abby Parrott Payson, this had meant tragedy; the Paysons had lost a son and a daughter to illnesses that could have been treated in a hospital. This personal knowledge, combined with Elizabeth's Red Cross experience and her closeness to the Episcopal Church and community at San Mateo, inspired her to act.

First she talked with Neptune Blood William Gallaway, minister at the Episcopal Church, who was desperately trying to reconstruct his earthquake-wrecked building. Yes, the Church would allow a health care facility on its property. Next Elizabeth consulted with Dr. W. C. Chidester, who consented to provide medical

A new high school, very dignified in style, was built in 1911 on Baldwin Avenue. Eventually it became the home of San Mateo Junior College.

Courtesy San Mateo County Historical Museum

leadership in the endeavor (and continued to do so until his death three decades later).

Elizabeth then hired Miss Beatrice H. Woodward to act as district nurse. Woodward had vast experience working in the slums of her native England and in similar places in New York and San Francisco.[58] Beginning in 1907, and for two years afterwards, Woodward lived in the rectory of the church. Elizabeth made it clear that if Woodward deemed it advisable, she would create a hospital for her. By 1908 a cottage, which was being built as nurses' quarters, was converted into an emergency hospital, ready to receive six patients.

Elizabeth kept close watch on the operations of the hospital. She quickly realized a larger building was necessary. By February 1909 the place could handle 24 patients. That year, Elizabeth also purchased the old Edward Taylor home across the creek for the long overdue nurses' quarters. This was the same structure that had once been the San Mateo House. Taylor had died in 1887, and his widow in 1899. The family sold the house to their long-time friend Elizabeth Mills Reid.

In 1911, yet another expansion was completed. Lewis Hobart designed a French Gothic wooden addition to the hospital, complete with solarium and square tower. In the early days this institution was known as Red Cross Hospital. But during World War I, because of the great work that the Red Cross was doing for the national effort, the name was changed to Mills Memorial Hospital to avoid any confusion.

Not all the public-spirited projects succeeded during

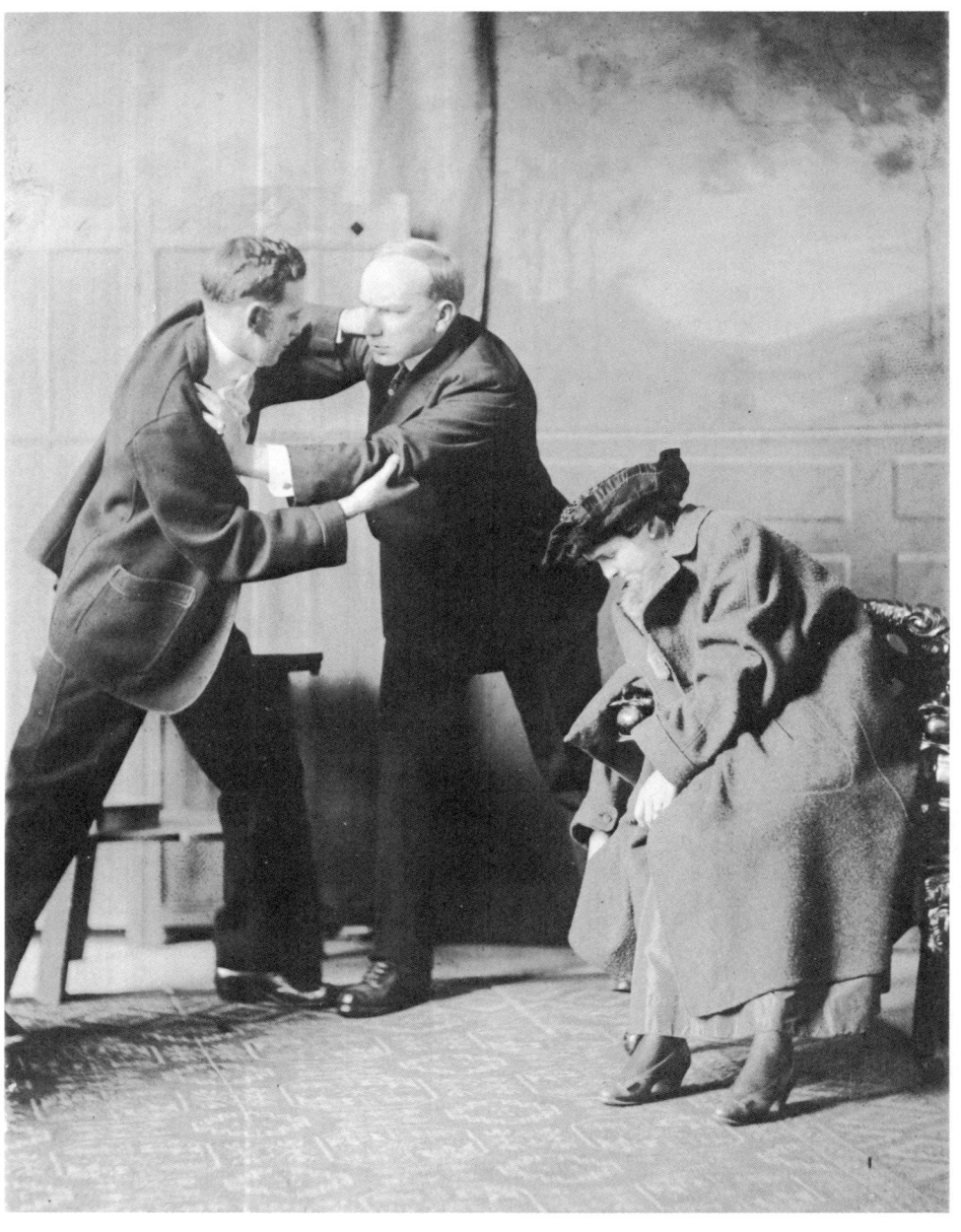

Horace Amphlett (center) and two unidentified thespians star in a play at the Community Center, circa 1915.
Courtesy Janet Boyer

But not owning its own water system did not impede San Mateo's progress. In 1909, recognizing its borders stopped short of the new residences northwest of town, San Mateo accomplished its first annexation, San Mateo Park. A year later the town stretched its southern border to bring in Hayward Park.

As America entered World War I in 1917, it was plain to everyone that the world was a different place. San Mateo itself had gone through a two-decade metamorphosis, from being a suburb for the elite of California society, to becoming a suburb for the middle classes of San Francisco and the Peninsula. Symbolic of this change, on October 6, 1917, Abby Parrott, the town's grand old lady, died at her beloved Baywood estate at age 89. She had had a cold for two weeks. Knowing she was going to die, she asked to be dressed in the brown habit of the Third Order of St. Francis for her funeral services. Father Callahan said the Mass, and the Archbishop of San Francisco read a passage from the Bible. The hymns she requested were sung. They buried her next to John Parrott in St. John's Cemetery.

SAN MATEO AND WORLD WAR I

ALL ACROSS AMERICA, ordinary life changed in April 1917 as the United Stated entered World War I. While San Mateans of all ages were affected, the War was of particular concern to children and teenagers. Beginning with the 1915-1916 school year at San Mateo High, the school board had provided a course in military training for boys. The State of California furnished weapons and an instructor. The students bought their own uniforms. William Lawrence donated a company flag.[59] The highschool students were always busy with Red Cross or bond drives. The manual training department had

these times of great accomplishment. Just before the turn of the century, the *San Mateo News Leader* led a concerted campaign to have San Mateo purchase its own municipal water supply. The town's trustees remained firm in their opposition. To this day, San Mateo's water is brought in by a private utility, with roots that go all the way back to Alvinza Hayward's San Mateo Water Works.

A costume party or pageant at the San Mateo Woman's Club in 1908 seems to involve a comic bride and groom.
Courtesy San Mateo County Historical Museum

students making crutches, splints, and fracture boxes for Camp Fremont in Menlo Park.

After the War started, when the first draftees from San Mateo were to leave for war in September 1917, primary school teacher Vera Emerson organized almost a thousand children, virtually all the pupils in the elementary system, to go to the railroad station to say farewell and sing "We'll Never Let the Old Flag Fall." After one year of war, 852 of the 967 children in the district owned war stamps valued at $6191.

The fervor to do everything possible for the War effort and for America in general may have gotten a bit out of hand with the formation of the "100% Club," which asked student members to constantly strive at 100% to better themselves and their community. Later a "75% Club" was formed for students with lower expectations.

When the war ended on November 11, 1918, San Mateans were ready to celebrate. The next day at one o'clock, an informal procession began on Main Street and wound its way through San Mateo, Burlingame and Hillsborough and then down to Redwood City and Palo Alto. The Levy Brothers supplied a float, a truck covered with flags and filled with children, including a miniature Uncle Sam, and a goat. A sign on the truck read "We got the Kaiser's goat." Another truck bore the Italian flag, and members of this community celebrated their native country's participation on the side of the Allies. The festivities on Main Street went on long into the night. The *San Mateo County News* commented that the party was highlighted by "community singing—an impromptu affair—led by a group of men who voiced the love of Italy in the singing of operas and all the national airs."

The famous influenza epidemic that swept the country just after the War also hit San Mateo. Once again the youth of the community seemed most affected. At San Mateo High, 100 of the 350 students were at home sick on any given day during the fall and winter of 1918.

LAW ENFORCEMENT

BEFORE INCORPORATION, law enforcement in San Mateo was carried out by a series of loosely appointed town constables and the county sheriff. After incorporation in 1894, the town hired its first marshal, Peter C. Rogers. A succession of marshals served during the period before World War I (Rogers, 1894-1898, Joseph P. Cummings, 1898-1900, Maurice F. Boland, 1902-1913, and Aldon A. McComb, 1913-1917).[60] In the early years crime in the town was minimal. In fact it was not until the reign of Marshal McComb that any records were kept regarding arrests.

San Mateo's modern law enforcement era began on April 17, 1917, with the appointment of Thomas F. Burke, first as Marshal and then, in 1922, retitled Police Chief. Burke was of Irish parentage (Thomas Sr. and Mary Leary), both born in County Gallway. They came to San Francisco in 1875. Thomas Sr.'s first job was to work as a guard at the Palace Hotel. Thomas Jr. was born in 1878. About 1880, the Burke family moved to San Mateo, where Thomas Sr. took a job with the Spring Valley Water Company.[61]

Burke went to Central School, and was a young member of the volunteer fire department. In 1904 he married Isabelle Curran, of a well-known Redwood City family. At the time of his appointment by Mayor F. P. Simmen and the town trustees, he was working as a mail clerk. Marshal McComb had died in office, leaving his successor with a small force of three officers, a couple of bicycles and a red model-T Ford, which had to be shared with the fire department. Not until the next year did the police get a vehicle of their own.[62]

Burke's first task as chief was to enforce the town's ban on sales of alcohol. Even before Prohibition was enacted as federal law, San Mateo experimented with laws designed to control saloons. In November 1917, Burke raided a "blind pig," or speakeasy, at a boarding house and Second and D. As we shall see, for the next three decades Chief Burke took San Mateo's police force from a small town operation to a modern institution.

FIRE—AGAIN!

THE ORGANIZATION OF A VOLUNTEER fire department did not stop the recurrence of disaster by fire in San Mateo. In fact between the time of the creation of the volunteer unit and 1920, San Mateo fire fighters responded to at least sixty blazes in and around the town. These included minor fires and bigger disasters, such as one that destroyed the public school in 1891, and the one that took San Mateo's great Peninsula Hotel in 1920. After the latter catastrophe, residents demanded improvement in public safety.

In the early days, the volunteer fire-fighters' primary mission was to make sure that a fire consuming a building did not spread. Usually the efforts were too late and too feeble to save the structure actually burning. George Kertell remembered that in the rare instance when the volunteers did arrive in time to save a building, they were given cash rewards with which they could organize "blowouts" to celebrate their victory.

In 1895, the town moved to organize its fire fighters by adopting Ordinance #16, officially creating a municipal fire department. Equipment then consisted of four hand-drawn hose carts.[63]

The capabilities of the department remained weak. The December 1896 fire at Alvinza Hayward's barn revealed some of the shortcomings. First, it was a struggle to pull the hose carts to the scene. Water from the nearby hydrant ran at a trickle because the water company had turned down the water pressure, as it did every night. The volunteer responsible for opening the water gate at Fifth Avenue and the County Road, to get a greater flow, slept through the alarm. Of course the barn burned down.

The fire at E. A. Husing's stable in October 1897 uncovered other problems. This time the nearest hydrant was 2000 feet from the structure. Hose from two carts had to be connected to reach the blaze. Meanwhile curious San Mateans drove their horse-drawn vehicles over the hose, breaking a town ordinance and nearly breaking the hose. The barn burned to the ground, but the nearby house was saved.

The San Mateo Woman's Club began raising money in 1903, and in 1905 purchased an $800 chemical engine for the department—its first horse-drawn fire apparatus. The horses were donated by Eugene de Sabla. Before this time, the volunteers pushed and pulled all of their equipment themselves.

In 1910, the passage of a bond issue allowed the department to buy its first motorized fire truck for $4800. In 1914 the Fire Department finally secured a permanent home at the rebuilt town hall (the site of Library Hall on B). This ended almost two decades of storing fire equipment in various stables and garages around town.

But San Mateo's love of its volunteer fire department became strained in 1919, when a bond issue to improve the water works and to purchase further equipment was turned down by voters. Members and officers of the department unanimously resigned. As the department was trying to reorganize itself, the greatest fire in San Mateo history occurred.

It started at 5:15 p.m. on June 25, 1920, in the attic at the Peninsula Hotel. The *News Leader* tells us that Edwin Thayer, a boy from Hayward Park, was passing by and saw the smoke. He ran into the hotel and alerted the staff. The telephone operator on duty "pluckily stuck at her post," calling for help and warning guests about the fire "until the wires burned out."

Coincidentally, the hotel's new manager, E. G. Borden, and his associates, Al Herert and D. J. Douglas, were at the *News Leader* offices that very moment, discussing their new plans for the hotel. Borden had just reopened the financially troubled Peninsula in April. They were telling the newspaper about a plan to construct a parking garage for the hotel, capable of accommodating 100 automobiles.

During the interview, the men heard the alarms. When they found out that the fire was at the Peninsula, "they jumped into their automobile and raced at full speed to the hotel," joining a crowd estimated at 1,000 to 2,000, to witness the four-hour blaze.

The San Mateo Fire Department was unprepared. Its Webb chemical engine was in the shop after having broken down on the railroad tracks a few days before. Chief George Bartlett was out of town. The lack of a pumping engine and poor water pressure made the work of the fire fighters futile.

In the absence of Chief Bartlett, Mrs. Elsa S. McGinn, Fire Commissioner and San Mateo's first woman town trustee, organized the fire fighters. Quickly she had the men connect a hose to a hydrant, but according to the *News Leader*, the water pressure was so weak "a small stream of water barely reached the roof." McGinn then sounded the cry for help to the departments of Hillsborough, Burlingame and Redwood City, who responded as quickly as they could. Menlo Park's contingent arrived within a half hour. By 6:30 San Francisco had also sent down a truck, two engines and several companies. One of the San Francisco vehicles had covered the distance in only 26 minutes. A San Francisco pumper used the water from the hotel's pool, as every hydrant in the area was taken. If their modern pressure

The Peninsula Hotel, once Alvinza Hayward's mansion, caught fire on the afternoon of June 25, 1920; it was the worst fire in San Mateo's history.
Courtesy San Mateo County Historical Museum

pumps had been on hand from the beginning, the building might have been saved, but the fire was too far gone by the time the San Franciscans arrived.

Early on, a troop of Boy Scouts joined bystanders who pitched in to save hotel furniture and the property of the guests. The *News Leader* reported: "Bureaus, dressers, tables, chairs, mattresses, bed clothing, and personal effects were dumped in confusion on the lawn, and many articles were thrown from second story windows. . . One fire man was seen to throw out a trunk, which broke open upon striking the ground with a smashing of glass and was seen to contain some guest's private liquor stock." As the fire was a slow one, taking some four hours to burn itself out, most of the Hotel's furniture and the possessions of guests were saved.

With all of this property sitting outside on the lawn, another problem developed. About seven o'clock Manager Borden and others began hearing rumors that some of the spectators were actually thieves and were "making a rich haul" by stealing whatever they wanted. Borden ordered the police to clear the grounds. One man was caught trying to carry off a mahogany table. Mrs. McGinn reported two seal-skin coats were taken. That night special deputies guarded the grounds.

By evening the magnificent tower had fallen, and the sumptuous rooms on the main floor were engulfed in flames, as hundreds watched from the lawn.

Courtesy San Mateo County Historical Museum

Marshal Burke went to work the next day "following the trails of petty thieves." He believed the reports of stolen property to be "greatly overestimated." A large amount of silverware at first reported stolen turned out to be in the possession of the Hotel's housekeeper, who had moved valuables in his automobile for safekeeping.

The hotel building itself was a total loss, much of it reduced to mere ashes. The value of the structure was estimated at $500,000. There was little insurance, and the new management predicted correctly that new funding for a hotel on that location was highly unlikely. On July 1, the Peninsula's owners staged an auction on the grounds, and almost everything the Hotel still owned was sold off.

The Peninsula Hotel was never successful as a business, but as a San Mateo landmark and symbol it was important. As the former home of Alvinza Hayward, it linked the past with the future. It was stately, and residents were proud of its appearance. Now it was gone, but people knew it could have been saved—just as Library Hall could have been saved 35 years previously.

The *News Leader* stated that "lack of adequate fire equipment" was responsible. The old volunteer firefighting regime was scrutinized. Mrs. McGinn was honored for her role in trying to save the structure. Soon after the fire, she called a meeting during which she "went on the war path," demanding and receiving George Bartlett's resignation.

With the fall of Bartlett and rise of McGinn a new era was dawning for San Mateo. The old village and town institutions were no longer adequate for the burgeoning middle-class town. Just as its struggle to emerge from village to town had started with a fire, now a new struggle, to become a city, started the same way.

NOTES

1. Thomas Nunan interviewed George Bartlett in his column, "Type High" of the *San Mateo Times*, May 21, 1937.
2. D. Gordon Bromfield, *The San Mateo We Knew*, 1957, p. 23.
3. Gary M. O'Neill, "Hermann Schussler and the Spring Valley Water System," *La Peninsula*, vol. XXVI, No. 2, August 1990, p. 9.
4. Wickert, *City*, p. 25.
5. "San Mateo, Burlingame and Belmont Souvenir," promotional pamphlet, circa 1895 published by *The Traveler* of San Francisco.
6. Stanger, *Peninsula*, p. 111.
7. Michell P. Postel, Sandi Tatman, Katherine C. Feallock, *Peninsula Portrait*, Windsor Publications, Northridge, California, 1988, p. 138.
8. Robert Y. Hayne, letter to the editor, *San Mateo Leader*, February 27, 1890.
9. Ringler, *San Mateo*, p. 21.
10. Bromfield, *San Mateo*, p. 80.
11. Betty Lochrie Hoag, "A Man of Charisma: "A.P. Giannini in San Mateo, California:" *La Peninsula*, Vol. XVII, No. 2, Spring 1973.
12. Frank M. Stanger, "Levy Brothers History," *La Peninsula*, Vol. XVI, April 1972.
13. Bromfield, *San Mateo*, p. 23.
14. Ibid. p. 24.
15. Ibid. p. 18.
16. Ibid. p. 140.
17. "San Mateo," *The Traveler*, promotional brochure cited in footnote 116.
18. Bromfield, *San Mateo*, p. 31.
19. Mitchell P. Postel, "More than a Grain: the History of the Salt Industry in San Mateo County," *La Peninsula*, Vol. XX, No. 3, Summer 1980.
20. Mitchell P. Postel, *The History of the Peninsula Golf and Country Club*, Peninsula Golf and Country Club, San Mateo, 1993, p. 21.
21. Henry Buffoni's interview with Aylette Cotton (see note, 102).
22. Edwin J. Halcron, "Swiss Echoes In California," Student Monograph #1493 in the archives of the San Mateo County Historical Museum, June, 1955.
23. Stanger, *Peninsula*, p. 104.
24. Winifred M. Burke was interviewed by Patricia Schmidt for the San Mateo County Historical Association on October 5, 9, 30 and November 2 of 1970.
25. Address of Aylett Cotton to the San Mateo County Historical Association, September 19, 1961.
26. Ibid.
27. Martin F. Suto, Melvin Cohn, F. J. de Larios, "San Mateo County Bench and Bar," *La Peninsula*, Vol. XXVII, No. 1, October 1991, p. 7.
28. Kae Marie Gifford, "San Mateo Woman's Club," Student Monograph #133 in the archives of the San Mateo County Historical Museum, May, 1938.
29. Bromfield, *San Mateo*, p. 42.
30. Ibid. p. 27.
31. Ibid. p. 41.
32. Letter from Pansy Jewett Abbott-Gish to Dr. David N. Thomas, Superintendant San Mateo School District, November 11, 1974, in the archives of the San Mateo County Historical Museum.
33. Burke interview with Schmidt.
34. Charles N. Kirkbride, "Memoranda," May 11, 1911, letter in the archives of the San Mateo County Historical Museum.
35. Bromfield, *San Mateo*, p. 24.
36. Hynding, *Frontier*, p. 146.
37. Francis A. Guido, "Electric Railways in San Mateo County — A History of the 'Forty Line,'" student monograph #100 in the archives of the San Mateo County Historical Museum, May, 1938.
38. *Souvenir Magazine of the San Mateo County*, San Mateo Leader, publisher, 1904.
39. Bromfield, *San Mateo*, p. 283.
40. George Kertell interview in the January 28, 1969 special 75th anniversary edition of the *San Mateo Times*.

Engine House No. 2 of the San Mateo Fire Department, in Hayward Park near Tenth Avenue, made a strong architectural statement for its time. The tower, built for drying canvas fire hoses, is beautifully detailed, and the wide barge-boards, projecting brackets, and brown shingle exterior make the building an outstanding example of the Craftsman style architecture popular during the early years of this century. Many bungalows in Hayward Park were built in the Craftsman style; the fire house was evidently designed to match them. This building, with its tower removed, is now used as a private home.

Courtesy San Mateo County Historical Museum.

Notes, continued

[41] Pauline Sullivan interviews with the *Times* on July 7, 1964 and February 26, 1983.

[42] Jostes, *John Parrott*, p. 218.

[43] Valentine, "Wisnom," p. 12.

[44] Minutes of the Building Inspection Commission, April 24, 1906 in the archives of the San Mateo County Historical Museum.

[45] R. H. Jury "San Mateo California," *Out West*, February 1908.

[46] Assessor records were compiled by Roland Giannini for the 1989 San Mateo Building Survey. They are now in the archives of the San Mateo County Historical Museum.

[47] Quotes taken from *La Peninsula*, Vol. VIII, No. 5, May 1956.

[48] Elaine Thomas, "The Italians of San Mateo County," *La Peninsula*, vol. XXI, No. 1, Fall 1981, p. 10.

[49] Bromfield, *San Mateo*, p. 49.

[50] Ringlar, Still, Tatman, "City," p. 5.

[51] Bromfield, *San Mateo*, p. 134.

[52] *1872 - 1942: A Community Story*, San Mateo Chapter, Japanese American Citizens League, 1981, p. 17.

[53] Vera Graham, "He Follows a Recipe for Longevity," *Times*, November 19, 1982, interview with Sayohei Kawakita on his 100th birthday.

[54] *San Mateo Buddist Temple 70th and 75th Anniversary 1910-1980*, published by the church in 1980.

[55] Japanese American Citizens League, *1872*, p. 59.

[56] Author's interview with Claire Mack, March, 1993.

[57] Mrs. C. N. Kirkbride, "History of the Peninsula Avenue Parent Teacher Associaton," February, 1935; manuscript in the archives of the San Mateo County Historical Museum.

[58] Beverly Hill, "History of the Hospitals of the San Mateo County" student monograph #326 in the archives of the San Mateo County Historical Museum, June, 1944.

[59] Gary Salzman, editor, *San Mateo High Through the Years*, San Mateo High School, April 1960.

[60] Louis Bortolin, "Police Chiefs of San Mateo," student monograph #1369 in the archives of the San Mateo County Historical Museum, 1953.

[61] Schmidt's Winifred Burke interview.

[62] "San Mateo's Police Department" *San Francisco Police and Peace Officers' Journal*, Christmas, 1940, p. 17.

[63] Jeff Barile, *San Mateo Fire Department 1887-1990*, San Mateo Fire Department, 1990.

CHAPTER V

The Town Becomes a City: 1920-1941

PROFESSIONALIZATION OF MUNICIPAL INSTITUTIONS

THE FIRE AT THE PENINSULA HOTEL on June 25, 1920, served as a wake-up call for San Mateo. Its residential areas were burgeoning, and the town was destined to become a city in a short time: its public institutions needed to keep pace. The volunteer fire department had proven no match for a fire that should have been contained, and it became the first branch of the town's government to be overhauled.

Taking the lead in that work was the community's first woman trustee, Mrs. Elsa S. McGinn. Women who stepped away from their traditional roles into political positions were rare in San Mateo in 1920. However, McGinn was well suited for prominence by family tradition. Her mother, Laura Catherine Redden, born in 1840 without the ability to hear, became a noted poet. At the age of 19, Redden began her professional life as an editor with a religious newspaper in St. Louis. She also wrote for the *St. Louis Republican,* under the pen name Howard Glyndon. During the Civil War, she was a Republican party correspondent, writing articles and poems about the War. She became a friend of Abraham Lincoln and Union generals James Garfield and Ulysses.S. Grant. In 1876, she married Edward W. Searing, an attorney, in New York. They had one daughter, Elsa.

Elsa also married an attorney, John L. McGinn; they said their vows in Nome, Alaska in 1904. John, a veteran of the Spanish-American War, went to Alaska as a prospector. In 1900 he was appointed Assistant United States District Attorney, and in that position saw to the conviction for murder of the first man ever to be hanged in Nome. In 1903, he opened a private practice.

John and Elsa, who by now had two children, moved to San Mateo in 1916.[1] Elsa immediately became a community leader. During World War I, she was active in a variety of patriotic causes. In 1919, she chaired San Mateo County's Liberty Loan Campaign. Among her strongest support groups was the San Mateo Woman's Club, which she headed for five terms. The governor of California appointed her Chairman of Community Service in San Mateo County in 1920.

In 1912 San Mateo had voted to incorporate as a city of the sixth class. Under state law, such cities could adopt a commission form of government, allowing elected town trustees to be assigned to different departments. This reorganization was approved by local voters, and went into effect in April 1913.[2]

As San Mateo's top vote getter in 1920, Elsa McGinn became San Mateo's first woman trustee, and received the important post of Commissioner of Public Health and Safety, which included overseeing the work of the Fire Department.

Looking south on El Camino in 1934: Central Park on the left is a cascade of foliage, bordered by the fine stone and iron fence installed by William Kohl when he owned the property.

Courtesy San Mateo County Historical Museum

John and Elsa McGinn

Courtesy San Mateo County Historical Museum

Her immediate task was to reorganize and better equip the Fire Department. But she soon took on more responsibilities. In 1921 she was named to the highly patriotic board on "Americanization" in San Mateo County. She became a trustee for the library. She joined the Red Cross committee combating the influenza epidemic. She also served as President of the County Federation of Women's Clubs, Vice President of the County's Peace Officers Association, and Vice President of the Peninsula Bureau of Chambers of Commerce and Civic Associations. She also became Commissioner for Public Works and sat on the County Board of Free Holders as it drafted a new county charter. When Mayor Thomas Brady became ill, McGinn was appointed San Mateo's acting mayor.

In 1926, after six successful years as a trustee, she ran in the Republican primary for the state legislature. She lost, but she stayed active, serving on the San Mateo Planning Commission from 1931 until 1952.

McGinn demonstrated her leadership only three days after the Peninsula Hotel fire, when she demanded that popular Chief Bartlett be dismissed from his office. The other trustees voted four to one to support McGinn.[3]

Volunteer Bruce Gibson, appointed as the new chief, immediately called a meeting of volunteers to discuss new equipment purchases and department reorganization. They agreed that a pumping engine for in-town fires and a chemical engine for grass fires were priority items. They also discussed the need for a fire alarm system.

McGinn made the purchase of the pumper her personal quest, and by 1921 San Mateo had two motorized engines at Fire Department headquarters. McGinn also saw to the professionalization of the department's personnel. Beginning in 1922, the Fire Department was placed under the command of Thomas Burke, who now assumed the role of both police chief and fire chief. Protecting San Mateo had become too big a responsibility to be managed by part-time volunteers.

By 1925, the Fire Department had three paid firemen and twelve volunteers. Recognizing that the continuous modernization of crime fighting and fire fighting techniques were advancing so fast that one man could not keep up with both, Burke resigned as Fire Chief in December of 1925.[4]

San Mateo hired Hugh Morris as its first full-time Fire Chief on January 1, 1926. Morris went to work to establish a training program, revamp the rules and regulations of the Department, and improve equipment. At his request, the city hired Lewis Degen, one of the world's foremost experts on fire alarms, to design a new alarm system. Degen had 14 alarm boxes installed throughout the downtown area and placed the switchboard in the firehouse on B Street. The service was fully operational by May 1930.

San Mateo's expenditure for equipment and professional services paid off in May 1934, when a fire at the new San Mateo Fox Theater broke out. The conflagration developed a backdraft, and only quick action by the well-trained firemen averted more property damage and possible loss of life.

By 1935, despite the effects of the national Depression on the city's finances, San Mateo had twelve paid and seven volunteer fire fighters. In 1937, when the Department answered some 261 alarms, its mechanized equipment consisted of three engines plus a 50-foot service truck, another truck, a coupe, a sedan and a 1,000-gallon tank wagon.[5]

In August 1940 the Department moved to the new downtown civic center on Ellsworth. Its headquarters was among the most up-to-date buildings in the state.

Later that year Ordinance 495 allowed for the creation of a Chief Fire Inspector and a Bureau of Fire Prevention and Fire Safety. Also in 1940, Chief Hugh Morris was named President of the Pacific Coast Fire Chief Association.[6] By the beginning of World War II, the Department had 25 paid staff members.

The Police Department also improved during this era. Chief Burke's original patrol consisted of three men and two bicycles. For a time the police at least had use of a red Model T Ford, when Burke was chief of both the fire and police Departments. The police department got its first automobile and motorcycle during the 1920s.

Unfortunately, Burke and his tiny force had plenty to do. The 1920s were, of course, the era of Prohibition.

For three years Thomas Burke (right) was chief of both the Fire Department and the Police Department. Below is the police force in 1929 (from left): Chief Burke, McNally (?), Ed Klimp, Jack Pease, George Martin, Hartnett (?), Manuel Trinta, and Tom Conners.

Courtesy Norman Burke

Top: Baywood, the beautiful mansion of the John Parrott family, was reduced to a pile of rubble by a fire on August 28, 1928, in spite of the best efforts of fire fighters. Below: The Fire Department in 1921 had a new ladder engine and a chemical unit (right), the latest equipment available, with whitewall tires on wooden spoke wheels.

Courtesy San Mateo County Historical Museum

On a sunny Sunday in 1934, when no one had much money to spend, people dressed up and went to Central Park for picnics, games, or climbing on the old cannon (right rear).

Courtesy San Mateo County Historical Museum

While San Mateans had been experimenting with their own "dry" laws for some time, the national Volstead Act made enforcement mandatory. Like other jurisdictions all over the country, San Mateo had trouble abiding by the letter of that law.

One of the first raids in the county took place in San Mateo in 1920. Chief Burke took two men named Bursa and Piccoli, operators of a speakeasy at the Union Hotel, by surprise. Piccoli backed himself up near a door and refused to surrender his liquor. Bursa hurled a bottle at officers, and a "spirited" but brief fight resulted until the two were subdued.[7]

As the years went on, illegal alcohol became big business locally. Rum-runners would land their cargo on the San Mateo County coast and truck it over the hill for distribution in San Francisco. Burke worked with federal authorities to choke off this supply. Tips from local citizens and other law enforcement agencies often resulted in the interception of quantities of hooch. While there was seldom any gun play, confrontations between the law and the lawless were often lively.[8]

Local bootleggers tended to be more of a problem than professional outsiders. They bought the stuff and even made it. Family legend has it that the Wisnom family—pioneer leaders in business and civic affairs—stored kegs of hooch in a barn at the back of their store.

Even Albert Chartier, who operated a restaurant in the Woman's Club Building at West Santa Inez and El Camino Real, was arrested in 1928 for selling "jiggle soup." The police raided his establishment and found a five-gallon demijohn of gin, a five-gallon keg of moonshine, and twelve bottles and vials of various "stylish" liquors.

The law allowed families to make wine for their own personal (or religious) use. Such laws were difficult to enforce, especially in a small town where the police knew everyone. Many Italians made more wine than their own families could use, and were not willing to throw it away. Among immigrant families, especially the Italians wine making continued throughout the period. Genevieve Altieri remembered her own family's wine making when they lived on Grant Street.[9]

Chief Burke worked seven days a week. He arrived at his office at 8 a.m., went home for dinner, and returned to work until 8 p.m. On Saturdays and Sundays, he took half the day off. (Burke, whose home was on Monte Diablo, never owned his own car; he walked to and from his office.) When Prohibition finally ended in 1933, Burke and his force were relieved.

San Mateo's quest to professionalize its services included the way the town itself was run. In 1922 the voters approved a new city charter, allowing for a somewhat experimental government in which popularly elected, uncompensated city council members would select a mayor from amongst themselves. The council appointed a city manager, who was responsible for directing the city staff. San Mateo was the first incorporated jurisdiction in San Mateo County to have a full-time, paid city manager, C.F. Price.

In another positive move the city purchased its first park. In 1922, the executors of the Kohl estate sought to sell sixteen acres at Fifth Avenue and El Camino Real. Under Mayor Thomas J. Brady, an $80,000 bond issue was successfully put before the voters, and Central Park became the first municipal park in the county. A small, half-acre parcel on Ninth Avenue was added later. Most of the plantings and pathways established by the Kohls remain today to remind us of what the old San Mateo estate looked like.

While no Parks and Recreation Department existed as yet, the Park and Boulevard Commission did. City employee Tom Pearson was reassigned from caring for roadway islands in San Mateo Park and became Central Park's first staff member. Pearson removed some fruit trees and installed a turfed baseball field—the first public recreation facility in the city. Before this, baseball games were played in an old corporation yard, later called East Side Park and today known as Martin Luther King Park.

BACK TO NORMALCY

BETWEEN WORLD WAR I and the Great Depression of the 1930s, the San Mateo elite tried to ignore income taxes and the changing shape of society and resume their comfortable lives.

Then the Borel Family began to break up their estate. In 1926 they sold a large parcel south of Arroyo Mocho to the San Mateo Polo Club, which set up three playing fields and a grandstand. Many members were friends of the family anyway. Besides, the major portion of the land still belonged to the Borels. In 1927 both San Mateo and Hillsborough became interested in annexing the estate. Aylett Cotton advised the Borels in favor of San Mateo, reminding them that their sewer ran through San Mateo and that the Hillsborough Police and Fire Departments were too far away.

It was also during the 1920s that Louis Bovet, a member of the family, built a beautiful English-style home on the Borel estate. In later years it became Chuck's Steak House. Today the Borel Bank and Trust building sits on the site.

During the 1920s the elite were able to regain some of their elegant life style. Blooded horses retained their stature among the elite sporting circles. Polo was played not only at the San Mateo Polo Club but on private fields at various estates in the San Mateo and Hillsborough area.

Interest in things equestrian probably reached its zenith in 1929 with the formation of the Gymkhanna Club on seventeen acres just east of the Beresford Country Club. The club's first president was the well-known Mrs. Nion Tucker. Its manager and instructor was Dr. H. Hordon. While it sponsored an annual horse show and race, the chief attractions of the Gymkhanna Club were the facilities catering to horses and their owners, and proximity to many trails throughout the nearby hills.[10]

By the early 1930s, things began to fall apart for the "horsy set." Fewer people could afford to maintain strings of polo ponies, or even to belong to polo clubs. Furthermore, the march of development south from the center of the city began to squeeze out stables and pastures. New suburban neighbors complained to the city council about flies.

In April 1931, notices were issued to stable owners in the south San Mateo area reminding them of San Mateo's sanitation ordinances. City Manager E. P. Wilsey now warned that if substantial progress toward compliance was not made within ten days of his communication, $300 fines would be levied. Among those notified were members of the Peninsula's highest social circles, including George A. Pope, Jr., Will Tevis, Jr., and Lindsey Howard. The exclusive Gymkhana Club was also notified.

Then ensued a standoff known as "the San Mateo Stable War," or "The Horse Fly War." The elite simply ignored these notices. Eventually, the City Council sat down with some of them, behind closed doors, with the press specifically excluded, and settled the matter by compromising on some of the ordinances—for a while. Eventually, the influx of housing projects in south San Mateo after World War II forced the equestrians out.

In the 1920s San Mateo became a paradise for golfers at the Beresford Club, which catered to prominent Jewish families of San Francisco and the Peninsula. Utilization was light enough so that playing times for women and children were not restricted, as was the case at other clubs.

Moreover, the course was in great shape, and members claimed that the food was the envy of San Francisco Bay Area clubdom. The Sunday buffet was particularly famous for cold cuts, salads, oysters, crab, smoked salmon and, always, a baron of beef. Ruth Steiner recalled that children made great use of the club, swimming in the pool and learning to play tennis from professional Merv Griffin, Sr. The club's ballroom and luxurious appointments made it a fine place for blossoming romance—whether pre-marital or extra-marital.

Liz Mack remembered that during Prohibition, although the bar, which overlooked the pool, was "officially" closed: "We carried our own bottles [in] and they would set you up."[11]

The Beresford Club's golf course was designed by the internationally famous Scotsman, Donald Ross. Of the approximately 400 golf courses Ross was responsible for during his career, he crossed the Mississippi only once, to design the one at Beresford. Getting Ross to come to San Mateo was largely the work of Walter Stettheimer, president of the club in 1922. Ross deliberately set his costs to discourage Stettheimer. But the architect was surprised when Stettheimer accepted Ross' conditions, including the highest fee paid to any golf-course designer up to that time. Beresford members committed $100,000 to rearrange and improve their course.

An important legacy bestowed upon the Beresford Club by Ross was his introduction of another Scotsman, Willie Nicoll, as golf professional. Nicoll later admitted that never having been to California before, he fully expected to encounter cowboys and Indians when he got off the train at San Mateo. But he quickly found his new home was far from primitive, and he enjoyed the club members and community of San Mateo immensely.

The feeling was mutual. Nicoll became an institution at Beresford. Men were taken with his classic, old-world approach to the game of golf, and women were charmed by his burr. Nicoll helped promote women's golf by developing some of the best players in the Bay Area, including Patty Berg, Dot Kielty and Helen Lengfeld. Between the 1920s and 1940s, he and Lengfeld organized a number of tournaments to focus women's attention on the game.

Not only was Nicoll popular at the club, but he was quite well known in town as well. He lived just two

The Wisnom family sold not only hardware but also Dodge automobiles in the early 1920s. And it seems they were in the hotel business, too.

Courtesy San Mateo County Historical Museum

blocks from the club, and had his hair cut at the local barber shop. A former caddy, Frank Gustafson, remembered that as young men during the Depression, he and his friends would hop the fence at the club and play a little golf when no one else was around. Nicoll always looked the other way.

During the 1920s, many San Mateo boys earned their first money as caddies at Beresford. In those days before the electric golf cart the club might use thirty caddies on a Saturday or Sunday. Among the boys who worked at the club were Bill O'Ferrel, who would become city clerk, and Claude Hirschey, who would become Mayor. Frank Gustafson says the crusty caddy master, a man named Wilson, advised the boys to watch the ball and not "drive the players nuts."[12]

Like the "horsy set," the Beresford Club had problems during the 1930s. The Great Depression adversely affected its members. The opening of another Jewish country club at Lake Merced in San Francisco in 1923 didn't help, either. By the beginning of the 1940s, the club's leadership had to make decisions that would forever alter its social make-up.

Ah Sam Florists, founded by brothers Lincoln, Gordon, and Arthur Leong and their sister Mable in 1933, in the depth of the Depression, was thriving in the early 1940s.

Courtesy the Leong family

Changing Ethnic Communities

For the ethnic communities of San Mateo, the period between 1920 and 1941 was full of change. For one group it meant extinction, for others economic and social acceptance, and for some a time of improvement in some areas and losses fueled by intolerance in others.

The saddest story involves the disappearance of Joseph Evencio, probably the last surviving descendant of the San Mateo Mission Hospice Indians still living in San Mateo. His grandfather had been Evencio Yocalo, the head man among the neophytes before the American takeover of California. Joseph's father, Pedro Evencio, was interviewed by Stanford professor Mary Sheldon Barnes in 1894.

Joseph became a caretaker for the Howards at Coyote Point in 1925,[13] tending boats and performing other services. Local legends, especially among children, abounded about this character with his dog and rifle (filled with blanks to scare off young trespassers). Joseph disappeared after Coyote Point was turned over to the Merchant Marines to create an academy during World War II. Thus the continuous four-thousand-year history of the native people of San Mateo ended—their final disappearance unmourned, hardly noticed at all.

San Mateo's Chinese community changed very little during this time. Unlike other groups, including the Japanese, who lived in ethnically mixed neighborhoods, the Chinese tended to live in certain pockets of town. A Chinatown of sorts still existed around First Avenue and the railroad tracks.[14]

Genevieve Altieri remembered the Chinese children as quiet and obedient, staying close to home and family, working after school, at family-owned laundries. She remembered that they all dressed similarly: "simple and neat [with] black pants that came just above the ankles and the high mandarin collared tunic, also in black." The children wore small black slippers. The girls "wore their hair short in a 'bowl' cut," and the boys had close-shaved heads. Their mothers had their long hair "pulled tight into a knot at the back of their heads."[15] The women of this community did most of their shopping at a store owned by Chow Yuke, who reportedly also ran a gambling operation in his back room.

Perhaps San Mateo's most successful Chinese family was—and is—the Leongs. Sam Shun Leong sold fruit and vegetables. In 1933, at the age of 19, his son, Gordon, borrowed $150 and opened a flower shop at El Camino Real and 28th Avenue. Gordon ran this very successful business, with his brother Lincoln and other members of the family, until he retired in 1982. Today, Ah Sam's is one of the city's oldest and best-known businesses.

During the 1920s, San Mateo's European-born populations grew, developing into mixed neighborhoods of Polish, German, Scandinavian, English, Italian and Irish. According to Genevieve Altieri the Europeans got along with one another and mixed well with Japanese and African-Americans in the same neighborhoods. The possible exception was Irish and Italian boys, who engaged in name calling and all-too-frequent fist fights.

The European group which grew most during that time was the Italians. Like the Altieri family, many came to America just before World War I. Some became farmers on the Peninsula. Some found their way to San Mateo, as the Altieris did in 1924.

Italian families living in San Mateo enjoyed the advantages of suburban living. The rural setting allowed for large backyard gardens, with room to keep poultry, rabbits, and even sheep.

Lincoln and Arthur Leong (left), with their mother, Mrs. Sam Shun Leong, and a cousin.

Below: Mable Leong, one of the founders of Ah Sam.

Courtesy the Leong family

As with many ethnic groups in San Mateo, the Italians had their own stores. Businesses such as Daba's, the Guido Brothers' and Rodolari's carried basic groceries, but also stocked pasta, olive oil, Italian spices, special cheeses, salami, anchovies (dried and salted), dried codfish, and freshly baked Italian and French breads. Stores like Daba's did a fair volume of business with phone orders, but for the Italian community, shopping at Italian-owned stores was an important social event.

The owners of the stores became leaders of the Italian community. Because many could speak and read English, they became links to the outside community. They explained bills, business documents and government papers, and gave advice to new immigrants.

Marco Daba was one of these community leaders. He arrived in New York in 1900 and came to San Mateo in 1909 to open a saloon and wholesale liquor establishment at Second and Main. After Prohibition closed his business, he started his grocery store in 1924, at First and B, moving it in 1929 to 42 B Street. He became a mentor for the Italian boys,

Mrs. Nui Takahashi, the new teacher at the Japanese Language School in 1922, somehow managed to control 35 very well-dressed children; only George Yamaguchi (top left) refused to conform. His sister, Shizu Yamaguchi Tabata (second from right, back row, wearing a big hairbow) recently identified many of these children: her brothers George, Kunio and Sike Yamaguchi, Masuo Nosaka, Mio Oida, Tomiko Ito, Grace Hashiguchi, Toshi Endo, Noriko Shiba, Sei Sakuma, Kiyo Sakuma, some of whom still live in San Mateo County.

Courtesy Japanese American Cultural League

helping them find jobs and move up in society.[16]

Daba was also a founder of the politically-oriented New Deal Italian-American Federation of San Mateo. The formation of this club in 1934 indicates the growing influence of the Italian community. Italian Americans gained political strength in the Bay Area—earlier than in any other part of the country—largely because of the activities of organizations such as this one. The New Deal Italian-American Federation eventually evolved into more of a social institution. In 1946, it changed its name to the Peninsula Social Club, and still maintains a building for its popular gatherings on B Street.

The years from 1920 to 1941 were of mixed blessings for Japanese citizens, who made considerable progress, but also faced lingering social intolerance. Much of the social history of the Japanese Americans of San Mateo during this period is related to their two churches.

Tetsuo Yamanouchi and his wife, Yoshiko, were leaders of the Buddhist Church; Yoshiko organized a Sunday school and a Women's Auxiliary. By 1929, the church had sixty members and began operating independently of the San Francisco church. In 1933, recognizing his work, the Nishi Hongwangi in Kyoto, Japan awarded Tetsuo a certificate for distinguished service, the first time such an award was given outside of Japan. Tetsuo died in 1930 at the age of 58 from a lingering illness, but the progress of his church continued. In 1939 the congregation launched a building campaign; their quarters within the Japanese language school at 504 Second Avenue had become too cramped. They purchased lots on South Claremont, but World War II interrupted construction.

Hidematsu Tamura, Tomoko Yamamoto and Masazo Shimizu founded a Japanese Christian Church in 1924. The congregation originally met in the Tamura home on North Grant Street. Later gatherings were held in the Congregational Church with services performed by Reverend Shokochi Hata of San Francisco.

At first, the Japanese Christian community identified most strongly with the Congregationalists. Then in 1925 Dr. Ernest Adolphus Sturge, a medical doctor and Director of Evangelism under the Presbyterian Board of National Missions, came out of retirement to help 69 members of San Mateo's Japanese community establish a church. Sturge had worked with Japanese Americans in San Francisco and other Japanese enclaves on the West Coast.

Sturge and his wife left Carmel to establish residence on Elm Street. Their home became a meeting place for the infant church. In 1926 the congregation became part of the Japanese Church of Christ of San Francisco. A year later it became known as the Japanese Independent Union Church of San Mateo.

In 1930, the congregation purchased property to construct a proper church. They were in the process of raising money when Dr. Sturge died in 1934. He left the church his home, valued at $5,000. In 1938, the church at 25 South Humboldt was dedicated in Dr. Sturge's memory. Final construction was interrupted by the War.

For many Japanese, life in America continued to be hard economically. Yoneo Kawakita's father had a job at the salt refinery until it closed during the Depression

People stood in line for the opening of the original Noah's Cafeteria, at 139 South B Street, in 1920.
Courtesy San Mateo County Historical Museum

(1931). Thereafter, his parents worked as domestics, but the family, like others, continued to live at the abandoned plant until it was purchased by L. C. Smith for his paving and asphalt business just before the war.[17]

For other Japanese families, however, these years brought substantial improvements. San Mateo became a place where Japanese families from all over San Mateo County visited. From as far away as Pescadero they shopped at the Takahashi store or went to the Buddhist or Christian Church. Many San Mateo Japanese were successful in the flower industry. The Imachi family established their nursery near 19th Avenue between El Camino and the railroad tracks. In 1919 they moved up into today's Hillsdale residential area, east of the present high school. East of the railroad tracks, eleven other Japanese chrysanthemum growers had nurseries that stretched from Laurel Creek to Belmont.

North of these growers, the Ishimaru family, who moved to San Mateo in 1931, established a nursery at Poplar and El Camino. Ishimaru catered in retail sales to local residents and not wholesale stock, as did most of his contemporaries.[18] Some families explored different business opportunities. Before the war the Endo family was well-known for car repair service.[19]

A certain sign of well-being and high spirits was the annual picnic in the Beresford area. The Buddhist Temple, Christian Church and Nippon Gakuen (the language school) organized the event for the entire Japanese community in San Mateo.

While the first generation (Issei) were generally satisfied with their new life, they did not lose their desire to return one day to their mother country. So that their children would not be ignorant of the ways of Japan, the

Issei insisted their offspring (the Nisei) attend Japanese language school. The youngsters spent a full day at public school, and then went to language school until almost 6 p.m. each day.

Despite this schooling, the Nisei developed their own attitude about America. They enjoyed going to public school. They formed their own Boy Scout Troops or Blue Jay Clubs. They formed their own judo and kendo clubs. They organized sports teams, and, in 1935, they even formed their own San Mateo branch of the Japanese American Citizens' League (the activities of the national organization began in 1930).

By law, the Niseis were American citizens. Unlike their parents, they could own property, and when they came of age, would be entitled to vote. They saw their future not in going back to Japan, but in staying in America.

The San Mateo branch of the Japanese American Citizens League focused on protection of their parents' rights and, as the war approached, loyalty issues. Meetings took place at the language school or at Sturge Cottage Church. The League also sponsored social activities for young members, including dances and celebrations at the Benjamin Franklin Hotel, Kloss Hall (built by the Congregational Church in 1922) or at the Masonic Temple.

Of all the ethnic groups in San Mateo, none faced more devastating racial intolerance than the Japanese, even before World War II. For example, in September 1930, when the language school prepared to build a new building on Cypress Avenue and Idaho Street, the plan was vehemently opposed by 48 residents of the district and eight other San Mateo citizens. The Nippon Gakuen had been on Second Avenue for eleven years and had out-grown its facilities. The protesters had no general objection to the building of a new school, they just didn't

want it in their neighborhood. San Matean Mike Boepple testified before the City Council that, "if the Japanese were allowed to cut into the sections, they would destroy the district."[20] The Council promptly formed a committee to find a "more suitable" location for the school "in the Oriental quarter of the city."

While no "Oriental quarter" formally existed, it was established practice among bankers and realtors that no Japanese resident could obtain a loan to purchase a house outside of the area from Fifth Avenue to Poplar and El Camino to Bayshore. Clearly discrimination was very much a reality before 1941, setting the stage for the internment measures taken in 1942.

San Mateo's still infant African-American community suffered similar restrictions before the war. Although fewer in number, this group had much in common with the Japanese-Americans. For instance, the roots of their community life can be traced back to the establishment of two churches.

In 1919, African-American community leaders such as Robert Holmes, Jesse Selby, Anita Miles, Robert Williams, Kelly Mack, Rose Jones, William Pinkstone, Mary J. Boutee, E. M. Brown, Mamie Davis and Harry Cox were working to organize a church. They received a big boost when Reverend J. B. Holmes, pastor at Cooper Zion Church in Oakland, crossed the Bay to assist with

Chef Noah Williams (opposite, top) had the magic touch in cooking. Diners in his tasteful Noah's Ark on Third Avenue (opposite) are obviously pleased with the arrangements.

Noah's Ark opened in 1923 (right), with lines of customers and shiny new cars parked in front. Noah Williams opened a third restaurant (above right) on El Camino in the 1930s, when the Chrysler Airflow design was shockingly modern.

Courtesy San Mateo County Historical Museum

Les Williams, Noah's son, became a well-known performer and dance instructor.

Courtesy San Mateo County Historical Museum

the house-to-house preaching that led to the organization of the African M. E. Zion Church of San Mateo.[21] By 1927, the congregation had constructed a building at 803 Monte Diablo, which was named the St. James African Methodist Episcopal Zion church. In 1938, the church moved to 825 Monte Diablo.

The second church, the Pilgrim Baptists, had a controversial beginning. The congregation wished to build on the east side, but residents protested, echoing arguments similar to those against the Japanese language school a couple of years previously. This time, however, city councilman Aylett Cotton championed the cause of the underdog.

Cotton went on to become a Superior Court Judge, and when the church was completed in 1937, he was asked to make a speech during the opening ceremonies in recognition for his work on the congregation's behalf. He admitted to the group that it was his first trip to the pulpit, despite the fact that there had been preachers in his family. He added: "the last two generations deteriorated and became lawyers."[22]

In general, the African-American community mixed well in those neighborhoods set aside for ethnic diversity. The prevailing view among Italian immigrants was that the blacks "worked hard and were clean and hospitable."[23] Most of the African Americans were laborers, but there were also entrepreneurs within this community. None became more famous than restaurateur Noah Williams.

Williams came from a family of famous cooks. His father, Noah Williams Sr., had been chef for the Rock Island Line. Noah Junior also became a railroad chef, eventually assuming responsibility for all food service for the Southern Pacific's Coast Division. Then he opened a restaurant in San Francisco across from the Palace Hotel.

About 1920, Williams moved to San Mateo and established Noah's Cafeteria at 139 South B Street. His old San Francisco customers remained loyal. They came down the Peninsula and lined up on the street for his famous baked ham or fried chicken. In 1923 Williams followed the new business trend and moved up from B Street to Third Avenue. The new restaurant, called Noah's Ark, was housed in the third building constructed on that block.

Noah's Ark was renowned not only for its food, but for its decor as well. Huge paintings of jungle animals (now in the possession of the County Historical

Museum) hung on the walls, and miniature iron beasts were suspended from chandeliers. Williams believed in advertising. An ad in a 1925 Orpheum Theater program stated that Williams had spent $40,000 to equip and furnish the restaurant and to create food that was "unsurpassed."

The Depression is blamed for killing off this landmark restaurant in 1931. Williams did operate another on El Camino Real, but it never achieved the fame and popularity of Noah's Ark.

But the story of the Williams family in San Mateo does not end there. Noah's son, Les Williams, became a well-known dancer. During the 1930s, he and a friend, Luther Smith, worked at a San Francisco dance studio in exchange for lessons. For a while the two had an act, "Mo and Les." After they broke up, Williams opened a successful dance studio on San Mateo Drive and became a well-known and popular figure on the Peninsula in his own right.

Right: Barney Williams, Noah's son, became an Eagle Scout, organized Scout Troop #48 in San Mateo, and led it to great accomplishments in the late 1930s.
Below: The second grade class at Lawrence School in 1919; Eva Garrett is at the far left in the third row.

Courtesy San Mateo County Historical Museum

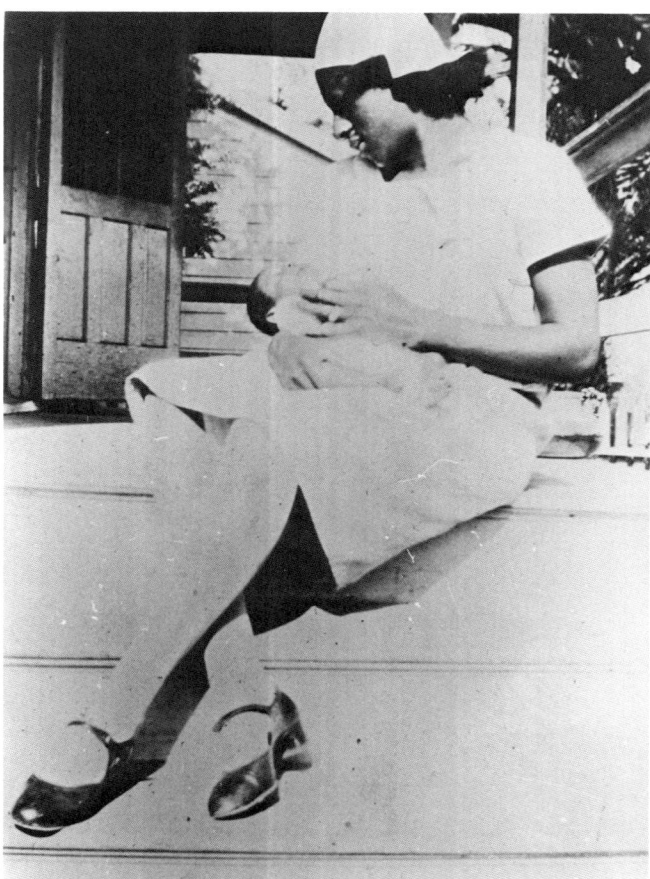

Eva Garrett Cullen, her husband Bill, and baby Lorraine lived near Third Avenue and Humboldt in 1929, when Kodak box cameras enabled anyone to take informal portraits like this one

Courtesy San Mateo County Historical Museum

FROM B TO THIRD

DURING THE 1920S AND 1930S, San Mateo's business district shifted back towards El Camino Real. Before the railroad, the County Road had been the site of most of the community's businesses. After the tracks were completed in 1863, the focus quickly shifted to B Street. Some 60 years later, with the growing popularity and affordability of the automobile, San Mateo's business section began to move back toward the highway. It did so by advancing up Third Avenue. The de Guigne family still owned most of the land between A (today's Ellsworth) and El Camino Real on the south side of Third. The development of this vital section of the downtown is credited to realtor D. A. Raybould.

D.A. or "Doc" Raybould was born in Salt Lake City in 1888. He graduated from the University of Utah, moved to the San Francisco Peninsula in 1911, and became a flying instructor at local airfields. For a time he was also the Peninsula correspondent for the *San Francisco Chronicle*. In 1917, he went to work for Paul Pinckney at the *San Mateo Times*, but later that year went to war, serving as a first lieutenant. At his suggestion, Horace Amphlett took his job at the *Times*.[24]

When he came back from the war, Raybould decided to go into real estate. In 1919, he joined M. J. Conway, a San Mateo realtor since 1912 with an office at 155 B Street. In 1922, Frederick M. Johnson joined the firm. Johnson specialized in residential property while Raybould instituted a business property department.[25]

Raybould dreamed of connecting the highway with the railroad station; he wanted to transform the narrow, unpaved Third Avenue into a high-class, 80-foot-wide thoroughfare with "Santa Barbara-type" shopping arcades, a restaurant, a hotel and a movie theater. San Mateo Drive would be extended through the property, and Fourth Avenue would run to El Camino Real. Such a move required the purchase, subdivision and development of the de Guigne estate.

Some laughed at Raybould's bold vision, but in August 1923, he arranged for Christian de Guigne's daughters, the Countess de Tristan and the Countess de Dampierre, to sell the property through Conway, Raybould and Johnson to the B. Getz Company of San Francisco for $80,000. At the time of the sale, the *San Mateo Daily News Leader* reported that Getz had already secured tenants for the theater and arranged for financing the hotel.

In June 1924, Raybould arranged for the donation of a ten-foot strip on Third from Ellsworth to El Camino Real. This gave Third Avenue an 80-foot width, allowing for diagonal parking and making it the widest business street on the Peninsula. As the Third Avenue scheme reached full speed, Raybould's firm moved a new office at 10 Third Avenue.

The first building to go up on the south side of the street (and the first concrete building in San Mateo) was the Caldwell building at 149 Third. Oddly enough, it was the only Third Avenue commercial property between El Camino and B not sold by Raybould and company. The Caldwell firm handled that first transaction and developed the property itself.

The next building to go up was a grocery store, and the third was Noah's Ark at the present site of Collins

---

The south side of Third Avenue, east of El Camino, was sold by the de Guigne family in 1923, opening the entire block to commercial development, and stealing the focus of downtown away from B Street. The Payson and Parrott parcels remained intact a little longer.

Courtesy San Mateo County Historical Museum

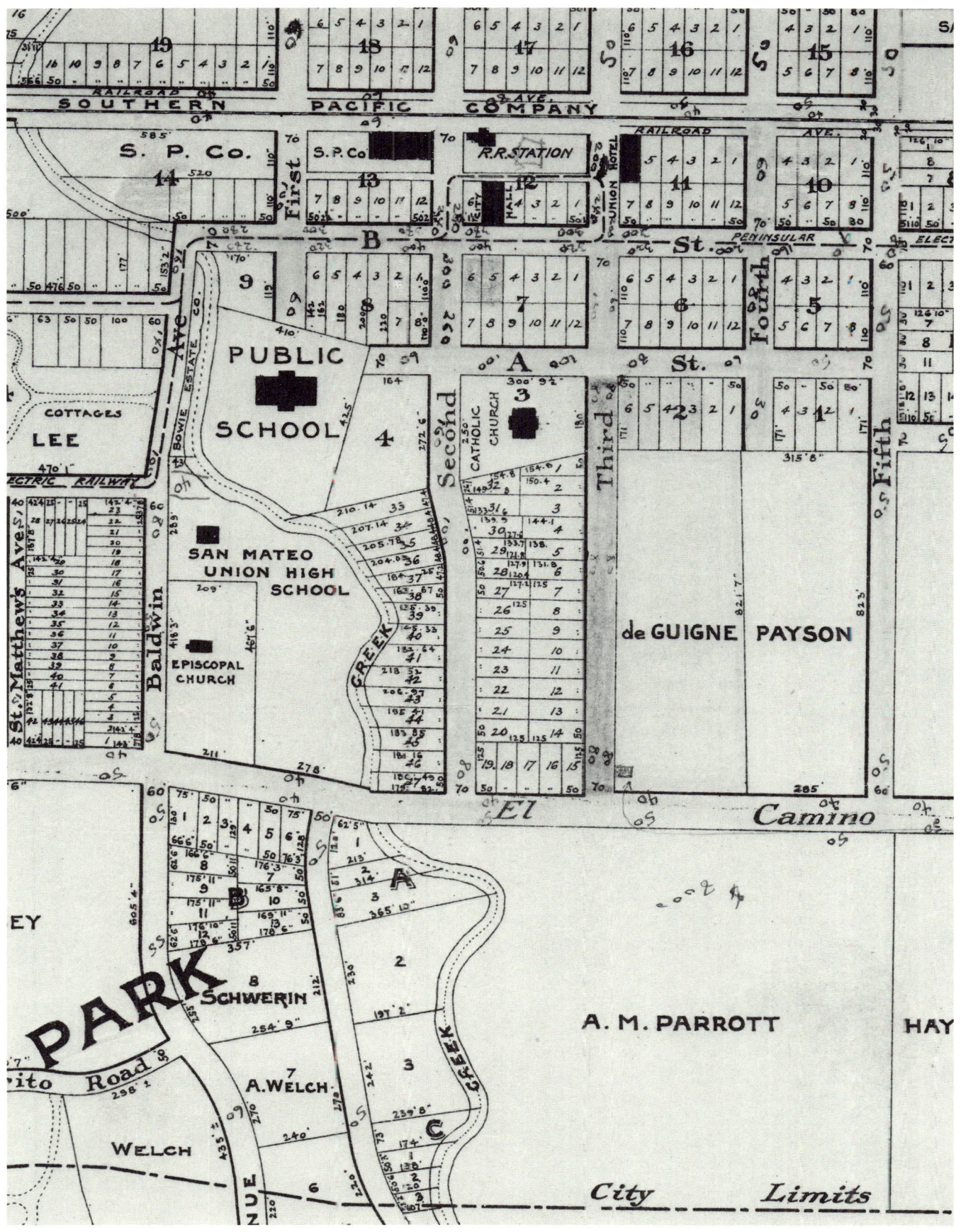

East Third Avenue was rapidly transformed in the 1920s. The Benjamin Franklin Hotel, the ornate San Mateo Theater, and Noah's Ark restaurant made the south side of the Avenue sparkle. The north side had not yet been developed.

Courtesy San Mateo County Historical Museum

Drugs on Third and San Mateo Drive. Then Standard Oil bought the parcel at Third and El Camino for $25,000 to build a service station.

By January 1925, San Mateans beheld changes they had thought impossible. The *Daily News Leader* suggested: "A person who had not been in San Mateo for three years and had not heard anything of the development during that time, would rub his eyes in amazement should he suddenly be placed in the center of Third Avenue between A Street and El Camino Real."[26] Among the new businesses were a Studebaker dealership, two grocery stores and Noah's Ark "with an investment of close to $100,000."

But the large projects had not even started. To make room for the San Mateo Theater, the old de Guigne mansion was moved to San Mateo Drive (it was demolished not long after). The movie palace cost about $250,000 to complete in 1926. Three years later its owners improved it considerably, buying equipment for motion pictures with sound.

The Benjamin Franklin Hotel was completed in 1927. Architect W. H. Weeks designed the block building: eight stories off the sidewalk, with a crowning ninth which was set back. Contractor Anton Johnson built the structure for $250,000. A. C. Franklin, president of the B. Getz Company, was the original owner. Only seven years after the destruction of the Peninsula Hotel, San Mateo had regained the status associated with having a "country" hotel—this one a much more successful endeavor.

With progress on the south side of the street in full motion, Raybould turned to the north side. To anchor the east end of the Street, the Medical Arts Building was heavily promoted. On the west end, Levy Brothers moved to 51 Third in 1931.

Edmond Levy chose the distinctive Tudor revival style of architecture to attract "people on the hill" to his upscale store. He also bought ten enclosed trucks so his employees could make deliveries anywhere on the Peninsula. Levy Brothers had everything: a grocery store in the basement; hardware, men's clothing and dry goods on the first floor, and millinery, women's clothing and toys on the upper floor. The mezzanine included a beauty shop.

Between 1931 and 1938, the north side of Third changed almost as dramatically as the south side had the previous decade. In place of a miniature golf course,

shabby buildings and open lots, brand new retail establishments sprang up, blending perfectly with the improvements across the street.

Indeed, San Mateo's commercial real estate vitality during the Depression years was unusual. In 1933 the Belmont Investment Company of Los Angeles purchased the building on the southwest corner of B and Third. The company's president, Carl H. Beal, explained why:

> We have carefully noted San Mateo's record during the Depression... and find it one of the most impressive in the United States. We cannot overlook that it leads all the prosperous Peninsula cities in building during the last five years with permits nearly reaching $7,000,000. In a city with that record, we do not think we can make a mistake when we choose the junction of B, a well established business street, with Third Avenue, which has had nearly 1000 feet of new building during the Depression years.[27]

In the early 1930s, one could park his car, rent a room, buy cigars, jewelry, or a chicken, play billiards, have lunch, and get his shoes repaired, all within about fifty feet on the west side of B Street between Second and Third Avenues.

Courtesy San Mateo County Historical Museum

In 1936, the now highly successful Raybould chose a new partner, Frank M. Bartlett, who had been in the Army Air Corps between 1917 and 1928. He came to San Mateo as an employee of the Curtiss Wright Company, which had purchased 500 acres for a flying field; today most of the land is known as Bay Meadows Race Track.

Since Raybould was also an aviator, the two made good partners. They launched a series of commercial developments along Fourth and Second Avenues, bolstering downtown San Mateo's move westward. Bartlett also became involved in civic matters, and served as President of the Chamber of Commerce for a while.

Bayshore and Third Avenue around 1930 gives no hint of the daily traffic snarls people endured sixty years later.

Courtesy San Mateo County Historical Museum

RESIDENTIAL REAL ESTATE BOOM

THE SUCCESS OF DOWNTOWN'S western expansion was the result of yet another real estate coup conceived by D. A. Raybould. In 1927, he engineered the sale of the Parrott estate for residential development, guaranteeing a new market for San Mateo's business community.

The Dunn-Williams Company of San Francisco had negotiated an option on the 375-acre parcel, but the asking price was steep, and the deal stalled. Tired of waiting for a breakthrough, Raybould approached local investors about a joint venture. He pledged $5,000, and other well-known local men such as J. E. McCurty ($10,000) and C. H. Kirkbride ($5,000), made commitments. He mustered $95,000, but was far short of the $850,000 needed. Raybould and his partners then approached their neighbor, A. P. Giannini, at his home Seven Oaks. At first, A. P. promised $200,000, but later, telling them "I will not let San Mateo and you down,"[28] he offered $650,000.

Giannini's bold move "stimulated"[29] the Dunn-Williams Company to offer $850,000 for the property. Captain Payson, president of the Parrott Investment Company, accepted the bid, and San Mateo County's greatest real estate deal, at least until that time, was done.

Almost immediately after the transaction was finished, brochures began to appear. Baywood, the promoters claimed, was a perfect residential area—close to the shops and activity of downtown, yet separate and aloof from it because of El Camino Real.

In July, listings for lots from $3,150 to $4,250 appeared. More than half the lots of the first subdivided unit were purchased in the first week. The first houses were built for affluent, professional people in the Tudor, Spanish and other revival-style architecture.

On August 5, 1928, in the midst of all the development activity, a fire destroyed the beautiful old Parrott mansion. It had been slated for demolition anyway. The house had stood since San Mateo was just a whistle stop; now it was only a memory—a part of history.

Despite its speed, the development of Baywood did not proceed without controversy. Early in 1929, the developers of Baywood Park announced plans to include a six-story office building and several shops of Spanish revival design west of El Camino. The merchants on B Street felt they already had enough competition from the Third Avenue businesses east of El Camino. New Baywood residents joined forces with the merchants, with Hein Goldman, San Francisco attorney and president of the local improvement association, heading their opposition. Since the developer's plan called for rezoning a part of West Third Avenue, the matter had to come before the City Planning Commission. After heated testimony, the Commission voted four to one against changing the zoning. D. A. Raybould cast the lone favorable vote.

But the developers did not go away. Two years later they tried again.[30] This time, the issue ended up on the ballot. In the election of November 1931, the proposed rezoning was defeated by a two-thirds majority.

The Second Homestead School served the children of San Mateo's burgeoning population in the 1930s.

Courtesy San Mateo County Historical Museum

Still, developers pretty much had their way during this era. Although it was the prevailing opinion of most San Mateans that no one would live east of the Bayshore Highway, "Doc" Raybould disagreed. He knew that new real estate opportunities would go with the new highway. So in 1926 he began buying Howard estate properties, mainly pasture and marshland. In March of 1928, as the roadway was being built through San Mateo, Raybould had already begun development of the Shoreview Tract. He also had begun commercial developments on both sides of the highway. In a perceptive move, he donated a 20-foot strip of land on both sides of the Bayshore for future widening projects. Besides Shoreview, he subdivided the Bayshore Highway Tract, Peninsula Manor, and the Howard Tract.

While Raybould was San Mateo's leading developer and real estate man during the 1920s and 1930s, he certainly was not the only one. Brisk sales continued on lots of the former Hayward estate during the 1920s. Owners built Tudor, Spanish and Colonial revival homes, as well as classic California bungalows.

Between 1922 and 1925, on the site of the Peninsula Hotel (the Hayward Mansion) the Glazenwood Tract was developed. The S. A. Born Building Company, principal owner and developer, planned a more upscale residential area, using predominantly Spanish revival architecture. Houses in the $5,000 to $13,000 range were built, larger than most of those nearby. This became San Mateo's first "restricted" real estate development: persons of certain races, national origins or religions were not welcome.[31]

Other residential developments initiated during these years included the San Mateo Villa and Bay Meadows Tracts on the east side of El Camino Real, and the Aragon, Homestead and Beresford subdivisions west of the highway. By the beginning of the 1930s, San Mateo's development was clearly marching south. The town's first shopping district outside of the downtown was built at 25th Avenue during that decade.

By 1920, the character of San Mateo as a middle-class suburban community had been established, and the rapid increase in residential areas catering to commuters made it even more so. Between 1920 and 1923, the town grew by more than 2,500 people—from 5,979 to about 8,500. Recognizing the increased demand for transportation, Southern Pacific augmented its commuter service from forty trains a day in 1921 to sixty in 1923. Street car service was also expanded. By 1923, the Three Cities Chamber of Commerce estimated that 85% of the residents of San Mateo, Hillsborough and Burlingame had a San Francisco working commuter in the family.[32]

By 1925, San Mateo's population was estimated to be 10,246, and by 1930 it was 13,444. While San Mateans owned 30 phones in 1900, they had 2,500 by 1920, and 10,000 by 1930. Enrollment in public schools increased during the 1920s from 1179 at the beginning of the decade to 1755 at its end.

At Hayward Park (formerly Homestead) School, on Fifteenth Avenue, the sixth and seventh grades show that integration seemed to be working well in 1930. The names written on the back of the picture are Chinese, Irish, German, English, Swedish, Italian, Hispanic, and French.

Courtesy San Mateo County Historical Museum

PUBLIC SCHOOLS AND THE CHALLENGES OF THE 1920S

THE INCREASE IN POPULATION during the 1920s put pressure on the school system to expand, at the elementary, high school and even junior college levels. San Mateo's educational leaders proved equal to the task.

As early as the fall of 1919, the PTA at Central School recognized its building was obsolete and launched a campaign to build a new one. Completed in 1922, it was built in a U-shape using a Spanish revival design, with eight rooms, an auditorium, an oil-burning heating system, and an electric bell and clock system. A separate building was created for seventh- and eighth-grade manual training and cosmetic science. Edward Lydon, school trustee and manager of the Beresford Country Club, planned the landscaping. In 1937, the school was renamed George Hall School in honor of the Superintendent, retiring after 43 years of service.

Also in 1922, Turnbull School at Poplar and Delaware opened. Named for school board member, William F. Turnbull, it too was built in the Spanish revival style.

In January 1923, residents southwest of town began agitating for a school in their area. Mrs. Jessie Ketchen is credited with leading the effort. Sometime around 1925, Beresford School, a one-room school house, was built. The locals called it "the school in the fields."[33] The presence of the flower industry in the area was evidenced by the fact that 50% of its students were Chinese or Japanese.

In 1924, San Mateo Park parents (northwest of El Camino Real), asked the city to turn over an old fire house to the School District so their children would not have to cross the highway. A year later, San Mateo Park School on Crescent and Clark was born as a two-room school house. Four years later it was rebuilt into a modern school.

Finally, Borel School, west of El Camino at Barneson and Shafter, was completed in 1929. Ten years later it became a junior high school.

At the beginning of the decade, Superintendent

San Mateo High School on Delaware Street, built in 1927, is almost unaltered today. When a student came up the walk toward the entrance and the clock tower, he knew he had arrived somewhere. The design and quality of construction reflect the value placed on education.

Courtesy San Mateo County Historical Museum

George Hall had three schools in his jurisdiction. By its end, he had seven, with more than 50 teachers.

One thing that did not change about George Hall's system was its emphasis on discipline. Genevieve Altieri, who went to school at Lawrence Elementary in the 1920s, recalled that "most of the teachers were unmarried," and that "they were great disciplinarians [who] took their teaching assignments very seriously." She remembered Miss Trimingham:

> A very stern woman [who] never hesitated to rap our knuckles with the ruler. She was an older woman and very tall. Her hair was pulled into a knot on top of her head.[34]

At Peninsula School, the PTA held fund-raising cantatas, operettas, and spring fiestas to help the school purchase a piano in 1923 and baseball suits in 1925. It helped build an auditorium in 1926. It also lobbied successfully for the appointment of a nurse to aid all the schools in the district.

During the early 1920s, San Mateans also took their first steps toward an institution of higher education. The state had passed the Caminetti Bill in 1907, allowing high school districts to create post-graduate curriculae.

However, it was not until 1921 that legislation was passed to finance such programs. Community leaders in the San Mateo Union High School District, such as Colonel Kirkbride, immediately organized a petition drive to create a San Mateo Junior College District. In February 1922, a ballot measure was approved, and the San Francisco Bay Area's second junior college came into existence shortly thereafter on the Baldwin Avenue high school campus.

At that time, the district superintendent was William Leon Glascock. Glascock was born in Indiana in 1883. His father had been a professor at Indiana University and a school superintendent. The younger Glascock graduated from Indiana University in 1905, took a master's degree from Stanford in 1906, and became principal of San Mateo Union High School in 1912. Glascock was a Mason, an Elk and a "progressive republican."[35]

In that first year, 1922, Glascock's college consisted of 33 students (17 of whom went out for the football team). The next year 40 students came from as far away as San Francisco on the trolley car from the north, Santa Clara County by train from the south, and the coastside by whatever means possible. No other institution like it existed on the west side of the Bay. Good students who could not afford tuition at a university now had a chance at higher education.

Because of the expanded student body, classes were held at the Baldwin campus and at the old Kohl Mansion in Central Park, six blocks away. Dorothy Dickie, a student at the time, remembered how her old jalopy, a red Essex, "always looked like a crowded cable car with riders hitching a lift to classes."[36]

Lecture classes in the old mansion were held in bedrooms with beautiful brocade wallpaper. The old study became the physics laboratory. Closets were used as offices. The kitchen became the girls' dressing room for gym class. School assemblies were held in the dining room, and dances in the living room.

Dickie recalled that the Kohl mansion originally had elaborate chandeliers, but "the prisms on the light fixtures soon disappeared, and all the students seemed to carry one for luck."

By 1924, the school had become so popular that additional classes had to meet in tents near the Kohl place. Despite crowded conditions, school spirit was high. The football team under Murius ("Furious") McFadden finished in first place in 1925, playing against four-year schools in the California Coast Conference. The baseball team was organized in 1927, and one of its original players, Bill Lawrence, eventually played for the Detroit Tigers. The basketball team won a state championship in 1928. Hessie Ballantine's bulldog, "Rival Goldstone," from her parents' Goldstone Kennels, became the school mascot. When Dorothy Dickie had a lot of blue and white crepe paper left over from a party, she donated it to the students for a dance, and blue and white became the school colors.

The success of the college and the burgeoning demands placed on the high school put pressure on the district to expand its facilities. On Armistice Day, November 11, 1926, the cornerstone was laid for a new high school on Delaware. Only a year later, the $600,000 campus opened. Now that it had a new high school campus, the district allowed the Baldwin Avenue building to become the college. A short time later the Kohl mansion was torn down.

Expanded space for the college certainly was needed. By 1927 it had an enrollment of about 400, and by 1929 it had 629.

THE CHANGING SOCIETY OF THE 1920S

THE PLACEMENT OF THE JUNIOR COLLEGE in San Mateo was indicative of the increased stature the city enjoyed during the 1920s. Its central location, progressive city government, and growing population made it the Peninsula's leader. During that decade, San Mateans continued to strengthen their existing public and private institutions and created new ones.

A shining example of this was the progress made at the city's library. Librarian Inez M. Crawford, who directed the Library between 1911 and 1937, led the successful effort to pass a bond issue to fund an expansion program which would triple the size of the library. The project was completed in two years, 1927 and 1928.

The sudden popularity and affordability of the automobile during the 1920s meant the City was constantly paving streets as subdivision after subdivision was laid out. The construction of the four-lane Bayshore Highway through San Mateo in 1928 and the completion of the San Mateo Hayward Bridge in 1929 confirmed the predominance of the car.

In the *San Mateo Times* during that decade, individual purchases of autos were covered as news stories, adding considerable social prestige to ownership. Even immigrant families like the Altieris of Grant Street bought a Buick sedan in 1926. During the 1920s, many automobile sales were handled by established merchants. The Wisnoms sold Dodges, while the Levy Brothers had the Buick dealership. Morbid evidence of how important the automobile had become is the fact that by 1930, more than a third of the deaths recorded at Mills Hospital were the result of highway accidents.

The 1920s were a very socially conscious period in San Mateo. The San Mateo Woman's Club reached a peak of popularity, and spun off two branches, the San Mateo Junior Woman's Club in 1921, and later the 20-30 Club, established to raise money for school programs. In 1924, chef Augustin Chartier opened his first restaurant in the Woman's Clubhouse at El Camino Real and Santa Inez.

For the men of the community, it became very important to be a Mason, Elk or Rotarian. The San Mateo Masonic Lodge was originally formed in Half Moon Bay in 1872, but in 1900 it moved to San Mateo. In 1903 a building committee consisting of Milton James Green, Jesse Penton, Joseph Levy and John Wisnom began planning for the creation of its imposing Temple, designed with columns said to be of the same dimensions as those of the Temple of King Solomon.

The San Mateo Woman's Club honored two former presidents: the redoubtable Elsa McGinn, in black dress and pearls, and Louise Rebele, to her left. Big hats with flowers were the rage in 1921.

Courtesy San Mateo Woman's Club

Ground was broken in 1909, and the temple was completed in 1910. By the end of the 1920s the lodge numbered 288 members from all parts of San Mateo County.

Similarly, the Elks Lodge had a significant countywide following by the 1920s. The organization was founded in 1908 with 80 members. By 1909, it owned a building on B Street.

In 1924 the city's first service club was organized. San Francisco Rotarian and San Mateo Park resident, Oscar Boldemann, of the Boldemann Chocolate Company in San Francisco, served as sponsor for the San Mateo Rotary Club and presided over its first meeting. Most of the early San Mateo members were already Elks and prominent in the community. Among the 16 original Rotarians were local attorney J. E. McCurdy, the club's first president; high school and junior college superintendent William L. Glascock; P. A. Oliver, President of the Peninsula Building and Loan Association; realtor Albert A. Rochex; Horace Amphlett of *The San Mateo Times*; Fred Beer, owner of San Mateo's Ford dealership and a mayor of San Mateo in the 1930s; Walter H. Cambridge, Rector of St. Matthew's Episcopal Church and President and Resident Manager of Mills Memorial Hospital; Robert Wisnom of the proud old family; and John R. Fairbanks, superintendent of the Leslie Salt works. The birth of the club was announced in the *Times* on January 25. It described the Rotary as "primarily . . . a group of business and professional men, who without secret vow, dogma, or creed, without question of their religion or politics, but each in his own way, have accepted the Rotary philosophy of service." This certainly distinguished it from the potpourri of secretive men's organization in the city.

In 1926, a group of San Mateo businessmen organized their own Chamber of Commerce and broke away from the Three Cities Chamber of Commerce, which had represented Burlingame, Hillsborough and San Mateo. Hugo F. Bettelheim served as its first president. Other founding members included J. E. McCurdy, M. A. Poss, Edmond Levy, Horace Amphlett, Bruce S. Gibson, and Joseph B. Gordon.

The all-Japanese Scout Troop #115, Taro Takahashi, Scoutmaster. The photograph dates from 1931.

Courtesy San Mateo County Historical Museum

By the end of the 1920s, Boy Scouting had become an important movement. In 1931, of the 24 troops in San Mateo County, seven were located in San Mateo, including one in the Beresford area.[37] Unlike many other organizations, the Boy Scouts were open to all ethnic communities of the city. Troop 115, organized about 1925, consisted of a mixed group of Italian, Japanese and other boys who met at Turnbull School.

During the early 1930s, San Mateo's first African-American Eagle Scout, Barney Williams, of the Noah Williams Family, organized Troop 48 after receiving sponsorship from a parents' committee who met with Williams at Hayward Park School. Troop 48 became one of the best in the Bay Area during the 1930s. Williams encouraged other Eagle Scouts to assume leadership positions. His boys wore a special uniform with a white and purple handkerchief. They made their own patrol flags. During the 1939 World's Fair on Treasure Island, Troop 48 scouts came in first, second or third in almost every competitive scouting event. Williams could not have been more dedicated. One year, he and his 40 boys reportedly camped out 100 nights. They took bicycle trips to San Francisco. Sometimes they visited Sutro baths or went swimming at the Fairmont Hotel swimming pool in order to work on merit badges. Many of the boys never realized that the reason their scoutmaster did not always follow them in their activities was that he was not allowed in many public places because of the color of his skin.

Racial prejudice was a very real factor during the 1920s and 1930s. A public membership drive for the Ku Klux Klan was launched in 1924, when the *San Mateo Times* carried a front page headline: "Ku Klux Klan Seeks Members in San Mateo." Applicants could write to a post office box. The tenets of the Klan were outlined, including the belief in "White Supremacy, Protection of Our Pure American Womanhood." The *Times* handled the story as if it were describing the activities of the Rotarians. There is no evidence to show how successful the Klan's membership drive was.

The *San Mateo Times* itself went through some important changes during the 1920s. Horace Amphlett took over the paper in 1920, after the death of Paul Pinckney. Amphlett, a graduate of San Mateo High School (class of 1907), had been an assistant postmaster under Thomas E. Byrnes and then an employee at the San Mateo National Bank before coming to work at the *Times* in 1917. He was also an amateur poet and playwright.

Despite his lack of experience, Amphlett proved a successful newspaper man. In 1924, he took a real chance and made the *Times* a daily in an already-competitive market, which included San Mateo's, *Daily News Leader,* the *Burlingame Advance,* and the *Burlingame Star.* All four papers vied for the same advertising dollars.

Apparently, the competition was as hard on the advertisers as it was on the newspapers. A group of businessmen formed a committee and asked that the newspapers merge. In 1926, Amphlett purchased the *Daily News Leader,* giving San Mateo one daily, while the two Burlingame papers combined about the same time.

Amphlett became one of the most influential men in San Mateo County. An outspoken leader within the business community, a member of the county's Republican Central Committee and a joiner of all kinds of clubs and associations, he based his philosophy on the premise that: "Only such newspapers as fill a definite need in the community, supporting its institutions, safeguarding its interests, and protecting its character abroad can hope to endure."[38]

Amphlett died in 1933, in his early 40s. A family trust ran the paper for ten years after that. Gradually, Amphlett's brother-in-law, J. Hart Clinton, assumed leadership of the paper.

Clinton was born in Quincy Massachusetts in 1905, graduated from Harvard Law School in 1929 and then came out West. In February 1933 he married Helen Amphlett, only nine months before her brother's death. When the Amphlett family trust terminated in 1943, Clinton was asked to take over.

The newspaper continued to thrive, even through the depths of the Great Depression. By 1940, the *Times* emerged as the county's leading newspaper, with a circulation twice that of its rival, the *Redwood City Tribune*.

In the area of health care, San Mateo also became a leader in the county. In November 1920 the San Mateo Preventorium was founded to care for children with pulmonary tuberculosis. The institution had some thirty beds. Private donations fully funded its construction. Mrs. Harry S. Dana led the fund-raising campaign. Through the years the Preventorium took great pride in handling children of the poor at no cost. It was located at Poplar Avenue and Claremont Street.

San Mateo's central location made it the right spot for the San Mateo County Community Hospital. By 1919, the County Board of Supervisors had recognized that its hospital and poor farm on Polhemus Road (built in 1891) no longer adequately provided for the needs of the county. That year they appointed a committee with a representative from each township to select a site for a new 89-bed hospital. The committee chose more than 20 acres belonging to Keyron and Margaret O'Grady in the south San Mateo area, on today's West 30th Avenue. The County purchased the property for $1,000 an acre.

Architect William Toepke designed the building, which cost $160,000 to build. Dr. Wood C. Baker became the hospital's first superintendent when it opened in 1923. County Community's original purpose was to serve patients with communicable diseases. Previously, only Isolation Hospital in San Francisco had provided that function for San Mateo County residents until 1923. A second mission for County Community was to take some pressure off Mills Hospital by accepting emergency highway accident cases.

In 1929, a nurses' residence was added to the site, and

J. Hart Clinton
Publisher of the San Mateo Times

Courtesy San Mateo County Historical Museum

in 1930 a second wing was built on the east side. By 1941 County Community had become the county's largest hospital, with some 200 beds.

During the 1920s, Mills Hospital expanded as well. In 1922, Mrs. Elizabeth Mills Reid provided funds to build a new 16-bed maternity ward on the site of the original hospital. She gave more money in 1928 to double the size of the hospital to about 125 beds. Reid thereafter made it clear that she believed the hospital should grow no more for fear "it would lose its personal touch."[39] Later appeals to acquire property and expand west of El Camino Real were not answered. Nevertheless, the presence of the hospital encouraged the establishment of nearby doctors' offices and related medical services. Eventually, the hospital would develop its facilities further.

Top: Mills Hospital was photographed in 1934 by Gabriel Moulin. Below: Mills Hospital nurses take a break in 1917.

Fabulous Failures

THE 1920S WAS A PERIOD of tremendous optimism in the United States. But while many dreams were realized, other proved too grandiose or unrealistic. These included ambitious plans to make San Mateo the home of movie studios to rival Hollywood, a scheme to create a Coney Island of the West at Coyote Point, and a quest to make San Mateo a center of aviation activity.

Movie making in San Mateo can actually be traced back to the endeavors of Sadie Lindblom before World War I. She had small studios located on B Street, but her venture lasted only a year or two until her funds ran out.

A much more ambitious project—to make San Mateo the next Hollywood—was promoted after World War I. Various politicians and civic groups lined up behind the idea. Organizers included such well-known San Mateo public officials as J. J. McGrath, who encouraged locals to buy $100 shares in what came to be known as Pacific Studios.[40] San Francisco Mayor James Rolph also pushed the project.

Bay Area investors felt that Southern California had been "shot to pieces"[41] and too many locations had to be "faked" in order to look like other sections of the country. Because most films were produced with rented equipment and facilities, it was believed that a fully-functioning studio at San Mateo would easily attract movie makers: San Mateo would become another Niles Canyon across the Bay, where some years before Charlie

Chaplin had made films before moving to Hollywood.

A 103-acre parcel was purchased for the complex, east of the railroad tracks, facing Peninsula Avenue in North San Mateo. Construction began at the end of 1920. According to its publicity managers, Pacific Studios would eventually accommodate 24 production companies. Architects for the project were Roy Purnel and Harold Stoner. John Jasper, who had quite a bit of Hollywood experience, was director of general production. About $500,000 worth of construction was completed, including two four-story film stage units with special effects equipment and film labs.

Unfortunately, only a handful of films were ever shot at Pacific Studios. Perhaps the most famous was "White Hands," a 35-mm, six-reeler completed in 1922 by Producer Max Graf and Director-Writer Lambert Hillyer. The cast included Hobart Bosworth as 'Hurricane Hardy," and Robert McKim, Elinor Fair and Freeman Wood. The America Film Institute describes the film as a melodrama featuring the evil sea captain, "Hurricane Hardy," who intends to do harm to a missionary girl while searching for treasure. However, the "White Hands" of a child (Baby Muriel) stop him, and he reforms. Location shooting included scenes at Coyote Point and San Francisco's Ocean Beach.

"White Hands" premiered at the Garden Theater in Burlingame and reportedly drew great crowds, but by and large, the Pacific Studios were a failure. As an independent, Pacific did not have the distribution outlets that its Hollywood competitors had. Pacific also lacked enough business to attract the necessary cadre of actors and technicians. After going through a string of owners, the studio finally shut down in 1929. The administration building and other structures once belonging to the studios still stand at 430 Peninsula.

NOT FAR FROM the Pacific Studios, David Stollery, the manager of the Howard Estate Company, envisioned Coyote Point as a sort of a grand amusement park. On June 28, 1921, the Three Cities Chamber of Commerce, with San Matean Fred Beer as Chairman, endorsed the idea. A group of investors formed the Pacific City Corporation and raised $100,000 to purchase 90 acres on the northwest side of the Point and 250 acres of submerged land.[42] According to *The San Mateo Times* of September 10, 1921, they intended to create a park that would rival New York's Coney Island.

In March 1922, Pacific City Corporation staged a dedication ceremony, celebrating the completion of the boardwalk. San Mateo Mayor Thomas J. Brady, Burlingame Trustee Frank Lindsay and David Stollery, representing the corporation, participated in a spike-driving contest. San Francisco Mayor James Rolph sent an airplane carrying three gold spikes over Coyote Point at 2 o'clock in the afternoon. A bag with the spikes was dropped on the boardwalk, and the contest began. Mayor Brady was the victor.

By late Spring 1922, $10,000 worth of lawns, shrubs and trees had been planted. Streets were laid out, water and sewage hookups were installed and a $60,000 dance pavilion was completed. Charles W. Iverson, proprietor of the Tarpin Hotel in San Francisco, installed the dance floor, which measured 125' x 80'. C. H. McFadden, dance director for 15 years in Oakland, took over that professional position at Pacific City, and Herman Heller, the most popular musical director in the city, resigned from the California Theater in San Francisco to become musical director. A ferris wheel and smaller rides, a railway, restaurants, concession stands and game booths were already in place. Nearing completion were the bath house, band stand, a 30-foot pier, a playground and the remainder of the electrical work. Tons of white sand from Santa Cruz were poured over the beach. Contracts with ferry boats and shuttle bus companies were signed.

Finally, on July 1, the Pacific City Company and the Three City Chamber of Commerce staged the formal opening. Some 27,000 people attended the first day. Another 51,000 came the next, and, on July 4, park officials counted 100,000 visitors.

From the early indications, Pacific City seemed a success. Genevieve Altieri remembered the spectacular nature of the place as a little girl: "There was a very big Ferris Wheel, a Merry-go-Round, a Punch and Judy Show and a band that played such lovely music." She also recalled "a very high slide." Meanwhile on the beach:

> Everywhere . . . were bright parasols, women and girls wore colorful Japanese Kimonos. The beach was alive with color. Everything had a restful festive feel, and as usual Mama brought along enough food to feed an Army.[43]

When Pacific City closed for the winter on November 12, 1922, the Company claimed to have had one million visitors in its first season. Plans for 1923 were already in the making. When the park reopened on May 19, the great roller coaster, "The Comet," billed as the second largest roller coaster in the United States, was ready to thrill the public.

But in the second season, the crowds diminished. Because of contamination from the growing bayside cities of Burlingame and San Mateo, swimming in the bay water had to be restricted. Competition from Playland in San Francisco and Neptune Beach across the bay hurt too. Money problems added up. A damaging fire in August did not help. When Pacific City closed for the winter in 1923, it did so for good. In 1925, the Howard family bought the property back for $188,000. For years huge remnants of Pacific City stood to remind San

Above: In the drying room at Pacific Studios, F. H. Thomason (center) hangs film on a huge spool to dry.

Left: the main entrance to Pacific Studios in 1920.

Courtesy San Mateo County Historical Museum

Above: The premiere of "White Hands" at the Garden Theater in Burlingame in 1922 drew a huge crowd, including two boys in knickers and caps. People apparently didn't worry about bicycle thieves.

Right: Hobert Bosworth draws a bead on Baby Muriel, who seems to have risen out of a very large vase.

Courtesy San Mateo County Historical Museum

Pacific City Amusement Park, northwest of Coyote Point, had a roller coaster, ferris wheel, dance pavilion (the domed structure at center) and a grand gateway in 1923. Ferryboats brought throngs of passengers from San Francisco and the East Bay to the pier for a day of pleasure.

Courtesy San Mateo County Historical Museum

Mateans of this failed venture. "The Comet" was finally torn down in 1933; the dance hall stood until 1946.[44]

San Mateo's ventures into aviation failed as well. Aircraft landed at the site of today's Bay Meadows even before the 1920s. In 1921, Walter Varney (later a founder of United Airlines), built a hangar. "Speed" Johnson took over the field in 1925, and in 1929 the Curtiss-Wright Company purchased Johnson's field and other properties in the vicinity to create a proper airport. Plans called for the expenditure of millions of dollars on the development of a flying school, shops, and a terminal for commercial flights. Curtiss-Wright assigned Captain Frank M. Bartlett to the project. Under his management two important Chinese pilots of World War II received training. General Woo Gan became chief of staff of the Chinese Air Force at Canton, and General Wong King Yue became commander of the entire Chinese Army Air Corps.[45]

But the Curtiss-Wright venture never made it. Competition from Mills Field, which had the City of San Francisco's financial backing, was bad enough before the Great Depression—after its onset, the viability of aviation was in question even at Mills. The Bay Meadows field was certainly doomed.

While the major portion of the Bay Meadows property became a horse racing track in the 1930s, an airfield of sorts existed into the 1940s. It was owned and operated by the track's founder, William P. Kyne. Another field, San Mateo Airport, existed east of the Bayshore Highway in today's Parkside residential area. For a while it was owned by "the two flying dentists,"[46] Dr. Joseph Lorenze and Dr. Cecil Smith. Both the San Mateo and Bay Meadows' fields were shut down after World War II because their flight patterns conflicted with various other local airports.

THE BRIDGE TO HAYWARD

NOT ALL THE SPECTACULAR IDEAS of the 1920s ended in failure. Since the early part of that decade, San Mateo leaders had discussed the need for a bridge to span the Bay and link the Peninsula with East Bay communities and the Central Valley. Even though the Dumbarton Bridge opened in 1927, there was still hope that a bridge would be built to San Mateo.

In 1923 the Three Cities Chamber of Commerce began an organized campaign toward that end. The Chamber explained that a bridge from Hayward to Little Coyote Point would connect the most northerly points on the Bay where the War Department would allow the building of a low-level bridge. The Chamber also pointed out that a bridge to Hayward would provide ready access to the Dublin Canyon, dubbed "the gateway to the two great river valleys,"[47] the Sacramento and San Joaquin. Finally, proponents claimed, the proposed route over bay waters presented relatively few engineering difficulties.

One of the necessary topographical changes was the blasting and removal of the knoll at Little Coyote Point. The Chamber's Secretary-Manager, D. C. Imboden, consulted with engineering firms on the West Coast and then went to New York City to get the advice of an old friend, John A. Bensel, State Engineer of New York. Bensel was interested in taking on the job himself, but he died just before a scheduled trip to California. An associate of his, Frank E. Webb, came to the Bay Area to pick up the pieces. He secured a franchise from the San Mateo County Board of Supervisors and a permit from the War Department to construct the bridge, but he was not able to secure financing, even after fund raising trips to San Francisco, Los Angeles and New York. He turned over the franchise to another engineer, Frank C. Towns of New York, who was associated with A. W. Devel.

While the engineering seemed matter-of-fact, it would require the building of a bridge more than seven miles in length. When completed, it would be the longest continual vertical lift highway bridge in the world, and it would cost $7.5 million.

In those days, before massive government building programs, the financing for this endeavor would have to come from private sources. Finally, banks in San Francisco, Los Angeles, New York and Boston were talked into supporting the endeavor. In September, 1927, in Wilmington, Delaware, the San Francisco Bay Toll-Bridge Company was incorporated, headed by attorney John T. Williams. A new fifty-year franchise was worked out with the San Mateo County Board of Supervisors.

The bridge was designed as a cantilevered span with a 300-foot-wide "Gothic" draw section over the shipping channel. The lift went up 35 feet, allowing for a 135-foot clearance. At first, the Three Cities Chamber pushed for a connection with the bridge approach at Ninth Avenue and Bayshore Highway. The idea was dropped, however, and the interchange was planned for Third Avenue and the Bayshore.

The construction contract was awarded on December 16, 1923. The bridge required 10,350 tons of reinforcing steel and 2,910 tons of structural steel. Local companies provided construction materials for the huge undertaking.

Cement for the piles and deck slabs came from Redwood City, where ancient oyster shells dredged from the Bay became part of the mix, prompting the County's premier promoter, Roscoe Wyatt, to call it "the bridge the oysters built."

Construction began on both sides of the Bay with the first pilings being driven into the mud on March 1, 1928. The Bethlehem Ship Building Corporation at Alameda precast the piles and floated them down the bay by barge. Altogether, 4854 piles were driven to support the bridge's deck. Bethlehem also fabricated the 35-foot,

The construction of the San Mateo - Hayward Bridge began in March 1928; only three months later, the piers and caps were in place (left), ready for placing the roadway slabs. Then the immense drawbridge sections (above) were barged into place.

Courtesy San Mateo County Historical Museum

reinforced concrete deck slabs and barged these 45-to 54-ton sections down the bay to be lifted onto the piles.

The greatest construction challenge was installing five huge central steel spans. They were manufactured in South San Francisco. The largest, middle span, was 303 feet long and weighed 613 tons. These sections were put in place with the help of "moon power." At high tide they were barged down and positioned on their piers. As the tide receded, the spans gently sank into position.

The pace of building was torrid. At one point, construction was being carried on at ten different places. Amazingly, there was only one fatality: field engineer J. R. Janson fell 57 feet on to a concrete pile.

When the two halves of the bridge finally converged in the middle of the bay, the alignment was only 1/16 inch off—a significant accomplishment. The bridge was completed in only fourteen months, four months ahead of schedule.

On Saturday, March 2, 1929, San Mateans enjoyed one of the greatest celebrations in the history of the city with the dedication of what was then called the San Francisco Bay Toll Bridge. Festivities began with a luncheon at the new Benjamin Franklin Hotel. City Attorney and well-known clubman, J. E. McCurcy, gave the keynote address. A parade began with the Stanford University Band leading a horde of officials from El Camino and Third Avenue down to Bayshore Boulevard.

At Bayshore and Third the official program commenced. The two masters of ceremonies were Horace Amphlett, chairman of the San Mateo County Bridge Committee, and I. B. Parsons, chairman of the Alameda contingent. The crowd endured an hour of speeches by such dignitaries as James Rolph, Mayor of San Francisco, Major General John Hines of the Ninth Army Corps, and Admiral Thomas G. Washington, commander of the 12th Naval District.

After the speeches, precisely at 3:30 p.m. Pacific time (6:30 in Washington, D. C.), President Calvin Coolidge pressed a button signaling the opening of the bridge. A bomb went off, releasing a gigantic American flag. Then the 91st Observation Squadron of the United States Army thrilled the crowd with an aerial show. Finally Miss Rae Wantland, secretary of the Bridge Company, cut the ribbon.

San Mateo Mayor Aylett Cotton had the honor of being the first to cross the bridge. Other dignitaries followed, and then the public was allowed to motor

On March 2, 1929, the bridge opened with a huge celebration, just one year after construction began. But after the excitement died down, traffic was much lighter than anyone expected.

Courtesy San Mateo County Historical Museum

On opening day in 1929, the Army Air Corps flew five biplanes over the bridge in tight formation; they are visible over the canal bordering Brewer's Island, today's Foster City.

Courtesy San Mateo County Historical Museum

across, free of charge, from 4:00 to midnight. It was estimated some 12,000 did so, lumbering across the new span three abreast. The next day, some 63,000 motorists crossed the bridge. Police reported at least 16 minor accidents, mostly rear-enders.

Horse drawn vehicles were originally allowed to cross the bridge, but even in the early years, bridge employee Alfred Luis remembered that only about four or five a year would make use of it. During hay baling season, hay wagons took three hours to make the crossing, even at night, when traffic was light.[48]

While the construction of the bridge was a tremendous success, its financial operation was not. Despite its novelty, the bridge lost $232,500 in its first year, and things got worse after that. Need for the bridge simply had not developed to the point where a profit could be made. The Great Depression, which almost immediately followed the bridge's completion, did not help bridge finances. A Richfield service station and a restaurant had been built at the toll plaza, but while the gas station proved a valuable fixture, the restaurant never opened and became offices for the bridge's staff.

William S. Rothrock, who went to work as an auditor for the bridge company in 1927 and worked his way up to bridge manager by 1940, recalled that various promotional campaigns were hatched to attract people to the bridge. The company's slogan, "Cross the Bay the Fastest way," graced signs from Grant's Pass to Los Angeles. During the summer, Rothrock and his wife drove into the hot Central Valley with brochures advertising the cooler coast, encouraging people to come west for rest and a dip in the ocean. They distributed cases full of the folders at gas stations. Another device was the "Follow the Orange Line." campaign. The company painted an orange stripe on the highway from Dublin Canyon across the bridge to Crystal Springs Road.

Despite such efforts, the average daily traffic—2,000 vehicles in 1929—dropped off significantly as the Depression rolled on. By 1935, the toll for a regular

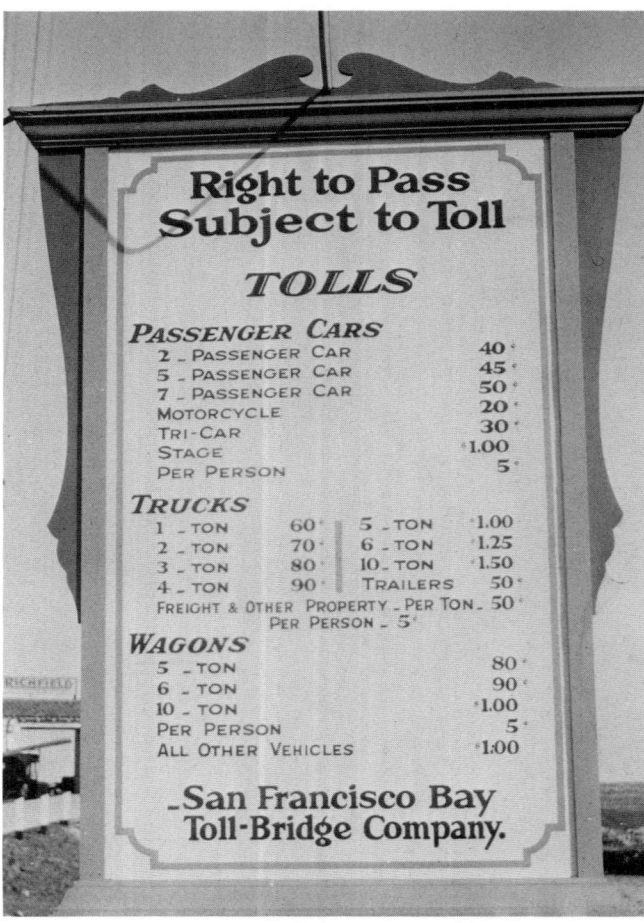

The initial tolls for crossing the bridge were modest, but had to be lowered later.

Courtesy San Mateo County Historical Museum

automobile was lowered to 35¢ in order to lure more travelers.

Originally, the bridge had lights similar to city street lamps. Rothrock remembered: "they worked fine too [but] in wet weather they made reflections on the pavement." This caused a light and shadow problem that particularly annoyed truckers. Rothrock told the fate of the offending lights:

> The truck drivers didn't like it, so they just carried .38s and shot [the lights] out. For a while we replaced them, but finally we gave up.[49]

The San Francisco Bay Toll Bridge Company operated the bridge until it was bought out by the state in 1951. Ironically, this was just at the time when increased development in the San Francisco Bay Area finally made the bridge profitable.

THE BLUES

IF PACIFIC STUDIOS, Pacific City and the new bridge were symbols of San Mateo during the 1920s, so was its very own baseball team, the San Mateo Blues.

As far back as stagecoach days, San Mateo youngsters played baseball. By 1924, a men's team, known simply as the San Mateo team, got together to play other local clubs. In 1924, a semi-pro Californian League was founded by baseball enthusiasts including San Mateo's Justin Fitzgerald. The new San Mateo team was named the Blues; Fitzgerald himself managed it for its first ten years.

Perhaps no San Matean evidenced the true spirit of baseball better than Justin Fitzgerald. Born in San Mateo in 1893, "Fitz" went to Santa Clara University, where he became known as a talented left-handed fielder. He came to the attention of the pro scouts, who recognized his considerable hitting and defensive abilities.

In 1911, just out of high school, he signed with the New York Yankees. But the promise of a brilliant career faded with an unfortunate injury. During a game early in the season, Fitz charged a ball from center field, picked up the line drive on one hop and hurled it home in time to throw out a base runner heading in to home plate. It was a spectacular play, but Fitz felt something snap in his arm the instant he let the ball go. From that time on, although he remained a great hitter and fielder, he had a "dead arm," limiting his value to any team.

In 1912 he was picked up by Portland, of the Pacific Coast League. After two seasons there he was sold to the San Francisco Seals, with whom he spent eight successful years. The team's Recreation Park was ideal for him. It had a short right field fence, which meant shorter throws; his weak arm was much less a detriment and his hitting continued to be sharp. In 1916, in fact, he won the Pacific League batting championship with a .316 average.

Such accomplishments were not wasted on pro scouts; in 1918 Fitz found himself back in the big leagues. Manager Pat Moran of the Philadelphia Phillies seldom played Fitz in the field because of his bad arm, but used him as a pinch hitter. Fitz kept a batting average of over .290.

In the midst of the 1918 campaign, Fitz married the socially prominent Ruth Wooley of Salt Lake City and returned to the Seals the next year under manager Charley Graham. There was plenty of baseball left in this San Matean. In 1920 he had his biggest year as a hitter, with a .336 batting average. He played with the Seals until 1922. In every year that he was with that club (1914-1917 and 1919-1922), he was counted among the league's top five hitters, batting over .300 in all those seasons except for the last. He also stole 40 to 50 bases every year he was with the Seals. In 1923, Fitz found himself back in Portland where he played for a brief time. Then he was traded to Salt Lake City, but refused to report there. He finished out his career in Sacramento and retired before the 1924 season.

As manager of the Blues, Fitz became an inspiration to those he coached. Sports editor Harvey Rockwell of the *San Mateo Times* described him as "quiet, studious, gentlemanly and tolerant, with a kind sense of humor." Rockwell claimed that the boys who played for him "felt a personal allegiance" to the man.

Fitz's popularity extended outside of the world of baseball. After returning to San Mateo he became quite a community leader. He even sat on the City Council for a few years.

The Blues played at Central Park. About the time the field got its night lights, in 1935, Fitz left the Blues to return to Santa Clara University as coach. He also scouted for the Detroit Tigers, and, eventually, for the Brooklyn Dodgers.

The Blues received their first major-league

Justin Fitzgerald and the San Mateo Blues, early 1920s.
Courtesy San Mateo County Historical Museum

In 1931 the Levy Brothers' beautiful new store on Third Avenue supplied groceries, liquors, gifts and housewares to the carriage trade. Some of the carriages now had rumble seats.   Courtesy San Mateo County Historical Museum

sponsorship in 1941, when the Brooklyn Dodgers took an interest. While the team was dormant during World War II, it was revived in 1948 by manager Paul Thiebaut and lasted another thirty years.

Fitz did not live to see the resurrection of the Blues. He died of a stomach disorder in 1945 at the age of 52. From that time on, baseball players and fans called the field at Central Park Fitzgerald Field in his honor. On August 21, 1960, the City of San Mateo made what had been an informal name an official title. More than a thousand people were on hand for the dedication of Fitzgerald Field. An editorial in the *San Mateo Times* remembered Fitz "as a man, small of stature and big of heart; short on words and long on action."

FROM TOWN TO CITY

DURING THE 1920S San Mateo changed dramatically from town to city. Its municipal services were significantly upgraded, and other public and private institutions followed suit. Grand plans for the future were hatched. Some failed, some succeeded. While there was little industry, San Mateo's health care institutions, social organizations, modern retail outlets and junior college made it the focal point of the Peninsula. Its status was symbolized by grand downtown buildings such as the Benjamin Franklin Hotel, San Mateo Theater and Levy Brothers Store. At the end of the decade its motto was "San Mateo, the City of Beautiful Homes"[50] With something like 85% of its working adults com-muting to San Francisco, San Mateo had fully become a suburb.

Still a common fixture were the old fashioned peddlers, selling produce, ice, ice cream, fish and baked goods, or offering services such as mattress packing, photography and dress making. Genevieve Altieri remembered a popcorn-and-peanuts man in a musical wagon:

> We could smell the hot roasted peanuts a block away. This vehicle was very unique; it was like a miniature glass house on wheels. A chimney went through an opening on the roof of this glass house and smoke came out of it.[51]

Also lingering around town were a variety of hobos and tramps. They were mostly regarded as harmless, asking for a meal in exchange for doing a little work. Altieri commented: "Mama fed many, and she would put them to work washing windows or digging up weeds."[52]

The Levy Brothers' shiny new delivery van and nattily dressed driver were a big change from the horse and wagon days.
Courtesy San Mateo County Historical Museum

Less popular were the colorful gypsies, regarded by some as "somewhat of a menace . . . nearly everyone feared them."[53]

> They would arrive with much fanfare. They sang and danced and played their tambourines and stepped in front of people as they walked on the sidewalks. They begged for money and insisted on reading palms.

An occasional circus came to town in those days. Off the train would come a parade of elephants, horses and a long line of brilliantly decorated wagons filled with "fierce looking lions and tigers and nervous monkeys." To Altieri, a little girl at the time, it seemed the parade lasted for hours.[54] Then, out in a field near Peninsula Avenue and Delaware Street, the children would watch the men erect the huge circus tents with the thrilling roar of the big cats in the background.

Even the telephone seemed a throwback to the old days. At the Altieri house, the phone was square and black and hung on the wall. There was no dial: "...whenever the receiver was lifted off the hook a voice would call out either 'Central' or 'Operator' or sometimes the voice would say 'Number please?'" The operator was always a woman, "and the greeting she gave would depend on the mood she was in." Of course the telephone was considered a "very serious instrument" to adults, but to kids "it was a toy...Funny how the operator in those days knew exactly who was calling so they were able to quickly trace the offending party."[55]

When the circus wasn't in town, perhaps the most popular place for children was Pantages Candy Store at 144 B Street. John Pantages made his own candy, and served up milkshakes and ice cream cones as well.[56]

For teenagers football was rapidly becoming the biggest thing on campus. Perhaps the greatest football moment in San Mateo High School history came on December 28, 1926, when the team played Covina High School of Southern California for the state championship and won 20 to 0.

CITY POLITICS OF THE 20S AND 30S

DURING THE 1920S AND 1930S, San Mateo's political leaders made crucial decisions in charting the course of the city. The era was highlighted by a number of successful bond issues, annexations, a progressive zoning

The Belmont Building brought refinement to the southwest corner of Third and B in 1933. Carefully restored after the 1989 Earthquake, it now holds a pizza restaurant.
Courtesy San Mateo County Historical Museum

ordinance, and a generally well-run municipal body. On the negative side were a series of squabbles that reached disturbing proportions.

San Mateo became a political town because of its prominence in the county. Many of the important social institutions such as Masons and Elks made their headquarters there. Some, such as the New Deal Club, had political interests. Despite San Mateo's lack of industry, the labor unions began meeting there, and built a headquarters, the Labor Temple, at 709 South B. By 1924, such organizations as the San Mateo County Building Trades Council, Carpenters Union, Hod Carriers' and Cement Laborers' Union, Electrical Workers' Union, Labor Council, Lathers' Union, Painters' Union, Sheet Metal Union, Plaster and Cement Finishers, and Teamsters' Union all gathered at this location. As the Great Depression dragged on, activities at the Temple became increasingly important.

As the 1920s and 1930s wore on, San Mateo County in general suffered through a period (that would last until the post-war era) of allowing election of sub-par officials to government. Some came under the influence of corrupt elements such as bootleggers and gamblers. While San Mateo seemed more immune to this trend than other Peninsula cities, it still had some shifty characters. One of the most controversial was James McGrath, who served as County Sheriff for five terms until he was finally voted out in 1950.

McGrath was born in New York City in 1892, but grew up in San Mateo, where his father ran a saddlery shop. On January 11, 1916, he became postmaster of San Mateo, an appointed position not governed by civil service regulations. While serving as postmaster, McGrath also worked as a mechanic in South San Francisco. He cultivated a wide range of friendships, joining the Elks Lodge and other civic organizations. In 1927, when Sheriff Brick McGovern died, McGrath saw a new political opportunity for himself. Because he had no law enforcement experience he called on his powerful friends to help him, and they managed to get him elected. Among these influential supporters was fellow Elk, Horace Amphlett of the *San Mateo Times*.

While his entire 23-year administration was "fraught with problems,"[57] rarely was there an outcry against him. The County's law enforcement capabilities were at times laughable, and while McGrath was rightly held responsible, the various Boards of Supervisors of the period provided little in the way of support to help reverse the situation, and the electorate kept putting the Sheriff back in office.

But they sometimes had no choice: McGrath was opposed in 1934 by powerful gambling boss John Marchbank of Daly City. Instead of running on a righteous clean-government platform, McGrath enlisted the help of his old friend Emilio Georgetti, a well known South San Francisco bookie, who was rumored to have "east coast connections." Marchbank was out.

On the other hand, San Mateo generated some pretty good political leaders too. Among the best of this period was Aylett Cotton, who, despite his high social status, became known as a champion of the underdog.

Cotton had played a role in cleaning up San Francisco politics. In 1909 he helped elect reform-minded Charles Fickert to the office of District Attorney. Cotton then served as Fickert's assistant from 1910 until 1920, when Cotton went into practice for himself.

While Horace Amphlett must assume part of the responsibility for giving San Mateo County Jim McGrath, he can take credit for helping convince Cotton to run for San Mateo City Council, the same year McGrath ran for sheriff, 1927.[58]

Cotton's driving concern during his early days in office was to push the city limits southward, with the slogan: "Extend San Mateo to Belmont!" Retired residents in the Beresford area resisted the campaign, fearing their taxes would go up. But Cotton argued that their property would become more valuable. He also promised better police protection. Because Beresford was outside Police Chief Burke's authority, Sheriff McGrath had responsibility for law enforcement. (Cotton later claimed that murders reported and unreported occurred there almost weekly, and that the area was infested with bootleggers, who vigorously opposed his annexation plan.) After a "tremendous election battle,"[59] Cotton's forces won the day. In 1929, the Aragon and Beresford sections became part of the city. In 1934, toward the end of his City Council days, he also pushed through the annexation of Bay Meadows and other property east of the Bayshore Highway.

As Mayor and Councilman, Cotton presided over many of the most important events of the era. He rode a steamroller at the ground-breaking ceremonies for the extension of West Third Avenue through Baywood. He cut the ribbon extending Bayshore Highway south from San Mateo. He participated in the opening of Bay Meadows Race Track. He helped with the campaign to lay out a municipal golf course near Coyote Point.

Cotton also became embroiled in a series of political tussles. One centered on the appointive positions of city manager, police judge and city attorney. The squabbling started in the spring of 1929 when rumors of dishonesty began to circulate about one-time town trustee and current police judge George A. Kertell. Well-known citizens such as Carl W. Elfving and Herbert A. Thayer

Aylett Cotton
Courtesy San Mateo County Historical Museum

wrote letters to the council attesting to Kertell's "absolute"[60] and "unquestionable"[61] honesty.

Nevertheless, in November 1929 the Council voted four to one to ask for Kertell's resignation (M.A. Poss opposed councilmen Taylor, Cotton, Sharon and Brady) effective December 31, 1929. In the meantime, on December 10, an audit proved Kertell had done nothing wrong. This did not sway the Council. Kertell was out.[62]

The Council also fired City Manager, Oscar F. Weissgerber, and appointed James Mulryan in his place. Weissgerber then ran for state assembly, but in the Republican primary of August 1930, he was crushed by Harry L. Pullman, 11,933 to 2,283. Weissgerberg was outraged. Even San Mateans had rejected him 2,103 to 495.

He moved to Southern California but kept track of the doings in San Mateo, hoping to return one day if politics changed. In February 1931, he wrote a personal letter to Kertell, analyzing what had happened to them:

> The one thing that I cannot forgive Taylor is that he as a Mason did not talk to both of us as a Mason and let us know in time so that we could

prepare ourselves. You can see through the whole deal in that it is a case of the Irish wanting to control and Taylor ought to see it by now. The whole deal is the Masons against the Irish and Taylor had better be told that now. That has been San Mateo's political background for years, you know that.[63]

In April, when Aylett Cotton was running for re-election, Weissgerber came across an ad put out by Cotton listing his accomplishments. Weissgerber commented: "They are a joke to me as Cotton never had an original idea in his life, and if it were not for some dead relatives he would not be where he is today." As for Colonel Charles N. Kirkbride, who apparently was also a political enemy: "He gives me a pain in the neck."[64]

In the election of April 1931, Cotton ran as a ticket with political allies Charles Cheney and John Casey, exhorting citizens to vote for "the three C's." They were also known as the candidates of the Citizens and Taxpayers League, and enjoyed strong support from City Manager Mulryan. The Cs won, while M. A. Poss of the old guard—the only councilmember who had opposed Kertell's ouster—was knocked out of office. One of their first moves was to remove J. E. McCurdy from his post as City Attorney.

Colonel Kirkbride had been City Attorney from San Mateo's incorporation until 1924, excepting his time in the Army during World War I. In 1924, he was replaced by McCurdy. Now in 1931, the pendulum had swung back. The Council appointed Kirkbride's law partner, Ernest A. Wilson, as City Attorney. Wilson held the office until 1946.

With the departure of McCurdy, the new council needed to reassure people that they had no intention of engineering a total "clean out" of the city's government. They made it plain that they would not threaten the popular chiefs—Burke of the police and Morris of the fire department.

In 1933 a new "independent" coalition won control of the council, ushering new allies Justin Fitzgerald and Emil Stein to the side of incumbent Charles Cheney. In 1935, Governor Frank F. Merian appointed Aylett Cotton to the Superior Court after the death of Judge Franklin Swart. He left the city council but continued to have an influence at the county level.

San Mateo's water supply was a hot political issue during the 1920s and 1930s. Before 1920, the City leaders had debated whether the town should own its own supply, but the argument was never resolved. In 1929, San Mateo could have bought the properties of the Pacific Water Company for $235,000, but the council failed to act. Instead, the California Water Service Company purchased San Mateo's water supply, along with several other holdings of the Pacific Water Company, in February, 1931. The state railroad commission fixed the price of the San Mateo property at $1,194,747. By December 1935, the California Water Service Company had spent $140,000 improving the system.

In early 1936, Mayor Frank Simmen called together a citizens' committee to reopen the question of purchasing the system.[65] In 1939 and 1940, Simmen continued to encourage San Mateans to make the move, but no action was ever taken. San Mateo's water supply is still owned by the California Water Service Company.

There was more direct action with the city's sewer system. By 1934, the system had become woefully inadequate. Its south outfall was a terrible threat to health, at one location running through an open ditch just east of the Bayshore Highway before dumping into Seal Slough. The outfall to the north was disgraceful as well. It had been built to accommodate 5,000 people, but was handling the waste of 10,000. The treatment plant would overload, and raw sewage often spill into the bay. The State Board of Health began investigating the matter, but in the November election, San Mateo voters approved an $85,000 bond issue, which was matched by a $38,000 grant from the federal government, to remedy the situation. The town of Hillsborough contributed another $18,000 toward the project, giving the City $141,000 to work with.

Another major step forward was the passage of a zoning ordinance in 1937 that helped plan the city's future. This provided four classes of land use: residential, commercial, light industrial, and heavy industrial, although no land was ever designated for the last classification.

During the 1920s and 1930s, despite rocky infighting, the city seems to have been efficiently run, with adequate services for the people. Even during fiscal year 1937-1938, widely regarded as the worst year of the nationwide Depression, San Mateo balanced its budget. Although disbursements for the entire year added up to only $365,654, that was enough money in those days for a wide variety of services. The police department received $44,528 (12% of the budget) and the fire department needed $41,671 (11%). There was also enough money for the library ($20,224, 6% of the budget) and recreation ($38,377, 10%).

Among the facilities supported by the recreation budget was a golf course. The municipal course out near Coyote Point was made possible through a work relief project in 1932. (Because it was laid out on a marshland, a special drainage system had to be installed.) Golf pro Jack Hart was hired by the city to run the operation.[66]

With two large parks—Central Park and the 19.5-acre

San Mateo dedicated a new Civic Center in 1940; originally built as Central School, the building was converted to offices, and a fire station was added (left).

Courtesy San Mateo County Historical Museum

Beresford Park—and a golf course now in its possession, the city passed an ordinance in November 1937 to create the grand position of Superintendent of Parks, Playing Fields, Golf Courses, Parkways, Street Islands and Trees. Stanley P. Pitcher was appointed to fill the position. Under Pitcher, many improvements were made at Central Park, including the addition of a playground, picnic area, recreation building, and tennis courts. Perhaps Pitcher's most lasting legacy at Central was his respect for the landscaping of the original Kohl estate. His work to preserve the original plantings gave San Mateo one of the most beautiful parks in the Bay Area.

POLITICS AND EDUCATION DURING THE 1930S

BY 1930, THE BAYWOOD residential area was becoming an attractive, upscale addition to San Mateo. But the new families found the city's educational system deficient. In the first few years, some Baywood children went to school in Hillsborough, but this created a few problems. For one thing, by 1934 the 31 students attending school in Hillsborough were diverting crucial state money away from San Mateo. Also, some Baywood parents claimed that Hillsborough wouldn't enroll some of their children for discriminatory reasons. Despite the Hillsborough board's denial of this charge, the issue exploded at a San Mateo School Board meeting in September 1934.

The *San Mateo Times* called it the "floor-of-the-Senate, all-talking-at once, word battle—the Battle of Baywood."[67] The San Mateo Board had decided that children living in Baywood would be obliged to attend San Mateo schools, with the exception of students who had been attending the Hillsborough School and were due to graduate that academic year. However, an "incensed" group of mothers, called the "Hillsborough faction" by the *Times*, wished to have things stay as they were, and stood up and said so at the board meeting. An even larger group of Baywood mothers countered that the "Hillsborough faction," led by Mrs. Anne S. Kaplan, "wanted to be exclusive." The Baywood group alleged "un-American" discrimination was practiced at Hillsborough School, and "only those children who were found 'desirable' were accepted."

Kaplan and her group finally gave up and walked out of the meeting. "Following the verbal fireworks," board members William F. Turnbull, E. C. Lydon and Frank Simmen decided to stick to their guns and refused to reverse their decision.

But the Hillsborough faction was not finished. They hired attorneys and continued to send their children to Hillsborough. In October, the *Times* claimed that the solution to the problem lay in passage of a proposed bond issue to build a Baywood school for $25,000. It had the support of the San Mateo-Burlingame Board of Realtors and other components of the business community. The *Times* editorial of October 5 asserted:

> More than a million dollars has been spent in Baywood-Aragon since the subdivision of this property and its addition to the taxable wealth of the city of San Mateo. It is one of the few successful subdivision operations of the Peninsula in the last few years and has attracted to our city a class of people for whose presence chambers of commerce of any city in the state would have spent a small fortune in promotion. It is capable of still further development, and for that reason

alone, as well as for the benefit of the families which have already invested their money and set up their homes there, the city of San Mateo should make proper school provision.

The development of Baywood, and consequently the development of the city of San Mateo is being retarded by the lack of school facilities there . . . Scores of families who might have chosen to live and build in Baywood Park have not done so because they found out that it was necessary to have their children cross the highway four times a day in order to attend classes.

In the October 23 election, with fewer than 1,000 ballots cast, the issue failed to capture the necessary two-thirds majority. A *Times* editorial said this failure represented a blow to the business development of the city.

Four years later, in May 1938, *The Times* announced a new plan for a massive update of the city's public elementary schools, supported by a specially appointed citizens committee. Its chairman, the well-known David J. Stollery, vice president of the San Mateo Chamber of Commerce, submitted a four-point program that called for enlarging Beresford School; constructing a school for the Baywood and Aragon districts; converting Borel School into a junior high school; and selling George Hall School (formerly Central School) to help finance the endeavor. Besides the sale, the committee hoped to obtain $100,000 in federal Public Works Administration funds and to use general tax money for the balance. The committee also mentioned the possibility of another bond issue attempt.

This proposal accidentally provided the solution to another problem. Mayor Frank Simmen wanted to build a new city hall and civic center. The old city hall on B Street had been built in 1914 to serve a community of 4,500 people. The city's population was now 22,000, and the needs of administrators, fire department and police force demanded expansion. Simmen believed the city could buy the George Hall School for a new Civic Center. With the money from the purchase, Baywood School could be built and improvements made at other schools as suggested by the citizens committee.

Architect W. H. Toepke was brought in to design a new firehouse. The old school's classrooms could be employed for offices and the auditorium converted for use as council chambers. While the original plan called for the police station and jail to move to the new plant, they could stay at the old city hall until all the necessary funds were obtained. Former San Mateo City Councilman and former judge George Kertell was one of a very few to oppose the plan.

On June 30, the *Burlingame Advance* announced a deal had been arranged between the city and the school board. The city would purchase the property for $100,000.

In August, a city election was held to pass a $145,000 bond issue for the purchase of the property and a start on construction. Help was anticipated from the Public Works Administration for at least a portion of the project. The bond issue passed, and the city requested federal aid. But by November 1938 it appeared the Public Works Administration would not be helping with the project. Mayor Simmen announced that the city would begin work anyway.[68] Plans were scaled back, and the police station and jail would have to remain on B Street.

Simmen continued his quest for federal assistance, but that help never came. In October 1939 construction got underway, and by May 1940 the new civic center was completed. The Chamber of Commerce, under its President Frank M. Bartlett, organized the dedication on August 18, 1940. The city allowed the Chamber a new office in the center. Both the *San Mateo Times* and the *Burlingame Advance* ran special celebration editions.

The beautiful Mission Revival architecture of the new Civic Center was enhanced by lawns, gardens, and a fountain obtained from the Golden Gate International Exposition at Treasure Island. The fountain had been built for the Mission Trails Building. It was special enough to warrant its own dedication on December 14, 1940. The fountain was a duplicate of one in Barcelona, Spain, centuries old and of a rare design. Its pool consisted of an eight-pointed star. Because of the revolution raging in Spain at the time, it was suspected that the original was destroyed, leaving San Mateo with only the one of its kind.[69]

While the civic center neared completion, the San Mateo school board continued to move ahead. It had Baywood School constructed in 1939, and in April 1940 it purchased four lots from the Borel Estate for $10,000 for additions to Borel School.[70] In May the Board passed a tax increase to raise capital funds for additions at the new Baywood and expanded Borel schools.[71]

San Mateo and the Great Depression

San Mateo was very lucky during the decade of the Great Depression. The city did not experience the influx of people fleeing the Dust Bowl, as did other parts of California, nor did it have long soup lines and destitute people constantly on the streets. Still, the optimism of the 1920s was dead. Business suffered, public institutions faced lean times, and people had a bleak outlook in general.

Public transportation during the decade continued to serve the commuters of San Mateo, but plans to extend the streetcar service south toward San Jose were curtailed.

In 1939 the Police Department had three motorcycles, a three-wheeler, and three radio-equipped cars, reasonably new.

Courtesy Norman Burke

While Third Avenue continued to look healthy, with all its new buildings, times were not good even for the established retailers. The Levy Brothers lost money in 1931, the first year in their new location on Third Avenue, and 1932 was even worse. Not until 1936 was the store truly profitable again.

Other proprietors, who lacked the staying power of Levy Brothers, went out of business. Store fronts remained empty for years. Nevertheless, Third Avenue continued to be the focus of the city's commercial enterprise. Restaurants, gift shops, a photographer, soda fountains and pharmacies all somehow survived.

Even in 1937, after seven years of economic disaster, San Mateo still had two banks, two savings and loan associations, four hotels, one newspaper, and 222 retail stores providing employment for 570 employees. Also producing jobs were the two hospitals. A variety of business luncheon clubs continued to meet regularly, including the Rotary, Lions, Kiwanis and a women's business and professional organization.[72]

Auto repair shops were one of the few growth businesses of those days. Henry Mituals opened a successful repair shop near Bayshore in 1931. During the early 1950s when the Bayshore was enlarged into a freeway, he moved east several blocks and opened a junk yard. Henry died in 1964, but his family continued the business into the middle 1970s.[73] For three decades youngsters growing up in the surrounding tract homes learned about junk-yard dogs, salt and shotguns from Henry and his kin.

Other businesses with a good chance at success were those which catered to the enjoyment of alcoholic beverages. When Prohibition ended in 1933, Tom Casey is said to have procured the first license to reopen a bar in San Mateo. He moved into an old smoke shop in the Benoit Building on B. Through the years, and a succession of owners, the bar was a hangout for members of the San Mateo Blues Baseball team and a haven for those who just wanted to "hang out with the guys." Old-timers recalled the bar had a famous Chinese short-order cook named Joe Bang, who wielded a cleaver at overly demanding customers. The establishment was also famous for its beautiful rosewood bar that could seat twenty.[74]

San Mateo Junior College changed dramatically in the 1930s. The institution was established to help those of modest economic means in good times. During the Depression, its activities and the hope it provided for young people became even more important.

In 1929, 626 students were enrolled at San Mateo Junior College. By 1934, the number had more than doubled, to 1,600. Young people who had no jobs and realized the importance of education poured onto the campus. In 1935, another junior college opened in San

The San Mateo Fire Department had seven vehicles, ranging from antique to modern, in 1937, before the move to the new Civic Center.

Courtesy San Mateo County Historical Museum

Francisco and took some of the pressure off overenrollment.

The college was led during those hard times by one of the great educational leaders in San Mateo County history, Charles S. Morris. The students called him "Jum," short for "Jumbo." At 6'4" and 210 pounds, the former track star was a big man, with great empathy for his students. He was appointed dean in 1931, when the college was still under control of the high school district. His driving motivation was that his institution was "the last chance" for many young adults. A typical student was Earle Marsh, who later recalled:

The world opened up for me at San Mateo. [Before coming here] I'd had some high school years at Lowell in San Francisco where I more or less messed around. . . so I couldn't get into Cal or Stanford. [At San Mateo] I was active [student body president, 1932]. . . and I got very good grades. I lived in the Peninsula Gymnasium catercorner across the street from the Baldwin campus. In exchange for collecting money from the people who used the gym and pool at night, and for cleaning out the pool every Saturday night (an allnight job, by the way, it had to be done by hand in those days), they let me sleep and study in the locker room.[75]

In a continuous quest to meet the community's needs, in 1936 Morris assigned administrator James Tormey the task of creating an adult school. Tormey expected 500 to sign up for the new evening program, but 1,500 came that first year. Morris, who went the first night just to see how things were going, found himself

The Police Department had 24 officers and a female dispatcher in 1939.

Courtesy San Mateo County Historical Museum

rushing to help register adult students. In 1937, the adult school program grew to include vocational training such as plumbing and welding courses. Eventually, Tormey extended the adult school to the campuses of the two high schools in the district (San Mateo and Burlingame) and still later to some 45 to 50 locations county-wide.

Morris' concern for the young people of the college was equaled by that of his wife, Carlena, called "Ma Jum" by the students. In the midst of the Depression, Jum discovered that two of his boys were sleeping in a cellar and living on canned food. Ma Jum took on the task of providing housing for such students as her personal crusade. She received permission from the college board, and then asked the "Mothers Club" to sponsor a program she would manage as a volunteer.

Carlena rented a house at 517 San Mateo Drive for $30 a month. She opened it for ten male students in February 1938. That fall she opened another residence in Burlingame for 13 boys. Each student was expected to pay $7.50 a month for rent and laundry. Boys wishing to enter the program applied to a faculty committee who judged the applicant according to his need, character and scholastic record.

The boys at each house elected their own managers, who reported to Ma Jum. She did the bookkeeping, paid the bills and made sure the houses stayed self-supporting. Every Sunday night Jum and Ma Jum visited both houses. Ma Jum later recalled that in the five and one half years that the houses functioned as dormitories, there was never any problem with the boys, their neighbors, or anyone involved.

Despite the Depression, San Mateo Junior College thrived as a place where positive experiences happened. Fred Roehr's choir had over 100 members. Physical education offerings included horseback riding (the stables are now the Elks Lodge on 20th Avenue).

Dorothy Herrington's French Club met at Mr. and Mrs. Chartier's popular restaurant in the Woman's Club building at El Camino and West Santa Inez. Eleanor Nettle, a student at the time, recalled lively dances at the college, featuring the Barnyard Bounce and the Chicken Romp.

It was also during the 1930s that sophomores perfected the fine art of torturing freshmen. Initiation lasted one week. Freshmen girls had to wear Levis, a plaid shirt, non-matching socks and a traditional blue and white ribbon. Boys also wore Levis and non-matching socks, and were required to walk with shoe laces untied and to wear a "dink" (a blue and white cap without a bill).

In 1937, the educational community recognized that the expanding programs of the college deserved special attention. The college was separated from the high school district and a new junior college board of trustees was elected. Morris became district president under the new system.

Morris and the new trustees began to plan for a future campus on 35 acres at Peninsula and Delaware (currently the site of the Woodlake Apartments), purchased in 1935. In 1939, the College constructed a 51,000-square-foot science building there for $350,000. Shuttle buses operated between the two campuses. The District's plan to move the entire college to the new site was interrupted by World War II.

Police Problems of the 1930s

WHILE BOOTLEGGING dominated Chief Thomas Burke's time during the 1920s, a variety of problems complicated his life during the 1930s. Among them was the completion of the San Mateo-Hayward bay bridge, a great engineering feat which came perhaps too soon. The private owners of the bridge had trouble keeping up with its maintenance and law enforcement.

Originally, the company employed just two motorcycle patrolmen, each working 56 hours a week, but this simply was not enough. At best, the long bridge was covered by one man. At worst, in the middle of the night, there was no law enforcement.

The bridge became the scene of a variety of crimes. The most notorious incident occurred in November 1933, when two kidnappers murdered Brook Hart, a 22-year-old graduate of the University of Santa Clara. Jack Holmes and Thomas Thurmond abducted the young man, the son of a wealthy San Jose family, hoping to receive a $40,000 ransom. The two stopped about half way out on the bridge, smacked their victim with a brick, bound him, weighed him down with cement blocks, and threw him into the Bay. One of the kidnappers allegedly fired a pistol at the young man as he hit the water. Holmes and Thurmond were caught and then lynched by a mob in San Jose, ending one of the vilest incidents in the history of California.

In 1934, three more kidnappers drove up to the toll gate at the bridge. They were armed, and were attempting to leave San Mateo County with their young victim. This time one of the patrolmen, Alfred Luis, was present at the toll booth and thought he heard a child shout for help. Luis hopped on his motorcycle and pulled the suspects over. The youngster was saved, and Luis received a letter of commendation from Alameda County district attorney Earl Warren.

In 1935 yet another incident involved the bridge. Jerome Von Braum Selz, a 26-year-old auto mechanic who worked at Third and Bayshore, killed 58-year-old Ada French Rice in her remote cabin in Woodside Glen. Selz, whom the newspapers later called "the Laughing Killer," beat her to death with a poker and discarded her body on Skyline Boulevard. Chief Burke, acting in cooperation with Sheriff McGrath, questioned Selz and suspected him of the murder.

Selz originally blamed the crime on an intruder he identified as Michael Baronovitch, a Bulgarian army officer. Later, Selz admitted he had killed this man too and dumped his body into the Bay from the San Mateo Bridge. Sheriff McGrath used grappling hooks to attempt to recover the body, but it was never found.

For Chief Burke, a more routine problem during the 1930s was illegal gambling, especially within the Chinese community. One of the most successful campaigns against gambling happened in 1935. San Francisco police had initiated an energetic crack-down which forced some of the operators to flee the city and come down to the Peninsula. Burke learned that three of the gambling houses had moved to Railroad Avenue in San Mateo. At nine o'clock one night, Burke and his officers used axes and crowbars to gain entry into the gambling dens. They netted 74 Chinese and Filipino gamblers in that single night of raids.

Gambling was a problem not just among a couple of ethnic groups. At the House of Merkel at 201 South B, right next door to City Hall, youngsters could buy sodas, read comics or buy cards or other notions. Adults could get cigars or a bottle of booze, play billiards—or place a bet on a horse at Bay Meadows.

Brothers Carl and Cuna Merkel came from Germany and opened their business in 1918. Long-time resident Robert Elfving remembered the Merkels as "two wonderful guys [who] gave the biggest ice cream scoops"[76] to the local children for a nickel. During the 1930s the brothers replaced their original building with the beautiful terra cotta one, still standing. But this center of social activity was raided at least once during the decade. Almost everyone in San Mateo knew it was a haven for bookies.

The opening of Bay Meadows in 1934 made San Mateo the target of bookie operations. Betting and other law enforcement issues which surfaced because of large crowds at the track made it necessary for Chief Burke to hire 17 special officers to keep order during the racing season.

Toward the end of the decade, as San Mateo's borders extended southward, the "hobo jungles" that had previously been a county problem became the city's. At the abandoned Leslie Salt warehouse and at neglected Southern Pacific buildings, homeless people, mostly men, created unsightly and unsanitary shelters. Periodically the public demanded their removal.[77]

In 1930 police did not even have radios in their squad cars for communication with their headquarters. Instead, a tower stood on the top of City Hall. When officers were needed, a beacon was lit, signaling that the patrolman should come in to receive instructions.

With such primitive equipment, and a lack of manpower, Chief Burke had to be resourceful. In 1931, realizing he could no longer guarantee the safety of

William P. Kyne, (right) founder of Bay Meadows Race Track.

Courtesy San Mateo County Historical Museum

Jockey Joe Ferguson on Seabiscuit, probably the most famous horse ever to run at Bay Meadows.

Courtesy San Mateo County Historical Museum

children walking to and from school, he initiated the Junior Traffic Patrol. At first only 8th graders were enlisted. They were equipped with hats and whistles and given the responsibility to assist smaller children in crossing busy streets. Burke asked officer Manual Trinta to organize the patrol, which in its first year numbered only a dozen or so youngsters. By 1933, the patrol was large enough to warrant a parade, and by the 1950s this auxiliary force numbered in the thousands.

By the time Burke neared his twentieth year as chief in 1936, the force had come a long way. There were three patrol cars, all equipped with radios, and a fingerprint identification bureau.[78] By 1940, Burke had a staff of 21, and had added three motorcycles and a three wheeler.

The Track, the Fair, the Park, and the Museum

The Bay Meadows story is largely about William Patrick Kyne, one of the great equestrian enthusiasts in California history. By the time of his death in 1957, Kyne was known for the creation of the daily double, night racing, quarter horse racing, Bay Meadows Race Track itself, and the legalization of parimutuel betting, which made it all possible.

Originally, Kyne wanted to be a priest, but he became entranced by "the sport of kings" after seeing his first horse race at Emeryville Racetrack in 1900. In 1910, when California banned horse racing, Kyne traveled to other states and even to Mexico, working as a bookmaker. In the early 1930s he led the campaign to legalize parimutuel betting in California, creating a state-controlled wagering system that included an automatic monetary return to the track and the state on every bet. It also established a California Horse Racing Board to oversee the track.

This aerial view taken before World War II shows El Camino crossing Third Avenue, near the bottom, just above the Benjamin Franklin Hotel. Alameda de las Pulgas angles in from left center, and passes Baywood School. The hills, here dotted with houses, are fully developed today.   Courtesy San Mateo County Historical Museum

In 1933, the state instituted the new system, and Kyne began planning where to open his own track. He chose the former McLellan ranch lands which were currently in use as the Curtiss-Wright flying field. Bay Meadows opened for racing on November 3, 1934. It was an immediate success, with some $100,000 in wagers on its first day.

Under Kyne, Bay Meadows became a leading force in racing. It was the first track in California to use the "tote" adding machines, simplifying parimutuel betting; it was first to use the photo finish; it was the first to install an electric starting gate.

Some of the most famous horses in the world raced at Bay Meadows in those early years: Charles S. Howard's Seabiscuit twice won the Bay Meadows Handicap; the famous English horse, Noor, first raced in America at Bay Meadows; Native Diver first ran at Bay Meadows and then set a record by winning 24 stakes.

Along with quality racing, another early Bay Meadows tradition involved charity. The track supported Children's Hospital in San Francisco in its earliest years with a Children's Hospital Day Sweepstakes. Part of the proceeds went to a building fund.

A year after its establishment, Bay Meadows became the site of the San Mateo County Fair. The beginnings of the fair go back to 1926, when the Burlingame-Hillsborough Flower Show was organized at McKinley School.[79] A year later, the exhibition moved to the San Mateo Junior College campus. By 1929, the name of the event had changed to the Burlingame-San Mateo Flower Show, sponsored by the San Mateo, Burlingame,

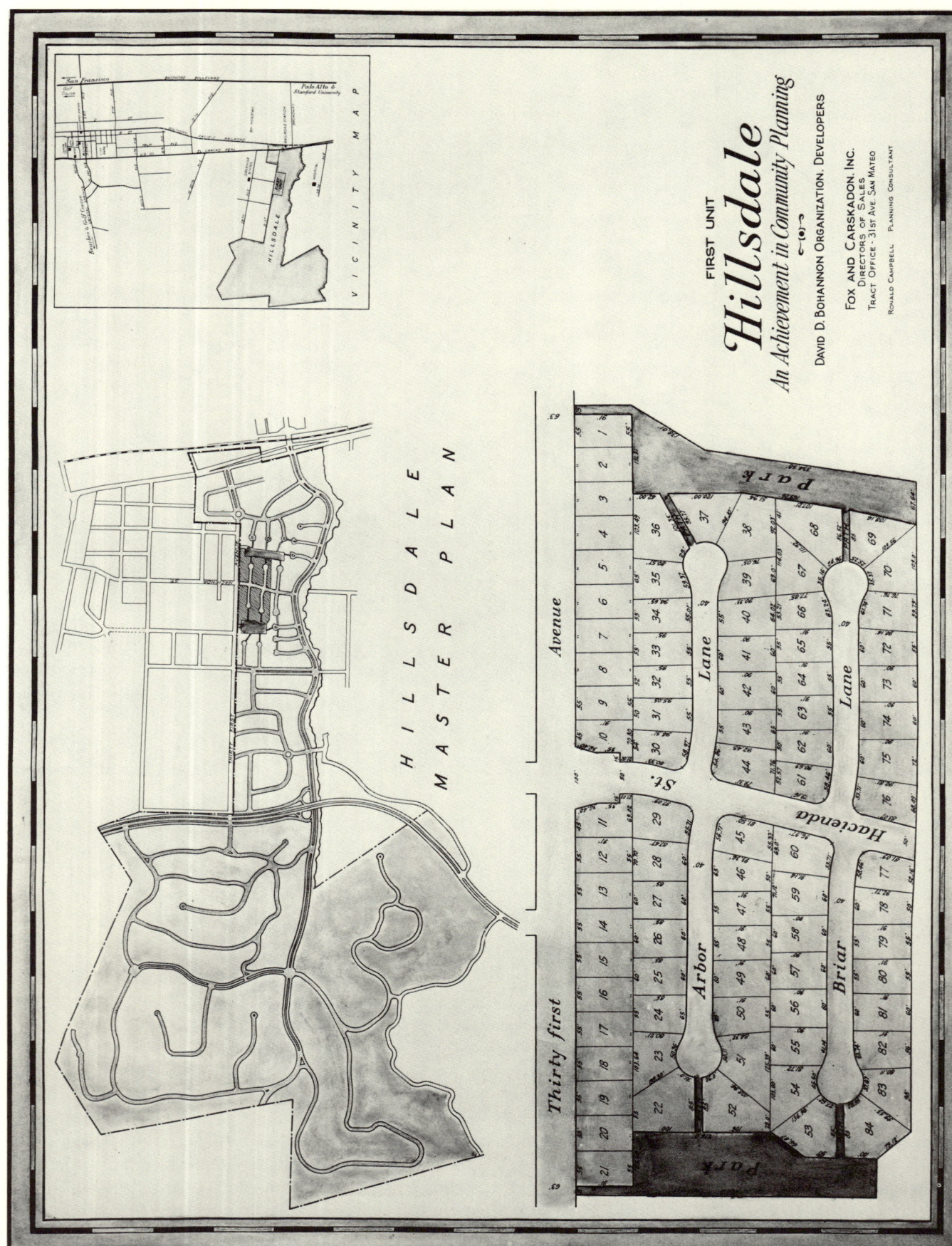

Hillsborough and Peninsula Gardeners Association. The next year, a parade was organized in conjunction with the show. The exposition was so popular by 1931 that a tent had to be erected over the tennis courts at the college because the school auditorium could no longer handle all the displays.

Between 1931 and 1934 the Depression halted the show, but in 1935 a group which included peninsula mayors, representatives of unincorporated areas, sponsors, and county manager William Kellogg met with the goal of creating a new fair. George J. Davis, superintendent of the San Francisco Water Department, was elected first president of what became the San Mateo County Fair Association.

Davis and his board appealed to Kellogg for financial assistance. The county had supported the parade, even after the festival had gone into hibernation. Kellogg agreed to help. Association board members Elmer Roberts, Bruce Gibson, Chester Lipman, B. G. Kost, and Davis each lent $1,000 to the endeavor

They selected Bay Meadows as the site of the revived fair. The four-day event, called the San Mateo County Products and Floral Fiesta, opened on October 10, 1935. No rent was charged by Bay Meadows for use of property, thanks to the California Jockey Club.

Unfortunately it rained the first day and only 300 people attended. But the next day the sun broke through, and 60,000 came to Bay Meadows and the fair over the remaining three days. The Fiesta featured a highly popular orchid display, the traditional big parade (then in its fifth year), a beauty contest, polo games, a pageant staged by hundreds of school children, exhibits of exotic birds and fish, and finally a fireworks display.

The Fiesta just broke even. The Association had piled up $29,000 in expenses, and it looked like it might be $2,700 in the red. But the state paid the balance under the California Horse Racing Act, which allowed parimutuel tax money to be spent on agricultural and district fairs. The Fiesta marked the true beginning of the County Fair as we know it today.

In 1937, a more reliable budget was established, with money committed from the state and the County Board of Supervisors. In 1938, a rodeo was added to the list of attractions. That year, on August 16, the San Mateo County Fair Association was officially incorporated as a non-profit organization.

Change was imminent in southern San Mateo when David Bohannon unveiled his plans for the first unit of the Hillsdale development. He soon had 84 houses completed, with 5,000 building sites planned, including commercial properties.

Courtesy Bohannon Development Company

The Fiesta of 1940 was special, featuring the tenth annual parade, sponsored by the San Mateo Junior Chamber of Commerce. The parade began at Broadway in Burlingame and ended at Bay Meadows. The theme was decidedly patriotic as the United States' entry into World War II seemed likely. According to the *Burlingame Advance*, flags flew while "scores of cowboys and cowgirls on well groomed horses" rode between "beautiful floats [and] decorated cars and wagons of ancient vintage." About 5,000 visitors attended the fair on opening day. They "thronged the racetrack grandstand and clubhouse, which were converted into a virtual garden paradise." Altogether, 28,000 attended the Fiesta during its four-day run.

After World War II, the Fair Board purchased 25 acres of California Jockey Club property adjacent to Bay Meadows to establish the formal fair grounds of today.

A racetrack, a fair and even a regional park became possible for San Mateo during the 1930s. In 1937, the Howard family gave permission to the City of San Mateo to establish a firing range at Coyote Point. By the end of the decade, many people were convinced that the county should buy Coyote Point for use as a recreational park. After public hearings in early 1940, the property was purchased. Even a yacht club was started in 1941, with Oscar Thayer as its first Commodore. But World War II interrupted progress toward a formal park at Coyote Point. It was instead turned over to the Merchant Marines for a maritime academy.

The idea to create the San Mateo County Historical Association originated with the manager of San Mateo County Chamber of Commerce, Roscoe Wyatt, in 1935. He thought a showcase for the county's rich past might attract people to the Peninsula. The *San Mateo Times* helped recruit supporters. Among the early leaders were Inez M. Crawford of the San Mateo Public Library; Lindley Miller, Rector of St. Matthews Church; Dr. Harold Taggart of San Mateo Junior College; Colonel Kirkbride; and the grand old-timer, George A. Bartlett.

In 1936, Wyatt was able to interest Dr. Frank M. Stanger of the college's history department in the activities of the association. Stanger soon assumed leadership of the organization, and began a campaign to establish a historical museum. Jerome Hamilton suggested placing the museum on the Junior College campus. In 1939, the request was made to the college trustees. "Jum" Morris liked the idea. After all, Dr. Stanger was from his own faculty, and Colonel Kirkbride, a member of the Association's board of directors, was a trustee of the college.

During the fall of 1940, a former French classroom was converted into a museum, and opened to the public in January 1941. The first object accepted into the museum's collection was Jerome Hamilton's map of Indian shell mounds in the downtown San Mateo area.

David Bohannon (right) streamlined the process of house-building. At Arbor Lane West (above), dozens of foundations, all poured at once, are ready for pre-cut lumber to arrive.

Courtesy Bohannon Development Company

Residential Expansion as War Loomed

Between 1920 and 1940, the City of San Mateo's population more than tripled, from 5,979 to 19,403. Most of this growth occurred during the 1920s. The spread of subdivisions meant businesses were needed outside the downtown area. The first opened in 1937, a store and office building on the northwest corner of El Camino Real and 25th. The distinctive art deco structure was designed to catch the eye of fast-moving motorists. By the end of 1941, the street also had a market (originally Lester's—later known as Humphrey's) and the Manor Theater.

The driving force behind the 25th Avenue development was Axel Johnson and his San Mateo Investment Company. During the early 1930s he fought against tacky roadside businesses in the area. Johnson and his allies were particularly annoyed with a Shell service station called "The Castle" with its "flamboyant display of gasolines and oils"[80] towering high above El Camino Real at 25th Avenue. Johnson successfully lobbied against further construction of that kind. He also

This signboard, remarkably three-dimensional, stood at the corner of El Camino and 31st Avenue, inviting passersby to have a look at Hillsdale.

Courtesy San Mateo County Historical Museum

staged special Sunday auctions, selling lots on 25th for $50 each ($80 for corners), even though the city didn't plan to pave streets in the area until 1940.[81] Johnson successfully developed "San Mateo Knolls," a section of the city between 39th Avenue and Belmont, where 400 homes were built by 1940.

Lawrence Clinton (L.C.) Smith came to San Mateo about the same time. L.C. was born in Rutherford, California in 1903. He worked his way up through the building industry from laborer to foreman to superintendent, and then went into business for himself. He was known internationally as a polo player and horseman, and was a key contractor of San Mateo streets and sidewalks as the city expanded before, and especially after, the War.

Like Johnson and Smith, Thomas J. Culligan, Jr. and his company, Conway and Culligan, got started in the early 1930s. He developed 250 homes in Howard Park, south of the high school. His firm became even more active in the post-war period.

Of all the developers who emerged in San Mateo during the 1930s and early 1940s, none would become better known than David D. Bohannon. Bohannon was born in San Francisco in 1898. His father, an inventor, and a socialist, founded the newspaper, *The California Socialist*.[82]

His father's greatest invention, the "spring wheel," was rendered obsolete by the balloon tire after World War I. Bohannon and his father then tried gold mining in Nevada. When that proved unsuccessful, young Bohannon returned to the Bay Area. In 1926, at age 28, David landed his first real estate job, selling property in the Devonshire Hills of booming San Carlos. Real estate was a wide-open business during the 1920s. After working for a series of less-than-honest men, he formed the David D. Bohannon Organization in 1928. His was one of the few real estate operations to survive the stock market crash of 1929.

Bohannon was the first builder in San Mateo County to use Federal Housing Administration loan guarantees. He built his first five houses in the Menlo Oaks area in 1934. Materials were cheap and labor cheaper. He sold the homes for between $3,500 and $4,500.

Bohannon became a nationally-recognized leader in real estate development and succeeded in instituting reforms in California to correct much of what he thought was wrong with the industry in the 1920s. As a national business figure, Bohannon traveled across the country to confer with other leaders in the field.

In the late 1930s, Bohannon became interested in San Mateo. He purchased the St. Cyr Estate, formerly Howard property, which included 15 acres in Hillsborough and 10 in San Mateo. Helen Strong, the divorced wife of Jean de St. Cyr, sold it to Bohannon for a reported $202,000 (the real figure may have been significantly lower). He built El Cerrito Manor on the land and employed the real estate firm of Raybould and Bartlett as sales agents. As part of the agreement, Bohannon agreed to save the property's Japanese garden.

An even more ambitious project was the Hillsdale development. In 1937, Bohannon began negotiations with Burleigh H. Murray of the original pioneer family

Hillsdale houses in Unit One were in the $5,000 to $6,000 range. What would they sell for today?

Courtesy Bohannon Development Company

to purchase 848 acres of Beresford lands, equivalent to a significant percentage of the entire City of San Mateo. The sale took years because of the Murray family's concern that the "character"[83] of the place be preserved. Among the guarantees Bohannon made was to preserve the "Murray Oak," a great tree that stood in the center of the old farm buildings. In 1952, Bohannon donated the site to the city for the Hillsdale Branch Library. The 300-year-old tree survived until 1963, when diseases weakened it, threatening the library, and it had to be cut down.

Three years after initiating talks with the Murray family, in April 1940, Bohannon finally bought the first 241 acres, with an option for the rest.[84] Bohannon and his staff decided to stage a public contest to come up with a more descriptive name than Beresford. Unknown to his staff, Bohannon entered his own choice, "Hillsdale," and it won.

The scope of the project was unprecedented in Bay Area history. Bohannon's plan called for the construction of 5,000 inexpensive and well built houses to be priced between $5,000 and $6,000. Nationally-known planning engineer Ronald L. Campbell, who was working for San Mateo County at the time, was called in as consultant. Bohannon actually went before the County Board of Supervisors to get their permission to allow Campbell to "moonlight." (Campbell eventually came to work full-time for Bohannon in 1946 as a vice president of his firm.)

Bohannon and Campbell, after studying subdivisions throughout the United States, envisioned a planned community with parks. Various designs and lot sizes would be used to avoid a monotonous tract appearance. Low, rambling California ranch houses were designed by architects Williams and Westell. Two-and three-bedroom homes had stucco, redwood and cedar exteriors, copper pipes, hot-air furnaces, and Venetian blinds.

The first 84 houses of "Hillsdale No. 1" were located on Hacienda near 31st Avenue and down Arbor and Briar Lanes. Sixteen were opened for exhibit on September 16, 1940, with one furnished as a model. According to the *San Mateo Times*, by December, eight of them had sold, and reservations were being taken on the second unit of houses already under construction.

Bohannon supported the sale efforts of real estate agents Fox and Carskadon by building an attractive entrance to Hillsdale on 31st Avenue, a little west of El Camino Real. Nearby a lavish billboard announced Hillsdale as "An Achievement in Community Planning."

Bohannon also replaced the railroad station. There had been a station at this location for many years, variously called Laurel Creek, Cottrell, Beresford and Bay Meadows. Bohannon offered Southern Pacific a new, attractive station to be built by him, at his expense in exchange for calling the station Hillsdale. Southern Pacific agreed, and the structure was dedicated in August 1941. Of colonial design, the new station stood only a few minutes' walk from the residential development. By that time 38 trains a day stopped at Hillsdale. Original Hillsdale home owners remember with fondness the camaraderie among the train commuters in those early days—perhaps engendered by the presence of the cocktail bar on board.

Southern Pacific was important to Bohannon for another reason. Most of his building materials, including practically all of the precut lumber, came in by train and were then trucked to the old Murray barn area (now at Hacienda and Hillsdale Boulevard). Precutting the wood and transporting it by rail saved Bohannon a great deal of money, which helped keep prices affordable.

In June 1941 Bohannon began construction on another 100 homes. These included larger windows, combination living and dining rooms, elevated bedrooms and sunken gardens. Bohannon's achievements were not overlooked by his colleagues; recognizing his innovative successes at Hillsdale, they named him as the first president of the National Association of Homebuilders in 1941.

Bohannon also began his commercial venture at Hillsdale before the War. On October 4, 1941, amid great fanfare, ground was broken for construction of an Andrew Williams Store on the site of today's mall. With 15,000 square feet, it was equal in size to the largest store in Northern California—at that time the Williams store in Oakland. Mrs. Doris L. Williams, president of Andrew Williams Stores, and San Mateo Mayor Frank Simmen assisted Bohannon with the ground-breaking ceremonies.[85] With the market's completion, residents of Hillsdale no longer had to go to 25th Avenue to shop.

AT THE BRINK

By the start of the 1940s, a growing San Mateo still had old-fashioned charm. Telephone dial service would not begin for two years. The entire municipal budget was only $376,000. The city's quiet character was captured by the motto on its official letterhead—"Homes—Sunshine—Flowers"—depicting a Greek goddess dropping flowers on Spanish haciendas along a California hillside.

But a national crisis was certainly on the minds of San Mateo's leaders. When in June 1940 the San Mateo City Council instituted the flag pledge, Mayor Frank Simmons alluded to "troubled times"[86] ahead. On October 8, 1940, the *San Mateo Times* announced that the League of California Municipalities had drawn up a resolution "prohibiting trespass upon and loitering about industrial plants and other property deemed essential to national defense." This included gas and electric plants, water works, communication lines, railroad tracks, and bridges. Fear of sabotage and foreign attack were real concerns of San Mateans on the brink of World War II.

NOTES

[1] Cloud, *History*, Vol. II, p. 64.
[2] City of San Mateo, *Annual Statement*, 1916-1917.
[3] Barile, *San Mateo Fire*.
[4] Letter from Oscar F. Weissgerber, City Manager, to Thomas F. Burke, December 23, 1925.
[5] City of San Mateo *Governmental Facts*, Sixteenth Annual Report, for the Fiscal Year 1937-1938.
[6] City of San Mateo, *Governmental Facts*, Eighteenth Annual Report, for the Fiscal Year 1940.
[7] Betty Sears and Alan Hynding, "The Not-So-Dry Years: Early Prohibition in San Mateo County, 1920-1926," *La Peninsula*, Summer 1980, Vol. XX, No. 3, p. 10.
[8] Interview with Norman Burke, the son of Thomas Burke, by the author on April 27, 1993.
[9] Genevieve Altieri, *The House on Grant Street*, Alsten Publications, 1978, p. 181.
[10] Official Catalog, *First Annual Horse Show and Race Meet, Gymkana Club*, San Mateo, May 24, 25, 1930.
[11] Postel, *History*, p. 23.
[12] Ibid, p. 22.
[13] *Burlingame Advance*, October 2, 1925.
[14] Author's interview with Kenge Takahashi on March 23, 1943.
[15] Altieri, *House*, p. 79-80.
[16] Michael Svanevik, "Daba: An Italian Grocer with Political Clout," *Times*, August 17, 1990.
[17] Author's interview with Yoneo Kawakita on March 23, 1993.
[18] Author's interview with Ed Ishimaru on March 23, 1993.
[19] Author's interview with Mariko Endo on March 23, 1993.
[20] "Japanese Language School Location Creates Big Stir in San Mateo; New Offer Made," *Advance*, September 3, 1930.
[21] Bill Cox, "A History of the African M. E. Zion Church of San Mateo, California," student monograph #1797 in the archives of the San Mateo County Historical Museum, 1958.
[22] Vera Graham, "Judge Cotton, Beloved Judge," *The Times*, January 2, 1965.

23. Altieri, *House*, p. 129.
24. Vera Graham, "Mr. San Mateo — Doc Raybould," *The Times*, October 16, 1965.
25. D. A. Raybould, *My Thirty Years as a Real Estate Broker, Subdivider and Developer*, Raybould's own scrapbook, pp. 2, 5, 21.
26. "Realtors Are Given Credit for Progress," *Daily News Leader*, January 26, 1925."
27. Raybould, *My*, p. 39.
28. Ibid, p. 67.
29. "Parrott Property Is Sold," *San Mateo Times*, February 15, 1927.
30. "Set Date to Hear Baywood Protests," *San Mateo Times*, July 9, 1931.
31. Linda Wickert, *City of San Mateo Historic Building Survey*, report section, San Mateo County Historical Association, City of San Mateo, September, 1988, p. 33.
32. "Union with S.F. to Give Boom-impetus," *San Francisco Examiner*, December 7, 1923.
33. Burke, *San Mateo*.
34. Altieri, *House*, p. 26.
35. Cloud, *History*, Vol. II, p. 309.
36. Mitchell P. Postel, "The Junior-Community College Movement of San Mateo County, 1922-1987," *La Peninsula*, Vol. XXIV, No. 2, October, 1987, p. 4.
37. Irene T. Miura, "Boy Scouts of San Mateo County, 1910-1940," *La Peninsula*, Vol. XXV, No. 1, April, 1989, p. 17.
38. Postel, *Peninsula*, p. 138.
39. Wickert, *City*, Survey Section.
40. Lorraine Thomason, "Theaters and the Motion Picture Industry of San Mateo and Burlingame," student monograph #703 in the archives of the San Mateo County Historical Museum, June 1945.
41. "San Francisco to the Front as a Motion Picture Center," *San Francisco Bulletin*, February 28, 1921.
42. Anne Kernohan, "History of Pacific City," student monograph #764 in the archives of the San Mateo County Historical Museum, June 1946.
43. Altieri, *House*, p. 25.
44. Hynding, *Frontier*, p. 255.
45. Bradford Evans, "Aviation History in San Mateo County," *La Peninsula*, April, 1944, Vol. II, No. 5, p. 2.
46. Jack Dowling, "Airports of San Mateo County," student monograph #766 in the archives of the San Mateo County Historical Museum, Spring 1946.
47. John A. Lowry, "History of the San Mateo - Hayward Bridge," student monograph #560 in the archives of the San Mateo County Historical Museum, June 1943.
48. Bob Lyhne, "The first Wondrous Bridge at San Mateo," *Advance Star*, October 18, 1967. This article contains a number of interviews with the bridge's original employees.
49. Ibid
50. Cloud, *History*, p. 141.
51. Altieri, *House*, p. 93.
52. Ibid. p. 130.
53. Ibid. p. 131.
54. Ibid. p. 133.
55. Ibid. p. 140.
56. Michael Svanevik and Shirley Burgett, "San Mateo goes Through its Rockwellian Stage," *The Times*, February 22, 1991.
57. Hynding, *From Frontier*, p. 229.
58. "Judge Cotton, 90, Dies, was Dean of Bench," *The Times*, April 16, 1965.
59. Vera Graham, "Judge Cotton, Beloved Judge Cotton," *The Times*, January 2, 1965.
60. Letter of May 27, 1929 from Carl W. Elfving to William Hendrickson Taylor in the archives of the San Mateo County Historical Museum.
61. Letter of May 25, 1929 from Herbert A. Thayer to William Taylor in the archives of the San Mateo County Historical Museum.
62. Letter of December 10, 1929 from C. E. Piatt to the San Mateo City Council in the archives of the San Mateo County Historical Museum.
63. Letter of February 19, 1931 from Oscar Weissgerber to George Kertell in the archives of the San Mateo County Historical Museum.

64. Letter of April 3, 1931 from Oscar Weissgerber to George Kertell in the archives of the San Mateo County Historical Museum.
65. "An Analysis of the Report of the Citizen's Committee Appointed by Mayor Frank Simmen to Study the Possibilities of Acquiring a Municipal Water System for the City of San Mateo," February 11, 1936.
66. May Aldrick, "History of Recreation in San Mateo," January, 1942, student monograph #416 in the archives of the San Mateo County Historical Museum.
67. "Social Angles Crop Right Out When Baywood Mothers Split on School Issue Before Board," *San Mateo Times*, September 28, 1934.
68. "Civic Center Work to Begin," *San Mateo Times*, November 16, 1938.
69. *City of San Mateo Governmental Facts*, Eighteenth Annual report, for the Fiscal Year 1940, p. 3.
70. "S. M. Schools Buy 4 Lots from Borels," *Advance*, April 18, 1940.
71. "S. M. Grammar School Raises Tax 30 Cents," *San Mateo Times*, May 25, 1940.
72. San Mateo Chamber of Commerce, "Facts and Figures - 1937."
73. John Horgan, "Dismantling Yard on Way Out," *Times*, April 22, 1974.
74. "Malley's May Move," *Times*, December 22, 1975.
75. Postel, "Junior-Community," p. 7.
76. Wickert, *City*, Survey Section.
77. Hobo Jungles Face Closing as Health Menace," *San Mateo Times*, March 24, 1939.
78. "Tom Burke Begins Twentieth Year as S. M. Police Chief," *Burlingame Advance*, April 20, 1936.
79. Mary M. Stanisick, "A History of the San Mateo County Fair and Flora Fiesta,", student monograph, #83-77 in the archives of the San Mateo County Historical Museum, January 16, 1981.
80. See the *San Mateo Times*, August 16, 1940 for a retrospective article and photographs of "the Castle."
81. Shirley Curtis, "South San Mateo History and Present Growth," student monograph #1135 in the archives of the San Mateo County Historical Museum, January 31, 1950.
82. Richard M. Stannard, "Loquacious Bohannon Loves to Tell His Story," *Redwood City Tribune*, September 27, 1963, and author's interview with David D. Bohannon on October 13, 1993.
83. Darryl D. Kenyon, "Hillsdale," 1977, student monograph #77-210-1 in the archives of the San Mateo County Historical Museum.
84. "Old California Rancho in San Mateo Sold," *San Francisco News*, April 12, 1940.
85. "Break Ground for Big Market in Hillsdale," *San Francisco Call Bulletin*, October 4, 1941.
86. "S.M. Council Initiates Flag Pledge," *Burlingame Advance*, June 4, 1940.

CHAPTER VI

San Mateo and World War II: 1941-1945

THE INITIAL SHOCK

Sunday, December 7, 1941, was going to be an important day at the Beresford Country Club. The club was run-down; the roofs leaked, the furniture was dilapidated, the carpets needed replacement, the grounds were looking shabby—even the golf course looked dry. The Depression was partly to blame, along with a second Jewish country club at Lake Merced, the advancing age of the members who remained, and burdensome assessments continually inflicted upon loyal members.

Some members favored selling off a substantial portion of the club and reducing Beresford from an 18 to a nine-hole course. But long-time golf enthusiast Helen Lengfeld and other important Beresford members such as Lloyd Liebes and Edgar Sinton opposed this and proposed to open membership up to non-Jews. After all, the Club needed new blood. Since Beresford's creation in 1912, the nearby Peninsula communities had grown considerably with new middle-class residents who could inject life into the old club. The club began offering "associate" memberships at only $9 a month with no initiation fee. New people—local, young and gentle—were interested. Among them was Ben Follett, whom Lengfeld personally recruited as a leader in the effort to revive Beresford.

Two different tasks lay before Lengfeld and company. First, the old members would have to recognize the state of affairs and agree to changes in the club. Second, new members would have to be enlisted. The task of appealing to the old members fell to the attorney Edgar Sinton. He was able to buy up the property holders' memberships at only $25.00 each—a trifling sum considering the value of the club's properties and the assessments already paid out.

Lengfeld, Liebes and Follett decided they could recruit new members by organizing a big golf tournament. They went into the local communities and signed up 300 potential members, a terrific turnout, for the event scheduled for December 7.

The morning weather was beautiful for December. Preparations went smoothly. But about an hour after the start of play, the news came that the Japanese had bombed Pearl Harbor. Those present remembered that a near panic ensued. Reservists and Guardsmen rushed to their units, familymen went home to protect their loved ones, caddies dropped their bags and left for home. Suddenly America was at war.

The next day, the reality of what had happened began to sink in. An assembly was called at San Mateo Junior College. Student Body President Cliff Pierce asked his fellow students to remain calm, to think clearly and not act out of emotion. Later he recalled that despite his words: "A lot of them didn't even take a deep breath." Many students immediately signed on with the various

Merchant Marines leap into the Bay during combat training at Coyote Point, 1942.

Courtesy San Mateo County Historical Museum

San Mateo Boy Scouts leading a scrap-metal drive were proud of their haul—as well they might have been. Two cannons have been brought in, apparently from Central Park, where they had rested for decades. The one at left is believed to have been a World War I cannon. These boys, like others all over the country, probably sang "Heil! (Neeah) Heil! (Neeah) Right in the Fuhrer's face!" as they went around collecting zinc jar covers and tin cans.

Courtesy San Mateo County Historical Museum

services. A number of their instructors did likewise, assuming teaching positions within the military. Pierce remembered one student, Jim Swett, "kind of a skinny kid" on his soccer team:

> All of a sudden he just didn't show up for practice one day, and the next thing we knew he had become a Marine pilot and was heading out to the Pacific.

Swett won the Congressional Medal of Honor for his heroism at Guadalcanal.

Many men and women from San Mateo quickly enlisted, some with special experience and skills, like real estate man Frank Bartlett. During the First World War, Bartlett had significant training responsibilities in the Army Air Corps. He did not retire from active duty until 1928. In early 1942, Bartlett was called back by the Air Corps and rose quickly to the rank of colonel. He became commanding officer of the Western Flying Training Command at Santa Ana, California, where he assumed responsibility for 148 installations in the west. Some 500,000 training courses were completed under his command between 1942 and 1945, for pilots, navigators, bombardiers and radar observers.

For everyone in San Mateo, everyday life changed suddenly. Those not going into the service realized immediately that the war meant sacrifice at home. In south San Mateo, construction of St. Gregory's Church under Father John T. Scanlon had begun that October. The parish had purchased a block of pasture land, formerly a goat ranch, including a dilapidated barn, a ruined windmill, an old cabin and a ranch house. The church's first service took place Sunday, November 30, in the Manor Theater. Its second meeting was December 7. Soon thereafter, at the church's construction site, the Army seized its copper drains and gutters for the war effort. Because of the continued shortage of building materials, the old ranch house, with only a pot-bellied stove and a wooden crate to sit on, became the rectory that January. The floors of the 50-year-old structure were shored up, and the house furnished. Amazingly the Army returned the building materials not long afterward. St. Gregory's Church was blessed by Archbishop John J. Mitty on Palm Sunday, 1942 (the building standing today was completed in 1954).

From today's standpoint it is hard to understand the fear that gripped people in San Mateo County. Dr. Frank Stanger of the Historical Association later explained: "In this war, for the first time in over a hundred years, Americans were threatened with foreign invasion, and this Peninsula was in the center of the potential invasion coast."² Aircraft bombing seemed a distinct possibility.

In anticipation of aerial attack, philanthropist Paul Fagan financed the construction of an observation tower just west of San Mateo on Skyline Boulevard. "Fagan's Tower" was equipped with a telephone. From the beginning of the war until 1943, volunteers manned this post and reported every visible aircraft to a screening center in San Francisco.

Another expected threat, more evil than outright attack, was sabotage. Crystal Springs Dam, west of San Mateo, seemed a likely target. In one stroke, San Francisco's water supply and the City of San Mateo itself could be wiped out with a well-placed explosive device. Traffic over the dam was detoured away, and guards were assigned to protect it.

Because World War II had already proven itself a "total war" for the children of other countries, steps were also taken to prepare the young for attack. Children were "dog tagged" with metal identification plates to wear on chains or ribbons around their necks. Schools practiced air raid drills.

Without doubt, the War created a sense of urgency in San Mateo never realized before or since. On the positive side, this diverse community found common ground. Since stagecoach days, San Mateo had been a place where people of different ethnic, religious and socioeconomic backgrounds had made a home. Differences between groups were largely tolerated. But no single issue brought together the community as a whole. During World War II, San Mateans found a

Guarding Crystal Springs Dam, 1942.
Courtesy San Mateo County Historical Museum

common cause. They fully believed in the righteousness of the American commitment to win the war against the Axis nations. Every single ethnic, religious and socioeconomic group was included. Everyone had a role to play. Everyone except those of Japanese heritage.

Above: On September 21, 1941, Japanese citizens marched on B Street to demonstrate their loyalty to America.

Left: Members of the Cultural League were pictured in an advertisement in the Burlingame Advance, September 17, 1941, proclaiming "We, TOO, are Americans! This is our country, our state . . . our home, our only home." From left, Hiroshi Ito, Sally Kawakito Tanouye, Joe Yamada, Fred Ochi, George Takahashi, Naoye Mayeda, M. Takahashi.
Courtesy Japanese American Cultural League

The Japanese Community and World War II

There is no doubt that citizens of Japanese ancestry were undeserving victims of the hysteria that gripped the west coast of the United States. Constitutional rights were disregarded by President Franklin Roosevelt's executive order 9066, which gave local military commanders authority to relocate people who might be judged loyal to an enemy nation because of ethnic background. In California, at Sixth Army headquarters at the San Francisco Presidio, the decision was made that the Japanese in California constituted a possible threat.

By 1941, about 200 Issei and 240 Nisei lived in San Mateo. The community's very active Japanese American Citizens League recognized that war with Japan would adversely affect Japanese Americans. In 1940, the League tried to participate in every civic event possible, promoting the local Japanese community's loyalty. During the County Fair's parade that year, the League entered a float which consisted of a huge American flag, 70 feet by 40 feet, carried by 50 of its members. Parade judges gave it the award for most unique. As war approached, the League even took newspaper advertisements proclaiming loyalty to the United States, California and San Mateo County.

The young men of the Japanese community knew they might be called upon to serve in the armed forces. By June 1941 seven had already been drafted. That month, one of Dr. Stanger's students at the Junior College completed a research paper on "Japanese Pioneers in San Mateo." K. Asai wrote that the Japanese Americans were "slowly but surely gaining a foothold in the community" and that they were "forever endeavoring to become a part of San Mateo."[3]

But these assurances were quickly forgotten after Pearl Harbor. Almost immediately, the Federal Bureau of Investigation rounded up and arrested Issei leaders. Bank assets of Japanese Americans were frozen (although later released). People were told they would be removed to camps east of the strategically important coast of California. They would have to make their own provisions for the property they were to leave behind.

The Congregational Church offered help to some of the families, and safely stored their belongings for the entire war. Some families, such as the Endos, successfully rented out their homes during this time. The Endos also

Kenge Takahashi of San Mateo (third from left) enlisted in the army and joined the 442nd Regimental Combat Team, one of the most highly decorated units in WWII. His friends are (from left) Frank Yano of San Francisco, Warren Yano of Fremont, and (far right) Joseph Ito, of Los Angeles.

Courtesy Japanese American Cultural League

At the San Mateo Civic Center, Volunteers build a USO dormitory for servicemen in San Mateo.

Courtesy San Mateo County Historical Museum

packed their automotive tools in a barrel of oil and buried it under their back porch. The Takahashis closed their store and got rid of their merchandise. They rented their house with the help of an honest realtor. The Yamanouchi family found an attorney and gave him the power to look after their Imperial Laundry, their home and other possessions.[4] Many placed their valuables in the old "Long House," the center of the Japanese community for decades. Unfortunately, vandals broke into it and almost everything was stolen or damaged.[5]

Most of the San Mateo Japanese were assembled at the Masonic Temple before being sent to Tanforan, a racetrack in San Bruno, where they waited to be sent to the interior. Yoneo Kawakita recalled that the day he was ushered off to Tanforan was the saddest of his life. It was May, and he was to graduate from high school in June. Right in the middle of the school day, he was pulled out. His lingering memory is watching all his schoolmates waving to him from classroom windows. However, the five or six students ready to graduate still had their chance. San Mateo High teachers went to Tanforan and gave these students their homework assignments (San Francisco schools simply awarded the students their diplomas before they left). Later, the high school gave these San Mateo Nisei their final exams. The teenagers had their graduation ceremonies at Tanforan.

San Mateo Japanese were joined by thousands of others at Tanforan. Then they were sent to wind-swept Camp Topaz in Utah, where San Mateans stayed together as much as possible. Despite what had happened to them, many of the young men volunteered for the army right out of Topaz. Most, such as Kenge Takahashi, fought in Europe with the 442nd Regimental Combat Team. This all-Japanese unit became the most highly decorated (for its size and length of service) in American military history. Others, like Yoneo Kawakita,

Servicemen and young women of San Mateo obviously enjoyed themselves at the USO.

Courtesy San Mateo County Historical Museum

were used as translators in intelligence work. These men became known as the "Eyes and Ears" of General Douglas MacArthur in the Pacific.

After a year at Topaz, the Japanese-Americans were given the option to leave the camp and move to Salt Lake City or another place, so long as they did not return to the West Coast. Many families, such as the Takahashis, stayed at Topaz for the duration. Others did go to Salt Lake City. The Endos opened an auto shop there. Hasuko Yamanouchi went to Salt Lake City to find employment. She needed money to pay her family's attorney to protect their property in San Mateo. She ended up working twelve hours a day at two jobs in other people's laundries, in order to save her family's laundry at home.

Many of the Japanese who moved to Salt Lake City found irony in their stay there: because the place had few Asians before their arrival, discrimination against them was relatively light. But they noticed with sympathy the harsh treatment of African-Americans by the white citizens of Utah..

MAKING DO ON THE HOMEFRONT

SAN MATEANS DID WHAT THEY COULD to assist the war effort. Ewald Peterson and E. Holm Arnold became involved in defense-related mill work on the former Wisnom property on Fifth Avenue. However, San Mateo's industrial contribution to the war effort was very light except for this endeavor.

Because of the booming wartime industry around San Mateo, the town grew rapidly, from 19,403 in 1940 to 26,804 in 1944. The number of children enrolled in elementary schools jumped from 1,923 to 2,626. People who worked in the electronics or steel industries in South San Francisco or at the burgeoning San Francisco Airport needed places to live.

Many African-Americans came to northern California

to work at the shipyards in South San Francisco. Discriminatory real estate practices made it difficult for these people to live in Burlingame or Belmont. Many came to live in San Mateo. They even formed a new church, the Macedonia Church of God and Christ.

Providing enough housing was a problem. Most of the big-time developers, such as David Bohannon, were busy with huge defense-related projects. But some small houses were built along the Bayshore Highway and in the Beresford region, and a number of old homes were converted into apartments.[6]

Along with the housing shortage, another wartime burden was rationing. Gas, meat, tin cans, mechanical parts—almost everything had value for the war effort. San Mateo Bridge employee Alfred Luis recalled that after gas rationing kicked in during the fall of 1942, traffic across the span fell to a mere 300 vehicles a day. At Wisnom hardware, rationing meant a shortage of small appliances, so the store stocked records and installed listening booths.

At the Beresford Club, times were really hard. The labor shortage meant there was little help for club operations. The plan to take in non-Jews had worked to an extent, and the name of the place was changed to the Peninsula Golf and Country Club, but by January 1945 there were only 59 members. President Ben Follett did what he could to keep the place going. He asked members to volunteer to help with the maintenance work. He rented rooms to jockeys from Bay Meadows, occasioning wild, noisy nights with short, thin and occasionally naked men running up and down the stairs and through the halls. He worked out a deal with the Benjamin Franklin Hotel to lodge the hotel's overflow guests. A certain member was let into the club, gratis, because he could obtain meat for the kitchen. Follett even arranged to have slot machines installed. They were legal in private clubs in California in those days, even though control of the machines was known to be in the hands of organized crime. Four slots came to the club late one night. They had cost $1,325, and they paid for themselves in a month.

The USO in San Mateo was a popular place for boys away from home.
Courtesy San Mateo County Historical Museum

Follett also secured a $59,000 loan from an insurance company and sold off 46 acres of surplus property for $46,000. All of these measures seemed extreme, but it is universally agreed within the Peninsula Golf and Country Club that Follett saved the day. The club now serves as a prestigious sporting and social institution.

HOME FRONT CONTRIBUTIONS

DURING WORLD WAR II, nearly every public or private organization had some wartime program to assist the nation. The city's Recreation Department was an important morale booster. It offered tennis instruction, crafts, tumbling, auto mechanics, children's supervised play, plane modeling, ceramics, dance, and men's softball. It operated a preschool, and organized a "Teen Canteen"[7] for high school youths. In 1944, the Recreation Department listed 88,000 participants in its activities.

The Police Department assumed some responsibility in civil defense matters. At the war's start the department lost some of its younger members to the draft and voluntary conscriptions. Luckily crime decreased during the War. In 1943, most of the 2,987 arrests were for traffic problems. By 1944 the department had more than regained its former strength with 24 employees, including the chief, captain, inspector, patrol sergeant, traffic sergeant, radio man, matron, 3 motorcycle officers, 10 patrolmen and 4 part-time school traffic officers. (A severe blow to the force was delivered that year when after 27 years of service, Chief Thomas Burke died in office. Robert O'Brien replaced him and held the position until 1950.)

During the war, the Fire Department undertook a program to augment its numbers by training volunteers as salvage workers and as engine crew members. It also gave considerable instruction in civil defense. By the end of the war, 85 auxiliary volunteers supplemented the 18 regular firemen.

The city also contributed to the war effort by expanding library services to help raise morale. Small stations were established at Mills Hospital, a shop on 25th Avenue, and other locations.

In conjunction with the local post of the American Legion, the city made another significant contribution in 1943 by allowing the erection of a dormitory in the Civic Center for servicemen on leave. Funds from William Kyne and Bay Meadows built the facility, which was promoted and managed by the Legionnaires. While the official charge for a night's stay was 50 cents, those without money were allowed a bunk for free. It was estimated that some 30,000 men made use of the dormitory before the end of the War.

Even the city's 50th birthday party took a back seat to the war effort. The *San Francisco Chronicle* of September 3, 1944 reported that San Mateans celebrated the occasion with a Victory Garden Harvest Fair. Their "Golden Jubilee" also featured a "colorful Pageant of Progress."

Private organizations did their part as well. The Red Cross was active, training citizens in first aid. Mills Hospital trained girls as aids in case an emergency overwhelmed the regular staff. Even the community theater group, the Hillbarn Players, visited troops in camps, helping to lift morale.

During World War II, every horse-racing track in the state closed in order to preserve resources—every one except Bay Meadows. As a morale booster for servicemen and the local population, the track was allowed to stay open, provided its profits were donated to the war effort. In the end, some $4,000,000 in funds were turned over to war relief and service organizations.

San Mateo took its civil defense very seriously during the war. Each block had an air raid warden. Blackouts were ordered and shelters arranged. Salvage campaigns were conducted frequently. Tin was especially valuable and was picked up at service stations. Tin drive promoters modeled a life-sized tin dummy and called it "Corporal Can."[8] The crude sculpture was paraded around San Mateo and Burlingame to aid in informing residents of the need for tin and explaining to housewives how to prepare empty cans for salvage.

The San Mateo Chamber of Commerce played an active part in the war bond campaigns. It gave out trophies weekly to stores selling the most bonds or war stamps. The competition was based on a percentage of what was sold the week previously, allowing the smaller stores to vie with the bigger outfits.[9]

Although San Mateo had an integrated population, it also had two USO stations during the War, one for white servicemen and one for blacks. The white facility was on Third Avenue and El Camino. Its free canteen was open from 8:30 a.m. to 11:00 p.m. every day. An average of 25,000 soldiers and sailors used this facility every month.

The USO for African-Americans on Second Avenue was also a very popular spot. There were also two privately-owned night spots for African-American servicemen, where soldiers and sailors were joined by the increasing number of blacks who had come to live here, often in houses formerly occupied by Japanese-Americans. Charles Sullivan's restaurant, "Sullivan's," was set up in the old Takahashi Store. There were great hamburgers, dancing, and an occasional card game. Claire Mack, a youngster during the war, recalled that most parents preferred their teenagers to visit Texena Sisson's "Little Harlem," where gambling was forbidden but the food was superb—especially the chili.

YOUNG PEOPLE WERE ALSO affected by the war. Most high-school boys expected to be part of the fighting in one way or another. Girls prepared for sacrifice as well.

The patriotic fervor among the boys at San Mateo High had always been high. During the 1939-1940 academic year a series of fist fights broke out over who was the best president—George Washington or Abraham Lincoln. When the War came in 1941, students canceled their Christmas dance.

School air raid drills became routine. With automobile parts and fuel unobtainable, students and faculty bicycled to school. Junior and senior boys took special physical education classes where they learned basic military commands and ran obstacle courses. The idea, of course, was to get them in shape for being soldiers.

Many new classes were offered to help the cause. Instructor Royal Ivory gave a course in gardening; produce that the students grew was used at home or given to war-related charities. Some students supplied the school cafeteria with vegetables they grew in their own backyard Victory Gardens. Mary Marshall taught a course on home nursing. The PTA funded the purchase of necessary equipment and supplies.

Coffee and doughnuts, and conversations with volunteers, helped boost servicemen's morale at the USO canteen.

Courtesy San Mateo County Historical Museum

The students formed their own organizations as well. Nearly 200 joined the "Victory Corps," in which young people learned how to prepare themselves for wartime employment. The Knitting Club made wool scarves which the Red Cross distributed to servicemen and women. Students gathered playing cards, records and coat hangers to give to the soldiers stationed at the Cow Palace. During the 1942-43 academic year, San Mateo High won a treasury flag award after raising funds and materials totaling $300,000 for war-related causes. Despite the war, students' spirits remained high. Since phonograph records were scarce, students listened to radios, went to San Francisco to see stage entertainment, and went often to the San Mateo Theater.

No peacetime institution in San Mateo County was more active in the war effort than San Mateo Junior College. Many women students (two thirds of the student body by 1944) worked for the Red Cross, or helped the wounded at Dibble General Hospital in Menlo Park. Occasionally, patients would visit the campus, some of them badly disfigured from their wounds. Frank Stanger remembered that they had a strong impact on the students, "bringing the realities of war"[10] to everyone.

Besides volunteer programs, the college offered classes in war preparedness. It became San Mateo's own decontamination station in the event of a gas attack. The San Mateo County Blood Bank was set up in an unused classroom. By the spring of 1945, 11,542 donations had been accepted from 5,436 different donors, of whom 69 were members of the "Gallon Club."[11]

At the new campus at Peninsula and Delaware, faculty members Fred Klyver and Erford McAllister organized a Victory Garden and canning project that became the best of its kind in Northern California. Administrator James Tormey noted that society ladies worked side by side with their servants, each managing their own little plot. People brought their produce, meat, or fish to the campus, where they were taught how to prepare the food for canning. By 1945, some 68,000 cans of food had been produced in this way. At the canning center, everyone participated. Tormey commented: "people of all races, colors, mixtures and everything else—every status in life, would find work right across these preservation tables."

Of all the activities sponsored by the college, perhaps none made more of an impact than its radar school, one of the best on the West Coast, teaching military personnel 22 hours a day, six days a week, to use the new electronic detection system. Eventually about 700 graduated from the 48-hour intensive course. Every hour of training was critical. Tormey recalled, "If Christmas Day came on Wednesday, too bad, Mac, this class is on Wednesday too."

While the college was the unquestioned leader of peacetime institutions in the war effort, San Mateo also had an important wartime institution especially created for the cause. The United States Merchant Marine Cadet Basic Training School was established at Coyote Point. Just before the War, only a roller skating rink remained as the last vestige of the old Pacific City. When the manager of the rink was called to service, the Point became practically abandoned—but not for long. Lieutenant Commander R. M. Sheaf, United States Naval Reserve, assumed command of the Coyote Point school. His design of the campus was utilitarian, but he resisted the temptation to clear cut the eucalyptus groves that were (and still are) present. Instead, he situated his twenty or so buildings within the groves, which made for an attractive campus. He left the vegetation and open space, so that when it returned to peacetime utilization after the war the school could continue as a beautiful campus and then as a regional park. Included with the improvements were a chapel, gymnasium, barracks, classrooms, an administration building, parade grounds and a swimming pool. Just a few months after the start of the war, the school was ready to receive its first 300 cadets. The school's dedication took place on August 29, 1942.

Training took ninety days and included classroom instruction and physical fitness.[12] In the second month students spent a night in a life boat with cold rations on San Francisco Bay. Lieutenant John Macauley, writing for the *U.S. Coast Guard Magazine* in December 1943, described his firsthand experience on one of these outings. He and 23 cadets left the dock in their boat at 4:30 in the afternoon. When they pulled away, everyone was singing and spirits were high:

> When we put into an anchorage further down the bay, there wasn't a bit of song left in any of us. We were wet and hungry, and our eyes were blood red from salt spray and the lack of sleep. Our arms were tired from rowing and bailing. There had been a storm on San Francisco Bay during that night.[13]

Those who successfully completed their ninety days at Coyote Point went to sea for six months for further training aboard a merchant ship. After that, they attended the King's Point Merchant Marine Academy at Long Island, New York before their final graduation as officers. Eventually some 5,000 went through the program at Coyote Point.

When Japan surrendered and the war ended, there was great rejoicing at Coyote Point. One cadet wrote:

> Japan surrenders . . . and suddenly the realization of what it meant . . . the snake dance . . . fire hoses . . . sudden liberty . . . and through it all, the wild surging hysteria and joy . . . and just as suddenly the sobering reality that it was all over . . . then the prayers of thanksgiving . . . and hope . . . and remembering those who would not come back . . . and the resolutions . . . fervent and sincere . . . that they had not died in vain. Then a short time later an unusual assembly . . . the speculation and the scuttlebutt . . . and finally the words from Captain Brady . . . your commander . . . "And so gentlemen, with the coming of peace the Cadet Corps has returned to the four-year course so that those of you who wish the sea as a career will be given the very best of training. Those of you who entered after July first are eligible and will remain at San Mateo until May of 46."[14]

And so in 1945 San Mateo set about the business of making civic improvements, expanding its population, and healing the wounds left by the war.

Notes

1. Postel, "Junior-Community," p. 10.
2. Stanger, *Peninsula*, p. 178.
3. K. Asai, "History of the Japanese Pioneers in San Mateo,", student monograph #330 in the archives of the San Mateo County Historical Museum, June 1941.
4. Author's interview with Hasuko Watanuki, February 12, 1993.
5. Author's interview with Yasuko Ann Ito, March 23, 1993.
6. Dolorita Falvey, "The Story of San Mateo, 1944," manuscript in the archives of the San Mateo County Historical Museum.
7. Stanger, *Peninsula*, p. 116.
8. Ibid, p. 185.
9. Letter from Henry F. Misselwitz, San Mateo Chamber of Commerce to Dr. Frank Stanger, March 27, 1950.
10. Postel, "Junior-Community," p. 10.
11. Stanger, *Peninsula*, p. 182.
12. "Cadet School Marks First Anniversary," *Burlingame Advance*, August 27, 1943.
13. John Macauley, "Merchant Marine Trains Em," *U.S. Coast Guard Magazine*, December, 1943.
14. *Bearings, Souvenir Edition*, May 1946 publication of the U. S. Merchant Marine Cadet School, San Mateo, California.

CHAPTER VII

Postwar Optimism and the Resulting Boom: 1946-1969

THE RETURN OF THE EXILED

The feeling of optimism generated by the conclusion of World War II spread across the nation, along with the belief that the world could be made over into a better place. Especially in California was this true. Service men and women who came here for the first time on their way to various military assignments decided to make new lives for themselves in the Golden State. Thousands of others had come for jobs in war-related industries, and they were determined to stay. Soldiers who were native sons returned from Europe and the Pacific. And so did those people who had been exiled because of distrust and prejudice.

As in many other places up and down the West Coast, San Mateo's bittersweet relationship with its Japanese American citizens resumed after the war. These people returned not just to piece their lives back together, but to do it in a way in which past injustices could not be repeated. Led by their heroic veterans, who had unquestionably proven their loyalty, bravery and ability, Japanese Americans would no longer simply accept "second class citizenship."

Among those returning from the fighting was Yoneo Kawakita, who served with MacArthur in the Pacific. For him the war will never be over. He lost friends, both Japanese-American and white. Meanwhile his family suffered through the humiliating internment. However, some of the bad feelings were tempered by the fact that the Hillsborough family whom his family had entrusted with their possessions had perfectly preserved everything—including the 1941 automobile they had bought just before the War started.

For those who had spent the entire war in the camps, the decision had to be made—what now? There was no government program to help these people re-establish their lives, to find housing or jobs. Many Issei found themselves totally lost to despair. Most of the San Mateo group who had been sent to Topaz returned, and on their return overwhelming challenges confronted them. Mariko Endo recalled, "God, we had to start all over again."¹ Former childhood friends like Claire Mack did not even recognize Joe Fujuiki. However, according to Edward Ishimaru, old friendships were rekindled rapidly. The Endo family found that to be true, too.

While things were far from perfect for the Japanese Americans of San Mateo, perhaps their return was easier than in other places. Out in the Central Valley, and in other agricultural communities where Japanese farmers competed economically with whites, things were worse. Attitudes were less conciliatory. In San Mateo, where a good number of the Japanese had worked as servants or in businesses which were noncompetitive before the war, the feelings seemed more warm. And San Mateo had a long tradition of diversity. Those who came back were familiar to the established members of the community.

Opposite: (left to right) Thomas Culligan, Jr., Andrew Conway, San Mateo Mayor Edward Reilly, and D.C. McGinnis, of the Federal Housing Authority, are ready to begin a development.
Courtesy San Mateo County Historical Museum

*Mrs. Ishie Takahashi
Photographed in 1977*

Courtesy Japanese American Cultural League

In fact, Japanese families who had well-known businesses before the war found it possible to resurrect their enterprises fairly rapidly. The Yamanouchi family re-opened their laundry business in 1945. They changed its name from Imperial Laundry to Blu-White Laundry and Cleaners, so as not to provoke resentment. The Endos dug up their barrel of tools and established a new auto shop on First Avenue and B Street. It took the Takahashis about six months to rent a place, but they also re-established their store.

Those who had to work for others found life more difficult. Edward Ishimaru, whose family had operated a nursery before the War, had to take a step backward and work as a gardener. He eventually became a mechanic for United Airlines.

Another problem was housing. Some who owned homes found their places in disrepair, and in some cases vandalized. For many others, who did not own a home before they left, it was hard to find any place to live. Some joined African American families living in barracks, once part of the Merchant Marine Academy at Coyote Point.

Exacerbating the situation for the Japanese, and African Americans too, were the many real estate restrictions applied to them. Realtors who considered selling to certain racial groups in Burlingame or Belmont might be blacklisted.[2] In San Mateo, racial covenants existed on the new development in the Shoreview district. This discrimination was especially painful because the houses constructed there were built as starter homes for returning veterans. They were also in the eastern part of the city, where minority groups had traditionally lived, while the western section of San Mateo had always been highly restricted.

Yet the postwar period did bring substantial gains to people who had long suffered from second class citizenship. After all, World War II had, in part, been fought against racial intolerance. The ideals espoused during the war were not forgotten. For the Japanese Americans the change in attitude was symbolized by the passage of the Walter-McCarren Act in 1952, allowing for the naturalization of the Issei, and also reopening Japanese immigration on a quota basis.

For San Mateo's Japanese Americans, the year 1952 was doubly momentous in that the San Mateo Elementary School District hired Kumiko Ishida as a teacher, the first non-white instructor in the district's history.

Slowly the Japanese Americans revived their former community affiliations. Sometime after 1950, through their Buddhist Temple and Sturge Presbyterian Church, they again sponsored Boy Scout troops. The Buddhist Temple itself was improved greatly. Under the leadership of Sanaye Ikeda a $36,000 auditorium was constructed in 1952. In 1958 Ikeda led an effort to build an adjoining chapel.

With restrictions partly lifted during the 1950s and 1960s, Japanese immigration to California increased, partly because of an economic depression in Japan. While most first went to the Central Valley to find work, a good number ended up in San Mateo, swelling the Japanese American community and greatly enlarging such institutions as the Buddhist Temple.

The healing process between Japanese Americans and San Mateo was formalized in 1963, when Mayor Roy Archibald proposed a sister city relationship to Mayor Tasuku Fujito of Toyonaka. Among the gifts exchanged was an El Camino bell, which was mounted near the entrance of the Toyonaka City Hall.

The sister city relationship sparked the development of another community project. Sometime in the 1950s, the San Mateo Gardeners' Association had offered to landscape and maintain a garden in a public location. No site had been settled upon until the creation of the sister city relationship, when a one-acre site in Central Park was suggested.

A Japanese Garden Koen-Kai club was organized with

The Japanese Garden in Central Park was dedicated in 1966, to mark the sister-city relationship between San Mateo and Toyonaka, Japan.
Courtesy San Mateo County Historical Museum

Sanaye Ikeda as chairman, Shiro Ishimaru and Masazo Shimizu, vice chairmen and Stanley Pitcher, Superintendent of the Parks Department, as honorary vice chairman. Nagao Sakurai, a Japanese born and trained landscape architect, was selected to design the grounds.

To get things going, the city granted start-up funds. More money was raised by the Koen-Kai. Work officially began on October 22, 1965. Many other organizations, companies and individuals—Japanese and from the community at large—contributed capital, materials and volunteer labor. The Gardeners' Association alone donated 6,000 man-hours. The City of Toyonaka contributed a handsome pagoda.

In August 1966 the city celebrated the completion of the garden with a dedication ceremony at Central Park and then a banquet at the Villa Hotel, where the Mayor of Toyonaka sat as guest of honor.[3]

The garden became a tangible reminder of the contributions of one of the city's important ethnic communities. Doris Batchelor of the *Redwood City Tribune* summed up its existence this way:

> Most of the men who gave of their skill, labor and money to create the garden are American citizens who, with their families, spent the years in "relocation centers" during World War II. But the bitterness of those years has not stood in the way of their giving to the city this jewel of a garden . . . that bespeaks peace, friendship and love.[4]

POPULATION EXPLOSION

SAN MATEO'S huge population increase in the postwar period included many African-Americans. Drawn to the Bay Area by wartime and postwar employment opportunities, but restricted from going to many other communities, San Mateo African-Americans encountered many of the same barriers the Japanese-Americans faced. They also made gains. African-Americans went before the School Board and City

Bayshore Highway near Bay Meadows, 1949, was one of the busiest and most dangerous highways in the country. Drivers had plenty of billboards to distract them.

Courtesy San Mateo County Historical Museum

Council to demand the hiring of black teachers. They succeeded when Evelyn Taylor and later George Dabney were hired.[5]

But the minority population did not keep pace with the exploding white population. In 1947, the African American population was 4.2% of the total, with whites at 93.4%. By 1950, the percentage of African Americans had shrunk to 2.9%, while the white population grew to 94.7%.[6]

Before World War II, San Mateo's total population was just under 20,000. By 1946, one year after the war, it was 30,613, a one-third increase in six years. Rapid growth continued in the succeeding postwar years. By 1948, the population was 34,133, and the average per capita income of a San Matean was one-third higher than the national average.[7]

While new residents immigrated from all over the United States, many came from close by. Future four-time mayor, John J. Murray, a native San Franciscan who lived on fog-bound 33rd Avenue, one day said to his wife Hallie: "Honey, I can't stand putting on my overcoat to water that little front yard," and resolved to move down the Peninsula.

Murray was acquainted with developer Axel Johnston, who was building houses on the site of a former victory garden southwest of 25th Avenue. Murray bought a lot for $2200 on Del Mar Way. The city would have preferred that Murray build a dwelling of Southern Colonial design to conform to the other homes in the neighborhood, but John had met an architect of the Frank Lloyd Wright school who talked him into a one-story house with a modern look. It would also be equipped with a new type of radiant and convection heating. The city opposed the design and the heating system, and delayed construction for many months. But Murray succeeded in building his dream house, which eventually was featured in the *San Francisco Chronicle* and *Sunset Magazine*. He also gained an unquenchable interest in San Mateo city government that would inspire him to run successfully for city council several times.[8]

By 1950, with a population of 41,782, San Mateo had spread out over 7,879 acres. While mostly residential in character, it did have commercial centers, which included five banks and two building and loan associations. There were also 19 churches. By 1957 the town had 65,999 people, eight banks, three savings and loans, and 30 churches.[9] By 1963, population reached an astonishing 77,250 people, living in 25,334 housing units.[10] In the seventeen years since the end of the war, the city's population had grown by 149%.

BOHANNON RESUMES
DEVELOPMENT OF HILLSDALE

WHERE WERE ALL THESE NEW RESIDENTS going to live? A group of energetic developers changed the face of the landscape in the San Mateo area from open fields, bayside marsh and grass-covered hills to block after block of housing. Depending on one's perspective, this might be construed as either the answer to every American's dream of owning his own home, or environmental disaster. Most San Mateans would probably find a middle ground between the two points of view. But no one can deny that the postwar developers were highly successful in identifying a market and providing a desirable product. Unquestionably the best-known of this entrepreneurial group was David Bohannon.

During the war, Bohannon's Hillsdale project lay dormant. The sites of future housing tracts were reserved for "victory gardens." By December 1942 all the original homes in Hillsdale were sold, including the models.[11]

While Hillsdale was inactive, its builder was not. Bohannon became involved in a variety of wartime housing activities. He built temporary housing for defense workers throughout the Bay Area, and some 3500 permanent homes, including 1500 in a "completely planned community" called San Lorenzo Village.[12] At one point during this development, a house was completed every 48 minutes.

Not long after the war ended, Bohannon returned to his San Mateo project. In June 1946 the *San Mateo Times* announced that work on "Hillsdale No. 3" would begin. Another 200 houses were to be started. Paving and widening of side streets and the extension of Alameda de las Pulgas south to Laurel Creek commenced. Hillsdale Boulevard was extendeded to the Alameda. The new Bohannon subdivision would occupy the area bounded by Laurel Creek on the south, 31st Avenue on the north, Alameda to the west and El Camino to the east.

In January 1947 the *Times* announced a 150-acre addition, "Hillsdale No. 4," extending north to 27th Avenue and west to Monterey. "Hillsdale 5 and 6," also planned, would extend far into the hill country. The 200 homes to be created on No. 4 were designed to sell for $12,000 to $20,000. In November 1949, Bohannon asked the city to begin annexing the area, before even a single home was completed.[13] The city complied, eventually taking a one-hundred-acre portion of the development, pushing the city limits relentlessly westward.

Bohannon's Hillsdale encompassed all the changes the housing industry experienced across the nation during the postwar period. His large tract development was quite unlike the prewar standard of lot-by-lot purchase and building by the individual owner. Before the War, there were builders like him, but they were essentially small operators who could put up only a few houses, sell them and move on. Not much planning or imagination went into them.

Bohannon was the prototypical big-time developer. He created whole communities, hundreds of houses at a time, with consideration for community, recreational, social and educational needs. Liberal lending policies by public and private institutions made this transformation possible in the postwar period. New materials and techniques brought into existence during the war also helped to cut prices and made large-scale construction feasible.

In 1949, Bohannon stated his purpose in creating Hillsdale:

> To take care of the forgotten man—the guy in the middle income bracket... He wants and needs a good home in good surroundings, but can't afford to pay the tab on a custom-built house. In Hillsdale, I have tried to give him the custom-built feeling at mass volume prices.[14]

He mentioned that part of his success at Hillsdale was due to his foresight some years before:

> I got the land when the price was right... So now I plan to make nothing on the construction of the house, but take my profit from the sale of the land.

Houses he had sold before the war for less than $7,000 were fetching $20,000 in 1949.

BOHANNON'S GENIUS was not only in constructing, but in promotion as well. He marketed his houses as living quarters for the new postwar middle class.

After he saw the 1948 movie "Mr. Blancings Builds His Dream House" with Cary Grant, Myrna Loy and Melvyn Douglas, he had an inspiration. The film, depicting all the nightmares associated with people building their own houses, rang true for millions of Americans. Bohannon reasoned that he could offer people their dream house, while saving them the pain of building.

In the spring of 1948, in partnership with RKO Films, Macy's Department Stores (which provided furnishings) and General Electric (which supplied the appliances), Bohannon constructed a "dream house" in Hillsdale, modeled after the one in the movie. After its completion the public was allowed to tour the "dream house," after paying an admission fee which was donated to the YMCA, Boy Scouts and Girl Scouts. Bohannon later sold the "dream house" for $19,000, but in the course of his effort he had introduced his product to thousands of potential buyers.[15]

In September 1954, Bohannon announced the development of another 40 acres in the hills to the west of his earlier developments, to include houses on Sunset Terrace, Verdun and an extension of 31st Avenue. This project came under some protest from residents down the hill, who were tired of construction noise, trucks, and mud. Nevertheless, building continued.[16] By 1961, the last of the houses had been completed, high up on 31st Avenue and West Hillsdale Boulevard, 1000 feet above those Bohannon had built twenty years before. As thousands realized their dream of owning a home, Bohannon made a fortune, and won award after award

Bay Meadows Airport continued in use until 1947

Courtesy San Mateo County Historical Museum

from regional and national organizations, testifying to his buildings' excellence.

Besides housing tracts, Bohannon also built apartment complexes. In April 1948 he unveiled a plan to build 503 apartment units on both sides of Hillsdale Boulevard. These "garden style" apartments would be similar to the Park Merced project in San Francisco. Bohannon later explained: "My idea was to give people who like apartment life a chance to enjoy the country." The development included 54 one-bedroom, 383 two-bedroom and 66 three-bedroom units. Also planned were garages for 479 automobiles and eight playgrounds for children. The complex would include machine washers and dryers, which would "eliminate unsightly lines full of clothing."[17]

This project met some opposition. The Planning Commission asked whether San Mateans wanted so much of their city to be devoted to renters. Some residents complained about the removal of some 300 trees. Nevertheless, the project won the Commission's approval. In February 1949 work began on a $10 million development, constructed in several sections.[18] By the fall of 1950 twelve of the buildings had been completed, with units renting for $125 to $144 a month.

Bohannon shocked Peninsula residents in 1953 when he sold the apartment houses for $7.5 million to an eastern realtor (actually this was a 99-year lease). By that time the complex had grown to 705 units. This transaction was the largest real estate transaction in San Mateo County history up to that time.[19]

While Bohannon sold his homes and disposed of these apartments, he held on to his commercial property and eventually converted it into one of the premier shopping centers in the world. In April 1948 he announced his first coup: Sears had selected the site for the placement of a store. When it opened in 1951, thousands attended the ribbon cutting.[20]

Bohannon later revealed that before the war he had planned to build a community shopping center to serve only local people. But during the war his plan changed:

> We had time to stop and survey and think. And we came to the realization in view of the population and merchandising trends, that we had a future regional center on our hands, a center designed to serve an area of up to 300,000 people, a center with practically all the merchandising units to be found in a big city's downtown district.[21]

Bohannon's commercial developments were as innovative as his houses and apartments. He had built residential developments with the automobile in mind, so his shopping center featured easy road access, vast

Pouring the concrete slab for the basement of Macy's store in Hillsdale, March 1954. The store opened only three months later.

Courtesy San Mateo County Historical Museum

parking accommodations and short walking distances from parking spaces to stores. He put retail stores in the center and surrounded them with parking.

Also part of his plan were underground facilities for truck loading and unloading of merchandise to help ease traffic congestion and add to the attractiveness of the center. This idea was borrowed from a Los Angeles shopping center with subterranean features. In August 1951, as the Cold War intensified and the Korean War raged, the San Mateo City Council requested that this underground area be made available as a civil defense shelter. Bohannon consented, helping his $20,000,000 project gain approvals.[22] The Korean War made construction materials scarce. However, in May 1952, the National Production Authority approved plans for Bohannon's mall and the Stonestown center in San Francisco.[23]

Macy's then announced plans to build a $6 million store at Hillsdale—its first suburban project in California. At the same time, Bohannon revealed his overall design for the 42-acre center, complete with three department stores and 75 shops.[24]

Ground breaking for Macy's took place in 1952.[25] On May 28, 1954, amid considerable fanfare, San Mateo Mayor Wesley P. Johnson and Martin A. Foss of the San Mateo County Board of Supervisors cut the ribbon. Also announced that spring was the $200,000 remodeling and expansion—by 8,000 square feet—of the former Andrew Williams supermarket, at that time a Mayfair.[26]

By 1956, Bohannon had 50 shops in place, augmenting the Sears, Macy's and Mayfair. In April 1961, ground was broken for a third "anchor" store, the Emporium. It was completed in September of 1962.[27] By 1970 the Hillsdale Mall included more than 150 stores and shops. Its $400 million in sales contributed greatly to the economic well-being of the city, adding significantly to the tax base.

A few argued that this had a negative effect on San Mateo. Certainly it changed the entire character of the city. Since stagecoach days the center had been near San Mateo Creek, between the tracks and El Camino. Now, suddenly, a regional suburban shopping center had changed that, and the commercial focus of the city had shifted south. In order to compete more effectively with Hillsdale and other shopping centers, the downtown merchants in 1957 organized a non-profit Downtown

L. C. Smith, the contractor who built the Nineteenth Avenue Freeway and installed most of the sidewalks in the city.
Courtesy San Mateo County Historical Museum

Association to promote their businesses in a unified way. The Association has been able to keep downtown business viable.

Suburban shopping malls are seldom thought of as centers of art, but once again the innovative David Bohannon did things differently. While the mall was under construction, Bohannon commissioned Benjamin "Benny" Bufano to create eleven granite statues to adorn his shopping center. Bohannon even had a studio built for the artist. By the fall of 1956 his eighteen tons of statuary had been completed. Except for "Saint Francis on Horseback," all the pieces depict animals, ranging in size from an 18-inch mouse to a 12-foot-high owl. At a dedication on October 15, $500,000 worth of art was unveiled to some 4,000 spectators, including California's Lieutenant Governor, Harold Powers.[28] Since that time, millions of people have enjoyed Bufano's art at Hillsdale.

When "Benny" died in 1970 he was mourned, in many knowledgeable circles, as the greatest artist in San Francisco Bay Area History.

Besides being a dynamo in real estate development and a patron of the arts, Bohannon was also influential in local politics. He was a perennial leader of the County Development Association and a major supporter of freeway projects and the improvement of the San Mateo Hayward Bridge.

Because his residential and commercial real estate successes were founded on the primacy of the automobile in the California life style, it is not surprising that Bohannon backed road development and opposed public transportation projects. In 1961 he spoke out against Bay Area Rapid Transit (BART), and led the opposition to its adoption in San Mateo County. For better or worse, Bohannon helped to keep BART off the Peninsula for many years.

More Developers

While David Bohannon was perhaps San Mateo's best known developer, he certainly was not the only one. A variety of builders accomplished projects comparable in scope to Bohannon's. Included in this lofty arena was L. C. Smith.

Smith, at one time an internationally-known polo player, had been very busy during the war, building roads, excavating, grading, and paving. In the postwar period, Smith became San Mateo County's premier sidewalk, street and highway developer, doing all the work for most Peninsula cities and completing projects throughout the Bay Area. Between 1957 and 1969, he was responsible for $250 million in road work alone.

Smith also became involved in residential construction. In 1952 his Concord Ranch Enterprises purchased Leslie Salt properties to develop 19th Avenue Park. The city approved plans in 1954, and Joseph Eichler's Moorepark Company began construction in 1955, using the designs of architects Emmons, Anschen and Allen. By 1956 the houses were finished, and virtually every one was sold. Smith then developed the Lauriedale area. In 1966 this southwestern section was annexed to the city.

Among Smith's largest commercial successes was bringing the $15-million Royal Coach Inn of Texas to his site on Bayshore and 19th Avenue (today the hotel is known as the Dunfey).

Smith, active in Democratic politics, became personally acquainted with President Harry S. Truman, Governor Edmund G. "Pat" Brown and State Senator (later United States Senator), Alan Cranston. These political connections could not have hurt him in his quest for government road-building contracts.

In local affairs, Smith worked hard with such men as

Typical of the postwar developments in eastern San Mateo was Shoreview, bordered by East Third Avenue crossing at the top, and Newbridge Avenue slanting down the eastern border. The area to the right, once the site of the San Mateo Airport, will soon be developed as Parkside.

Courtesy San Mateo County Historical Museum

Judge Francis W. Murphy to rehabilitate and employ "the out-of-luck, the criminally convicted, the helpless." After Smith's death in 1973, the Judge's son, attorney William F. Murphy, remembered that Smith had "never turned away a man sent to him for help."[29] Smith was also a substantial supporter of the San Mateo Boys' Club.

Axel Johnson and the San Mateo Investment Company developed enormous projects after the War. By 1951, the firm had built a thousand houses within its San Mateo Knolls 1, 2, 3 and 4, with 5 in the works. The San Mateo Investment Company also built 2,500 houses in San Mateo Terrace, while constructing individual houses on contract in the Aragon and Baywood sections as well.[30]

Like Bohannon, Smith, and Johnson, the firm of Conway and Culligan came back strong in the postwar period. In January 1947 they announced plans to develop $10 million in residential real estate, mostly east of El Camino Real. In June they began construction on a commercial tract at 37th Avenue. In 1949 they won an award from the National Association of Home Builders for their San Mateo Village development. In 1955, they completed housing tracts in the area once occupied by polo fields west of El Camino Real and east of the Peninsula Golf and Country Club. The new Elks Lodge and Serra Catholic High School were built in the same vicinity. Also in 1955, the firm finished 500 houses in the Fiesta Gardens area.

After the war, Raybould and Bartlett returned to their developments in the Bayshore Highway tract, Peninsula Manor, College Park, Bayshore Acres and Shoreview. In 1945, Raybould was also involved with the $250,000 purchase of the Caldwell estate, which encompassed the downtown block extending from Second to Third Avenues on San Mateo Drive, for the purpose of modern commercial development. In 1948 the firm helped to liquidate the John Barneson estate (formerly part of the San Mateo Homestead), converting pasture land into 65 lots to form Aragon Terrace and Vernon Terrace.

Raybould was also involved in the $300,000 purchase of the historic 20-acre Mounds Estate. Duncan Hayne had built an Italian villa which was acquired in 1915 by Mrs. Cyrus Walker. She held many parties there during San Francisco's Panama Pacific International Exposition. During the 1920s the estate was purchased by Hugo Lorder, a shipping magnate formerly with the Dollar Lines. The property included a 3200 foot frontage on El Camino Real. Its great natural feature, the mound, rose 130 feet above the surrounding towns of San Mateo and Hillsborough and was capped with the 30-room mansion.

The original development plans called for nine Hillsborough and forty San Mateo lots, including 14 apartment sites around the old mansion, which would not be touched.[31] However, the structure was demolished, and in 1954 a "super-luxury" apartment house called "The Mounds" was built on its site. Developers McCann, Keys and Day of Redwood City heavily promoted the "panoramic view of the entire bay area"[32] seen from every unit. Each of the 18 two-bedroom, two-bath apartments, with 1500 square feet plus a large lanai, rented for the princely sum of $350 and up.

A variety of smaller developers also took advantage of opportunities and successfully developed properties. In 1950, the Hanson Brothers established Glendale Village on the site of the old McClellan home on 36th Avenue. The Parkside Development Company created a tract, complete with a shopping center, south of Shoreview on the site of the San Mateo Airport. South of Parkside other tracts included Hillsdale Manor, Marina Gardens and Los Prados.

Darcy's Marina, Parkside Development and Los Prados Homes sponsored a contest to rename Seal Slough to an appellation more inviting to future home owners. The winners were Mr. and Mrs. Charles Hice, who came up with Marina Lagoon.

East of Marina Lagoon and west of rapidly developing Foster City, the Philben Corporation announced plans in 1964 for the construction of an "Aquatic City."[33] The $200 million project called Mariners' Island was to include a 51-acre trade mart and convention center, hospital, 20 acres of recreational and cultural amenities "patterned after the famed Tivoli Gardens in Copenhagen," apartments and houses for 7,000 people, and four acres of light industry. The development was annexed to San Mateo as planned, but many of the envisioned improvements never came about.

In July 1965 Mayor Hugh A. Wayne served as the master of ceremonies for the opening of the $18-million Woodlake Apartment Complex on Peninsula Avenue, on property formerly occupied by San Mateo Junior College. A variety of celebrity sports figures were also on hand, since the complex stressed physical fitness with its $500,000 fully equipped and staffed spa, seven swimming pools, four tennis courts and paddle ball courts. The project also boasted a beautiful man-made lake. Woodlake's developers believed that the 35-hour work week would soon be the norm for Americans, and that leisure activities at home thus would become increasingly important. Architects Wurster, Bernardi and Emmons and landscape architect Lawrence Halprin planned accordingly, and included a closed circuit television system capable of bringing first-run movies to every one of the nearly 1,000 units. The Woodlake Apart-ments quickly became a mecca for "swinging singles." By 1967, the project had also won a variety of design awards, including ones from the American Institute of Architects, *Homes for Better Living* and

Sunshine Cottage, on the Borel Estate, was home to the Arts Council in 1973.

Courtesy San Mateo County Historical Museum

American Home magazines.

Of all the developments which materialized in the San Mateo area, perhaps the most interesting was the one the city chose not to annex. During the 1960s, T. Jack Foster's watery Foster City rose up from the marshes. One would assume that expansion-minded San Mateo would adopt this new community. But the Foster City project was heavily financed by the State of California through its Estero Municipal Improvement District. Any city choosing to annex Foster City would have to replace EMID and assume EMID's indebtedness. The San Mateo City Councils of the time steered clear of the liability.

THE LAST ESTATE

ONCE, THE SAN MATEO AREA had been dominated by the great estates of some of the most famous capitalists of the West. By 1961, only one of these remained within the city limits: since the time when San Mateans had called themselves villagers, the Borel family had owned the large, beautiful piece of property west of the highway and south of the center of town, surrounding Arroyo Mocha. The Borels had occupied this land longer than any other family on original property. But now the pressures of development would affect even them.

In 1961 a large section of the very center of the estate was condemned by the State of California in order to make way for the 19th Avenue Freeway (now called the J. Arthur Younger Freeway). A suit was brought to determine the value of the land, based on whether or not it should be commercially zoned, a designation achieved while condemnation was in process. In June 1962 the family won the commercial status, along with an $890,000 settlement for a 150-foot strip through the western portion of the property. In August it was awarded another $578,000 for six acres. The family had originally asked for $1,000,000 for this parcel, but the state had offered only $380,000.[34] Once the settlements were made the family determined to divide up the remaining property and develop it.

Years later, newspaper columnist John Horgan of the *San Mateo Times* wrote about what the old Borel estate had meant to kids born in the late 1940s and early 1950s. While the property was privately owned "there was little attempt made to keep us out":

> There was always something marvelous about the old place. Even though aspects of it were beginning to deteriorate after World War II, the estate was a radical departure from our day-to-day bouts with parents, teachers and other fronts of reality. The neighborhood kids, suburbanites all, flocked to the crumbling fences surrounding the estate each day after class as if it were some kind of formidable Oz . . . We regarded Borel land . . . as our own.[35]

The old Borel Chapel, where Alice Borel was married, was used as the Hillbarn Theater for many years.

Courtesy San Mateo County Historical Museum

While a proposal did surface to convert the estate into a park, this was not given very much consideration. Instead, Horgan wrote, "Quickly, almost obscenely, the familiar trappings of the place were stripped away." Bulldozers appeared on the scene, the old buildings came down, fields and gardens were leveled, trees were torn away, and a cement culvert replaced Arroyo Mocho.

One casualty of the project was Borel's chapel, which had been used part of the year by the Hillbarn Players theater group. The chapel also had been a hangout for kids, and, for a while, a place where tramps slept in the rafters. It was demolished in November 1961. Today's Highway 92—El Camino Real cloverleaf sits right on its site.

The Players had been formed by Robert Brauns, Ralph Schram and Sam Rolph as part of the College of San Mateo Adult Education program in the early 1940s. Its first theater was an old barn west of El Camino, near 41st Avenue. The group then moved to the Borel chapel until it was closed in 1950 because of fire hazards. For two years the Players performed on the college campus, then returned to the refurbished chapel. When the chapel was demolished in 1961 the group moved to Carlmont Village Shopping Center in Belmont. Finally, in 1968 they opened the doors of a permanent home in their own building in Foster City.[36]

The final insult to the Borel property occurred on June 8, 1962, when the fine old mansion of Antoine Borel burned to the ground. Some suspected juvenile arsonists were at work, but the cause of the blaze was never proved. Members of the family, some weeping, arrived on the scene to witness the abandoned house's last moments.

Many held an emotional attachment to the old estate, but Antoine Borel's grandchildren and great grandchildren realized they owned a very valuable piece of property. By 1961, the center of the city had moved closer, and the land was destined to become a major crossroads. In Superior Court the family essentially split the estate in two. The 30-acre eastern portion was taken by the Bovet branch of the family, who formed the Borel Estate Company. The 70-acre westerly portion was awarded to the Cotton side.

Before the final conversion of the property was to be

Third Avenue in 1947 is full of sleek new cars. The Medical Arts Building gives weight to the left side, just beyond massive St. Matthew's Catholic Church, which was demolished in 1982.

Courtesy San Mateo County Historical Museum

completed, one of the heirs invited the public to gather firewood. John Horgan recalled the spectacle:

> A horde of [people] descended on the property. It was like something out of the death scene from "Zorba the Greek." It was so hectic that one eager soul wanted to rip the paneling out of a house which was still occupied. He was asked to wait.

Both family groups correctly envisioned hundreds of millions of dollars in development. By 1967, the Owens Illinois Building at 1700 South El Camino Real was ready to be occupied, and the Borel Shopping Center was only about a year away.[37]

TRANSPORTATION—KEEPING PACE

THE POSTWAR PERIOD saw little advancement of public transportation on the Peninsula. In fact, as far as rail transportation goes, reversals were the order of the day. In 1944 the voters of San Francisco elected to purchase the Market Street Railway, which included the "40 Line" to San Mateo. In December 1948 city leaders decided to curtail this streetcar extension to the Peninsula as a cost-cutting measure. Privately operated bus lines served the area until 1969, when the city of San Mateo contracted with San Mateo Transit for this service.

Of course, the postwar period was dominated by the automobile. By 1950 the San Francisco-San Mateo stretch of Bayshore Highway (as yet without a divider strip) had become one of the most traveled and most dangerous sections of road in the world. Constant improvement through the 1950s and 1960s made it safer and accommodated ever-increasing numbers of automobiles.

Perhaps the most controversial transportation issue of the period was the establishment of the cross-town expressway known as the 19th Avenue Freeway. The need

The old electric railroad line, which had served San Mateo for more than forty years, was deemed obsolete, and was removed in 1949. Here the #40 line, its sign reading "Cemeteries, Burlingame, San Mateo," stops at the train station.

Courtesy San Mateo County Historical Museum

for this road was discussed at least as far back as the early 1950s, when the approach to the San Mateo-Hayward Bridge began at Bayshore and Third Avenue and wound its way out to the Bay. Westward traffic to the coast had to move through downtown San Mateo and up Crystal Springs Road, which was then a state highway. A 19th Avenue freeway would take a much more direct route through a dairy pasture (now Foster City), straight up to Skyline, eventually connecting with Highway 1. According to local proponents, the road would become the Sierra-to-the-Pacific by-way.

For San Mateo developers the plan was very advantageous. L. C. Smith supported it (and eventually did most of the construction). He wished to develop nearby properties that would benefit by good transportation. David Bohannon fought for the 19th Avenue Freeway. It would help with his grading operations along local hillsides: at the time he had no choice but to have his trucks transport dirt through residential portions of town to bayside fill sites. The new freeway would also eventually connect his newest westside subdivisions with the Bayshore Freeway.

In July 1955 the San Mateo City Council unanimously adopted a resolution asking the state to develop the highway. In exchange, the city pledged to take responsibility for Crystal Springs Road as a city street, providing for its maintenance at city expense.

The state devised a plan and presented it to the city. By October 1956 the plan had become the object of considerable debate. Led by Fiesta Gardens Home Improvement President John R. Barber, local citizens complained that the freeway would be an unsightly obstruction of the beautiful skyline, that it would create additional noise and fumes, that debris from auto accidents would fall onto nearby houses and residents, and that property values in the immediate area would be greatly reduced. Speaking in favor of the project was David Bohannon. Most of the 400 or so present booed and hissed as the developer made his presentation. Bohannon cautioned the Council not to be influenced by "pressure groups."[38]

After five hours of "wrangling," Carrol M. Speers made the motion, and the Council voted four to one to support the plan with the addition of "specific amendments" requesting the state to provide attractive landscaping and to construct underpasses instead of overpasses wherever possible. Councilman Victor G. Binsacca cast the lone negative vote.

In February 1957 the issue surfaced in Sacramento. David Bohannon and L. C. Smith spoke in its support, and the project cleared all political and bureaucratic hurdles. In October 1961 work began.[39]

Hillsdale High School (top), 1960, and Sunnybrae Elementary School, 1948; the horizontal designs illustrate the architectural values of the era.

Courtesy San Mateo County Historical Museum

For many San Mateans, the great change in the landscape was hard to take. Long-time residents such as educator Winifred M. Burke lamented over the "fallen eucalyptus, pines, bay and oak a century old." She worried that only "old-timers" would weep over "the despoiling we are forced to witness." But soon a generation of citizen ecologists would take up the cause of protecting the local environment.

In the meantime, the postwar period meant creation of new streets and roads and the improvement of old ones throughout San Mateo. Perhaps no single intersection in the City received more attention than Hillsdale and El Camino. The shopping center, Bay Meadows, and nearby railroad tracks created considerable congestion there. Then in 1959, a horrible accident occurred at the intersection: a baby was killed, trapped in its mother's car which was stalled on the tracks. The City Council asked the state for $1,000,000 to create an underpass here.[40] While this request was being processed, the city also began considering lowering El Camino at Hillsdale. The Council approved plans for this underpass in the spring of 1962. In 1963, bids were accepted for the $2,100,000 job of undergrounding Hillsdale at the tracks. The state provided $891,000 of the necessary funds.[41] Later that year the state granted $825,000 more toward the $1,650,000 El Camino Real underpass. The County Board of Supervisors contributed $112,000 toward the El Camino project.[42]

EDUCATION—KEEPING PACE

THE UNPRECEDENTED INCREASE in San Mateo's population during the postwar period was primarily due to an influx of families, and families needed schools. In many other parts of California, the educational system buckled. Children were forced to attend half days in overcrowded classrooms. But San Mateo's school system kept pace with growth on every level—elementary, secondary and junior college.

When the boom began in 1945, San Mateo was already building a new school. Back in 1938, the elementary school district had paid $8,300 for 4.7 acres on South Delaware, south of 10th Avenue, from Roland Borden and Associates of American Homes Inc. Plans had been drawn up during the war years, and Sunnybrae school opened in 1945. The school's modern design influenced the construction of San Mateo elementary schools to come, with single level, airy classrooms opening onto individual play yards and gardens. The

When the war was over, the Merchant Marine Academy at Coyote Point became home to a new campus of College of San Mateo. All the major buildings are gone now.
Courtesy San Mateo County Historical Museum

property for Laurel School on 36th Avenue was purchased during construction of Sunnybrae, and the new campus was completed in 1946.

That same year, San Mateo Schools Superintendent Albion Horrall died in office at the age of 55. His assistant, Walter Jack, took his place. Jack had been principal of Peninsula back in 1929, and had also been principal at San Mateo Park School before becoming Horrall's assistant in 1945. During eleven years as Superintendent, Jack presided over a virtual explosion in elementary school education. By all accounts, he met the challenge admirably. He started with eight schools and finished with 19.

Shoreview school opened in 1948. Two years previously, condemnation proceedings had to be employed to purchase the property, which was being used as a duck farm. The construction site was on an old native mound, where an ancient body was discovered and sent to the County Historical Museum. As opening day approached, the school's furniture was destroyed in a train accident in Ohio, and the school had to open with folding tables and chairs. Shoreview's new principal, John Daly, watched as the carpenters, painters and other workmen departed almost exactly as classroom supplies and children arrived. For the nine schools that followed during Jack's tenure, similar stories of pressing need, rapid construction and hectic openings are told. These schools included George Hall (1950), College Park (1950), Meadow Heights (1951), Albion Horrall (1953), San Mateo Knolls (1953), A. J. Abbott (1954), Fiesta Gardens (1955), Parkside (1956) and Buena Vista (1956). By the time Jack retired in 1957, there were 10,089 children in the elementary school system.

Within the high school system, the need for more buildings was also urgent. In 1949 the San Mateo Union High School District began negotiation with David

This sturdy Art Deco building was San Mateo Junior College's second campus, built in 1937 on Peninsula Avenue. Just twenty years later it was sold, demolished, and replaced by the Woodlake Apartments.
Courtesy San Mateo County Historical Museum

Bohannon for land for a high school. Finally, in 1956, Hillsdale High opened. It was followed by Aragon High, which had been scheduled to start classroom instruction in September of 1960, but because of a steel strike, did not admit students until February of 1961.

Both schools were designed by architects John Lyon Reid and Partners. Their "New Brutalist Style" drew considerable comment by architecture critics. One well-known local reviewer, Alan Temko, described the schools as products of their time. Of Hillsdale, he wrote: "Confronting a suburb littered with TV aerials, the school asserts its own disciplined ideal of rational order in a technological age." He concluded that the design suggested an Orwellian "hemmed-in, troglodytic . . . dream of technocracy, as if the year were already 1984."[43]

In the postwar period, San Mateo Junior College continued to occupy a primary position in San Mateo and the Peninsula. Its small buildings on the Baldwin Avenue and Peninsula Avenue campuses soon became overcrowded. By 1947 enrollment swelled to 2,000 full-time and 4,500 adult students, with 77 instructors. The G. I. Bill helped local veterans who wished to continue their education; the optimism of the times was demonstrated by their eagerness to learn and get ahead. Formal dinner dances at the Benjamin Franklin Hotel were full of gaiety, symbolizing the better future these young people knew they could achieve.

In order to relieve overcrowding, the classroom facilities at Coyote Point's 24-acre former Merchant Marine Cadet School were officially leased in 1947. Now the College was located on three campuses. Students and instructors were hard pressed to zip across town in order to make all their classes. French instructor Dorothy Herrington, recalled:

> One year I had a 9:00 class in the Baldwin building and a 10:00 class at Coyote Point. Of course I couldn't get from the Baldwin class to my car and drive to Coyote Point and park and get to class in the ten-minute interval so I had to leave the Baldwin class a few minutes early and maybe arrive a few minutes late at the Coyote Point classroom—utterly out of breath.[44]

Regardless of such inconveniences, the college continued to expand and improve. In 1948, a "Parents' Nursery School" was formed to assist young adults with their children; the project gained national acclaim. The school's jazz band, which included budding entertainer Merv Griffin, was widely popular.

In 1952, the junior college's great inspirational leader "Jum" Morris died while attending a championship basketball game. Two years later the school changed its name from San Mateo Junior College to College of San Mateo, or CSM, as many have referred to it ever since. The name change reflected the fact that CSM was no longer a junior college, but a community college. Some college officials said that the name was changed so that the new initials would be the same as those of Charles S. Morris.

In 1955, the College's new President, Elon Hildreth, called on a nationally-known architectural firm to plan the future college site at Coyote Point. Hildreth also proposed that the Baldwin Avenue campus be traded to the Navy for use as a naval reserve training school.

Barneson Heights in the 1950s was full of flower gardens and hothouses. Then it was sold to College of San Mateo.
Courtesy San Mateo County Historical Museum

However, many local people felt Coyote Point was not worthy of their college. The *San Mateo Times*, League of Women Voters, American Association of University Women and the downtown business community opposed the site and complained that not enough community input had been gathered. They were worried about sound problems at the Coyote Point location, which was directly under the flight path of San Francisco International Airport. Moreover, they thought the Point was too small for long-range expansion.

In July 1956 Hildreth resigned under pressure from intense opposition. Politically astute Julio Bortolazzo, who took his place, was clearly the right person in the right position at the right time. Some admirers called Bortolazzo "the bulldozer with a brain"[45] because of his ability to get things done.

Joining Bortolazzo was newly-elected trustee Eleanor Nettle, who had been president of the League of Women Voters and a strong critic of Hildreth. With her support and that of other members of the Board, Bortolazzo organized a 29-member citizen's committee to study the college expansion and give recommendations. Community consensus on the future siting of the college would be absolutely essential if adequate funding was to be found. In a shrewd maneuver, the College asked James Wood, publisher of the *Burlingame Advance Star*, and J. Hart Clinton, publisher of the *San Mateo Times*, to act as co-chairmen. Clinton later quipped, "whatever came out of the committee would have the support of the press."[46] Bortolazzo appointed William A. Goss, an economics professor, as Assistant Superintendent and Director of Research to assist the committee, which met 19 times between November 1956 and July 1957.

The results of the meetings were decisive: the Baldwin Avenue campus was "disposable," the Peninsula campus was too small, airport noise at Coyote Point would be a problem and any expansion there would require bay fill. Then came their bombshell recommendation. The committee envisioned a major four-campus institution to cover the entire county. Noting demographic studies which predicted tremendous need

By 1963 the new campus of College of San Mateo was nearing completion, and landscaping had begun.
Courtesy San Mateo County Historical Museum

for higher education in the near future, the committee held that three campuses should be constructed on the bayside of the county, north, central and south, and that an additional campus be located on the coastside. The first priority was the establishment of the central campus, on a 95-acre parcel of Barneson Heights (later referred to as College Heights) which would include 40 acres for buildings, 30 for athletics and 25 for parking. This site was originally suggested by David D. Bohannon; its adoption guaranteed construction of the 19th Avenue Freeway. Otherwise, how would the students get to school?

To finance this measure the committee suggested selling the Baldwin Avenue and Peninsula Avenue properties. The Peninsula Avenue site alone brought $2.7 million, for property that had cost $110,000 in 1937. The rest of the money was to come from a bond issue.

In 1957 the College Trustees adopted a 25-year plan based on the findings of the Citizens' Committee. Their first move was to put a $5.9 million bond issue on the ballot. It passed with a better than 3-to-1 majority.

In 1958, the District purchased 153 acres for $1,125,730 to establish the future CSM. The ground-breaking took place January 21, 1960. Kenneth W. Van Gundy, who had been chairman of the bond campaign and was at that time the President of the San Mateo Chamber of Commerce, was among the honored guests. Grading was completed by September, and contractors Theo G. Mayer and Sons began construction of 410,000 square feet of campus structures in February 1961. On September 20, 1963, after the expenditure of some $19 million, the college opened for classes. It was dedicated on December 8, 1963.

The design of the costly new buildings drew the wrath of architectural critics. One reviewer called the J. C. Warnecke and Associates design "one of Northern California's most pompous yet empty formalist compositions."[47] Nevertheless, the hard-earned new campus was built on a foundation of community love and respect for a college that had proved itself to be more than just an educational institution during the war.

The San Mateo County Historical Museum also moved up the hill. In 1959 the College agreed to finance half the cost of building a new home for the Museum. Representatives of the Museum Association, including J. Hart Clinton, Mrs. David D. Bohannon, George N. Keyston, Paul A. McCarthy and Dr. Frank Stanger went before the San Mateo County Board of Supervisors to request the additional $50,000. College representatives Julio Bortolazzo, Eleanor Nettle, Robert A. Taver and G. W. Bromfield supported the request. The supervisors agreed, and the county finally had what everyone thought then was a permanent home for its historic heritage.

The campus library had not yet been finished when the new campus opened. Students used a lounge area as study room. The card catalog and circulation desk were placed there, and a book mobile outside provided reserve and reference materials. But by the end of 1963, the 35,000-volume library was fully functional.

In 1964, the innovative district made use of federal grants to create a public television station, KCSM. CSM became the first educational institution in northern California to broadcast from its own television station. Faculty and students staffed the station, whose first program was "Health for Better Living." KCSM's first live broadcast featured a debate between incumbent Congressman J. Arthur Younger and his opponent W. Mark Sullivan. By 1965, KCSM was producing fourteen live shows a week. This and other achievements earned it national attention through an article in *Time* magazine on March 5, 1965.

The nationally turbulent 1960s were reflected locally by KCSM's "Inquiring Student" program, which covered significant student involvement in controversial topics. One especially provocative segment was titled "Evolution or Revolution to Solve Campus Problems?"

In 1968, KCSM won a Broadcast Media Award for its series "Dimensions: The Universe" directed by Nina J. Martin, featuring astronomy instructor Michael Chriss.

By June of 1968, CSM had a total student body of 22,000, with 9,000 day students and 13,000 night students—the largest enrollment of any community college in the state. That fall its south county sister college, Cañada, opened for classes and began taking the pressure off. The District's third campus, Skyline College in San Bruno, was dedicated in 1970. The coastside college never materialized.

Municipal Institutions— Keeping Pace

As the transportation and educational systems grew to accommodate the population increases of the postwar period, so did almost every department within the city's government. For the San Mateo Public Library, this meant library branches. As early as 1947, David Bohannon promised to donate land in the southern part of the city for a library site in exchange for approvals on his Hillsdale Garden apartment project. However, progress was slow. In the meantime, the library opened a "book station" at Beresford Park School, containing some 200 volumes. In 1950 this facility was expanded to take up an entire classroom. A year later, the city secured a lease and moved the library into a building owned by the San Mateo Investment Company on 25th Avenue, where it remained until 1957.

In the meantime, on December 12, 1952, Bohannon deeded appropriate lots on Hillsdale and Hacienda to the city for the purpose of establishing a branch library. In 1957 voters approved a bond issue for construction of the Hillsdale Library, serving the southern part of San Mateo.

The city also moved to provide a facility in the eastern section. In 1954, commercial space was leased in the Shoreview Shopping Center. In 1966, the Marina Branch Library was constructed on property purchased by the city on Susan Court.

With two branch libraries established, the city turned its attention to its 63-year old main library at South San Mateo Drive and Second Avenue. Mills Hospital was planning an expansion and wished to purchase the property. The city resolved to move the Library to 55 West Third Avenue and began planning a modern facility. The 35,000 square foot structure would require a $1,200,000 bond issue. A. L. Stoner led the political campaign which succeeded in September of 1966. Architect William Gay Garwood designed the new facility. On December 15, 1968, under Mayor Roy Archibald and Librarian Pauline Coleman, the Central Library was dedicated.[48]

By 1950, the Police Department consisted of 49 officers, two secretaries and three part-time crossing guards, contrasting with the wartime force of 25.

In 1950 Robert O'Brien, a native of San Mateo, a San Mateo High football hero (he was on the 1926 state championship team) and a popular member of the force since 1930, retired. Martin McDonald took his place.

During the 1950s the Department outgrew its station in the old 1914 City Hall building. Voters passed a bond issue to build a new 30,000 square foot building on Delaware. The station was completed in 1962 and was described then as one of the best in the state. By that time the force had a total payroll of 105 people. Six years later, it had risen to 122, with 91 full-time officers plus supporting staff. The Police Department was now a modern, large urban force, with a $1,430,943 annual budget.

The Fire Department also kept pace. In 1947, a bond issue funded two new station houses—one at 27th Avenue and Edison, and another on Fourth Avenue and Humboldt—to be added to the downtown headquarters in the civic center and the station on Bellevue. The two new stations became operational in 1948. In 1953 a $220,000 bond issue allowed reconstruction of the Bellevue Station and the construction of another new station, at Barneson and Alameda. In 1957 a sixth station opened at 1812 South Norfolk.

In 1954 the Department suffered a tragedy. Captain Julius Meghinasso suffered a heart attack while leading fire fighters at 1616 South Norfolk, in the Parkside area. His death marked the first time in the city's history that one of its Police or Fire Department personnel died in the line of duty.

During the postwar period, while fighting fires and inspecting for safety violations remained the Fire Department's primary task, it was also concerned with the Cold War and the possibility of nuclear attack. During these years, the Department distributed nearly 20,000 civil defense pamphlets. In 1952, the Fire Alarm Bureau established an attack warning system. Even into the 1960s, department personnel found themselves stocking fallout shelters at the San Mateo High School auditorium, the delivery area under the Hillsdale Mall and the Emporium basement. At one point, the shelters contained enough medical supplies, sanitation kits, food, water, and radiation measuring devices to serve nearly 35,000 people for two weeks.

In 1962, after 47 years of service—ten as a volunteer and 37 as Chief—Hugh F. Morris retired. He had taken the young department from a paid staff of two to a force of 105 professionals working in six modern station houses. Morris was replaced by Noe Chanteloup.

That same year, the San Mateo City Hall was moved to 330 West 20th Avenue. The old civic center was then demolished, to be replaced by an office-medical-residential development. The city moved into a building built by the Mobil Oil Company for its offices in 1953. The move symbolized the city's shift southward, but was not an universally popular one. Some thought city hall belonged downtown; others did not like the political dealings that had initiated the change. Among the disenchanted was John Murray, who ran that year for City Council as a protest. He lost by only 200 votes. Two years later he tried again and won.

When the city hall was razed, the old city seal, with a rose, the sun and railroad tracks on it, was also replaced. After much debate, in 1966, Councilman Hugh Wayne prevailed in having his own design accepted; it included the old Murray oak and the San Mateo Hayward Bridge.[49]

For the children of the city, one of the postwar's

*Merv Griffin,
one of San Mateo's most successful alumni.*
Courtesy San Mateo County Historical Museum

greatest happenings was the coming of Etta Latta "the train lady" and Oris Latta "the train man"[50] to Central Park. In May 1948 they purchased a 14-passenger miniature coal-burning replica of Southern Pacific's "Daylight in the Midwest" for $10,000, and had it shipped to San Mateo by truck. Oris himself laid the track. The Lattas originally charged nine cents a ride to avoid the entertainment tax on any activity costing ten cents or more. They ran the train every day during the summer, and on weekends during the winter. The engine took 45 minutes to warm up and spewed fumes and smoke, so about 1953, the Lattas converted it to a cleaner, diesel-burning engine. Bob Bianachi bought the train in 1977 and nine years later converted it again, this time to battery power. The train still runs at Central Park, to the delight of a new generation of children.

Regional Institutions—Keeping Pace

During the 1920s and 1930s, San Mateo had become the county's center for a variety of important institutions. Among them were the County Fair, the regional park at Coyote Point, Bay Meadows Race Track and two fine hospitals. While World War II interrupted progress, in the postwar period this trend continued.

There was no County Fair during the war years, but between September 27 and October 5, 1946, the event was reborn at Bay Meadows. The theme was Pan Americanism. That year fair manager Norvell Gillespie flew to Central and South America to make arrangements for daily shipments of exotic tropical flowers. Of course the Peninsula's own flower growers were also featured, and eight garden clubs were involved.

The fair featured horse racing in the afternoons and Hollywood entertainment at night. Bay Meadows' William B. Kyne took a special interest in seeing the fair succeed.

The Fair Board purchased 25 acres adjacent to Bay Meadows from the friendly California Jockey Club to begin making a home of its own. Construction began almost immediately. In 1948 the Hall of Flowers became the first building completed on the new fairgrounds. That year the entire event took place at the fairgrounds for the first time.

The 1949 Fair was noted for a grand waterfall, a 150-foot-long brook, and a lake with a tropical island in the center, complete with orchids and other lush vegetation.

Through the years improvements continued. By 1953, the Home and Industry Community Building, Agricultural Building and Fiesta Bowl had been built. In 1956 another 23 acres were added to the property. In 1958 the Administration Building and Home Arts Building were completed. In 1960 the twin industrial buildings were installed.

Out at Coyote Point, prewar ideas also were re-examined. After the College moved to the Heights, the county again began thinking of the 30 acre Coyote Point site as a recreational center. By 1965, it already had a yacht harbor, swimming beach, rifle range, and a junior museum.

The history of the junior museum began back in 1953. The San Francisco Junior League and the National Foundation of Junior Museums acquired a quonset hut and a warehouse, formerly used by the Merchant Marine Academy, to house a museum dedicated to educating the young about the natural history of the Peninsula. In 1954, the original Coyote Point Museum opened to the public. It would evolve into one of the Bay Area's most unique cultural assets.

Bay Meadows continued to be one of the premier race tracks in the country. William Kyne introduced quarter horse racing after the war. In 1946 he also became the first person to fly a horse to a race track when he flew El Lobo from Los Angeles to San Francisco International Airport.

In 1956, Kyne died, and his wife Dorothy took over as president and general manager. In 1959, Joseph Cohen was appointed to the dual position. Cohen built the training track just west of Bayshore Highway in 1960, and added a nine-hole golf course to create revenues on non-racing days. Famous jockeys who raced at Bay Meadows during the postwar period included Johnny Longden (who won his 3,000th race at Bay Meadows—he eventually won 6,032!) and Willie Shoemaker.

Another privately held regional institution that did very well in the postwar period was J. Hart Clinton's *San Mateo Times*. The conservative, pro-development newspaper continued in its role as the leading daily in the county. During this period it also purchased several weeklies in the north county. In 1964 the *Times* moved into new, larger facilities on Amphlett Boulevard.

Society and Politics in Post-War San Mateo

While public and private institutions raced to keep up with the postwar population explosion, so did religious groups. Many new congregations were formed during this period. Notably, in 1951, the Jewish people in the area formed their first synagogue in San Mateo, Peninsula Temple Beth El.[51]

Also on the move were some of the long-established churches. The Catholics were very active. In 1954, the congregation at Saint Gregory's in south San Mateo began construction of their new church under Reverend John T. Scanlon. At St. Matthew's parish, Father Henry J. Lyne assumed leadership after the death of the legendary Irishman, Timothy Callahan, in 1937. In 1948 Lyne was made Monsignor and moved to San Francisco. His place was taken by Irishman Edward J. Meagher, who saw to the building of a new church in the Shoreview area in 1954, named St. Timothy's, after the patron saint of the unforgettable Callahan. St. Timothy's soon became its own parish. A year later, Meagher did the same with the western portion of San Mateo by forming the St. Bartholomew's parish.

In 1956, Father Meagher died and was replaced by Father Bernard C. Cronin, Ph.D., the first native Californian to assume leadership of this church. As the venerable St. Matthew's approached its 100th anniversary as a congregation, Cronin began to nurture the idea of building a new church. In July 1962, the decision was made to go forward. Ground was broken in 1965 at One Notre Dame Avenue within the 7 1/2-acre church property that already included a school, the convent of the sisters of the Holy Cross, residential facilities for four priests, and offices. The Church was dedicated on May 8, 1966.

The old San Mateo Blues baseball team was resurrected after the war. In 1948, manager Paul Thiebaut brought semi-pro action back to Central Park with the formation of a new team, the Guadalupe Blues. In 1954, the team revived the old San Mateo Blues moniker and played until 1978. During that time, Thiebaut helped produce more than 100 professional players, 12 of whom made it to the big leagues. On Sundays, hundreds of fans would turn out to watch the Blues play other northern California teams. In his thirty years of managing the team, Thiebaut never had a losing season.[52]

Not missing a beat, the San Mateo Woman's Club remained active in the postwar period. In 1947, it became the first women's club on the West Coast to initiate a training class for the Junior Olympics (the Elks Lodge adopted this program in the 1960s). In 1950 the Woman's Club began assisting the Children's Receiving Home, which became Poplar Center. In 1965, the women converted their Club House Foundation into a scholarship fund. In 1968 they helped to form the Friends of San Mateo Library as the new main facility opened. Over the years, the Club has continued to support the library with gifts, including films for the audio-visual section.

Private clubs blossomed during the postwar period. The Elks Lodge moved in 1954 from its cramped home on B Street, where it had existed since 1909, to the site of the former Howard stables on 20th Avenue. The larger area allowed for many expanded activities. Today the Lodge has more than 2,000 members.

The Peninsula Golf and Country Club was booming. The once lightly-used facilities were now hives of activity. By 1954 the club had 323 members. These new middle-class members of the postwar period joined when the club made memberships available to non-Jews. The new members used the club to its fullest value: many found the dues expensive, and they were determined to get every dollar's worth out of their recreational investment.

By the late 1950s, parties at Peninsula had become society news stories in the local papers. Half-page pictorial spreads told who attended, what they wore, what the party's theme was, and who organized the event.

Children also made great use of the place. During the lazy summer days of the 1950s and 1960s, mothers would drop off their offspring to spend the day around the pool or on the golf course under the direction of the club professional. As many as 30 or 40 junior golfers were on the club's team at any given time during the period.

J. Hart Clinton celebrates the 100th birthday of the San Mateo Times.
Courtesy San Mateo County Historical Museum

Women's golf remained important. Club professional Willie Nicoll and long-time member Helen Lengfeld continued to sponsor events to develop interest. In 1948, they achieved their greatest goal when they attracted the Women's Trans-Mississippi 18th Annual Championship Tournament, the first time the Trans-Mississippi had met in California. Among the well-known women on the organizational committee were Miss Dot Kielty, Mrs. Jim Ferrie and Mrs. Bob Hope.

Club members were sad to say goodbye to their popular pro, Willie Nicoll, in March 1954. They staged a huge party for him, and gave him a trip to Scotland as a vacation. He had not been back to his home since he had immigrated to America. When he returned, he did not immediately hang up his clubs; for some time he gave golf instruction at the new nine-hole course at Bay Meadows.

Bud Ward, a former U. S. Amateur champion, took over for Willie. Ward was a well-known and gregarious sports figure who attracted other professional athletes to the Peninsula Club. Often noticed on the greens or in the clubhouse were members of the San Francisco Giants baseball team, such as Jimmy Davenport and Alvin Dark.

During the postwar period, San Mateans were still concerned with national and international problems. The Korean War was regarded as a highly serious matter. As during World War II, the elementary schools resumed the practice of "dog-tagging" the children. In the event of attack, San Mateo's young would have their names, addresses, blood types, religion and specific medical information recorded on metal plates hung around their necks.

In order to offer moral support to American fighting personnel, the San Mateo City Council, the Chamber of Commerce and the American Legion adopted the 25th "Tropic Lighting" Division commanded by General J. S. Bradley. "Operation San Mateo" was kicked off with a party at Central Park. The project's goal was to obtain one gift for every man in the Division. The co-chairmen of the steering committee, Dave McCullough and Robert M. Brown, arranged to have Sea Scouts stationed on business district corners throughout San Mateo, where they accepted gifts from thousands of residents.

San Mateo was more or less calm politically during the postwar period, although from time to time the business developers and the homeowners engaged in battle. A particularly active battleground was the office development west of El Camino, near Baywood. Hugh Wayne protected business interests for many years from his seat on the City Council. Wayne had lived in the area since 1938. His first job on the Peninsula was as an ad man for the *Burlingame Advance*. In 1946 he established *Peninsula Life* magazine, which lasted a couple of years. He served as Chairman of the Republican Central Committee of San Mateo and President of the San Mateo Chamber of Commerce. When the business interests of the community felt they needed better representation in City Hall, they persuaded Wayne to run. He became somewhat of an institution in his 22 years on the Council. He served several times as mayor, and worked tirelessly for the promotion of the city.

Despite his presence, during the 1960s, zoning laws made it difficult to create commercial strips and light industrial complexes. The new requirements did allow for office building developments, and, on the old Borel Estate and in the hills on the west side, internationally-regarded companies such as Fluor Mining, Hughes Air West, and dozens of lesser-known firms established office buildings, creating jobs for thousands of workers.

Only down at the post office did the "old ways" seem to last throughout the postwar period. In 1946, James J. Kehoe, a Navy veteran who had served in the Pacific, was appointed postmaster at San Mateo by President Harry Truman. Kehoe was a good friend of Jim Farley, who had been a postmaster during the Roosevelt Administration. Kehoe's was the last presidential appointment for the position of local postmaster in the United States.[53] Kehoe ran unsuccessfully for Congress as a Democrat, but was eventually elected to the San Mateo City Council. He served as postmaster for 41 years, becoming somewhat of a celebrity before retiring at age 75 in 1987.[54] Carol Conroy, San Mateo's first woman postmaster, replaced Kehoe.

THE NEW BRIDGE

OF ALL THE ASTONISHING CHANGES in the postwar period, none was more spectacular in appearance or important to the future than the augmentation—essentially the replacement—of the San Mateo-Hayward Bridge.

In 1929, the daily traffic across the bridge averaged about 2,000 vehicles a day. During the Depression and the war years, traffic dropped off substantially, prompting many to question the wisdom of having built the bridge in the first place. But in 1946, the average moved back to 2,000, and by 1951, when the State of California purchased it, the bridge was serving 5,200 vehicles a day. That year the State stimulated use by reducing the toll from 50 cents to 35 cents. While the bridge cost the state about $5 million and required another $3 million in repairs through the years, it paid off the bonded indebtedness in ten years instead of the scheduled seventeen because of unforeseen increases in traffic.

The San Mateo Chamber of Commerce was first to realize that the drawbridge would not be capable of handling the ever-increasing numbers of cars. By 1955 daily use had reached about 9,000 vehicles. The Chamber's Land Planning Committee, headed by David Bohannon, decided to work on two projects: improvement to the bridge—perhaps creating a second span—and the establishment of a major league baseball stadium at Bay Meadows (the Giants, of course, were still in New York, and there was no Candlestick Park). With the blessing of Chamber President, Dr. Hartzell Ray, the committee met with State Assemblyman Richard Dolwig who pledged his aid for the bridge project.[55]

The Chamber then organized a Bridge Committee to

promote the project. Members Kenneth Van Gundy, Henry Felt, Basil Waters and Chamber manager Ken Brown went across the bay to meet with representatives of the Hayward Chamber of Commerce to officially kick off a political campaign.[56] Eventually, Assemblymen Louis Francis and Carl Britschgi cosponsored a bill in the Assembly, and Richard Dolwig, by that time a State Senator, introduced a companion bill in the Senate, calling for an investigation of the matter.

The first San Mateo - Hayward bridge (right) lasted only forty years before deterioration made a new bridge necessary, at nearly ten times the cost of the original.
Courtesy San Mateo County Historical Museum

The wheels of government turn slowly, and at great cost. The Division of San Francisco Bay Toll Crossings conducted the $200,000 study for the State Toll Bridges Authority. The report said that the bridge's concrete trestles were in a state of continuing deterioration, with cracks caused by the corrosion of reinforcing steel. This condition, the survey noted, had been recognized by its owner only seven years after the bridge's opening in 1929. Over the seven years the state owned the bridge, $2.5 million had already been spent on structural repairs. The structure was deemed below state standards, and because increased usage was inevitable, the study called for the immediate creation of a "parallel span."[57]

Indeed, the traffic count was mounting fast. By 1967, the old bridge was handling 16,000 vehicles a day, even with an average of seven lifts for ships each day, which completely stopped traffic. While the lifting action itself took only four minutes, delays because of mechanical failures could take up to an hour and a half.

Soon after the report was issued, planning for the new bridge commenced. An additional span with another drawbridge was initially proposed. But David Bohannon convinced San Mateo County officials to fight against the double drawbridge concept.[58] State officials decided an orthotropic design, in which a steel roadway deck is part of the support construction, was most appropriate. This would allow for a low profile, most desirable because of the proximity to San Francisco International Airport. An airplane crashing into a high structural portion of the bridge during a time of low visibility was a nightmare to be avoided.

Many such bridges had been completed in Europe. However, this project would call for orthotropic sections 5500 feet long, and a 750-foot center span which would become the longest girder span in the United States. The State contracted with Hans Grassl of Dusseldorf, Germany, as a special consultant[59] to cope with these engineering difficulties.

The center of the new bridge was to be constructed without a lifting section. Therefore, it had to have a 132-foot clearance so that ships could pass underneath. It would have six lanes, as opposed to the old bridge's two, and would be hooked up to the proposed 19th Avenue Freeway instead of winding north along the bay to Third Avenue and the Bayshore Freeway.

Construction began on July 17, 1961 and was completed six years later. Perhaps the most spectacular part of the bridge's creation involved the placement of the gigantic center steel girders which were built in Richmond, California by Murphy Pacific Bridge Builders. In order to mount this section, Murphy's *Marine Boss*, a 300 foot-long derrick barge with a 285 foot boom (one of the largest in the world), moved each of the 520 ton girders in place, 138 feet above the Bay. The last girder flew an American flag, traditionally associated with "topping out"[60] or finishing a construction project. As the girder was held suspended over the Bay, hordes of photographers took photographs from an old World War II landing craft, specially commissioned for this promotional work. This final portion of the construction took only 17 minutes to accomplish.

The State of California spent $70 million on the bridge; just Murphy Pacific's work cost $27,146,000.

The soaring lines of the new bridge made the old bridge look quite antique.

Courtesy San Mateo County Historical Museum

(The old bridge had cost only $7,500,000 in total.) The 1100-ton center span of the old bridge was barged to Richmond in 1968, where it was sold as scrap to Murphy Pacific for $57.20.[61]

Kenneth Van Gundy, Chairman of the "Twin Cities" Bridge Dedication Committee, organized the opening ceremony and celebration for October 20, 1967. Some 500 public school musicians were on hand from San Mateo and Hayward.[62] United States Senator George Murphy clipped a metal ribbon. Governor Ronald Reagan had been invited to share the honor, but Murphy quipped that Reagan was too "busy reading his mail."[63] A motorcade of new cars provided by automobile dealers in San Mateo and Hayward joined a parade of classic autos in crossing the bridge. An "Aquacade" flotilla of boats from the Coyote Point and Hayward Yacht Clubs was led by the Coast Guard and sailed under the bridge during the dedication.

The San Mateo-Hayward Bridge accumulated a variety of awards for its design and construction. The American Society of Civil Engineers selected it as the "Outstanding Civil Engineering Achievement of 1968." The American Institute of Steel Construction made it their "Most Beautiful Bridge" in 1968. But the most important thing about the bridge was that it was completed just in time. In 1966 about 5,600,000 vehicles crossed the old bridge. By 1970, 9,100,000 vehicles used the new one. The Bay Area and northern California's transportation network was augmented at a crucial moment in the state's history.

THE SALAD YEARS

THE LATE 1960S were years of well-deserved pride for San Mateans. The completion of the new bridge and the projected link to the coast via the 19th Avenue Freeway was to make San Mateo one of the most important crossroads in California. (Of course, the freeway to the coast has still not been accomplished.)

The same year the bridge was completed, a $900,000 contract was signed for the building of San Mateo's new main library. Also in 1967, recreation centers at Beresford, Lakeshore and Central Parks were opened, and a new clubhouse was completed for the Municipal

On Third Avenue in the late 1950s, business was good. Cars have have lost their flowing lines and now have jutting tailfins. The San Mateo Theater has lost its tall sign.

Courtesy San Mateo County Historical Museum

Golf Course at Coyote Point. Finishing touches were put on City Hall on 20th Avenue that year. The commercial boom in the city continued as a $2.5 million project on L. C. Smith's property along the 19th Avenue Freeway was announced, with powerful new retail tenants. The City Council had even dealt with the delicate integration problem by endorsing the San Mateo Elementary School Trustees' plans for busing.[64]

By 1969, the population of San Mateo had topped 79,000. The people were led by a healthy city government, bolstered by $200 million in retail sales, with two major shopping areas—Hillsdale and the downtown, and eleven other smaller centers. There were five public parks, 38 churches, 32 public schools, seven private schools, three libraries, thirteen banks, seven building and loan associations, eleven motels and four hotels.

That year was the city's 75th anniversary of its incorporation in 1894. A Silver Anniversary committee was organized with L. C. Smith as its chairman. One major event was the unveiling of a 13-foot redwood statue of Father Junipero Serra, at Aragon Circle and El Camino Real. The two-ton likeness was carved by artist Kenyon Kaiser of Eugene, Oregon, and was given to the city by the Serra Club of San Mateo. Other celebrations included the dedication of the $550,000 Martin Luther King Recreation Center and a huge parade in August.

The parade was far and away the greatest event of the year. Smith himself directed the activity. Some 3,000 people took part in it. It started at Bay Meadows, went up to Hillsdale Mall, then on to 25th Avenue, across to the downtown, then back to Bay Meadows via Delaware. The judges' stand was erected on South Delaware. While Smith placed a great emphasis on "equestrian participants," much of the promotional material, in the style of the 1960s, dealt with the participation of beautiful young women. Sandra Wahlstrom, "Miss Diamond Jubilee," was widely photographed and described as the 5'4", 18-year-old blonde. Little was said of her academic ambitions. One press release established ogling as a good enough reason to see the parade:

> Girl watchers will have their day, too. Hundreds of beauties will be in evidence among the queens and majorettes and fancy-dressed cowgirls and scores of lovelies on floats and carriages.[65]

In 1969 many San Mateans still referred to their town as "The City of Flowers" or even "The Paris of the Peninsula." The optimism of the times was summed up by Emerson Murfee, president of the San Mateo Chamber of Commerce, who wrote a special column in the special 75th anniversary edition of the *San Mateo Times*:

> The city of San Mateo, on its 75th anniversary, finds itself a healthy, growing community of balanced homes, commercial life and industry in one of the finest climates in the world.
> Splendid public schools, private schools, beautiful churches and expanding playgrounds, as well as golf course, marina, yacht harbor, excellent public tennis courts, athletic fields and recreational facilities are available to its citizens.
> The College of San Mateo is one of the most beautiful in the West and has some of the finest facilities of any junior college in the country.
> Fire and police protection are models of modern efficiency and public service, from the excellent storm drainage system to playgrounds supervision is of first quality.
> Two major hospitals, two convalescent hospitals, and a large number of physicians, surgeons, dentists and specialists provide excellent medical attention, equipment and facilities. The city's most recent survey indicated there were 263 physicians and surgeons and 74 dentists.

Many San Mateans believed they had created an almost perfect city. But not even "The Paris of the Peninsula" could withstand the national and international problems that soon affected every city in the United States. San Mateo developed some home grown problems as well.

Notes

[1] Author's interview with Mariko Endo, March 23, 1993.
[2] Author's interview with Yasuko Ann Ito on March 23, 1993.
[3] Ira Newman, "A Thing of Beauty" *San Mateo Times*, August 27, 1966.
[4] Doris Batchelor, "Building a Peninsula Oriental Garden," *Redwood City Tribune*, February 6, 1968.
[5] Author's interview with Claire Mack, March, 1993.
[6] "San Mateo Facts and Figures," San Mateo Chamber of Commerce, 1950.
[7] Floyd Healey, "Freeway to the Future — San Mateo County," *San Francisco Chronicle*, June 28, 1948.
[8] Author's interview with John J. Murray, March 16, 1993.
[9] "San Mateo-City of Roses, Facts and Figures," San Mateo Chamber of Commerce, 1957.
[10] "Housing: San Mateo California" City Planning Dept., Arthur Sullivan, City Manager, 1963.
[11] "Hillsdale Planned Its War Homes" *San Francisco Chronicle*, December 13, 1942.
[12] Stanger, *Peninsula*, p. 233.
[13] "City Asked to Annex New 20 Acre Hillsdale Tract," *San Mateo Times*, November 1, 1949.
[14] Derek Parmenter, "Housing: The Big Package," *San Francisco Chronicle*, May 22, 1949.
[15] "Dream House Work Started," *San Francisco Examiner*, May 9, 1948, and Ray Spangler, "Under the Courthouse Dome," *Redwood City Tribune*, July, 1948.
[16] Darryl D. Kenyon, "Hillsdale," student monograph #77-210-1, in the archives of the San Mateo County Historical Museum, 1977.
[17] "Plan to Build 503 New San Mateo Apartments," *San Mateo Times*, April 4, 1948.
[18] "Hillsdale Starts 204 Apts." *San Francisco Chronicle*, February 6, 1949.
[19] "S.M. Apartments Sold $47,500,000," *San Mateo Times*, October 3, 1953, and the author's interview with David D. Bohannon on October 13, 1993.
[20] "Thousands at Opening of Sears' San Mateo Store," *San Mateo Times*, March 22, 1951.
[21] John Lyman and John Hubbard, "David Bohannon's Dream... And How It Grew" *San Mateo Times*, July 31, 1954.
[22] "Bohannon Gives City Pledge on CD Shelter," *San Mateo Times*, August 18, 1951.

23 "Bohannon Sees Early Start on Big Structure," *San Mateo Times*, May 20, 1952.
24 "Macy's Plans Big Store in Hillsdale," *Burlingame Advance*, May 28, 1951.
25 "Macy's Ground Breaking," *Burlingame Advance*, October 28, 1952.
26 "Food Center Planned in S.M. Shopping Area," *Redwood City Tribune*, April 24, 1954.
27 "Ground Broken For New Hillsdale Emporium," *San Francisco Call*, April 8, 1961, and "'Big E' Here Will Open Wednesday," *Burlingame Advance*, September 9, 1962.
28 "18 tons of Bufano Art to be Shown at Hillsdale," *Burlingame Advance*, October 3, 1956, and "Thousands See Bufano Statuary Dedication," *San Mateo Times*, October 15, 1956.
29 "City Pays Tribute to Developer Smith," *San Mateo Times*, August 4, 1973.
30 Vera Graham, "Golden Era Looms for County," *San Mateo Times*, September 19, 1951.
31 "Famed Mounds Sold for $300,000," *San Mateo Times*, April 18, 1946.
32 "Super-Luxury Apartments," *San Francisco Chronicle*, August 2, 1959.
33 "Developers Propose Huge 'Aquatic City,'" *Burlingame Advance*, June 5, 1964.
34 "$578,000 Price Set for Six Acres," *Burlingame Advance Star*, August 27, 1962.
35 John Horgan, "The Vanishing Wilderness," *San Mateo Times*, January 18, 1975.
36 Alice Phillips, "From Farm to Chapel to Shopping Center," *Burlingame Advance Star*, May 22, 1968.
37 "Borel Shopping Center Expected to Become a Peninsula focal Point," *San Mateo Times*, October 19, 1967.
38 "4 to 1 Vote Follows Five Hour Wrangle; Proponents Hissed," *San Mateo Times*, October 18, 1956.
39 Scott Thurber, "Time—And Cars—Move On," *San Francisco Chronicle*, October 6, 1961.
40 "City seeks $1,000,000 Underpass for Hillsdale," *San Mateo Times*, July 2, 1959.
41 "$2,100,000 Grade Plan Sealed Bids On Hillsdale RR Crossing Set," *San Mateo Times*, April 16, 1963.
42 "State to Pay Share of Hillsdale Interchange," *San Mateo Times*, July 23, 1963.
43 David Gebhard, Roger Montgomery, Robert Winter, John Woodbridge and Sally Woodbridge, *A Guide to Architecture in San Francisco and Northern California*, Peregrine, Smith, Inc., Santa Barbara, 1973,. p. 123.
44 Postel, "Junior-Community," p. 11.
45 Ibid. p. 13
46 Ibid. p. 14.
47 Gebhard, *Guide*,. p. 123
48 "Dedication Program, New Central Library," December 15, 1968, in the archives of the San Mateo County Historical Museum.
49 "A Button-Busting Symbol of Pride," *Burlingame Advance Star*, April 17, 1966
50 Gael P. Gouveia, "Twenty Years With a Really Friendly Railroad," *Redwood City Tribune*, September 3, 1968.
51 Russel Mentz, "The Jews of San Mateo County," student monograph #80-6 in the archives of the San Mateo County Historical Museum.
52 Kirk O'Niel, "Victorian Days Looks for San Mateo Blues Players," *San Mateo Weekly*, July 22, 1992.
53 Vera Graham, "A Parting Blast at Postal Service," *San Mateo Times*, July 24, 1987.
54 San Mateo Postmaster to Retire," *San Mateo Times*, July 24, 1987.
55 "State Asked to Build Parallel S.M. Bridge," *San Mateo Times*, August 4, 1955.
56 "S.M. Span to Open Oct. 20," *San Mateo Times*, October 6, 1967.
57 Official State Report: Start Work Now on S.M. Parallel Span," *Burlingame Advance*, December 21, 1958.
58 Author's interview with David D. Bohannon, October 13, 1993.
59 "A New Landmark to Rival Golden Gate, Bay Bridge," *San Mateo Times*, October 19, 1967.
60 Dave Glick, "Giant Girder Links Nation's Longest Span," *Burlingame Advance Star*, July 19, 1967.
61 "Scrap One Bridge," *Burlingame Advance Star*, July 26, 1968.
62 "S.M. Span to Open Oct. 20," *San Mateo Times*, October 6, 1967.
63 Wally Burke, "Look But Don't Touch ..Yet," *Burlingame Advance Star*, October 22, 1967.
64 "San Mateo City Setting Record of Achievement in Busy Year," *San Mateo Times*, October 19, 1967.
65 "75th Anniversary Committee," press releases of August 7, 1969 and August 16, 1969, in the archives of the San Mateo County Historical Museum.

Diminutive sculptor Benjamin Bufano was commissioned to create the sculptures which adorn Hillsdale Mall. Having delighted generations of visitors, they are an excellent example of the value of fine art to enhance a commercial setting. This figure is called "St. Francis on Horseback."

Courtesy Bohannon Development Company

CHAPTER VIII

Highs and Lows in the Modern Age: 1968-1993

Legacy of Rapid Growth

During the postwar period, the greater part of the built environment of today's San Mateo materialized. Most of the houses, apartments, shopping centers, bridges, freeways, roads, streets, sidewalks, schools, office buildings, libraries, recreation centers and churches that San Mateans live in, work in, visit and use were constructed in the two and a half decades following World War II. But this tremendous development did not come without cost. In the years that followed, San Mateans were forced to deal with the social, economic, environmental and governmental changes that came on the coattails of rapid growth. National and international problems—inflation, the Vietnam War, tax revolts, environmental crises and racial tensions—have all affected San Mateans.

Racial Unrest

During the mid-1960s all of America became involved with matters of desegregation. While San Mateo had always been a diverse community without any specific minority group cornered in a ghetto, there were geographic lines which could not easily be crossed by certain people. The racial make-up of elementary schools was visible evidence of this. Depending upon surrounding neighborhoods, some schools were mostly black or Asian, while others were mostly white.

In October 1965 a meeting on minority problems was called by the superintendent of schools. Citizens and school staff thereafter met regularly to propose programs. In 1966 a community-wide conference on de facto segregation in the schools met at the College of San Mateo. Some 700 people attended. In December an "Administrative Transfer Plan"[1] was adopted, and 45 students from Lawrence and Turnbull Schools were selected as the first to be bused to other schools, thus beginning the desegregation process. Parents from the two schools met in January, and on February 20, 1967, the busing began, with the 45 students fanning out to ten other schools.

The success of this early experiment prompted the San Mateo Elementary Teachers Association to pass a resolution supporting the plan, and to call for full desegregation of all city schools. More progress followed. In April Mary Jo Howell, an African-American woman, was elected to the school board, and in May more busing programs were approved.

Then minority group leaders pointed out inequities in the personnel practices of the District. In October 1967, of 521 teachers in the system, only 9 were African-American (1.7%), 13 Asian (2.4%), and 5 Hispanic (1.1%). All 36 principals were white.[2]

Similar figures existed in the high schools. San Mateo High had the most racially diverse population: of 1814 students, 173 were African-American, 202 were Asian and 70 were Hispanic. Yet, of the 81 teachers, only two were African-American and two Asian; there were no Hispanic teachers. All five principals and assistant principals were white, as were all five counselors.[3]

These inequalities were echoed in city government. In 1967, of 443 employees working for San Mateo, 17 were Asian, but only five were African-American and just two were Hispanic.[4]

259

At the San Mateo High School prom in 1952 (from left): Walter Black, Ada Lax, Claire Cullen, Cornell Meeks. Claire Cullen Mack was to become San Mateo's first African American Councilwoman.

Courtesy San Mateo County Historical Museum

During the late 1960s, as political activism rose all over America, a San Mateo group called "Action Now" was formed "to improve, foster and promote the general economic and social welfare of low-income residents of East San Mateo."[5] Among its original leaders were Mack McCoy, Gerald L. Monroe and Claudette Bell. A major issue addressed by Action Now was the employment practices of San Mateo's tax-supported institutions.

While San Mateans were in the midst of trying to resolve their racial problems, on April 4, 1968, Dr. Martin Luther King, Jr., was assassinated. The whole country was thrown into crisis as enraged African-Americans took to the streets and riots erupted throughout the United States.

In San Mateo, about a thousand high school and College of San Mateo students marched on City Hall. Mayor John J. Murray told Police Chief Martin McDonald to "get your ass over here,"[6] and called on African-American minister Rufus Cooper of Saint James Church for help. Cooper, a well-known figure in the community, had been an army chaplain, and everyone knew him as "Chappy." When one of the youths climbed up the city's flagpole, yanked down the American flag and replaced it with the North Vietnamese Flag, Chappy peacefully had the North Vietnamese flag taken down. (Later that year, during the holidays, Chappy's Saint James Church was fire-bombed; Murray and other leaders assisted the congregation in quickly repairing their sanctuary.) Mayor Murray invited everyone into the city hall where all would have a chance to speak. Electronic sound hook-ups were rigged so those outside could hear. Murray's one rule was to stay off the subject of Vietnam. This was to be a time to talk about Dr. King. The next day the Mayor led a memorial march from Central Park to San Mateo High. Murray and others spoke; Bay Area television stations covered the proceedings. In the end, San Mateo escaped violence. Police reports showed the two-day period to be more free of crime than a normal weekend.

Here, as in the rest of the country, pressure was applied to hasten the goals of Dr. King so that his death would not be in vain. The new recreation center on Monte Diablo would be called King Center. Less than three weeks after the assassination, citizens from Belmont to Millbrae came together to form the San Mateo Area Business Leadership Council. Members included labor officials, educators, minority group representatives and local government figures. Mayor Murray, who was also the executive director of the Peninsula Manufacturers Association, headed the Council. Richard De Lancie of the URS Corporation served as secretary, and Ron Fick, great-grandson of Antoine Borel, was treasurer. The goals of the council included improving communications, reviewing education issues and providing more jobs for minorities.[7]

That summer the City Council went still further when it formed the 25-member Human Relations Commission to reinforce the Council's commitment to existing federal and state anti-discrimination laws. The Commission was asked to go beyond those statutes to create more harmony within the community. An $18,515 budget was approved for this purpose.

By November, the Commission was making headlines. Chairman Eleanor Curry targeted the Elks Lodge, just across the street from the City Hall. Members of the Commission called for changes in the Elks' national by-laws, demanding that public officials withdraw from membership until this was done.[8] Other

Rudolph Lapp, instructor and liberal leader at College of San Mateo, speaks at an anti-war demonstration at San Mateo City Hall.
Courtesy San Mateo County Historical Museum

issues addressed by the Commission included complaints of youths against the police, individual cases of housing discrimination, problems in the high schools and employment difficulties faced by minority people.

Into the 1970s the Human Relations Commission not only worked to solve San Mateo's racial problems, but also served as a model for increased awareness among citizens who wished to participate in their community's government. Other official municipal groups established during this period included the Public Works Commission, the Youth Advisory Council, the Greater Downtown Commission and the Housing Advisory and Appeals Board.[9]

CAMPUS UNREST

SAN MATEO did not escape these emotional times without some violence. It did happen here—on the hard-earned new campus of the College of San Mateo. Student activism almost began as soon as the move up to the hillside site was achieved. In the spring of 1964, as the "free speech movement" was affecting other colleges and universities throughout the nation, Robert Coleman, president of the Associated Students at the College, wrote a letter to the Board of Trustees asking permission to have Mickey Lima, Chairman of the Communist Party of Northern California, give a speech. The request was supported by Superintendent Julio Bortolazzo and several faculty members. The Trustees agreed to the request as long as an opposing viewpoint would be allowed to be heard. Tom Lantos, an economist at San Francisco State, agreed to counter the communist speaker.

Having a communist address the students of the College of San Mateo created quite a sensation in this relatively conservative community, and more was to

A rally at College of San Mateo drew a huge crowd of young people who were deeply distressed about America's role in the Vietnam War. Rudy Lapp is the speaker. Congressman Pete McCloskey is seated at right.

Courtesy San Mateo County Historical Museum

come. With the escalation of the Vietnam War, a peace movement developed on campus. History professor Dr. Rudolph Lapp led a contingent of faculty and staff to Washington D.C. to present President Richard Nixon with a petition signed by 2,500 people, asking that the country's tax money be spent on education and not war. A temporary art exhibit displayed on campus included a doll, representing the Vietnamese people, with an American flag stuck through its forehead. Members of various veterans groups grew angry at what they saw as an anti-American message and demanded that the Board of Trustees close the art show. The Board instead adhered to its policy of encouraging freedom of expression and allowed the exhibit to remain. The trustees became victims of crank telephone calls, vandalism of personal property and threats against family members.

In racial issues, the College was also active. Since 1958 Professor Lapp had offered classes in Black History. The College of San Mateo was the first institution of higher learning outside the South to have such a course.

Also impressive was the College's highly regarded "Readiness Program." After the Watts Riots in Los Angeles in 1965, the College began to analyze its services to the African-American community. It discovered that of its 8,000 day students, only 87 were black, and of these, 90% would probably drop out in their first semester. There was no bus transportation from East Palo Alto, where a large number of potential black students lived.

Superintendent Julio Bortolazzo wanted action. That fall, the College Readiness Program (CRP) was designed to offer financial aid and tutorial assistance for minority students. During the summer of 1966, its pilot program included 39 students, 37 of whom completed their summer classes and enrolled that fall. By 1967, 256 students were benefiting from the program, aided by 87 student tutors. In 1968 the number reached 400, and by 1969, 700. The success of the program was noted in the Journal of the National Education Association.

Unfortunately, while the program quietly helped students, it did not quell the increasing disharmony on campus. On March 27, 1968, citing student unrest, a recently failed bond issue and internal administrative problems, Superintendent Bortolazzo resigned. Some nine months went by before he was replaced. In the meantime, Dr. King was assassinated, and the College went through its lowest period.

Student activists in 1968 believed the CRP was not getting enough support. On October 8 they staged a march on campus, and on October 15 they actually seized the administration building. Acting superintendent Philip Garlington called for help from the San Mateo Police. It took 50 officers to clear the building and free the staff.

The unyielding Garlington was then confronted in his office by a contingent of "older looking students"[10] who demanded he hire Aaron Manganiello to the staff of the CRP. Manganiello was working as a volunteer at the time. The students threatened to "off" Garlington unless he complied. Garlington's reaction was to request CRP's African-American director, Bob Hoover, to remove Manganiello from the campus. Hoover responded that he was "not the campus bouncer." The Board then banned Manganiello from the campus and suspended Bob Hoover.

This set off a series of unfortunate events. Hoover was a popular figure on campus among students, faculty and administrators. Even College of San Mateo President Robert L. Ewigleben asked for Hoover's reinstatement. At a student rally, African-American student Pat Girard gave up her Homecoming Queen title to protest the suspension. The student newspaper, the *San Matean,* reported that she "gracefully lifted up her fist, a gesture symbolizing Black Power." Hoover "praised Miss Girard's abdication," and remarked that this kind of action "reflected upon her consideration for her black sisters and brothers rather than her own accomplishments."

The November 22 *San Matean* reported a number of racially sparked fights in the cafeteria. Three bombs went off, two at the administration building and one in a classroom. Luckily, no one was hurt.

Activists then scheduled a rally for Friday, December 13. President Ewigleben promised to keep the number of law enforcement officers down to a bare minimum to reduce tension. Off-campus personalities such as Bruce Franklin from Stanford University and several activists from San Francisco State participated. But things got out of hand. The *San Matean* reported, "approximately 150 students, mostly black, raced through the halls of CSM . . . destroying property and injuring onlookers." The rampage began about 1:45 p.m. and ended about an hour later. Students grabbed pipes used by the gardeners along the grassy areas of the campus. The *San Matean* noted that some got other pipes "which appeared from nowhere just before the destruction began, as did a mobile medical unit."

> Three instructors, Stan Scott, George Angerbauer, and Lorne MacDonald were attacked and beaten in the Electronics Building, which also received the worst damage. Several students were injured, some seriously, and one co-ed was reportedly pushed down a flight of stairs by the strikers, landing in a pile of broken glass. . . . Aaron Manganiello, forbidden by court order to appear on the campus, was seen frequently throughout the day.[11]

By the time the police arrived, the activists had moved off campus. Altogether some $8,000 in property damage had been perpetrated, including substantial vandalization of the student newspaper office. Under these difficult conditions the new Chancellor-Superintendent of the district, Clifford G. Erickson, took over that December. His first board meeting was held in the school's gymnasium before 300 intensely interested participants who discussed ethnic issues at the College.

Meantime, in an emergency meeting of faculty and administration, President Ewigleben outlined his plan for action. On Monday, December 16, students found 250 police from throughout the Bay Area on campus. CSM was now a "controlled campus" to which only students, faculty and employees would have access. Every vehicle trying to enter the campus was stopped. Most students, including the *San Matean* editorial staff, agreed that this was a necessary step.

Unfortunately, the action did not stop trouble. Activists evidently organized reprisals against the new tough stand. During Christmas vacation, some of the trustees and members of the College's administrative staff received threatening telephone calls. Five shots were fired into a house that had formerly belonged to trustee Carl Ward. Bullets narrowly missed two young girls sleeping inside.

On January 7, 1969, someone fired a rifle into Philip Garlington's home. Later his house was fire-bombed; the blaze was ignited in his garage, directly under his bedroom. Garlington and his wife got out, but barely escaped death. He later remembered that the fire was so hot, "it melted my pen, my glasses frame and my comb together." His two family automobiles were totally destroyed. A police report described his Ford LTD as "a possible Pontiac."[12]

San Mateo police and other law enforcement agencies countered these attacks by providing 24-hour protection for the trustees and top administrators. Patrol cars passed their homes every half-hour. The police also tapped their telephones. When school resumed in early 1969, some administrators reportedly kept baseball bats in their offices and packed pistols in their briefcases for self-protection.

DURING THE SPRING SEMESTER, tensions seemed to ease. Superintendent-Chancellor Erickson reconciled with Bob Hoover, not merely offering him his old job back, but asking him to head a readiness program for the entire district. In February, outside speakers were again allowed on campus.

But the tumultuous times were not over. In the fall of 1969, protest against the Vietnam War was building. On October 15 hundreds of students attended a campus rally. By the spring of 1970, rallies that had once drawn dozens now drew thousands. The U.S. invasion of Cambodia compelled many students to protest. For administrators and faculty members, these rallies were extremely frightening, not because they were disorderly, for they were indeed quite peaceful, but because of their large size and the potential for disaster.

Just after the Cambodian invasion, a mass gathering of students successfully urged the trustees to adopt resolutions calling for U.S. withdrawal from Indochina. After this victory, the students marched on San Mateo's City Hall. A crowd of 2,000 presented a petition to Mayor Hugh Wayne, asking that the city also condemn the war.

A group from College of San Mateo traveled to Washington to present a petition to Pete McCloskey, asking congress to spend money on education, not war. From left: John Milligan, Rudy Lapp, an unnamed student, Ed McBain of the Skyline faculty, Ray Merkel, student leader and Vietnam veteran, and McCloskey. The inscription reads "To Rudy Lapp: Congratulations on a superb lobbying job. Pete McCloskey, M.C."

Courtesy San Mateo County Historical Museum

The long-range effect of student activism on the College of San Mateo campus was a loss of favor among voters. Two bond issues went down to defeat during the late 1960s. The second, in 1968, inspired Julio Bortolazzo to resign. This bond campaign not only failed to earn the necessary two-to-one majority; it did not get even a simple plurality. The *San Mateo Times* became particularly critical of the College's "controversial programs." It felt the original "brilliant concept" of the four-campus plan "came apart with the development of activist programs."

After 1970, the turmoil tapered off. In 1973, Glenn Smith became the new Chancellor of the San Mateo County Community College District. One of his immediate objectives was to smooth over the hard feelings of the late 1960s.

SAN MATEO AND THE VIETNAM WAR

BESIDES THE STUDENTS at the college, other groups protested the Vietnam War in San Mateo. In April 1970 the San Mateo Peace Center, along with other groups, sponsored a march from the Hillsdale Shopping Center to Central Park. The few hundred protesters included the very young and very old, carrying signs saying "Vietnam, Love it or Leave it" and "Get out of Vietnam."

Yet most people in San Mateo had a fairly conservative attitude about the War. Their support, not so much for the cause of the fighting but for the men and women who were making great sacrifices for their country, was clearly revealed by the city's adoption of the "Screaming Eagles."

San Mateo's home front activities during World War II were legendary. During the Korean War, the city adopted the 25th "Tropic Lightning" Division. But the city's actions taken during the Vietnam War were unique. At a time when many Americans turned away from their soldiers, airmen and sailors, San Mateans did what they could to express their appreciation to their armed forces.

It started in 1967 with a letter from 19-year-old Sergeant Joe Artavia to his 26-year-old sister, Linda Giese, of San Mateo. Artavia was in Vietnam with the 101st Airborne Division, known as "the Screaming Eagles." He wrote his sister that morale was low in his division. The men got very few letters from home and felt forgotten. Artavia suggested that perhaps Giese could start a letter-writing campaign in San Mateo to bring up the spirits of his companions "as high as the clouds."13

Giese thought about the request and, full of emotion, went before Mayor John Murray and the City Council and talked them into action. On March 4, 1968, the men of the 101st Airborne were proclaimed "Adopted Sons of San Mateo." Years later, Mayor Murray recalled: "In those days, everybody was ducking anything at all favorable to the Vietnam War, so we were really running against the tide." In fact, this action was unique during the Vietnam War.

San Mateans took to this cause with great enthusiasm. Between 1968 and 1972, they sent some 4,000 packages of cookies and candies, along with thousands of letters. A room at the new library was dedicated in the Screaming Eagles' honor. San Mateo's Pop Warner football team began calling themselves the Screaming Eagles.

Tragically, Artavia was killed during a skirmish in the mountains southwest of Hue. Giese, then an unhappily married mother of two children, decided not to cancel a trip she had planned to Vietnam. She wanted to visit the men of her brother's company during the Christmas season to lift their spirits, if she could. She was received warmly by the men. She eventually married her officially assigned escort, Lieutenant Stephen Patterson.

In 1972, when the war ended, San Mateo was the only community in the United States to honor returning veterans with a parade. On July 4, 1981, in order to rekindle these feelings, the city organized a reunion parade featuring the 101st. Some 110,000 people turned out to celebrate San Mateo's heart-warming relationship with these airborne soldiers.

Back at Fort Campbell, Kentucky, the 101st Division's headquarters, one should not be surprised that a street is named "San Mateo." Nor should anyone wonder why the post museum includes photographs of the people of this far-away California town.

Henry's Garage, a junkyard near Bayshore and Nineteenth Avenue, was for decades a favorite haunt for local boys, who picked up valuable information about car parts, grease, and junkyard dogs.

Courtesy San Mateo County Historical Museum

ECONOMIC ACTIVITY IN THE RECENT PAST

WHILE INFLATION and energy crises affected all Americans during the 1970s and 1980s, these decades were good ones for San Mateo business interests. In April 1976 the Chamber of Commerce estimated that visitors coming to San Mateo for conventions and meetings spent about $6,345,000 within city limits, a huge increase from the $33,000 spent by business visitors in 1950. This change reflected a great expansion of office space in the city, making it a business headquarters for many important companies.

But these figures do not reflect income from more casual visitors. At numerous events at the County Fair Grounds and Bay Meadows, the Chamber estimated another $155,165,682 was spent in 1976.

The 1970s and 1980s were particularly prosperous at Bay Meadows. In 1969, Joseph Cohen retired, and Robert Gunderson became general manager, and then president in 1973. Gunderson made many improvements to the track during his tenure. He also established "Ascot Day" in 1972, to honor an equestrian tradition

The Parkside Shopping Center in East San Mateo, built in the 1950s on the site of the San Mateo airport, was clearly a sign of the future. People could buy almost anything they needed within a hundred yards of their parking places. Compare this picture to one on page 173.

Courtesy San Mateo County Historical Museum

established in England long ago. Perhaps most important to the future of Bay Meadows, in 1985 Gunderson promoted a bill sponsored by State Senator Ken Maddy to legalize "off track betting." This allowed racing fans to place bets on horses running at Bay Meadows from fairgrounds and racetracks throughout the state. By the end of the 1980s Bay Meadows had more than 600 employees, and was second only to San Francisco International Airport in its contributions to the county's tax base. Among the 1500 or so horses at running Bay Meadows were some of the most famous in recent history. These included Gate Dancer, winner of the Preakness and Super Derby; Determiner, winner of the Kentucky Derby; Majestic Prince, winner of the Kentucky Derby and Preakness; and Citation, the great triple crown winner.

During this period another old San Mateo business, the *San Mateo Times*, continued to prosper. In 1972 publisher J. Hart Clinton retired from practicing law to devote all his time to the paper. In 1973, the *Times* purchased its strongest competitor, the *Burlingame Advance Star*. By 1980, the newspaper hit a record circulation of 50,000. In 1987 Clinton's son, John, took over as publisher. J. Hart Clinton died in 1992 at the age of 87.

The *Times* did experience some new competition beginning in 1989. Jerry Fuchs, who ran a string of weekly newspapers in San Mateo County, launched the *San Mateo Weekly*, with Kirk O'Neil as its editor.

In terms of an old family returning to an old business, no story could equal the establishment of the Borel Bank. In November 1978, Harold Fick, great-grandson of Antoine Borel, announced with nine others the organization of the Borel Bank and Trust Co. The bank opened in 1980 in the Borel shopping center. Its philosophy rested on personal service and remaining a single unit bank, with no branch offices. By 1985, Borel Bank was successful enough to warrant construction of a new building to house it and other offices. Chuck's Steak House, which had once been a home on the old estate, and "Sunshine Cottage," built in the 1800s as a guest house, were torn down to make room for the new building.

In 1978, the same year Borel Bank was started, Bay View Federal Savings and Loan Association made San Mateo its corporate headquarters and built a 12-story building on El Camino Real. The firm, started in 1911 in the Bay View-Hunters Point section of San Francisco, by 1978 had 24 branch offices; within three years it would have 41.

Construction, especially commercial construction, proceeded rapidly during this period. In September 1969 ground was broken for the new corporate headquarters of California Casualty on Alameda de las Pulgas, on the site of the old orphanage. Architects John Carl Warnecke and Associates designed the structure. California Casualty was formed in 1914 in San Francisco as the California Casualty Indemnity Exchange. After much growth it decided to move its 450 employees and its $4 million annual payroll to San Mateo. The new offices cost $5 million.

In downtown San Mateo, a lot of the new construction involved Mills Hospital, which began expanding in 1969. On the west side of El Camino Real, at Fourth Avenue, the McKeon Construction Company put up the tallest building in the city; in 1973 the 14-story structure became the home of Bell Savings and Loan.

Of all the businesses attracted to San Mateo in those days, none compared in importance to the arrival of the investment company, Franklin Resources Inc. In 1972 the company moved to San Mateo from New York because it had just acquired a San Mateo company that had a much superior data processing capability. While Franklin grew steadily during the 1970s, it was in the 1980s that it experienced phenomenal success. In 1984, the company had $3.6 billion in assets. By 1985 it had $10 billion,[14] prompting *Forbes Magazine* to declare Franklin the "Best Small Company in America."[15] The incredible growth continued. By 1986 the firm had amassed $15 billion in assets,[16] and by 1988 it had a staff of 1700, making it easily the largest employer in the city of San Mateo.[17]

During just the 1970s, the amount of money spent on construction in San Mateo increased by 225%.[18] In the early 1980s the trend continued. Among the new developers on the scene was Joaquin De Monet. Of German-Jewish heritage, he had fled across Asia and the Pacific to escape the Nazis during World War II. During the postwar period he became a successful builder. Monet constructed 284,000 square feet of office space in San Mateo, east of the Marina Lagoon at Highways 92 and 101. This development came in the form of two pyramid-shaped buildings: the first, a six-story affair, was completed in 1985, and the second, of ten stories, in 1986.

Probably the greatest transportation improvement of the 1970s and 1980s was the completion of the $33-million Highway 92—101 interchange.[19] Construction began in March 1982. The finishing touches were finally applied in 1985, concluding a 30-year effort by the city to link the San Mateo-Hayward Bridge to the 19th Avenue Freeway to the College of San Mateo and beyond.

While the 1980s held much in the way of progress, San Mateans said good-bye to some old friends during the decade. In 1982 the 84-year old former St. Matthew's Catholic Church, long since replaced, was razed. In 1981 a 15-week labor strike halted the milling operations of the venerable Peterson and Arnold plant. While it survived the strike, the firm came back only as a provider of finished woodwork. In 1988 Joe Greenbach, Jr., owner of the Villa Hotel, Villa Chartier Restaurant and Lanai Lounge, decided to close the old restaurant and lanai to make room for a new development.[20] The face of San Mateo had changed substantially.

ORGANIZED OPPOSITION TO DEVELOPMENT

WHEN THE CELEBRATION of San Mateo's 75th anniversary got underway in 1969, most citizens regarded it as an event dedicated to past accomplishments, present achievements and future prospects. But some saw it as a chance to pause in the busy subdividing and building to reflect on what had been lost and what could be saved. In December 1968, a group of citizens prevailed upon the City Council to adopt a Heritage Trees Ordinance, to "preserve the remaining great trees . . . the living landmarks which tie the city to its past"[21] as an official part of the celebrating. Before this time, except at their museums, it is hard to detect much organized concern among San Mateans to protect their natural and historic environments.

Then, during the 1970s, the national environmental movement took hold, and San Mateans rose up en masse against development. No better example of their dedication can be found than their fight to "Save Sugarloaf."

In June 1971 the Cargus Corporation, once known as the San Mateo Investment Company, proposed that a hilly region west of town known as Sugarloaf become part of the city's general plan. The proposal called for annexation of this property and then the creation of an "Adult Community" for 5,800 people, plus construction of some office buildings. The project hoped "to create a development which will obtain a reasonable utilization of the site while preserving the wooded character of the hillsides and valleys." Of the 305.5 acres involved (18.9 lying in Belmont), 60% would be preserved as park and open space.

Civic-minded people such as San Matean Jane Baker opposed the plan. She maintained that the portions of

The construction of the Highway 92 Freeway, here crossing El Camino, with the railroad tracks and Delaware Street above, meant the loss of the last large open space—the Borel estate—left in central San Mateo. A new financial and commercial center grew up on the land where young San Mateans had wandered about at will for many years.

Courtesy San Mateo County Historical Museum

Sugarloaf that would be "saved" were unusable slopes anyway; that no economic and environmental studies had been completed; that the top of the mountain would be removed to fill a valley to the east, requiring 2 1/2 years of earth moving; that the offices and apartment buildings placed on top of Sugarloaf would ruin the last uncluttered hillside in San Mateo; that residences for 5,000 people would comprise a very high density development; and that the project would change the course of Laurel Creek, one of the few natural streams still existing in San Mateo.

The battle lines were drawn. The City Council Chambers became the war zone. Under Mayor John Murray, the Council favored of the developer's proposal, believing in San Mateo's traditional reliance on new development to bolster the city's economy and tax base. But this was not a good enough reason for many citizens.[22]

Among those entering the fight were environmental organizations such as the Committee for Green Foothills and the Sierra Club. Everyone expected such a stand by these groups. Joining them were a variety of homeowners' organizations within the city. Again, because of the earth removal and other inconveniences expected in the neighborhoods, this opposition was more or less anticipated. More surprising was the support generated by the "Save Sugarloaf" people from the American Association of University Women, the League of Women Voters, the Central Labor Council, the San Mateo Junior Women's Club and a variety of churches. A measure of their strength was a petition drive which netted some 7,000 signatures.

The Save Sugarloaf Committee prepared a skillful publicity piece with a photograph showing what the hill looked like, and in a drawing, how it would appear, based on a Cargus Corporation rendering, if the project were to go forward. Obviously, a massive change in the landscape would occur if the proposed cuts were allowed and the hill flattened. The piece also showed what this meant to neighboring residential areas. The hauling of nearly 3.5 million cubic yards of dirt would result in "dust . . danger . . BLASTING!!! traffic" and noise for many months.

After some nine months of wrangling at the City Council level, the issue of annexation finally made its way to the voters. Because the county would require further environmental studies and had in place a program for open space, a successful no vote would doom the developer's project. The annexation bid resulted in an overwhelming victory for open space advocates. Environmentalism was now a force to be respected in the formerly pro-development city of San Mateo.

Jane Baker built a following that enabled her to run successfully for City Council in 1973. In 1975 she became the first woman mayor of the city since the days of Elsa McGinn.

In 1978 a vastly scaled-down version of the developer's plans was accepted, allowing for some construction at the base of Sugarloaf. About 200 acres were annexed to San Mateo. In 1988, with the help of the Trust for Public Land, the city bought 187 acres of the property to be set aside as a limited access public park.[23]

The Sugarloaf fight was perhaps the most spectacular, but not the only battle won against development. In 1989 home owners in the Fiesta Gardens neighborhood fought off the construction of a massive exhibition hall at nearby San Mateo Expo Center (formerly San Mateo County Fairgrounds) which had been intended for the huge annual Semicon computer show. The Expo Center eventually lost the Semicon show to the Moscone Center in San Francisco.

The latest in the efforts of neighborhood groups to topple the dreams of developers occurred in 1991, when they secured revised height limits on new construction in the the city. Back in 1985, after much debate, the city had settled on a "compromise downtown plan," limiting buildings to 120 feet in height.[24] By 1991 this did not seem restrictive enough to neighborhood groups who did not like the continued development of the downtown as a dense high-rise center. The City Council disagreed, so the citizens' group managed to place the issue on the November 1991 ballot in the form of "Measure H," calling their campaign committee "San Mateans for Responsible Government."

Opposing this group were the "Citizens for San Mateo's Future." The San Mateo Chamber of Commerce backed the pro-development group. Former Mayor Jim Chalmers became the business community's spokesman.

Despite their considerable efforts, the Chamber's group was defeated that November. Not only did Measure H succeed, but both of the Council members up for re-election, Jane Powell and Tom Mack, who opposed H, were defeated as well. Pro-H incumbent Jane Baker was returned to office. Newcomers and pro-H advocates Jerry Hill and Claire Mack were elected. Mack became the first African-American to sit on the San Mateo City Council.

All over San Mateo the new regime meant change. Developers scrambled to alter plans. Many projects were scrapped, including one backed by the San Mateo County Historical Association to build a cultural center on the site of the old train station.

270　History of San Mateo

The Battle of the Malls

According to David Bohannon, the battle between the Hillsdale and Fashion Island Malls began one day in the mid-1970s, when he failed to make a binding deal with Bullock's Department Stores. Bullock's then turned to Ernest W. Hahn, a developer in Southern California, whom they had worked with before. Bohannon contends that Bullock's put Hahn up to the San Mateo Mariners' Island project. Before that time Bohannon and Hahn had been friends. When Bohannon confronted Hahn with his opinion that two regional malls in San Mateo could not survive, Hahn's response was something like "business is business."[25] The fight was on.

In Ernest Hahn, Bohannon had a worthy opponent. Like Bohannon, he had relatively modest roots. Hahn's father was a German immigrant who came to the United States as a baker. During World War II, Ernest served in the Navy as an electronics technician. After the war he became a contractor who specialized in building shopping centers. In 1967 he moved into the development field. His first project was the highly successful La Cumbre Plaza in Santa Barbara. Others followed, and by the mid-1970s he was a nationally-known figure.[26]

Opposing him was the aging Bohannon, who in 1975 had already retired, leaving the presidency of his company to his daughter, Frances Nelson, perhaps the most powerful businesswoman in the history of San Mateo County.

In 1977, Hahn began making known his plan for the $60-million Mariners' Island Shopping Center. Citing statistics showing that the new center would boost the local economy and expand the tax base, he began to garner support. About the same time, Hillsdale announced plans for a $43-million expansion. The Bohannon group did not reveal that they were closing a deal to bring a Nordstrom department store into the picture. San Mateo's City Hall did little to discourage either party; city officials hoped that both might succeed.

By this time, Hahn had become known as the second largest developer of shopping centers in the United States. Hillsdale would be in a fight for its life. The Bohannons joined a growing group of environmentalists, downtown merchants and community activists in opposing the new center. In March 1978 the issue came before the City Council for approval. So great was the interest in the matter that the meeting was moved to the Performing Arts Center at San Mateo High. Some 700 people attended, most of whom opposed the plan. More than 30 speakers testified for and against. Those in favor were hissed and booed. Some were even shouted down. At one point David Bohannon got up and pleaded with the Council to kill the project. With his voice "rising and falling with emotion,"[27] he delivered a rousing speech, prompting many in the audience to stand up and cheer. Ignoring the clamor, the Council approved the plan.

This was hardly the end of the matter. Bohannon decided to help mount a referendum. Various groups united to place "Measure D" on the November 1978 ballot. The now $72-million project was hotly debated. By October 23 a total of $391,363—nearly $10 for each of San Mateo's 40,112 registered voters—had been contributed to the campaigns, for and against, by just the two developers ($274,539 by Bohannon and $116,824 by Hahn). Even more was spent before election day. In the end, the people of San Mateo voted in favor of the free enterprise system. Hahn won again. Now the two developers would have to compete for tenants and eventually do battle in the marketplace.

Hillsdale soon found itself falling behind. While Hahn had most of his approvals in hand, Hillsdale was still in the planning stage. In February 1976, Hillsdale finally unveiled plans and targeted September to start construction.[28] This proved far too optimistic. Bohannon Development did not receive final approval from the City Council until November 3, 1980.[29] By this time the cost of remodeling and expansion had swelled to $57.5 million. Hahn had a two-year head start, and would complete his center in the fall of 1981, quite possibly catching Hillsdale under construction during the crucial Christmas Season.

But Hahn must have been shaken by the magnitude of the Hillsdale expansion plan. It would increase the square footage to 1,300,000, most of it in a climate-controlled, enclosed mall, encouraging shoppers to come at night or during bad weather. Most ambitious were the proposed 120,000-square-foot Nordstrom and 83,500-square-foot Mervyn's. Parking was to be increased from 5,000 spaces to 5,800. Still, 50 to 60 conditions were levied upon Hillsdale by the city, including one hotly debated demand for 156 bicycle racks, capable of accommodating 1400 bicycles. Councilwoman Jane Baker worried that the parking spaces would be too small. Despite all the red tape, Hillsdale was going to happen.

In September 1981 the $75-million Hahn shopping center, now known as Fashion Island, opened to the

---

Opposite: Donna Richardson (left), Mayor of San Mateo, and Frances Nelson, president of Bohannon Development Company, cut the ribbon to open the Hillsdale Mall in November, 1981.

Courtesy Bohannon Development Company

public. Its 856,934 square feet included four majors: J.C. Penney, Liberty House, Montgomery Ward and Bullock's (which featured a unique, teflon-coated, fabric roof), with some ome 60 smaller stores filling in the rest.

Hillsdale did not let Fashion Island stay in the limelight for long. Its own construction proceeded close to schedule. The old supermarket was torn down. Improvements in "Phase I" included the enclosure of the mall and the addition of an upper deck of shops. "Phase II" would be the opening of Nordstrom and Mervyn's.

The Phase I opening celebration was arranged for November 1981, in time for Christmas, and for head-to-head competition with Fashion Island. The preview party was attended by 500 guests, including the most important people in government and business on the Peninsula. Also on hand were David Bohannon, his wife Ophelia, and Frances Nelson, who had become "the driving force behind the massive updating."[30] Balloons in holiday colors and baskets of poinsettias were suspended throughout the interior. Benny Bufano's statues were set in landscaped areas. The party fare was sumptuous. San Mateo City Council members were quoted as "adoring" the improvement.

Work on Phase II resumed in January 1982. Both Nordstrom and Mervyn's were completed before Christmas, allowing Hillsdale to be at maximum strength in competing with Fashion Island during the busiest season of the year. Hillsdale had doubled its square footage in two years, leaping from 100 stores to 150, against Fashion Island's 113.

Just before the Christmas season of 1982, *San Mateo Times* reporter Ken McLaughlin interviewed Hillsdale and Fashion Island representatives about the upcoming duel for shoppers. He noted that Nancy Brekke, marketing director at Fashion Island, seemed "somewhat worried about the competition."[31] The Hillsdale people exuded confidence.

Within less than a decade the Bohannon family and Hillsdale would prove itself twice: first in showing there really was not room for two regional shopping centers in San Mateo as Fashion Island failed, and second in going toe-to-toe in a retail war with a nationally known developer—and winning.

TROUBLES FOR POLICE AND FIRE DEPARTMENTS

THE LATE 1960S AND EARLY 1970S were troubled times for American society. The crime rate surged. Inflation put pressure on families. Tension within communities intensified. The greatly expanded city of San Mateo was not immune to these national trends.

For the San Mateo Police Department, the spreading drug problem and the growing violence in the United States were both brought home in brutal fashion on May 23, 1968, when one of its best, Sergeant Gordon Joinville, in the process of an investigation, was murdered by Zachary Lillard, a manufacturer of LSD, on the streets of San Mateo in broad daylight. The 34-year-old Joinville left a wife and two children. He has the unfortunate distinction of being the only San Mateo policeman ever killed in the line of duty up to the present. Lillard fled to San Francisco. After an intensive four-day search, he was apprehended there.

Meanwhile, the San Mateo Police Department made arrangements to bury one of their own. The funeral possession to Skylawn Memorial Cemetery, west of town, consisted of 38 motorcycles, the hearse and 192 automobiles. Mayor John Murray stood at graveside and presented an American Flag to the widow.

Lillard's story was far from over. Evidently he had a following of his own. Folk singer Joan Baez became one of his frequent visitors. He later escaped from Santa Clara County jail and had to be captured again. Finally on February 4, 1969, he was found guilty of murder, and on March 14, 1969, sentenced to death in the gas chamber at San Quentin. However, Lillard was saved by the United States Supreme Court decision of 1972, outlawing the death penalty.[32]

For police and firemen, the increasing dangers of their professions were matched by skyrocketing inflation in the 1970s. Many government employees felt they lagged behind other wage earners, who were keeping their salaries at least even with cost-of-living increases.

On July 1, 1973, the firemen in San Mateo organized Local 2250 of the International Association of Fire Fighters. This Union would soon gain national attention. By July 1974 unrest was evident among both police and fire fighters in San Mateo. A salary increase offered by the City Council was rejected as being far too low. Fire Chief Arthur Koron had been in office for only nine months when, on August 7, members of Local 2250 walked off their jobs.

Widespread media coverage of the strike generated fear, which led to confrontation and feelings of betrayal. While fire-fighters monitored the department's radio frequency throughout the crisis, and responded voluntarily to calls when they thought they might be needed, the strike was resented by many residents, who felt caught in the middle. Fighting fires was one of the principal reasons the town had been organized to begin with. First with volunteers and then professionals, San Mateans had traditionally taken great pride in the department. Now it seemed that those who had been equipped and paid to protect them were walking away.

For the fire fighters, it was a matter of family survival in those inflationary days. At the opposite pole stood the besieged City Council, trying to be fiscally responsible, not wanting to set a precedent by giving in to a union which

Victorian Days in the Park, sponsored by the San Mateo County Historical Association, draws thousands to Central Park each year. In 1994 the affair will mark the celebration of the San Mateo Centennial, and the launching of the book you are reading at this moment.
Courtesy San Mateo County Historical Museum

had, in the Council's view, organized an illegal strike.

The strike rendered San Mateo's seven fire stations ineffective. The strikers rallied at city hall to begin picketing. Police were summoned, but no violence resulted. Management personnel and firemen from other cities were called in to protect the city. Before noon Governor Ronald Reagan, who was prepared for this, had the California Division of Forestry fire fighters on the scene as replacements.

That afternoon San Mateo city employees at the corporation yard walked off their jobs in support off the fire fighters. Workers at the sewage treatment plant did likewise. Many police officers sympathized with their brothers in the fire department, but they did not strike. Off-duty officers joined the picketing for a while, until they were ordered not to do so.

There was picketing all over town—at city facilities and projects, even in front of the homes of city council members. At six a.m. on August 9, pickets appeared at Bay Meadows and the County Fair Grounds. The Fair was in progress at the time. The surprise move closed Bay Meadows for the day. A little more than twelve hours later, Local 2250 was served with a restraining order against picketing in these crucial locations. At that moment the city also presented the union with a $1.5 million lawsuit.

While the suit was later dropped, it did have a somewhat sobering effect. On August 12, city employees who had joined the strike began returning to their jobs. But the international union was not yet finished. It began pressuring politicians in Sacramento to remove the state aid, which was allowing the City Council to stick to its tough stand. This pressure had no result.

After nearly two weeks of the strike, relations between the state fire fighters and the picketers became strained.

In the meantime the city offered a 9% pay increase, along with the threat that if this was not taken at once, every striker would be fired. The San Mateo fire fighters unanimously rejected the proposal.

Finally, after nearly three frenzied weeks, the city offered a 15.6% raise over an 18-month period, and agreed that there would be no retaliation against the strikers. San Mateo fire fighters went back to work on August 26. To say things went back to normal after the strike would be stretching the truth. In fact, bitter feelings are still expressed by both sides when describing the incident today, more than twenty years later.

Nevertheless, the fire department was still one of the best in the state. Before the strike, in 1969, it had opened its seventh station at De Anza and Highway 92. By that time the department had 129 employees. During the late 1960s and into the 1970s, the department began regearing itself from its civil defense responsibilities, a remnant of the Cold War period, to more general disaster preparation.

The department more than proved itself in this endeavor on October 17, 1989. At 5:04 p.m. on that day, as the San Francisco Giants prepared to play the Oakland Athletics in a World Series game at Candlestick Park, just up the Bayshore Highway, a 7.1 earthquake struck the Bay Area. In six hours the fire department responded to 80 calls. No lives were lost, but a building on Third Avenue collapsed, and some 800 chimneys were damaged.

Actually, San Mateo came out of this quake amazingly well. Some noted later that tennis enthusiasts on the courts over the parking garage at Central Park never stopped their play. The next day, the San Mateo Municipal Golf Course was crowded, as always. Traffic did not appear much lighter than on a normal day. The *San Mateo Times* was able to recover from a power outage and print all its editions for October 18.

CONSERVATISM IN CHANGING SAN MATEO

SOCIETY'S RAPID CHANGES in the 1960s and 1970s resulted in a conservative backlash. The feeling that government on every level had assumed too much power and was spending too much money became political dogma across the nation and especially in California. San Mateo was no exception.

In 1978 San Mateans overwhelmingly supported Proposition 13 (the Jarvis-Gann Initiative), designed to cut property taxes. Despite dire predictions, the city remained in relatively good shape (although some insist the damages from Proposition 13 are only now, in the 1990s, becoming apparent). In March 1979 City Treasurer John de Russy explained that state allocations, sales tax revenue increases and good investments made by the city with its reserves allowed the city government to remain healthy.[33]

In fact, it seems never to have missed a beat. In 1970, the city's budget came in at about $10.4 million. By 1980, despite the "Tax Revolt" of 1978, the municipal budget came to $26.8 million. In April 1981, apparently in order to bolster a conservative image, support business and limit government, San Mateans elected Florence Rhoads and Aaron Hoffman to the City Council. Nevertheless, by 1985 the budget had risen to $50.6 million, which included $10.3 million for capital improvements to repair the city's aging infrastructure.

Conservative San Mateans faced challenges in the 1980s that forced them to act against their own principles. Despite their desire to slow down social change and freeze government spending, the evolving nature of the city's population—a population in need of ever-increasing services—simply would not allow them to do so. Almost all at once, San Mateo's population became much more ethnically diverse, older, and in certain neighborhoods vastly poorer.

In 1960, 94% of San Mateans were considered to be white (this included the small Hispanic population). Only 2% were African-American. Much of the remainder was made up of Asian groups, many of which had deep roots within the community.

By 1970 the ethnic makeup of San Mateo was changing. New immigrants from a variety of backgrounds were arriving. The white population decreased to 90.72%. African-Americans climbed to 3.62%. During the 1970s, the diversifying trend continued. Among the more noticeable newcomers were people from the Pacific Islands, especially Tonga. The Tongans, deeply attached to their Mormon and Methodist churches, arrived full of hope, only to be disappointed in many cases. Because of deep-seated cultural differences, they found some difficulty in adjusting into California society.[34]

By 1980 the white population had retreated to 77.7%. In fact, the population of San Mateo itself had declined from 78,991 in 1970 to 77,561 in 1980. There were 11,374 fewer white people living in the city. Meanwhile, the non-white population had increased by 236%.[35] African-Americans did not participate in this upward trend; their population fell from 2,862 in 1970 to 2,686 in 1980. Nevertheless the nonwhite population increased from 7,330 to 17,274. Asians and Pacific Islanders represented 5,955 of this number, and Hispanics, many newly arrived, numbered 7,160, or 9.1% of the entire population. Much of the increase in the ethnic communities occurred in the old central district of San Mateo, where the white population plummeted from 46% in 1970 to 32% in 1980.

San Mateo's population also became older during this period. In 1960, as the baby boomers grew up, 35.17% of San Mateans were still under the age of 18. By 1970, the percentage dropped to 19.51, and by 1980 it was a mere 10.58%.[36] Between 1970 and 1980 the median age of all San Mateans rose from 21.6 to 29 years. The senior citizen population of the city grew numerically and in political power. Issues that most affect older Americans came to the forefront.

Ordinary San Mateans became involved in such issues as housing for seniors. This concern was evident in 1984, when the San Mateo Rotary Club began its "Rotary Hacienda" project, to build a low-rent senior housing complex in the Hillsdale area.[37] The facility was opened in 1989.

At the other end of the socio-economic spectrum, work began in 1986 on the Peninsula Regent, designed as a "swank senior residence,"[38] which included extensive health coverage as part of its attractive package. Developer BAC Associates searched nationally for the right location to establish this community for "healthy, active seniors." They were attracted to San Mateo because of its established older population, convenient shopping, and neighboring Mills Peninsula Hospital, which agreed to provide long-term and acute care for its residents.

The senior population demonstrated its political

clout with the opening of the Senior Center on Alameda de las Pulgas, across the street from Beresford Park. The center came out of a 1985 study by the City Council. It had appointed a 15-member task force to determine the needs of seniors in San Mateo. The center had been one of the recommendations, and a bond issue in 1987 enabled the project to go forward. In July 1990 the $6.5-million facility opened with a happy celebration.[39]

San Mateo by 1980 was also coming face to face with poverty. The rising cost of housing was a contributing factor. During the ten-year period, 1970 to 1980, the average value of a house in the city increased 307.4%. Even though the $10,942 average household income in 1970 had risen to $22,196 by 1980, the percentage of people living below the poverty line had increased from 6.17% in 1970 to 7.14% in 1980. Unfortunately many of those living in that category were less than 18 years old (14.61%), and in the ethnic communities of the central area, 44.75% of the children lived below the line.

Changes in the make-up of San Mateo's population put a huge strain on the city's services in the 1980s. Yet even by 1989 this strain was not clearly evident. In that year the city balanced its budget. No one rose to challenge the three incumbents, Paul Gumbinger, Jane Baker, and Florence Rhoads in the City Council election, so the city called off the election and saved itself $20,000.

In August, however, the cracks began to show. City Manager Richard DeLong announced he would retire after 13 years on the job. This might not have been taken as a bad omen except that at the same time Deputy City Manager Ken Brooks and DeLong's executive secretary Margaret Chin announced their retirement as well. Then Fire Chief Art Koron and Director of Public Works Bob Bezzant announced they were leaving. While Arch Perry was named to replace Bezzant, the rest of the positions were held vacant so that the new manager could "build his team."

Then, on December 1, 1989, DeLong let the other shoe drop. According to Terry Robertson of the *San Mateo Times*, he "glumly told the City Council's five members that the cost of city services was outpacing the city's income, and they were faced with the hard task of raising taxes and/or making significant budget cuts."[40]

The mess was left to the Council and its new manager, Arne Croce (formerly city manager of Los Altos), in 1990. Talk of a utility tax was vehemently opposed during Croce's first year, while the controlled-growth factions fought development projects that might bring in needed revenues. The *Times* and the *Weekly* were full of bitter letters to the editor. City hall "watch dog" citizens prowled the aisles at Council meetings. The formerly quiet city turned contentious, and stayed so until the 1991 election and the installation of the new controlled-growth regime.

CULTURE AND SOCIETY IN RECENT SAN MATEO

SINCE THE LATE 1960S, San Mateo has produced several home-grown artists. Two of the best known have their work displayed in public places.

Painter Robert Loomis was active with the San Mateo Recreation Department for some years. He studied Monet and other French Impressionists and noted that they often did their best when depicting their own home towns. Believing that he should also paint what "he knows and appreciates," Loomis decided to begin creating scenes of San Mateo in the early 1970s. Many of the buildings that were central to his work have since disappeared, giving the paintings historical value as well as being fine pieces of art. In 1972 the city began to purchase some of the works for its library. Loomis eventually produced some 40 paintings of San Mateo.[41]

A second famous artist was metal sculptor Al Guibara. Probably Guibara's best-known work for San Mateo is his "Leon," the life-sized bronze giraffe in Central Park. Guibara presented "Leon" to the city as a gift in 1978. He named the giraffe for his father, who once operated a toy store on Fourth Avenue.

In the area of cultural affairs for San Mateo, and indeed throughout the area, KCSM continued to be a shining light. In 1974, the station won an Emmy from the Academy of Television Arts and Sciences in the category of "Outstanding Achievement: Community Affairs" for its production, "A Deaf Adult Speaks Out."

As the station's creative potential continued to increase, by 1975 its facilities had become inadequate. Its signal was weak, reaching only a portion of San Mateo County, and it could transmit only black-and-white in a world that demanded color. The cost of improvements was prohibitive until 1977, when station KDTV wished to change its position on the dial to channel 14, occupied by KCSM. In exchange KCSM would pick up $425,267 worth of modern color equipment. Additional government grants, $300,000 from the United States Office of Education alone, helped with the change-over. The College District, under Chancellor Glenn Smith, put up $90,000. As the new channel 60, KCSM suddenly had color capability and a 1.5-million-watt capacity, reaching a potential audience of 4,000,000 viewers.

Down at Central Park, the San Mateo Arboretum Society established its headquarters in the old Kohl pump house in 1977. Since that time, the Society has moved to restore the house and has made major plans for improving the gardens at Central Park for the City's Centennial in 1994.

By the middle 1960s, one of the community's most revered women, Mrs. Yoshiko Yamanouchi, a resident

Gordon Ashby designed unique exhibits at the Coyote Point Museum, which has become an important center for environmental studies.

Courtesy San Mateo County Historical Museum

since 1915, wife of the legendary Tetsuo Yamanouchi, founder of the Buddhist Temple, seemed to symbolize the Japanese experience in the United States with her family's successes in the laundry business. Yet she felt something was missing. In 1968, in her spacious back yard on East Fifth Avenue, she built a scaleddown version of Japan's famed Katsura Villa. Prince Toshito had begun building the original landmark back in the 1600s. Architectural historian Alan R. Michelson has called the San Mateo reproduction a "faithful. . . synthesis of the earlier building's features."[42]

This teahouse was built not for utilitarian use, but to provide space for social interchange and the appreciation of the culture of old Japan. Here visitors could practice calligraphy, read poetry, or observe the elaborate tea ceremony. The tea house was fabricated in Japan and then brought to the United States in 100 crates. Japanese craftsmen lived with the family on East Fifth Avenue for eight months as the replica, the only one of its kind, came together. It complements the 16th-century-style Muromachi garden, created in 1953, which is also on the property. The garden was featured in *American Homes* magazine in 1962. The first public event was held at the tea house on September 25, 1968, when the American Association of University Women held a benefit there for the College of San Mateo's scholarship fund. Mrs. Yamanouchi enjoyed the Katsura for five years until she died in 1973.

In 1979 the San Mateo County Historical Association staged its first Victorian Days in the Park, an arts, crafts and history festival. The event has grown into San Mateo's grandest annual celebration, attracting tens of thousands of people. Victorian Days were initiated because, under Proposition 13, county funding for the association's museum at the College of San Mateo was dramatically slashed. Under Board member Don Ringler, with the help of Executive Director Herbert Garcia, a professional promoter was employed to organize the first festival. After a few years, the Victorian Days became strictly a volunteer affair, with a perennial chairwoman, Carole Groom, in charge.

Since the city's 75th birthday party in 1969, perhaps no anniversary has been better observed than San Mateo

High School's 75th in 1977. Chairmen Noe Chanteloup, Sam Goodhue, Harold Fick and Thomas Reimer began planning the celebration in 1974. The three-day series of events in November 1977 required the help of 300 volunteers. Some 7,200 people attended the different functions, which included an open house, a tennis tournament and a dinner-dance at the County Fairgrounds. Among those on hand to help with the party was Merv Griffin (class of 1942), who sang for an hour. An honored guest was Mabel Moore Paul, member of the school's first graduating class (1905).[43]

Of all the cultural achievements made in San Mateo in the recent past, perhaps the greatest is the vastly improved Coyote Point Museum. In 1976 the museum revealed its plans, drawn up by Spencer Associates, architects, and exhibit specialist Gordon Ashby. In June 1978 the County Board of Supervisors approved the project, provided that the Museum Association raise all necessary operating revenues in the future.

A fund-raising campaign brought in $1.3 million in government grants, plus another $1.6 million from private sources.[44] The museum opened in 1981 to good reviews. Its advocacy of environmental sensitivity has set new standards in the way museums interpret their subjects. After a successful fund raising campaign in 1991, the museum opened an adjoining Wildlife Center.

Another magnificent project, the building of a new $9-million YMCA, was announced in 1984. Its massive fund raising drive and the recent completion of the project represent a huge achievement for residents of San Mateo and people up and down the Peninsula.

Toward the Future

AT ONE POINT, not long ago, one might have predicted that San Mateo would be the city of condominiums. In 1979, when the Woodlake Apartment complex gave tenants the option to buy their units, some 400 of the 990 decided to do so, while 200 apartments were reserved for seniors. All over town "co-op" conversions took place. Some new buildings were constructed as "condos." That same year, Grosvenor Properties, Ltd., announced plans to build a $60 million, six-story complex on Laurel Street across from Central Park. The 143 units would be of premium quality, with the latest improvements. However, after the project's completion, sales were slow, thanks to high mortgage interest rates and problems with the economy. Units were rented instead from $800 to $4000 a month. Since that time, the condominium "mania" has tapered off.

In 1984, the city looked to the future by remodeling its city hall. Back in 1972, the city had had to rent a house trailer and place it at the rear of the building to relieve the space crunch. The 1984 plan called for expanding the 1953 building and updating its interior. Eighteen months and $3 million later, the project, supervised by City Treasurer John de Russy, was completed, and city employees moved out of their trailer.[45]

• • • •

WHAT IS SAN MATEO'S FUTURE? Business experts, government officials, social innovators, and, of course, residents all would like to know. They can make predictions, but no one can really see past today.

Who would have guessed two hundred years ago that the beautiful stretch of land on both sides of San Mateo Creek, where natives had lived for centuries and a mission outpost was being constructed, would in a short span of time become an important crossroads, a home for tens of thousands of people, and a business, social, and cultural center? In this centennial year of San Mateo's incorporation, looking back and contemplating how much change has occurred is an important step to take, because we certainly have the capability to change much more.

Today many San Mateans have mixed feelings about their city. They want economic development to continue because it is essential to the well-being of the community, but they want to protect environmental and historical legacies as well. Diversity has always been a San Mateo characteristic—never so much as now. And those who have studied San Mateo's history can see in this diversity the very strength that will enable it to face the future. Business interests, home owners, ethnic groups, different generations and political groups all seem to be able to make themselves heard at the appropriate moment. To some, progress seems agonizingly slow. But the end result is a democratic, socially responsible, economically sound community. When the arguments are finally finished, San Mateans are galvanized into action, and great achievements are realized. This is historical fact.

NOTES

1. San Mateo City School District, "Significant Dates - San Mateo Integration Activities," May 25, 1967.
2. San Mateo City School District, "Racial and Ethnic Distribution of District Employees," November 21, 1967.
3. California State Department of Education, Bureau of Intergroup Relations," San Mateo Union High School District, San Mateo High, Racial and Ethnic Distribution of Employees, Racial and Ethnic Distribution of Public School Enrollment," November 10, 1967.
4. Robert W. Coppock, Director of Personnel, City of San Mateo, "Public Employment Survey, Summary Sheet," 1967
5. "Action Now," Articles of Incorporation, 1967, in the archives of the San Mateo County Historical Museum.
6. Author's interview with John J. Murray, March 16, 1993.
7. San Mateo Area, Business Leadership Council, "Press Release," April 23, 1968, in the archives of the San Mateo County Historical Museum.
8. Walt Wright, "Judges, Councilmen Should Quit Elks" *Burlingame Advance*, November 27, 1968.
9. Vera Graham, "Aging San Mateo Looks Strong," *San Mateo Times*, January 2, 1980.
10. Postel, "Junior-Community," p. 20.
11. Ibid. p. 21.
12. Ibid. p. 22.
13. Jane Gross, "Suburb is Reliving Two 60s Love Stories," *New York Times*, June 29, 1988.
14. "Franklin Mutual Funds Top $10 Billion Assets," *San Mateo Times*, June 25, 1985.
15. "Franklin: Best Small Company in U.S.," *San Mateo Times*, October 21, 1985.
16. "Franklin Lightening Flashes On," *San Mateo Times*, January 6, 1986.
17. Chris Kenrich, "Franklin Resources of San Mateo," *Peninsula Times Tribune*, November 6, 1988.
18. Vera Graham, "Aging San Mateo Looks Strong," *San Mateo Times*, January 2, 1980.
19. Vera Graham, "It Was a Boom Year for San Mateo," *San Mateo Times*, January 4, 1986.
20. Vera Graham, "Villa Chartier, Lani to Close," *San Mateo Times*, April 20, 1988.
21. San Mateo 75th Anniversary Committee, *Heritage Trees*, City of San Mateo, Mrs. Harold E. Atkinson, editor.
22. Author's interview with Jane Baker, March 17, 1993.
23. Mario Dianda, "City Buys Mountain," *Peninsula Times Tribune*, April 16, 1988.
24. Vera Graham, "Compromise Downtown Plan Ok'd," *San Mateo Times*, June 21, 1985.
25. Author's interview with David D. Bohannon on October 13, 1993.
26. Don West, Harold K.. Streeter, "And Now, the Men Who Brought You Measure D," *San Francisco Examiner*, November 2, 1978.
27. Vera Graham, "Mariner's Isle Plan Approved," *San Mateo Times*, March 15, 1978.
28. Vera Graham, "Hillsdale Expansion Detailed," *San Mateo Times*, February 10, 1978.
29. Vera Graham, "Hillsdale Center Wins Approval," *San Mateo Times*, November 4, 1980.
30. Vera Graham, "Hillsdale Opens Expanded Mall Area," *San Mateo Times*, November 19, 1981.
31. Ken McLaughlin, "A Tale of One City — with Two Regional Malls," *San Mateo Times*, September 28, 1982.
32. Lori Piacente, "Sergeant Gordon Joinville: The First Police Officer In the History of San Mateo Killed in the Line of Duty," 1988, student monograph #88-172 in the archives of the San Mateo County Historical Museum.
33. Vera Graham, "San Mateo Reports Being 'Fiscally Fit' Despite '13,'" *San Mateo Times*, March 17, 1979.
34. John Horgan, "Island Culture Contrasts Sharply with Urban Pace," *San Mateo Times*, September 8, 1976.
35. Vera Graham, "Minority Population in San Mateo More than Doubles," *San Mateo Times*, January 13, 1983.
36. Vera Graham, "Census Study of San Mateo's People," *San Mateo Times,* September 1, 1983.
37. Vera Graham, "A great year for San Mateo," *San Mateo Times*, December 21, 1984.
38. Vera Graham, "Swank Senior Residence Will Break Ground this Fall," *San Mateo Times*, August 16, 1986.
39. Modesto Fernandez, "New Senior Center Opens with Celebration," *San Mateo Weekly*, August 1, 1990.
40. Terry Robertson, "SM Loses Manager, Gains Fiscal Headache," *San Mateo Times*, December 30, 1989.
41. Vera Graham, "Resident Artist Preserves San Mateo's Past," *San Mateo Times*, August 30, 1982.
42. Alan R. Michelson, "Katsura Tea House," *Historic Resources Inventory Addition for the City of San Mateo*, May 16, 1991.
43. Gail Bernice Holland, "Biggest Event in 75 years at San Mateo High" *San Mateo Times*, November 28, 1977.
44. Mary Jane Clinton, "Their Dream Becomes Reality," *San Mateo Times*, May 16, 1981.
45. *City of San Mateo, Annual Report 1986*, January, 1986.

The following persons or organizations have demonstrated their support for the San Mateo Centennial and for the San Mateo County Historical Association by ordering this Centennial History in advance of publication. Their names are inscribed here as sponsors, and as Citizens of San Mateo in 1994, the Centennial Year.

A

Stephanie and Alan Abel
Carol Boulden Abrahamian
Albert A. Acena
Greg and Tracy Aguilar
Ah Sam Florist
Brent and Cori Ahlvin
Jean M. Ainsworth
Dominic and Evelyn Albano
Dominic and Helen Albano
Mr. and Mrs. Raymond Allara
Don and Gloria Allen
George J. Allen
Lorre Morris Allison
Gaitano and Maria Aloise
Myrtle and Tony Aloise
Mr. and Mrs. Joseph Amable
Sam and Karen Amato
Dean and Joy Anderson
Dr. and Mrs. William W. Anderson
Mr. & Mrs. Stanley T. Andrews Jr.
Hoshie T. Anjo
Mrs. Hoshie T. Anjo
Gordon and Jean Anthony
Dino and Cindy Antoniazzi
Len and Terri Appiano
Sharon Loucks Atkins
Ms. Carolyn J. Atkinson
Ms. Carrie Atkinson
Greg and Dorothy Atkinson
Jeff and Barbara Atkinson
Joe and Cordula Atkinson
Larry and Karen Atkinson
Lavina Parsons Atkinson
Mr. and Mrs. Alex Aycinena

B

Joe and Mary Bacchetto
Mr. and Mrs. Joseph Bacchetto Jr.
Douglas & Tamera Bacchi
Ted & Linda Backman
Jim and Bettye Bailey
Jane Baker
Mr. & Mrs. H. William Baker
Paul & Helen Baker
Richard and Barbara Baker
Mr. & Mrs. Carl S. Balch
Mr. & Mrs. Joseph Baldanzi
Frank & Mary Baldanzi
Frank A. Baldanzi
John and Lydia Baldanzi
Mr. Joseph Baldanzi Jr.
Mr. and Mrs. Joseph Baldanzi
Joseph A. Baldanzi Jr.
Thomas and Marjorie Baldenweck
Florence E. Bale
Glen N. and Elizabeth M. Bale
John E. Bale

Robert & Annamarie Balian & Family
Stevan & Laura Balian & Family
John J. and Jane Balles
Lee and Jody Baly
Walter J. Bank
Sherry Bennett Barbour
Eleanor and Thomas Barile
Maureen and Jeffrey Barile
Colleen D. Barnes
Fred & Betty Barnes
Kevin D. Barnes
Richard L. and Marjorie E. Barnes
Mrs. Judith Webster Barton
Mr. and Mrs. James G. Battey
Anna Karuntzos Baudoin
Bay Area Land Watch
Carlos Bazan
Marian Allen Beale
Daniel and Judy Beatty
William and Sylvia Beckerley
Helen R. Bedesem
Walter & Joan Beering
Carol J. Belo
Anne and Edward Bena
Benjamin Franklin Hotel
The Benner Family
Barbara Bennion
Dennis and Sue Bennion
Jerry Bennion
Richard and Bonnie Slade Bennion
Richard, Kelly and Alex Bennion
Tom and Sharon Slade Bennion
Mr. & Mrs. Harald J. Benson
Everett H. Berberian
Peggy Berlese
Mrs. Esther Bernardo
Michael L. J. Berube
Mr. & Mrs. R.V. Bettinger
David A. & Judith A. Biasotti
Palma Biasotti
Albert and Anne Bigley
Russ and Jessica Biglow
John and May Blaisdell
Rona D. Blevins
Nancy and Charles W. Block
Richard & Susan Blois
Jonathan Bloom
Jordan and Judy Bloom
Michael Bloom
Nicole Bloom
Pearl and Ernie Bloom
Bill and Carol Boes
Mr. & Mrs. Sewall Bogart
Ken and Betsy Bogel
David D. Bohannon
Edward and Doris Bohn
Albert and Connie Boido
J.E. Boling

Larry and Dorothy Borba
Manuel & Peggy Borba
Arthur L. and Dale K. Borland
Tom and DiAnn Bormes
Karla Muller Bostic
Henry & Betty Bostwick
Arthur (Boz) Bosworth III
Leda Claire Bosworth
Bob Bottari
Ken & Jean Bottari
Scott Bottari
Dorothy Grace Boyasian
Andrew and Janet Boyer
Mr. & Mrs. Robert Brahm
 (Margo O'Brien)
Donald Martin Branson
Tom Branson
Fritz and Sue Brauner
Barbara N. Bray
Chandler Briggs
Mary A. Brodzin
Geoffrey W. Bromfield Jr.
Daniel and Lillian Brooks
Allan and Kathy Brown
Horace D. & Mariellen Brown
June and Tony Brown
Clare and Simon Brown
Jerome J. Brozell
Dr. and Mrs. Gene Bruce
Mr. and Mrs. R.C. Bruno
Stanleigh Bry
Robert and Frances Buckingham
Shirley Burgett
Mrs. John Everett Burke
Mr. & Mrs. Norman T. Burke
Dr. & Mrs. Richard Burns
Mr. & Mrs. Harry T. Burton
E.J. Burwell

C

Judge Thomas B. Caldwell, Ret. &
 Moira Caldwell
California Water Service Company
Patrick and Dolores Callagy
Harold and Lois Callahan
H. A. Cahalan, Jr.
California State Library
John & Pat Canzian
Shiela A. Canzian
Jane L. Carboni
Victor and Gayle Carboni
Robert and Joseph W. Carcione, Jr.
Dawn Cardona
Sally and Amos Carey
Roy B. Carlson
Mr. & Mrs. Wallace Carlson
Barbara B. Carleton
Barbara Bohannon Carleton

Carlmont Capital Group, Inc.
Dr. Marilyn I. Carmona
Kristel Sellman Carter
Lisa M. Casazza
Mr. & Mrs. Louis M. Caserza
Hector & Angela Castro
Joseph Celotti
Mary and Victor Celotti
Jim & Liz Chalmers
Marcia H. Chase
Emily J. Chavez
Oscar and Nancie Lee Chavez
Santina P. Chelone
Nessie E. Chesebrough
Nivia Chong
Alison J. Choppelas
Christopher N. Choppelas
Jonathan G.J. Choppelas
Dr. & Mrs. Nicholas G. Choppelas
David and Barbara Chow
Maralene Church
Ruth and Gene Ciranni
City of San Mateo, Community
 Development Department
Mr. & Mrs. Allason N. Clark
Eleanor Roe Clark
Robert & Eleanor Clark
Marilynn & James Clarke
Chris and Lois Clausen
Francis and Mary Jean Clauss
Mary Ellen Clauss
Kenneth and Maureen Clayton
John and Nina Clinton
Nicholas Codianne
Edwina Coffing
Judge Melvin E. and Nita Cohn
Ralph & Linda Cole
Colma Historical Association
Max & Jacqueline Cologna
Tom & Linda Cologna
Mrs. Jennie T. Colson
R. Frank Coltart
Concar Enterprises, Inc.
Mr. & Mrs. D. Stephen Coney
Al Conrad
Barbara Conrad
Mr. & Mrs. Thomas L. Constantino
Christopher P. Conway
Dr. & Mrs. Joseph V. Cook
Mrs. Marie-Louise Johnson Cook
Robert G. Cook
Darcie and Michael Cookson
Mr. and Mrs. David Cookson
Heidi and Peter Cookson
Alexandra Mendes Cooley
Richard Cooley Family
Mr. & Mrs. George Cope
Robert W. Coppock
Lynn and Lance Corcoran
Mr. & Mrs. Jack Corey
Harry P. Costa
Frank and Kathleen Costaglio
Louella L. Costaglio
Jeanne M. Costin

George Cover, C.P.A.
Dona and Charles Cowan
George and Vivienne Craig
Mr. & Mrs. Thomas Craig
Frances Mary Cravens
Cris and Bill Crawford
Doris Batchelder Crawford
Helen R. Creighton
Mario & Jean Crispieri
John and Susan Critchlow
Arne and Carol Croce
Thomas Culligan
Bob and Jan Cummings
Jack and Debi Curry
Cypress Lawn Cemetery

D
Raymond J. Daba
Tressa E. Dabkowski
Daly City Public Library
Mr. & Mrs. Thomas J. Daly
Dr. & Mrs. Sonny H. Da Marto
David P. Damia
Eugene & Nancy D'Amico
Dan Newell Inc.
Harry M. Davis
Marie & Ernest Davis
Gail Davison
Stewart & Irene Nystrom Dawson
Debra Dayton
Monte and Mel Dayton
Dominick and Gail DeBellis
Ed. R. Decker
Douglass and Dorris Decherd
Jack and Margery DeFigueiredo
Froilan I. De Guzman
Mr. & Mrs. Shawn DeLuna
Louis B. and Lillian M. Dematteis
Denn and Susan Denning
Marvin and Nancy Dennis
Mr. & Mrs. Robert Desky
Charles DeSoto
Frances and Joseph DeVol
Victoria and Norman DeVol
Daniel Lido Dias
Michael Lido Dias
Sharon Diercks
Graham and Joanne Dilks
Don and Carol Dill
Mr. and Mrs. William F. Diskin
Joan and Larry Diskin
Dr. & Mrs. F. Gene Dixon
Mr. Alexander Djerassi
Mr. Dale Djerassi
Charles and Ruth Dodane
Irving and LaVon Doughty
Mr. & Mrs. Oswald Drews
William and Lois Drieslein
Richard and Debora Duncan
Candy Ducato
Dunfey San Mateo Hotel
Bob and Diane Dupont
Louis and Maxine Duranti
Anne M. Duskin
Elizabeth and Allan Dyson

E
Ray Ebersole
Vit Eckersdorf
Kenn and Lois Edwards
Francis and Margaret Egan
Margaret Egan
Clift and Ann Ehrhard
Dr. and Mrs. Charles H. Eid
Mrs. Viola Eikerenkotter
Ernest and Eleanor Elliott
Mike and JoEllen Ellis
Gary and Margaret Emich
Helen Hughes Empey
Mr. & Mrs. I.H. Encoyand
Enes, Inc., Late Bloomers
Joseph and Lois Erasmy
Elizabeth Ervin
Mr. & Mrs. William P. Ervin, Jr.
Harrison and Rita Estabrook
Bob and Joy Estupinian
Edward Everett IIIrd
Lois Almen Everett Heidi Ethridge

F
Ed and Elva Fabris
Robert and Betty Fahs
Mrs. Louis Falletti
E.L. "Geno" Fambrini, ECV
Mr. & Mrs. Ronald L. Faulk
Robert Faulkner
Mr. and Mrs. J. Sherry Feehan
Lynne Feely
Ellen Fender
Mr. & Mrs. Rick A. Fenton
The Ferguson Family
Bradley Borel Fick
David Bovet Fick
Mr. & Mrs. Harold Fick
Mr. Ronald G. Fick
Ronald G. and Valerie P. Fick
Stephen and Abbie Fick
Ted and Liz Field
Jane and Al Figone
David and Marian Finkelstein
First Baptist Church of San Mateo
Charlotte and Paul Fish
Dorothy W. Fisher
Mr. & Mrs. Kenneth L. Fisher
John and Pauline Fisher
Robert and Margareta Fisse
Carl W. Flach
Helen Nash Fleming
Richard and Mary Fletcher
Rob and Susan Flint
George and Nancy Fogerson
Mr. & Mrs. T. Jack Foster, Jr.
Dorothy Fowler
Fox and Carskadon
Colleen and Paul Franke
Franklin/Templeton Group of Funds
Joanne Fraysse
Louise and Bill Freedman
David W. and Janet K. Freeman
Thomas R. Friebel

John and Gabby Fuller
George and Eva Fulvio
Linda R. Fulvio
Mr. & Mrs. Emmett Funke
Richard and Janet Fusco

G
Ruth and Ralph Gaines
Philip A. Galu III
Frank and Grace Galioto
Ena H. Gall
Brian Gallaway
Howard and Marthine Gallaway
Suzanne and Frank Galli
Charles and Madeleine Gambony
Alfonso L. and Eva Dora Garcia
Ralph and Jean Garcia
Marian M. Gardner
Norman and Angela Gardner
David and Linda Gargiulo
Bradley and Gina Garibaldi
Mr. & Mrs. Philip Garlington
William J. Gastrock
Ron Gaydos
George Hall School
Mr. Denni D. Ghilarducci
Roland and Celeste Giannini
Albert and Maxine Giannotti
Benedetta Adele Gianoli
Robert P. Gianuario
Ted and Marie Gibsen
Gilbrech Financial Services
Mr. & Mrs. Thomas P. Gilmer, Jr.
Allan and Geraldine Giorgetti
Marilyn A. Gjerdrum
Mr. and Mrs. Robert F. Gleason
Glendale Federal Bank
Roger and Dorene Goad
Mr. & Mrs. Richard Goddard
Goldrath Family
Mary T. & Frank E. Gomes
Ms. Polly Gomes
Mr. and Mrs. Jose L. Gomez
Gene and Barbara Gorden
Lynelle Bennett Gordon
Gramercy On The Park
Gramercy Marcom Services
Gray Line of San Francisco
James J. Gray
Kent and Dyan Grealish
Jud and Cecile Green
Beth Greenhalgh
Nancy and Jerome Green-West
Maximillian and Helen Gretsch
Mark and Joan Gribble
Janet Griffiths
Hanni Grindrod
Carole Groom
Grosvenor Properties Ltd.
Sunny and Jerry Grotsky
Richard and Patti Gruber
Helen Gruber
Russ Guard

Helen C. Guarisco
Paul and Louise Gumbinger
Yael Gurse

H
Mrs. Carl Hagstrom
Ronald and Carryl Hall
Mr. & Mrs. Lee E. Ham
Lillian and Dan Hamburg
Mr. and Mrs. Peter F. Hamilton
Mrs. Susan Hamlin
Mr. & Mrs. Hans Hansen
Martin and Carol Harband
Mr. & Mrs. Donald F. Harle
Harman Chiropractic Center
Dennis D. Harman
John W. Harney Jr.
Katy C. Harney
Michael P. Harney
Scott T. Harney
Evelyn Harper
Taylor and Theo Harrell
Cecelia E. Harris
Edmund and Marilyn Harris
Louis and Linda Harris
Sanford and Mary Grace Harris
David C. Harrison
Mr. & Mrs. Roger Hartelius
Mr. & Mrs. William M. Hartmann
Mary Jean A. Haski
Tracy and Mark Hathaway
Dr. & Mrs. David Hayashi
Helga Hayse
Dennis and Jane Heckman
Joyce, Mark and Heather Heels
Jack and Maggie Heffernan
Lois and Walt Heim
Mr. and Mrs. Murray M. Hemming
Mr. and Mrs. Raymond Hemming
Mr. & Mrs. Clifford G. Henry
Dwain and Barbara Henry
Jerry and Sky Hill
Herb and Catherine Hill
Richard and Doris Hill
Taryn Hill
Hillsdale High School
Hillsdale Transmission
Wayne and Micky Hinthorn
Peggy Hintz
Historical Society of South San Francisco
Norah and Ira Hocherman
Michael and Lauren Hoffmann
Barbara and Richard Holm
Marion C. Holmes
Daisy Hom
Ila Homsher
E. Crane Honeysett
John Hopfenbeck
John and Sandy Soal Hopkins
Mr. & Mrs. Russell P. Hora
John and Gigi Horak
Elizabeth N. Horn
William G. Horn, Jr.
Mary Hould

Mr. John R. Houghton
Scott and Amanda Howard
Stephen H. Howell
Supervisor Tom Huening
Don and Mary Hughes
Karen and Dan Humber
Linda Humber
Barbara B. Hunter
Peter S. Hurlbut
Mr. & Mrs. J. Wesley Huss
Norman and Margreta Husted
Robert and Ruth Hutter

I
George and Aileen Ikuta
Tim and Michelle Inama
Ince Family
Robert H. and Judith Ipswitch
William J. and Mary Iracki
Yasuko Ann Ito
Larry and Marie Ivich
Carl and Mary Izzard

J
Helen and Donald Jaffe
Lowell and Helen James
Paul and Linda James
Dr. and Mrs. Robert E. James
William Alec James
Mr. and Mrs. M.M Jamieson
Michael and Elisabeth Jamieson
Mary H. Janney
Wally and Linda Jansen
Carl and Sena Jansen
Dell and Oleda January
Peter G. Jean
Daniel M. and Carol C. Johndrow
Johnsen & Bruun Opticians
Mr. & Mrs. Charlton F. Johnson
Edwin and Mary Jo Johnson
F. Deborah Johnson
Mr. & Mrs. John E. Johnson
Michele and Christina Johnson
Paul and Jean Johnson
Mrs. Phyllis H. Johnson
Thomas and Cay Johnson
Tori Johnson, Casey and Shaun
Andrew and Margaret Johnston
Mr. & Mrs. Jess Jones
Nelson and Diana Jones
William E. Jordan M.D.
Lupe Montoya Julius
Sharon McLaren Junge
Jan Jungnick-Smith
Junipero Serra High School
Herman and Jane Jurkovich

K
Ambassador Robert F. Kane
The Karimimanesh Family
Adrianna and David Karp
Paul and Mark Karuntzos
Theodore L Karuntzos

Miss Tomoko E. Kashiwagi
Juana Kavanaugh & Family
Mr. & Mrs. Jack M. Keeney
John and Olga Keeney
Donald W. Kelley
Jack and Kristine Kelley
Anne and Charlie Kelly
Jim Kelly
Kevin and Nancy Kelly
Lucille E. Kenney
William F. and Susan E. Kenney
Bill and Marion Kessler
Brian G. Kestner
John and Ginny Kiely
Sharon Kipp
Mr. & Mrs. Bruce Charles Kirkbride
Mr. & Mrs. Harold E. Kirkbride
Carl and Ann Kistner
San Mateo Downtown Kiwanis Club
Mr. and Mrs. Donald O. Kocmich
Masayuki and Anne Marie Kodama
Kathryn A. Koerner
Priscilla J. Koernig
Larry and Ruth Kollerer
Rosalyn Koo
Jerry and Gladys Kosro
Dr. Angela Kraft
Darius V. Kraft
Peter D. Kraft
Dr. and Mrs. Robert A. Kraft
Eunice and Howard Kraus
Robert and Maureen Kremers

L
J. Lacey
Mr. & Mrs. Ray Lagomarsino
John and Janet Lamb
June W. Lamb
Margaret C. Lanphier
Roberta and Jack Landers
The Hon. Tom Lantos
June L. LaPoint
Robert L. La Point
Douglas F. Lambert
Melvin B. Lane
Margaret Lanphier
Bernard Lanusse
Catherine Lanusse
Rudolph M. and Patricia T. Lapp
Richard and Joan Larson
Bernice and Kenneth Lauder
Ann and Paul Leake
The LeClair Family
Ken and Marilyn Lee
Mr. & Mrs. Richard J. Lee
Sue and Art Lempert
Supervisor Ted Lempert
Mr. and Mrs. Ernie Lena
Lincoln and Nellie Leong
Joyce and Tony Leopardo
James K. and Charlotte M. Leslie
Ralph and Mem Levin
Mathew McCarthy Levy &
    Kevin McGrath Levy

Don Leydig
Ed and Gay Liesse
Tonya Light
Mr. Christopher J. Lim
Mr. and Mrs. Carlo Lindsey
Drs. Paul and Jeanne Linquist
Jon M. Liss
Catherine Littmann
Bob and Jean Lloyd
Barry F. Lockwood
Barry B. and Clotilde A. Lockwood
Susan M. Loftus
Frank and Leslie Lohmeier
Linda Philpott Londerville
Long's Drugs
RIchard and Patricia Lopez
Thalia and Stephen Lubin
Edwin M. and Jerilynn Lucia-Johnson
Joe and Eleanore Lucido
Mr. and Mrs. Alfred Luddy
Mr. and Mrs. John Ludeman
Louis J. Luini
Carolyn and Jerry Lyon
Daniel Laurence Lyons
Kerry Marie Lyons
Tara Kathleen Lyons

M
Claire L. Mack
Elizabeth L. Mack
Harold L. Mack III
Tom Mack
Mr. and Mrs. J. Paul Madden
Kimm and Paul Marotta
Pauline Markas, Librarian, Serra High
Gerald and Clara Martell
Michael and Margaret Martinelli
Mr. James K. Mason
John and Louise Mason
Mrs. Marleen C. Mason
William J. Matson
Jo Ann Mattner
Dr. and Mrs. Paul H. Mawdsley
Mary L. and Ted Mayer
John Maylan
Jan Maze
Ethel Wright McCann
Mike and Margo McCann
Harold McCarthy
Dennis L. McClanahan
Katherine V. McClanahan
J.W. McClenahan Co.
Dorothy McConaughey
Loretta A. McClurg
Michael S. and Christine M. McCoy
Pam McCubbin
Jan McCune
Ronele and Scott McCurdy
Fielding McDearmon
Charlotte and Jeff McFadden
Doug and Ricki McGlashan
Peter J. McGrath
Catherine Marie McKay
Joy and William McLemore

Maura K. McMahon
R.J. McMills
Shirlee and Larry McMills
Michael and Sheila McQuade
Elissa and Lon McQuillin
Rosalind Cargill McRoskey
Medicross Pharmacy
Chuck and Daisy Meister
Msgr. Ferdinand Mempin
Menlo Park Historical Association
David and Marianne Mersereau
Wallace and Patricia Mersereau
John H. Messerschmidt
Francis Lengfeld Meyer
Mr. & Mrs. Kenneth D. Meyer
MHA Environmental Consulting, Inc.
Harry and Jean Michelsen
Peter F. Michelson
Dr. & Mrs. Robin P. Michelson
Mrs. Albert G. Miller
Alice Miller
Mr. and Mrs. Arjay Miller
Bruce and Adrienne Mitchell
Malcolm Mitchell
Mary and Hugh Mitzner
Dan Moisan
Alexander and JoLanta Moissiy
Al and Marjorie Molakidis
Daniel J. Monaco
Pat and Vickie Montgomery
Brian Thomas Mooney
John and Carol Mooney
Terri Ann Mooney
Gary and Terri Moore
Barbara H. Moran
Mr. & Mrs. James M. Moran
Rose and Bill Moran
Dean and Renee Moresco
Dick and Arlene Morgan
Mark and Tara Morgan
Gladys E. Morris
Jackson A. and Carol L. Morris
Lorraine E. Morris
Stewart and Margaret Morrow
Gary and Sandra Morton
Sue and Ray Moses
Harvey and Ann Mowry
Marshall Moxom
Robert Muehlbauer
Corinne Falvey Mullane
Joseph and Jenell Mullane
Michele Muller
Mrs. Dexter C. Mulliken
Mr. & Mrs. Edward V. Murphy
John and Elizabeth Murphy
Joanne Fleming Murray
John J. Murray
John J. Murray Jr.
Maureen M. Murray
William B. Murray
Jean M. Muzio
Darryl and Eleanor Myers
David Conrad Myers

N

Nagle, Krug & Winters
Colette P. Nassutti
Jo Ann Nassutti
Mark P. Nassutti
Denise and Greg Nelson
Frances Bohannon Nelson
Mr. & Mrs. Karl Nelson
Mr. & Mrs. Richard W. Nelson
Winifred Iliohan Nelson
Karin Sellman Nesse
Grethana Neuhaus
Dan Newell Inc.
James W. Newell
Steve and Jennifer Newell
Carolyn Nichols
Laura and Paul Niebuhr
Mr. & Mrs. Stuart Nixon
Dorothea and Roger Nolan
Northwest Information Center
Barbara Vignassa Norris
Emperor Norton, ECV #1
Chief John and Lynne Walcha Norton
Bob and Mary Ann Notz
Ichiro Numa
Paul and Aileen Nystrom

O

Donald and Anne Oakes
Hank and Mary Jo Obayashi
Dr. and Mrs. John B. O'Brien
Mrs. Robert E. O'Brien
Helen and Ronald O'Connell
Mary Sue O'Connell
Mr. & Mrs. James C. O'Keefe
Jean Ogren
Mrs. Teresa Beltramo Oklobzia
Margaret Bromfield Olian
Katie and Howard Oliphant
Lloyd and Janice Olsen
Karalyn Patrice Ortega
Kevin Michael Ortega
Kazu Oshima
Doris Osterling
Marguerite Ott
Dan Owen
Mr. & Mrs. Robert Oyster

P

Betsy and Bill Pace
Pacific Gas & Electric Co.
Pacifica Historical Society
Tadeusz and Susan Pacwa
Ian B. Paget
Mr. & Mrs. C.R. Pai
Palm Avenue Motors, Inc.
Karole Sellman Palmberg
Mr. Hall Palmer
Catherine and Alan Palter
Mr. & Mrs. Raymond Paneri
Stan and Corina Panko
John Pantages
Henri and Paulette Pardeilhan

Robert and Carolyn Pardini
Dr. and Mrs. Thomas G. Parker
Kim and Alan Parnass
Mr. & Mrs. William G. Parrott
Mr. and Mrs. William G. Parrott Jr.
Al and Adriana Paulazzo
Kirsten Borel Paull
R. Christian & Heather Borel Fick Paull
Frank E. Peabody
Mr. Joseph Benedict Pecora
Mrs. William W. Penaluna
Joyce H. Pennington
Peninsula Assn. for Retarded Children & Adults
Peninsula Ballet Theatre School
Peninsula Community Foundation
The Peninsula Regent
Peninsula Symphony
Chuck and Joan Peradotto
Gaston and Peggy Periat
Jacqueline and Elizabeth Periat
Marilyn Carlson Perry
Michael and Laura Peterhans
Anne D. Peter
Mary E. Peters
Gordon J. and Arlene M. Petersen
Christopher Albert Peterson
Janice K. Petty
Mr. & Mrs. Richard K. Pfeifer
Beth and Lee Phillips
Jim and Bo Phillips
Ray and Beth Phillips
George M. Philpott, Sr.
Mr. & Mrs. George M. Philpott, Jr.
Jessie Eitel Phinney
Joyce and Wilson Pinney
Louis and Diane Pitto
Niels A. and Mary L. Ploug
Podesta Construction
Poplar Center of San Mateo County
Mr. & Mrs. Bernard Postel
Mr. Donald Postel
Mr. Scott Postel
David G. Powell
Former Mayor Jane Powell
Jim and Valerie Powers
Mr. & Mrs. James Presta
Clyce Preston
Mr. & Mrs. Gilbert H. Price
Jonie and David Pulsifer
Kathryn E. Puterbaugh
Diane Pyke

Q

Joseph and Gayle Quadt

R

Mrs. Dorothy Radyk
Lida Irvine Raimondi
Walter and Mary Griffin Ramseur
Carol and Jim Rankin

Chris and Wei-en Raymond
Elizabeth Kirkbride Reinhart
Janet Rehe
Beth D. Remington
Jim Remington
Joyce Remington
Florence and John Rhoads
Enes and Bill Rice
Gilbert and Sally Richards
Bert and Bernice Rifas
Pat Riley
Linda Macdonald Risdon
Tom and Sharon Slade Roach
Mrs. Bessie Robbins
Barbara Downie Roberts
George and Leanne Roberts
Mr. & Mrs. Robert E.M. Roberts
Mr. and Mrs. Hugh E. Robertson
Renette Robillard
Darlene L. Robinson
Tyrone and Cathy Robinson
Mr. and Mrs. John M. Rodgers
Russell Ivan Roeckel
Ken Roed
Elizabeth Morris Roehr
Marjorie J. Rogers
Ken Rolandelli
Bettye and Jacques Roos
Joyce and Edward Rosenstiel
Mark and Martha Ross
Rotary Clubs of San Mateo County
Jack and Claire Roudebush
Stephen and Joanne Rovno
Mr. Russell Ruhlen
John F. Rusk
Patricia A. Ryan
Dale C. Ryman

S

Nelson and Victoria Saad
Nilima and Umesh Sabharwal
Carolyn J. Sadler
Helmuth and Anni Saggau
Harriett E. Saign
St. Matthew Catholic School
St. Matthew's Catholic Church
St. Matthew's Episcopal Day School
Mr. & Mrs. Harry Y. Sakai
Mr. & Mrs. Harry Y. Sakai
Mr. & Mrs. Harry Y. Sakai
Bert and Janice Salvato
Jeff and Jill Salvato
Howard and Jane Samuel
Harriett E. Saign
San Mateo Chamber of Commerce
San Mateo County Expo Center
San Mateo-Foster City School District
San Mateo Photography
San Mateo Public Library
Vivian and Danielle Sapper
Mr. & Mrs. James A. Sarrail
Neil and Mary Sasinowski
Clayton and Grace Saunders

Timothy C. Saunders
Colin and Julie Savage
Charles and Mary Anne Sayler
Nancy Scammell
Dan and Sallie Scannell
Paul and Judy Scannell
Joe and Dorothy Scheufler
Carol and Alton Schick
Thelma Schilber
Mrs. Derry W. Schillaci
Mrs. Alfred C. Schmidt
Mr. & Mrs. Chauncey Schmidt
Ed and Ruth Ann Schmidt
Mrs. Reinhold Leah Schmidt
Carl and Gertrude Scholl
Richard and Connie Schram
Joanne Schunter
Robart and Marion Schwantes
Karen Anne Schwarz
Ann L. Schwengels
Bill and Barbara Scott
Betty Sears
Mary Ide and Henry Secrest
The Seguines
Daniel Todd Seinworth
Harold and Nancy Seinwerth
Harold H. Seinwerth Jr.
Seton Medical Center
Jack Shackleton
Carolyn Shavel
John and Mary Sheehan
Elly and Steve Sherr
Gerald Shields/Geraldine Giacomini
Eunice Loy Shimozono
Scott and Sheila Sigmund
Richard L. Silver
George L. Sinclair
Marian A. Sinton
Marilyn Sirpis and Michael Dean
Michael and Barbara Slaughter
Louise S. Smith
Ms. Constance L. Smith
Dem Smith
Mrs. Ethel V. Smith
Mr. and Mrs. Glenn P. Smith
Josefina Barrios Smith
Robert E. Smith
Robert and Joanne Smith
Charlyne Sternberg Smith
Mr. & Mrs. Robert W. Smith
Thomas McGinn Smith
David and Sylvia Smoot
Susan and Laurence Snydal
George, Charlotte and Carol Soal
John and Alice Sodek
Edith Sofos
Mr. & Mrs. Stephen Sofos
Glenn Sonagere
Deke and Joanne Sonnichsen
Benny R. Souder
LeRoy L. Spahn
Nita and Ray Spangler
Kristi Cotton Spence
Robert L. Spence

Mrs. Robert E. Spence
Cheryl Spolar
Donn and Lisa Spolar
Joseph and Martha Spranza
Fran and Ray Stafford
Mr. and Mrs. Victor Stagnaro
Peter Stansky
David and Kathryn Steinbaugh
Ruth and Paul Steiner
Thomas S. Stephany
Michael J. Stephany
William J. Stephany
Bob and Betty Stevens
Lash Stevenson
Al and Harriet Stickney
Dr. and Mrs. Mark S. Still
Lena Storheim
Thelma and Karl Storheim
Fred and Paula Strebel
Lash Stevenson
Margo Hamberg Struble
Robert and Juliane Sullivan
Sunnybrae School P.T.A.
William B. & Suzanne Philpott Sullivan
Frances Savitsky Sutcliffe
Michael and Pam Svanevik
Mr. & Mrs. William D. Swackhamer
Pamela Swain
John Swanberg
Phyllis Stewart Swanson
Mrs. Robert Sweatt
Bob and Carolyn Sweyd
Joe and Claire Sweyd
Cindy and Matt Swinnerton
Mr. & Mrs. W.A. Swinerton
Charles and Gayle Syers
Charles and Claudette Syme

T
Mrs. Eleanor Alt Tabel
Talbots Toyland
Jauw and Lourdes Tan
Yolanda Y. Tarango
Dr. & Mrs. William Tatomer
Carol Taylor
Margaret Elaine Taylor
Polly and Ted Taylor
Mr. Raymond A. and Doris L. Taylor
Ty and Joyce Tekawa
John Tennyson
Roger and Mina Tennyson
Scott Tennyson
Paul and Maria Thiebaut
Eleanor and Harold Thiewes
James and Beverly Thivierge
Lloyd and Jeanne Thivierge
Carolyn L. Thomas
Irene M. Thommen
Maggie Timeus
Barbara Cahalan Tingvall
Alex and Jan Tom
Mrs. Harry W. Tracy
Trag's Woodwork & Designs
John, Kim and Michael Tragoutsis

Hoa Tran
Campbell Trangmar
Karen and Roberta Tremain
BeBe and Roger Trinkner
Alvin and Doris Troyer
Gary and Vina Troyer
Wells Wadleigh and Elizabeth Tsuji
Barney F. Tumey
Ethel Parnell Turner

U
Robert and Carole Ughe
Daniel J. Ullyot
Harold Ulrich
Nolan and Mary Untiedt

V
Donald and Colleen Van Kirk
Helen I. VanWinkle
Jack and Pauline Verducci & Family
Mr. & Mrs. Walter H. Vielbaum
Mr. & Mrs. Joseph Vignassa
The J.T. Vitugs
Vocker Kristofferson and Co. CPA's

W
Wells Wadleigh and Elizabeth Tsuji
Walgreen Drug
Mr. and Mrs. Leonard Walkden
Leo and Barbara Wall
Mr. & Mrs. Y.H. Wan
Helen C. Ward
Inez M. Ward
Reverend James J. Ward
John and Mary Anne Ward
Gretchen and Doug Warner
Sallee and Wayne Wash
Ron and Christie Weaver
Chris and Aiko Weber
Katherine M. Weber
Keith Weber
William C. Weber, Jr.
Kirsten C. Weiss
Raymond F. and Charlene A. Weiss
William J. and Faye R. Weiss
Mr. Floyd E. Welch
Mr. & Mrs. Floyd E. Welch
Christina and Cecil H. Wells, Jr.
David L. Wendt
Larry and Hanna Wenrick
Constance Poss Werder
Mrs. Ona Westigard
Silas P. Wheaton
Connie J. White
John Rider and Linda White Whitesides
Mark H. Whitman
Abigail and Henry Wilder
John and Eunice Wilkes
Robert R.& May-Blossom Wilkinson
Robert and Ann Williams
David and Michele Wilson
Clyde R. Wirgler Family
Dorothy Wirgler
Dick and Dean Wilhelm

Jann and Pat Wilkus
Mr. & Mrs. Charles F. Wilson, Jr.
Win-Door Service
Bill and Evelyn Winnegar
Robert N. Wisen
Allison Ward Wisnom
Stacey Walker Wisnom
Irving and Josephine Witt
Mr. and Mrs. Thaddeus Wojcik
Don and Darlynne Wood
Woodlawn Memorial Park Association
Erminia (Minnie) Beltramo Woodman
Pat Wong
Evelyn and Larry Wright
Katherine Wright
Larry and Evelyn Wright
Merna and Larry Wright Jr.
Robert Wright

Y
Jeffery and Susan Yarne
Alicia Marie Yates
Councilman Gary and
    Mrs. Linda Yates
Fred and Melanie Yeager
Derek Yee
Lee and Lilly Yee
Kathy and Donald Yent
David You
Jill Young-Diener
John F. and Carol C. Young
Jimmie J. and Carolyn C. Yuen

Z
Christine M. Zarringhalam
Linda S. Zimdars
John and Patricia Zoboli
Gregory N. Zompolis
Muriel Coll Zompolis

INDEX

A

A. Herrlich and Co.: 34
A.A.U.W.: 246, 269, 276
A.J. Abbott School: 244
Abbott, Pansy Jewett: 122-123, 141
Ackley and Maurison: 20
Action Now: 260
Adams Tom Ricks: 54
Adams, J.J.: 55, 77, 82
African Americans: 143, 162, 167, 168, 223-224, 230-232, 259-263, 274
African M.E. Zion Church: 168
Ah Sam's Florists: 162-163
Alameda de las Pulgas: 61, 78
Albion Horrall School: 244
Alemany, Joseph S.: 58
Aleut Indians: 9
Alice Borel: 117
Alley, B.F.: 77
Allsop Co.: 40
Alt, William Carl: 77
Altieri family: 178
Altieri, Genevieve: 159, 162, 177, 183, 194-195
American Association of University Women: 246, 269, 276
American Legion: 84, 225, 252
American Protection Assn.: 76
Ames, J.P.: 73
Amphlett, Helen: 181
Amphlett, Horace: 146, 170, 179, 180-181, 189, 196-197
Ancient Order of United Workmen: 84
Anderson, Fred: 76
Andrew Williams Store: 213
Angerbauer, George: 263
Anti-Japanese Laundry League: 141
Anza, Juan Bautista de: 5
Aquirre, Juan Bautista: 4
Aragon High School: 245
Aragon Terrace: 238
Aragon Tract: 175, 238
Arboretum Society: 275
Archibald, Roy: 230, 248
Arena, Luis: 15
Arenas, Cayetano: 15
Argüello family: 15, 34
Argüello, José: 14
Argüello, Luis: 14
Armitage Orphanage: 120
Arnold, E. Holm: 223
Arroyo Mocha: 239
Arroyo Mocho: 78, 122
Arroyo San Mateo: 5
Artavia, Joe: 265
Arts Council: 239
Asai, K.: 221
Ascot Day: 265
Ashby, Gordon: 276, 277
Asian Americans: 274
Asistencia: 9, 15
Atherton, Faxon D.: 73
Austin, Alexander: 49
Automobiles: 111
Auxiliary Civic Club: 119
Aviation: 187
Awastos: 6
Ayala, Lieutenant Juan Manuel: 4

B

B Street: 40, 43, 46, 54, 73, 75, 76-77, 84-85, 91, 101-102, 103, 108, 122, 125, 129, 138
Baba, Ishiye: 141
Baby Muriel: 183
Baden: 31, 125
Baker, Jane: 267-269, 271, 275
Baker, Wood C.: 181
Baldwin & Howell: 112, 126-127
Baldwin Avenue: 9, 40, 122
Ballantine, Hessie: 178
Bank of America: 138
Bank of California: 79
Bank of Italy: 134, 138
Bank, Joe: 201
Barber, John R.: 242
Barnes, Dr. Mary Sheldon: 33, 162
Barneson Avenue: 117
Barneson Heights: 246-247
Barneson, John: 112, 238
Baronovitch, Michael: 204
Barroilhet, Henri: 79, 85
Barrows, H.F.: 91
BART: 236
Bartlett Harness & Saddlery: 43
Bartlett, A.T.: 77
Bartlett, A.T.: 76, 84, 91
Bartlett, Frank: M.
Bartlett, Frank M.: 187, 200
Bartlett, George A.: 91, 94, 149-150, 156, 209
Baseball: 192-194
Batchelor, Doris: 231
Bay Area Rapid Transit: 236
Bay Meadows Airport: 234
Bay Meadows Racetrack: 117, 205-210, 225, 250
Bay Meadows Tract: 175
Bayshore Acres: 238
Bayshore Cutoff: 39, 98, 136
Bayshore Highway: 175, 232
Bayshore Highway Tract: 175, 238
Bayview Federal Savings & Loan: 267
Baywood: 33-34, 45-47, 130, 146, 174
Baywood Tract: 174, 199-200, 238
Beechey, Captain Fredrick W.: 13
Beeger, C.: 91
Beer, Fred: 183
Beiyor, G.: 78
Bell Savings & Loan: 267
Bell Telephone Co.: 75
Bell, Claudette: 260
Bellevue Avenue: 97
Belmont: 3, 230, 240
Benjamin Franklin Hotel: 36, 166, 172, 189, 194, 224, 245
Benoit Building: 201
Bensel, John A.: 187
Beresford: 142
Beresford Club: 224
Beresford Country Club: 116-117, 160-161, 176, 217
Beresford Park: 98, 199
Beresford Park School: 248
Beresford School: 176, 200
Beresford Tract: 175
Beresford train stop: 111
Berg, Patty: 161
Bertilotti, E.: 102
Bethlehem Ship Building Co.: 188
Bettelheim, Hugo F.: 179
Bezzant, Bob: 275
Bianachi, Bob: 249
Bickford, James R.S.: 77, 82, 84, 91
Billings, Frederick: 61
Binsacca, Victor G.: 242
Birmingham, Father Peter: 58
Bishop Armitage Church Orphanage of California: 81
Black, Walter: 260
Blanchard, Lady: 41
Blood donation, WWII: 226
Blu-White Laundry: 230
Blues baseball team: 192-194, 201, 251
Boepple, Mike: 167
Bohannon, David: 117, 210-213, 224, 233-236, 238, 242, 245, 247-248, 252, 253, 271
Bohannon, Mrs. David: 248, 271
Boland, Maurice F.: 148
Boldemann, Oscar: 179
Bolton, J.R.: 63
Bolton, James R.: 61
Bonner, Robert: 125
Borcia, Diego: 14
Borden, E.G.: 149
Borel Bank: 266-267
Borel Bank & Trust: 160
Borel Chapel: 118, 240
Borel Estate: 34, 65, 79-80, 117, 118, 200, 239-241, 252, 268
Borel family: 79, 117, 160, 239
Borel School: 176, 200
Borel Shopping Center: 241
Borel, Alfred: 79
Borel, Alice: 240
Borel, Antoine: 79, 84-85, 117, 118, 121, 126, 240, 260, 266
Borel, Grace: 79
Born Building Co.: 175
Borough, Marie: 124
Bortolazzo, Julio: 246, 248, 261-264
Bose, Father Leonard W.: 11
Bosworth, Hobart: 183
Boutee, Mary J.: 167
Bovet family: 240
Bovet, Louis: 160
Bowie Estate: 23
Bowie, Alexander J.: 80
Bowie, Henry P.: 23, 80, 142
Bowman, Father William: 58
Boy Scouts: 149, 166, 179-180, 218, 230, 233
Bradley, Gen.J.S.: 252
Brady, Thomas J.: 156, 160, 183
Brandenstein, M.J.: 116
Brauns, Robert: 240
Brekke, Nancy: 272
Brewer family: 120
Brewer, A.L.: 77, 81
Brewer, Dr. William: 67
Brewer, Lyman: 84
Brewer, Mrs. A.L.: 81
Brewer, Mrs. Francis C.: 124
Brewer, Reverend A.L.: 58
Brewer's Island: 111
Brewer's Military School: 31
Bridge, San Mateo-Hayward: 187-192
Briggs, Fergusson and Co.: 98
Britschgi, Carl: 253
Bromfield, Beatrice: 109
Bromfield, D. Gordon: 21, 95, 97, 102, 108-110, 111, 119, 124, 129, 138, 139
Bromfield, Davenport: 97, 126, 135

INDEX

Bromfield, G.W.: 248
Bromfield, John D.: 108
Bromfield, Mrs. Davenport: 118
Brooks, Ken: 275
Brookside: 30, 33-34, 35, 45
Brown brothers': 124
Brown, Allen: 33
Brown, D.: 94
Brown, Dennis: 82
Brown, E.M.: 167
Brown, Edmund G. "Pat": 236
Brown, Ken: 253
Brown, Michael: 77
Brown, Robert M.: 252
Brown, William H.: 82, 84, 91, 93
Buckmaster, Miss L.A.: 61-62, 64-65, 120
Bucknell, James : 70
Buddhist Church: 141, 142, 164-165, 230
Buena Vista School: 244
Bufano, Benjamin: 236, 258, 272
Bugbee, S.C.: 61
Bullock's department store: 271
Burke family: 119
Burke, Thomas F.: 148, 150, 156-160, 197, 198, 204-206, 225
Burke, Winifred M.: 117, 121, 122-123, 243
Burlingame: 14, 15, 101, 136, 149, 230
Burlingame Advance: 180, 200, 209, 220, 252, 266
Burlingame Country Club: 116
Burlingame Star: 180
Burlingame train station: 16
Burlingame-Hillsborough Flower Show: 208
Business Leadership Council: 260
Butler J.E.: 67
Butler, Hattie: 62
Butler, J.E.: 72
Butterfield Overland Mail: 26
Butterfield Stagecoach: 35
Butterfield, John: 26
Byrnes family: 119
Byrnes house: 75
Byrnes James: 102
Byrnes, James: 34, 73, 74, 84, 92, 102
Byrnes, Thomas E.: 180
Byrnes' Store: 56, 57
Byrnes' Union Hotel: 83

C

Caldwell Building: 170
Caldwell estate: 238
California Casualty Building: 61
California Casualty Co.: 267
California Home and Farm: 98
California Horse Racing Board: 207
California Indians: 31
California Jockey Club: 209
California Supreme Court: 72-73
California Water Service: 198
California, Its Gold and Its Inhabitants: 22
Callahan, Father: 136, 146
Callahan, Timothy: 58, 118, 250
Cambon, Pedro: 6
Cambra, Rosemary: 1
Cambridge, Walter H.: 179
Camp Fremont: 147
Camp Topaz (internment camp): 222-223, 229
Campbell, Ed: 102
Campbell, Ronald L.: 212
Carey Saloon: 57
Cargus Corporation: 267-269

Carnegie Foundation: 144
Carnegie, Andrew: 144
Casey family: 119
Casey I.I.: 67
Casey, Kate: 91
Casey, Peter: 58
Casey, Tom: 201
Casey, John: 198
Catholic Archdiocese of San Francisco: 81
Catholic Church: 131, 135
Central Labor Council: 269
Central Library: 248
Central Pacific: 41
Central Park: 40, 47, 49, 82, 160, 178, 193, 199, 230-231, 249, 251-252, 260, 272, 275
Central School: 122, 123, 131, 136, 143, 176, 200
Chalmers, Jim: 269
Chamber of Commerce: 200, 225, 247, 252, 256, 265, 269
Chanteloup, Noe: 249, 277
Charles B. Polhemus: 58
Charquin: 6
Chartier, Albert: 159
Chartier, Augustin: 178
Cheney, Charles: 198
Chidester, Dr. W.C.: 145
Children's Hospital: 208
Children's Receiving Home: 251
Chin, Margaret: 275
China Camps: 80
Chinatown: 77, 139
Chinese: 77, 119, 139-140, 162, 176, 204
Chinese shrimp fishermen: 80
Chriss, Michael: 248
Chuck's Steak House: 160, 266
Church, Reverend E.: 64
Citation (race horse): 266
Citizens and Taxpayers League: 198
Citizens for San Mateo's Future: 269
City budget: 198
City Council: 242-243, 252, 260, 272, 275
City Hall: 249, 255, 260, 277
Civic Center: 156, 200, 249
Civic Club: 118-119
Claremont Avenue: 52, 125
Clark estate: 126
Clark, Charles: 45
Clark, Mrs. J.G.: 81
Clinton, J. Hart: 181, 246, 248, 250-251, 266
Clinton, John: 266
Cloud, Roy: 21
Cohen, Joseph: 250, 265
Cold War: 235, 249
Colegrove, J.S.: 79
Colegrove, John S.: 117
Coleman, J.H.: 112
Coleman, Pauline: 248
Coleman, Robert: 261
Coleman, Thomas: 82, 94, 135
College Heights: 247
College of San Mateo: 240, 244, 245-248, 256, 259-264, 267, 276
College Park: 238
College Park School: 244
Collins Drugstore: 172
Colma: 125
Committee of Vigilance: 22, 33
Concord Ranch Enterprises: 236
Congregational Church: 52-54, 59-61, 94, 164, 166, 221
Congregationalists: 117, 131

Conroy, Carol: 252
Conway & Culligan: 211, 238
Conway, Andrew: 229
Conway, M.J.: 170
Cook, David S.: 24-26, 61
Cook, Elinor: 24-25
Cook, Eliza: 25
Cook, Ellie: 62
Cook, Evenlyn Mae:: frontispiece
Cook, Harriet: 24, 62
Coolidge, Calvin: 189
Cooper Zion Church: 167
Cooper, John B.: 25
Cooper, Rufus: 260
"Corporal Can": 225
Cotton family: 240
Cotton, Aylett: 117-118, 160, 168, 189, 197-198
County Board of Supervisors: 68, 71-73, 243
County Fair: 208-209, 221, 250
County Fair Association: 209
County Fair Grounds: 272
County Historical Museum: 94
County Poor Farm: 49, 119
County Road: 47, 67, 97, 101, 111
County Road (El Camino): 117, 118, 121, 122, 125, 127
County seat: 33, 71
Cox, Harry: 167
Coyote Point: 1-2, 6, 9, 14, 31, 80, 96, 99, 101, 109-111, 162, 182, 198, 209, 227, 230, 245-246
Coyote Point Museum: 250, 277
Coyote Point Regional Park: 250
Cranston, Alan: 236
Crawford, Inez: 178, 209
Crawford, Inez Mabel: 119
Crime: 204-206, 225
Croce, Arne: 275
Crocker family: 145
Crocker, Charles Templeton: 120-121
Crocker, Jennie: 120
Cronin, Father Bernard C.: 250
Crystal Springs: 56, 112
Crystal Springs Canyon: 40
Crystal Springs Dam: 3-4, 75, 96, 97-100, 110, 113, 136, 219
Crystal Springs Hotel: 57
Crystal Springs Quarry: 59
Crystal Springs Road: 33, 47, 96, 102, 111
Cullen, Claire: 260
Culligan, Thomas Jr.: 211, 229
Cummings, Joseph P.: 148
Cummins, Thomas: 65
Cuneo, Clarence: 135
Cuneo, Clarinda: 138
Cunningham, James: 81
Curran, Isabelle: 148
Curry, Eleanor: 260
Curtiss Wright Co.: 187

D

Daba, Marco: 163-164
Daba's: 163
Dabney, George: 232
Daly City: 136
Daly, John: 244
Dana, Mrs. Harry S.: 181
Darcy's Marina: 238
Dark, Alvin: 252
Daughters of the American Revolution: 11

Davenport, Jimmy: 252
Davis, George J.: 209
Davis, Mamie: 167
de Anza, Lt. Col. Juan Bautista: 4
de Dampierre, Countess: 170
de Guigne estate: 136
de Guigne family: 170
de Guigne II, Christine: 130
de Guigne mansion: 172
de Guigne, Christian: 46, 115, 170
de Guignes' family: 47
de Haro, Commandant José: 14
de Lancie, Richard: 260
de Monet, Joaquin: 267
de Peyster, Nicolas: 16, 19, 21, 25-26
de Russy, John: 277
de Russy, John: 274
De Sabla Road: 23
de Sable, Eugene: 148
de Tristan, Countess: 170
Deacon, James: 94
Deacon, Joseph A.: 92
Degen, Lewis: 156
Delaware: 40
Delaware Street: 97
DeLong, Richard: 275
Dempsey, Father: 77
Dempsey, Father Dennis F.: 58
Depression, the: 161, 164, 169, 181, 187, 191, 196, 200-204, 209, 217, 252
Dermott, Hugh M.: 77
deseño for Rancho de las Pulgas: 14
deseño for Rancho San Mateo: 16
Determiner (horse): 266
Devel, A.W.: 187
Di Martini family: 138
Diaz, Ben: 117
Dibble General Hospital: 226
Dickie, Dorothy: 178
Dickie, George W.: 84, 101, 118
Discovery of gold at Coloma: 16
Dolan family: 119
Dolwig, Richard: 252-253
Donahue mansion: 82
Donahue, Peter M.: 39, 49, 58
Donald Station: 40
Donald, John: 29, 30, 31
Donald, Sara: 39-40
Donald, Sarah: 30
Donnan, Sarah: 52
Donnelly, D.W.: 124
Donohoe, Joseph A.: 47
Donohoe, Mary E.: 47
Doolittle, James H.: 112
Dougal, William H.: 9, 20
Dougherty, Dick "Beefsteak": 57-58
Douglas, D.J.: 149
Douglas, Melvyn: 233
Dow, William: 59
Downtown Association: 235-236
Dubbers, Henry: 47
Duggan, John: 136
Dumbarton Bridge: 198
Dunfey Hotel: 236
Dunn Williams Co.: 174

E
Earthquake: 9, 129-136, 143
East Palo Alto: 15, 262
East Side Park: 160
Easton family: 145
Easton, Ansel I.: 28, 52, 61

Easton, Mrs. A.J.: 63
Easton, Reverend G.A.: 58
Ebright, A.W.: 124
Education: 199-200
Educational Assn. of San Mateo: 65
Edward Walker's Hotel: 77
Eichler, Joseph: 236
El Arroyo Mocho Creek: 117
El Camino Real: 4, 9, 49, 127, 268
El Cerrito: 23
El Cerrito Avenue: 135
El Cerrito Manor: 211
El Lobo: 250
Electric railroad: 241
Electricity: 109
Elementary Teachers' Association: 259
Elfving, Carl W.: 197
Elfving, Robert: 204
Elks Lodge: 179, 196, 204, 238, 260
Ellsworth: 58, 81
Ellsworth Avenue: 120
Ellsworth Street: 118, 125
Embarcadero: 15
Emerson, Vera: 147
Emmons, Anshen & Allen, arch.: 236
Emporium: 235, 249
Endo family: 165, 221, 223, 229-230
Endo, Mariko: 229
Episcopal: 136
Episcopal and Catholic churches: 119
Episcopal Church: 59, 60, 65, 120, 131, 135
Episcopal Diocese: 120
Erickson, Clifford G.: 263
Eto, Miss Kunie: 142
Eureka Gardens: 56
Evans, George: 41
Evencio: 15
Evencio, Joseph: 162
Evencio, Pedro: 33, 162
Evergreen: 52
Evergreen Cemetery: 81
Ewigleben, Robert L.: 263

F
F.B.I.: 221
Fagan, Paul: 219
Fagan's Tower: 219
Fair, Elinor: 183
Fairbanks, John R.: 179
Fairmont Hotel: 180
Farley, Jim: 252
Farnard, James M.: 94
Farrell, Tom: 41
Fashion Island: 271-272
Federal Bureau of Investigation: 221
Federal Housing Administration: 211
Felt, Henry: 253
Fenians: 41
Ferguson, Joe: 206
Ferrie, Mrs. Jim: 251
Fick, Harold: 266, 277
Fick, Ron: 260
Fiesta Gardens: 238
Fiesta Gardens School: 244
Fifteenth Avenue: 127
Fifth Avenue: 40, 47, 127
Figueroa, José: 13
Fire: 81-82, 83, 84, 91-92
Fire Department: 91-95, 119, 131, 132, 148, 155-158, 198, 200, 225, 248-249, 272-274
First Avenue: 52, 73, 101, 125

First School House: 30
First stagecoach line: 19
Fisher & Bartlett: 77
Fisher and Bartlett building: 76
Fisher Hotel: 91
Fisher, G.H.: 84
Fisher, George H.: 76
Fitzgerald family: 119
Fitzgerald Field: 194
Fitzgerald, Justin: 192-194, 198
Fitzgerald, Al: 133
Flarity family: 119
Fleishhacker, Herbert: 116
Fleishhacker, Mortimer: 116
Flood, James: 80
Florence Musto: 144
flower industry: 116, 142
Flower Show: 209
Fluor Mining Co.: 252
Flynn, John: 83
Follett, Ben: 217, 224
Font, Padre: 9
Font, Padre Pedro: 4
Football: 195
Forbes magazine: 267
Ford, Mrs. A.B.: 119
Fortnightly Club: 118
"40 Line" railway: 241-242
Foster City: 80, 111, 239
Foster, Jack T.: 239
442nd Regimental Combat Team: 221-222
Fourth Avenue: 46-47, 73
Fox & Carskadon Co.: 212
Fox Theater: 156
Fox, B.F.: 30
Fox, George: 30
Fox, Judge B.F.: 33
Fox, Sarah: 31
Fox, Sarah W.: 29
Francis, Louis: 252
Franklin, A.C.: 172
Franklin, Bruce: 263
Fremont Street: 143
Friends of the San Mateo Library: 251
Fries, William: 117
Fuchs, Jerry: 266
Fujito, Tasuku: 230-231
Fujiiki, Joe: 229
Future of San Mateo: 277

G
Gallaway, Neptune Blood W.: 136, 145
Gamble, John: 120
Gamble, Professor John: 65
Garcia, Herbert: 276
Garden Theater: 183
Garlington, Philip: 262-263
Garrison, William K.: 63
Garwood, William Gay: 248
Gate Dancer: 266
Gazette: 26
General Electric: 233
Geneva Chapel: 117
George Hall School: 176, 200, 244
Georgetti, Emilio: 197
Getz, B. Company: 170-172
Giannini, A.P.: 102, 134, 138, 174
Gibbs, Augusta: 120
Gibbs, George W.: 120
Gibson, Bruce: 156, 209
Gibson, Bruce S.: 179
Giese, Linda: 265

Gillespie, Norvell: 250
Girl Scouts: 233
Glascock, William L.: 177-178, 179
Glazenwood: 81
Glazenwood residential area: 112
Glazenwood Tract: 175
Golden Gate International Exposition: 200
Goldman, Hein: 174
Goldstone Kennels: 178
Goode, Mabel: 124
Goodhue, S.C.: 59
Goodhue, S.G.: 84
Goodhue, Sam: 277
Goodhue, Samuel: 34, 52, 77
Goodspeed Corners: 75
Goodspeed, I.R.: 75, 77, 83
Gordon, Joseph B.: 179
Goss, William A.: 246
Governor Newton Booth: 70
Graf, Max: 183
Grant, Cary: 233
Grassl, Hans: 253
Green, Milton J.: 178
Greenbach, Joe Jr.: 267
Griffin, Merv: 245, 249, 277
Griffin, Merv Sr.: 161
Griffith Street: 125
Griffith, Agnes Maria: 49
Grosvenor Properties, Ltd.: 277
Guadalcanal: 218
Guadalupe Blues: 251
Guibara, Al: 275
Guido brothers: 163
Guido family: 138
Guido, Francisco: 138
Gum Street: 122
Gumbinger, Paul: 275
Gunderson, Robert: 265-266
Gustafson, Frank: 161
Gymkhanna Club: 160
Gypsies: 194-195

H

Haas, Walter: 116
Hahn, Ernest W.: 271-271
Half Moon Bay: 34, 56, 57, 58, 71, 75, 132
Half Moon Bay-San Mateo toll road: 55
Hall & Crandall: 21
Hall, George: 121, 122, 123, 177
Hall, Mr. Albert L.: 118
Halprin, Lawrence: 238
Hamada, Toku: 140
Hambletonian: 41
Hamilton, Jerome: 210
Hanson Brothers Co.: 238
Haraszthy, Agostin: 68, 75
Hart, Brook: 204
Hartnell, W.E.P.: 15
Harver, Daniel: 77
Hata Merchant Tailor Shop: 140
Hata, Shokochi, Rev.: 164
Hata, Tokumatsu: 140
Hatch, Charles J.: 91, 93
Hatch, Harry: 101
Havens & Toepke: 144
Haver, David: 25
Hayne, Duncan: 238
Hayne, Judge Robert Y.: 101
Hayne, Robert Young: 47
Hayward Addition: 126
Hayward Chamber of Commerce: 252
Hayward estate: 70, 80, 111, 133, 144, 175
Hayward family: 70
Hayward, Mary: 70
Hayward Park: 123, 126, 127, 146, 149
Hayward Park School: 180
Hayward, Alice: 70, 118
Hayward, Alvinza: 41, 61, 67-68, 71-75, 77, 81, 91-92, 98, 111-112, 117, 127, 139, 146, 148, 150
Hayward, Carrie M.: 70
Hayward, Charity: 68-69, 70, 112
Hayward, Emma: 70
Hayward, Kate: 70
Hayward, Nellie: 70
Hayward, Sammy: 70
Hayward, Sophie: 118
Hayward's Landing: 80
Heller, Herman: 183
Hellman, I.W.: 116
Heney-Webb Alien Land Law: 142
Henry's Garage: 265
Herbst Brothers Genl. Store: 101
Herbst, Charles: 101
Herbst, William: 101
Herert, Al: 149
Heritage Trees Ordinance: 267
Herling, Joseph: 75
Hermance, Mrs. H.P.: 144
Herrington, Dorothy: 204, 245
Herrlich, August: 78
Hesmon: 13
Hice, Charles: 238
Hildreth, Elon: 245-246
Hill, Howard: 33
Hill, Jerry: 269
Hillbarn Theater: 117, 240
Hillsborough: 13, 15, 23, 67, 101, 149
Hillsdale: 75, 111, 208, 210-213, 233-236
Hillsdale Garden: 248
Hillsdale High School: 243, 245
Hillsdale Library: 25, 35, 212, 248
Hillsdale Mall: 249, 258, 271-272
Hillsdale Manor: 238
Hillsdale Station: 212
Hillyer, Lambert: 183
Hines, Major Gen. John: 189
Hintz Building: 135
Hintz dry goods shop: 106
Hirschey, Claude: 161
Hispanic Americans: 274
Hobart, Lewis: 145
Hobart, Walter: 45, 132
Hoffman, Aaron: 274
Hoge, Colonel J.P.: 73
Holmes, Rev.J.B.: 167
Holmes, Robert: 167
Holy Cross Cemetery: 126
Homes, Jack: 204
Homestead: 117, 120, 121, 122
Homestead School: 121, 122-123
Homestead Tract: 34, 175
Honolulu: 21
Hoover, Bob: 262-263
Hop Yick Co.: 139
Hope, Mrs. Bob: 251
Hordon, Dr. H.: 160
Horgan, John: 239-240, 241
Horrall, Albion: 244
House of Merkel: 204
Houston, A.H.: 61
Howard estate: 41, 97, 99, 175
Howard family: 33, 37, 59, 124, 187, 209
Howard Jr., George H.: 80
Howard Tract: 175
Howard, Adeline Taylor: 28
Howard, Agnes: 23, 52
Howard, Agnes Poett: 80
Howard, Charles S.: 207
Howard, Eleazar: 21
Howard, George H.: 22, 23, 52, 59, 60, 61, 63, 80
Howard, George Jr.: 23
Howard, Lendsey: 160
Howard, W.D.M.: 15-16, 21-23, 33, 39
Howard, W.H.: 97
Howell, Mary Jo: 259
Hughes Air West: 252
Hull, Henry: 102
Human Relations Commission: 260
Humboldt Street: 74, 97
Huntley, Henry Vere: 22, 33
Hurt, Principal D.E.: 67
Husing Brothers: 46, 54, 77
Husing, E.A.: 84, 92, 102, 112, 148
Husing, Henry: 28, 29, 36

I

Ikeda, Sanaye: 230-231
Imachi family: 165
Imboden, D.C.: 187
Imperial Laundry: 140, 141, 142, 222, 230
Incorporation: 81, 101, 102
Independent Cornet Band: 76
Indian: 31
Indian shell mounds: 210
International Association of Fire Fighters: 272
Ireland: 77
Irish: 77, 138
Irishtown: 119
Irwin, I.N.: 28
Ishida, Kumiko: 230
Ishimaru family: 165
Ishimaru, Edward: 229-230
Ishimaru, Shiro: 231
Issei: 165
Italians: 123, 138, 143, 163
Italian American Federation: 164
Ito, Hiroshi: 220
Ito, Joseph: 221
Ito, Tomisuke: 140, 142
Iverson, Charles W.: 180, 183
Ivory, Royal: 225

J

J.C. Street Co.: 55
Jack, Walter: 244
Jacobson, Charles: 76
Jail: 109
Janson, J.R.: 189
Japanese: 141-142, 143, 217
Japanese American Citizens' League: 166
Japanese American Cultural League: 220-221
Japanese Americans: 115, 123, 140, 162, 164-167, 176, 219-223, 229-231
Japanese Assn. of America: 142
Japanese Christian Church: 164
Japanese Church of Christ: 164
Japanese Garden: 230-231
Japanese Independent Union Church: 164
Japanese Language School: 142, 164, 165-166, 168
Japan's surrender, WWII: 227
Jarvis-Gann Initiative: 274

Jasper, John: 183
Jaszynsky, L.: 75-76
Jennings Building: 135
Jennings Livery stable: 125, 130
Jennings, Truman: 91
Jensen Buildings: 135
Jensen, "old": 135
Jinville, Gordon: 272
John Donald: 33
Johnson, Anton: 172
Johnson, Axel: 210, 232, 238
Johnson, Charles H.: 93
Johnson, Frederick M.: 170
Johnson, Wesley P.: 235
Johnson, "Speed": 187
Jones, Rose: 167
Jordan, A.H.: 59
Judah, Mrs. H.: 81
Junior Museum: 250
Junior Olympics: 251
Junior Traffic Patrol: 206
Junipero Serra statue: 255
Jury, Richard H.: 100

K
Kaiser, Kenyon: 255
Kane, M.: 77
Kaplan, Anne S.: 199
Kashiwagi, Shiro: 141
Kataoka, T.: 140
Katsura Villa: 276
Kawakita Yoneo: 222, 229
Kawakita, Sayohei: 140
Kawakita, Yoneo: 164
Kawakito, Sally: 220
KCSM: 248, 275
Kehoe, James J.: 252
Kellogg, William: 209
Kertell, George A.: 129, 133, 135, 148, 197-198, 200
Ketchen, Jessie: 176
Keyston, George N.: 248
Kielty, Dot: 161, 251
Kimball, Florence: 124
King's Point Merchant Marine Academy: 227
Kirkbride, Charles N.: 100, 102, 123, 124, 144, 174, 198, 209
Kirkbride, W.D.: 118
Kiwanis Club: 201
Klerck, Claus: 75
Kloss Hall: 166
Klyver, Fred: 226
Knapp, S.H.: 93
Knight, S.L.: 55-56
Knights of Pythias Library: 144
Knight's stage: 102
Knitting Club: 226
Kodiak Indians: 9
Koen-Kai Club: 230-231
Kohl estate: 118, 160, 199
Kohl mansion: 178
Kohl, C. Frederick: 49, 118
Kohl, Captain: 91
Kohl, May Elizabeth Godey: 118
Kohl, William H.: 49, 118
Korean War: 235, 252
Koron, Art: 275
Koron, Arthur: 272
Kost, B.G.: 209
Kotzebue, Otto von: 13

Krumm, John: 11
Ku Klux Klan: 180
Kuhio, Prince Jonah: 65
Kumiai, Rodo: 142
Kyne, Dorothy: 250
Kyne, William P.: 187, 205-210, 225, 250

L
Labor Temple: 196
Laguna School District: 124
Lantos, Tom: 261
Lapp, Rudolph: 261-263
Lathrop, Benjamin G.: 61
Latta, Etta: 249
Latta, Oris: 249
Laurel Avenue: 68
Laurel Creek: 3
Laurel Creek Stock Farm: 79
Laurel Creek Subdivision: 98
Laurel Hall: 62, 64, 67, 84
Laurel Hall Academy: 120
Laurel School: 244
Lauriedale: 236
Lawrence house: 75
Lawrence School: 123, 177, 259
Lawrence, Bill: 178
Lawrence, James M.: 73
Lawrence, Sarah: 73
Lawrence, William B.: 74, 91, 94, 146
Lawrence, William H.: 73, 91, 123
Lax, Ada: 260
Le Warne, Hallie: 120
Leader: 100, 101, 132
Leader Building: 135
League of Women Voters: 246, 269
Leary, Mary: 148
Lee, Ant: 139
Lee, Ching: 139
Lee, Robena: 62
Lengfeld, Helen: 161, 217, 251
Leong, Arthur: 162-163
Leong, Gordon: 162-163
Leong, Lincoln: 162-163
Leong, Mable: 163
Leong, Sam Shun: 162
Leslie Salt Co.: 115-116, 140, 143, 179, 205, 236
Leventhal, Alan: 1
Levy Brothers: 58, 102, 108, 135, 147, 172, 178, 194-195, 201
Levy, Adrien: 103
Levy, Armand: 103
Levy, Edmond: 172, 179
Levy, Edmund: 108
Levy, Fernand: 102
Levy, Joseph: 103, 112, 178
Levy's store: 131
Lewis, John: 118
Library Assn.: 143
Library Hall: 84, 85, 91, 92, 95, 102, 119, 122, 125, 131, 135, 143, 148, 150
Library, Public: 198
Liebes, Lloyd: 217
Lilienthal, Jesse W.: 116, 117
Lillard, Zachary: 272
Lima, Mickey: 261
Lindsay, Frank: 183
Lions Club: 201
Lipman, Chester: 209
Little Coyote Point: 187
"Little Harlem": 225

Lobitas: 56
Loma Prieta Earthquake: 273-274
Longden, Johnny: 250
Loomis, Robert: 275
Lorder, Hugo: 238
Lorenze, Joseph: 187
Los Prados: 238
Loveland and Bowman: 33
Low, F.F.: 61
Loy, Myrna: 233
Luis, Alfred: 190, 204, 224
Lydon, E.C.: 199
Lydon, Edward: 176
Lyman, Chester S.: 16
Lyne, Father Henry J.: 250

M
MacArthur, Gen. Douglas: 223
Macauley, Lt. John: 227
MacDonald, Lorne: 263
Macedonia Church of God and Christ: 224
Mack, Claire: 225, 229, 260, 269
Mack, Kelly: 167
Mack, Liz: 161
Mack, Tom: 269
Macondray, Captain F.W.: 29-31, 33-35, 45-47
Macy's: 233, 235
Maddy, Ken: 266
Maggi, John: 138
Mahe, Gustave: 78, 94, 120
Maher, Abby Eastman : 45
Main Street: 40, 73, 75, 85, 102-103, 125, 147
Majestic Prince: 266
Manganiello, Aaron: 262-263
Manor Theater: 210, 218
Manson, A..H.: 64
Marchbank, John: 197
Maria Kip Orphanage: 81
Marina Branch Library: 248
Marina Gardens: 238
Marina Lagoon: 238
Mariners' Island: 238, 271
Market Street Railway Co.: 126
Marsh, Earle: 202
Marshal, Dr. B.: 75
Marshall, Mary: 225
Martin Luther King Park: 160
Martin Luther King Recreation Center: 255
Martin, Nina J.: 248
Masonic Lodge: 178
Masonic Temple: 166, 222
Masons: 196
Mayeda, Naoye: 220
Mayer, Theo: 247
Mayfield: 39
Maynard house: 75
Maynard, John C.: 73
McAllister, Erford: 226
McCann, Dick: 73
McCann, Keys & Day Co.: 238
McCarthy, Paul A.: 248
McComb, Aldon A.: 148
McCoy, Mack: 260
McCullough, Dave: 252
McCurdy, J.E.: 179, 189, 198
McCurty, J.E.: 174
McDermott, Hugh: 77
McDonald, Martin: 248, 260
McDougal, John: 33

McFadden, C.H.: 183
McFadden, Murius "Furious": 178
McGinn, Elsa S.: 149-150, 155, 156, 269
McGinn, John: 155
McGinnis, D.C.: 229
McGintry, Mrs. Mary: 56-57
McGowen, P.H.: 75
McGrath, J.J.: 182
McGrath, James: 196-197, 204
McKeon Construction Co.: 267
McKernan, Hugh: 82, 84
McKernan's Saloon: 83
McKim, Robert: 183
McLaren, John: 80, 84
McLaughlin, Ken: 272
McLellan house: 238
McLellan, David: 4, 79
McLellan, Edgar: 139
McLellan, Orelda: 79
McLellan, Rod: 35
McLellan, Tom: 41
McLellan, William: 139
Meadow Heights School: 244
Meagher, Father Edward J.: 250
Measure D: 271
Measure H: 269
Medical Arts Building: 172
Meeks, Cornell: 260
Meghinasso, Julius: 249
Mellus and Howard: 15-16
Mellus, Henry: 15, 21
Menlo Park: 15
Menlo Park: 149
Merchant Marine Academy: 162, 209, 216, 227, 230, 244-245, 250
Mercy High School: 49, 118
Merkel, Carl: 204
Merkel, Cuna: 204
Merkel, Ray: 264
Methodist Church: 131
Mexican Independence: 13
Mexican-American War: 15
Meyer, Rabbi Martin A.: 117
Meyerfield, Morris: 116
Mezes, Simón: 15
Mezes, Simón M.: 63
Michelson, Alan R.: 276
Miles, Anita: 167
Millbrae: 14, 145
Millbrae School District: 124
Miller and Lux ranch: 31
Miller, Lindley: 209
Miller, Mrs. Lindley: 11
Mills estate: 145
Mills Field: 187
Mills Hospital: 14, 15, 145, 181-182, 225, 248, 267, 274
Mills, D.O.: 28, 61, 63, 80, 145
Mills, Elizabeth: 145
Mills, Robert: 79
Mission Outpost: 58
Mission Rock: 10
Mission San Francisco de Asis: 6, 9, 16
Mitty, Archbishop John J.: 218
Mituals, Henry: 201
Mobil Oil Co.: 249
Mocho Creek: 79
Monroe, Gerald L.: 260
Monterey: 6, 13
Moore and DePue: 77
Moore, John: 91

Moore, John G.: 96
Moorepark Co.: 236
Moraga, Lieutenant José Joaquin: 4, 6
Moran, Ella: 91
Morgan house: 80
Morgan Oyster Co.: 79
Morris, Carlena: 203-204
Morris, Charles M.: 202-204, 209, 245
Morris, Hugh F.: 156, 157, 249
Morse, Charles M.: 75, 84, 91
Morse, Dr. L.D.: 75, 84
Morse, John: 55, 77, 92, 135
Morse, Mary E.: 84
Morton, J.B.: 33
Morton, John: 135
Mounds: 99
Mounds Estate: 238
Mountain Joe: 75
Mr. Blandings Builds his Dream House: 233
Mulryan, James: 197
Municipal Golf Course: 255, 274
Muphy Pacific Bridge Builders: 253
Murfee, Emerson: 256
Murphy, Francis W.: 238
Murphy, George: 254
Murphy, William F.: 238
Murray brothers: 79
Murray Oak, the: 212, 249
Murray, Burleigh H.: 211
Murray, C.A.: 77
Murray, C.T.: 77
Murray, Calvin: 35, 79
Murray, Hallie: 232
Murray, John J.: 232, 249, 260, 265, 269, 272
Murray, Lemuel T.: 35, 79

N

Nagaya: 140
National Guard of California: 22
Native American: 1-8, 162
Native American Heritage Commission: 1
Native Californians: 1-8, 13, 15
Native Diver (race horse): 207
Native Sons of the Golden West: 84, 85, 92
Nelson, Frances: 270-272
Nettle, Eleanor: 203, 246, 248
New Deal Club: 196
New West: 40
Newhall, H.M.: 63
Newhouse, Samuel: 115
News Leader: 100, 149
Nichols, Henry: 57
Nicoll, Willie: 161, 251-252
Nineteenth Ave. Freeway: 239, 241-242, 247, 253, 254, 267
Ninth Avenue: 47, 101, 133
Nippon Gakuen: 165
Noah's Ark: 168-169, 172
Noah's Cafeteria: 168
Nolden, William: 102
Noor (race horse): 207
Nordstrom department store: 271
Notting, E.W.: 67
Nunan, Thomas: 74

O

Oak Lawn Villa: 70, 71
Oakes, Tony: 26-28, 54
Occidental Hotel: 56
Ocean Shore Railroad: 102
Ochi, Fred: 220

Odd Fellows: 76, 85, 92
Odd Fellows Building: 108, 135
Ohlone Families Consultant Services: 1
Ohlones or Coastanoans: 1
Oliver, P.A.: 179
101st Airborne Division: 265
Oregonian, The: 21
Orphanage: 83
Ortega, Dona Maria de la Soledad: 14
Owens Illinois Building: 241
O'Brien, Robert: 225, 248
O'Ferrel, Bill: 161
O'Grady stock farm: 124
O'Grady, Keyron: 45, 117, 181
O'Grady, Margaret: 181
O'Neil, Kirk: 266

P

Pacific and Atlantic Railroad Co : 39
Pacific City: 182-187, 227
Pacific Gas and Electric Co.: 102
Pacific Greyhound Lines: 137
Pacific Mail Steamship Co.: 28
Pacific Studios: 182-187
Pacific Water Co.: 198
Pacifica: 9
Palo Alto: 3
Palo Alto Times: 100
Palou, Francisco: 6
Palou, Padre: 33
Panama Pacific International Exposition: 238
Panic of 1873: 79
Pantages, John: 195
Parent Teacher Assn.: 144
Parks & Boulevards Commission: 143-144, 160
Parkside Development Co.: 238
Parkside School: 244
Parkside Shopping Center: 266
Parrott estate: 41, 130, 174
Parrott family: 45-46, 52, 81, 101, 118, 125, 132
Parrott Investment Co.: 174
Parrott, Abby: 47, 118, 146
Parrott, Abby Josephine: 46
Parrott, John: 33-34, 41, 45, 47, 63, 81, 92, 146
Parrott, Mary Katherine: 46
Paul, Mabel Moore: 277
Payson, Abby Parrott: 145
Payson, Capt. A.H.: 46-47, 53, 101
Payson, Capt. Edward: 174
Payson, Christine: 47
Payson, Grace: 47
Payson, John Jr.: 47
Pearl Harbor: 221
Pearl Harbor attack: 217
Pearson, Tom: 160
Pebble Beach: 121
Peckham, B.A.: 94
Penington, Charles: 36
Penington, William: 36
Peninsula Avenue: 101
Peninsula Avenue School: 123
Peninsula Community Book: 21
Peninsula Golf & Country Club: 116-117, 224, 238, 251
Peninsula Hotel: 112, 113-114, 117, 127, 133, 148-149, 150, 155, 156, 172, 175
Peninsula Manor: 175, 238

Peninsula Manufacturers Assn.: 260
Peninsula Rapid Transit: 126, 137
Peninsula Regent: 274
Peninsula School: 122, 144, 177
Peninsula Social Club: 164
Peninsula Temple Beth El: 250
Penton, Jesse: 178
Performing Arts Center: 271
Perry, Arch: 275
Perry, Thomas H.: 77
Pescadero: 55, 56, 58, 71-72, 75, 165
Peters, Cal N.: 10
Peters, Mary Eleanor: 11
Peterson & Arnold Co.: 267
Peterson, Ewald: 223
Phelps, T.B.: 63
Philben Corporation: 238
Pico, Pío: 15
Pierce, Cliff: 217-218
Pigeon Point: 56
Pilgrim Baptist Church: 168
Pinckney, Paul: 170, 180
Pinkstone, William: 167
Pioche, F.L.A.: 79
Pissis, Albert: 118
Pitcher, Stanley: 231
Pitcher, Stanley P.: 199
Planning Commission: 234
Plouff, George: 83, 84
Poett, Agnes: 21
Poett, Joseph Henry: 22
Polhemus family: 68
Polhemus, Carolina: 62
Polhemus, Charles: 47, 49
Polhemus, Charles B.: 39, 40, 61, 73, 97
Polhemus, Josie: 62
Police Department: 148, 157-159, 198, 204-206, 224-225, 248, 272-274
Politics: 195-196, 199-200
Pomponio: 15
Poor Farm,: 181
Pope, George A. Jr.: 160
Poplar Avenue: 97, 109
Poplar Street: 125
Population: 200, 210
Population figures: 175, 259, 274
Population increase: 255
Population, wartime: 223
Portola, Captain Gaspar de : 3
Portsmouth Square: 19
Poss, M.A.: 179, 197, 198, 235
Potter, J.C.: 77
Powell, Jane: 269
Powers, Lt. Gov. Harold: 236
Powers, Maurice: 30, 80
Prefabricated house: 22
Presbyterian Church: 164
Presidio at Monterey: 4
Price, C.G.: 160
Price, William Z.: 91, 92
Pringle: 78
Pringle-Pioche house: 79
Prohibition: 148, 157-060, 161, 163, 201
Proposition 13: 274
Public Library: 144, 248
Public schools: 68, 69, 121, 176-178
Public Works Administration: 200
Pullman, Harry L.: 197
Purissima: 56
Purnel, Roy: 183

R

Racial unrest: 259
Radar School, SMJC: 226
Railroad Avenue: 40, 92
Railroad House: 73, 77, 82, 83
Ralston, William C.: 26, 79
Rancho Buri Buri: 14, 15, 16, 19, 33
Rancho de las Pulgas: 14, 16
Rancho San Mateo: 14, 15, 22, 23, 31, 37, 52
Rawls, Buckskin Bob: 56
Ray, Hartzell: 252
Raybould & Bartlett Co.: 211, 238
Raybould, D.A.: 170, 172-175
Reagan, Ronald: 254, 273
Recreation Centers: 254
Recreation Department: 224
Red Cross: 225-226
Red Cross Hospital: 145
Redden, Laura C.: 155
Redwood City: 15, 34, 56, 71-72, 91, 125, 136, 149
Redwood City Democrat: 120
Redwood City Tribune: 181, 231
Reid, Elizabeth Mills: 145
Reid, John Lyon, Arch.: 245
Reid, Mrs. Elizabeth Mills: 181
Reid, Whitelaw: 145
Reilly, Edward: 229
Reimer, Thomas: 277
Remington, Charles & William: 28
Republican Party: 70
Rey, Jacques J.: 78
Rhoads, Florence: 274, 275
Rice, Ada French: 204
Rice, Dr.: 77
Richardson, Donna: 270-271
Ricks, Tom: 73
Rincon Hill: 28
Ringler, Don: 276
Rivera, Captain Fernando : 3
RKO Films: 233
Roberts, Elmer: 209
Robertson, Terry: 275
Robinson, Alfred: 14
Robinson, George H.: 94
Rochex, Albert A.: 179
Rockwell, Harvey: 193
Rodolari's: 163
Roedel, Mrs. Philip: 118
Roedel, Philip M.: 102
Roehr, Fred: 204
Rogers, Peter C.: 101, 148
Roland Borden & Assoc: 243
Rolph, James: 182-183
Rolph, Sam: 240
Roos, George: 116
Roosevelt, Pres. Franklin: 221
Rose, Mrs. Andrew W.: 70
Ross, Donald: 161
Ross, George C.: 112
Rotary Club: 179, 201, 274
Rothrock, William S.: 191
Royal Coach Inn: 236

S

Sacramento: 19
Sadie Lindblom: 182
Saint Bartholomew's Church: 250
Saint Catherine's Catholic Church: 11
Saint Cyr estate: 211
Saint Cyr, Jean: 211

Saint Dennis Chapel: 58
Saint Francis Hospital: 133
Saint Gregory's Church: 218, 250
Saint James Church: 260
Saint John's: 81
Saint John's Cemetery: 52, 146
Saint Louis: 26
Saint Margaret's School for Girls: 120, 124
Saint Matthew's Catholic Church: 54, 241, 250, 267
Saint Matthew's Catholic School: 45
Saint Matthews Episcopal Church: 11, 117, 120, 135-136, 145
Saint Matthews Guild: 84-85
Saint Matthews Hall: 65, 73-75, 120, 124
Saint Timothy's Church: 250
Sakurai, Nagao: 231
Salson: 3, 6, 9
Salt Lake City: 223
San Andreas Valley: 77
San Bruno: 14
San Bruno Mountain: 4, 14
San Carlos: 4
San Feliz: 56, 57
San Francisco: 13, 19, 21, 26, 45, 132, 135, 149
San Francisco & San Jose Railroad: 36, 39, 40-41, 61
San Francisco & San Mateo Electric Railway: 125
San Francisco Bay Toll Bridge Co.: 187-192
San Francisco Chronicle: 117, 225, 232
San Francisco Examiner: 118
San Francisco Fire and Earthquake of 1906: 127
San Francisco Fire Department: 22
San Francisco Giants: 252
San Francisco International Airport: 246
San Francisco Junior League: 250
San Francisco Midwinter Fair: 16
San Francisco Mission: 3
San Francisco Presidio: 6
San Francisco Seals: 192
San Francisco State: 263
San Francisco Telephonic-Telegraphic Co.: 75
San Francisquito Creek: 3-4, 14, 39
San Gregorio: 55, 56, 57
San Jose: 19
San Lorenzo Village: 233
San Matean, The: 263
San Mateans for Responsible Government: 269
San Mateo & Half Moon Bay Turnpike Co.: 54
San Mateo Adobe: 11
San Mateo Airport: 187, 266
San Mateo & Burlingame Exchange: 125
San Mateo Arboretum Society: 275
San Mateo Blues: 192-194, 201, 251
San Mateo Boys' Club: 238
San Mateo Chamber of Commerce: 179, 200, 225, 247, 252, 256
San Mateo City Council: 235, 242-243
San Mateo City Hall: 249
San Mateo City Homestead Assn.: 78
San Mateo Community Hospital: 181
San Mateo County Blood Bank: 226
San Mateo County Board of Supervisors: 55, 92, 101, 235, 248
San Mateo County Community Hospital: 181

INDEX

San Mateo County Fair: 208-209, 221
San Mateo County Gazette: 27, 34, 71
San Mateo County Historical Association: 209, 269, 272, 276
San Mateo County Historical Museum: 244, 248
San Mateo County News: 147
San Mateo Creek: 3, 9, 10, 14, 19, 74, 80, 96, 97, 122, 136
San Mateo Daily News Leader: 170-172, 180
San Mateo Drive: 122, 125, 144
San Mateo Expo Center: 269
San Mateo Flower Show: 208
San Mateo Gardeners' Assn.: 230
San Mateo Gas Light Co.: 102
San Mateo-Half Moon Bay Road: 34, 102
San Mateo-Half Moon Bay Stage: 92
San Mateo-Hayward Bridge: 80, 178, 187-192, 204, 236, 242, 249, 252-254, 267
San Mateo Heights: 124
San Mateo High School: 113, 124, 131, 144-148, 178, 180, 195, 221, 225-226, 249, 259-260, 271, 276-277
San Mateo Homestead: 68
San Mateo House: 20, 26, 28, 29, 41, 54, 61, 145
San Mateo Improvement Co.: 79
San Mateo Investment Co.: 210, 238, 248, 267
San Mateo Junior College: 49, 194, 201-209, 217, 226-227, 238, 245
San Mateo Junior College District: 177
San Mateo Junior Woman's Club: 178, 269
San Mateo Knolls School: 211, 238, 244
San Mateo Land Assn. Building: 135
San Mateo Leader: 122-123, 126, 130, 135, 139
San Mateo Mutual Building & Loan Assn.: 102
San Mateo National Bank: 180
San Mateo News Leader: 146
San Mateo Park: 125, 127, 129, 146, 176
San Mateo Park development: 79
San Mateo Peace Center: 264
San Mateo Planning Commission: 156, 234
San Mateo Point: 109
San Mateo Polo Club: 160
San Mateo Preventorium: 181
San Mateo Public Library: 144, 178, 198, 248
San Mateo Recreation Department: 224
San Mateo Road: 71
San Mateo Rotary Club: 179
San Mateo School District: 67, 124
San Mateo semi-centennial: 225
San Mateo Terrace: 238
San Mateo Theater: 172, 194, 226
San Mateo Times: 74-75, 96, 100, 123, 130-133, 136-137, 170, 178-179, 180-183, 194, 199-200, 233, 239, 250-251, 256, 264, 266
San Mateo Transit: 241
San Mateo Union High School District: 120, 244
San Mateo Villa: 34, 78
San Mateo Villa Tract: 175
San Mateo Village: 238
San Mateo Water Works: 73 146
San Mateo Weekly: 266, 275
San Mateo Woman's Club: 117, 118-119, 144, 148, 155, 159, 178, 204, 251

San Mateo Young Ladies Institute: 58, 62, 64
San Pedro Valley: 9
Sanchez family: 19
Sanchez, José de la Cruz: 14, 33
Sanchez, Norma: 1
Sands, William: 77, 84
Santa Clara Mission: 3
Santa Clara University: 192, 204
Santa Cruz: 56
Sanchez, José de las Cruz: 15
Savage, Reverend M.I.: 60
Save Sugarloaf Committee: 269
Scanlon, Fr. John T.: 218, 250
Schilling, August H.: 115
School busing: 255
Schram, Ralph: 240
Schussler, Hermann: 96-97, 136
Scott, General Winfield: 26
Scott, Stan: 263
Scrap-metal drives: 218
Screaming Eagles: 264-265
Sea Biscuit: 206-207
Sea Scouts: 252
Seagram, S.E.: 30
Seal Slough: 238
Searing, Edward W.: 155
Sears Roebuck: 234
Seaside: 56
Second Avenue: 73, 75-77, 118, 122, 125, 142-144
Secularization of missions: 13-14
Selby, Jesse: 167
Selby, Thomas H.: 61, 63
Selz, Jerome von Braum: 204
Senior Center: 275
Serra Catholic High School: 238
Serra Club of San Mateo: 255
Seven Oaks: 102, 138, 139
Shalshon: 3
Sheaf, Lt. Comm. R.M.: 227
Sheehan family: 119
Sheehan, Bart: 125
Sherwood, Mrs. Charles: 11
Shimada, Sekko: 142
Shimizu, Masazo: 164, 231
Shoemaker, Willie: 250
Shoreview School: 244
Shoreview Shopping Center: 248
Shoreview Tract: 175, 230, 237, 238
Shrewsbury & Smith: 130, 135
Sierra Club: 269
Simmen, Frank: 148, 198-200
Simpkins, E.W.: 100
Sinton, Edgar: 217
Sisson, Texena: 225
Skidmore, James E.: 54
Slot machines: 224
Smith, Austin E.: 23
Smith, Cecil: 187
Smith, Glenn: 264, 275
Smith, L.C.: 164, 211, 236, 238, 242, 255
Smith, Luther: 169
Sneath, R.B.: 61
Soto, S.: 140
South Ellsworth: 40, 65
South San Francisco: 3, 14, 125
Southern Pacific: 41, 77, 132, 133, 135, 136-137, 175, 213
Speers, Carol: 11
Speers, Carrol M.: 242
Spencer Associates, Arch.: 277

Spencer, T.: 65
Spring Valley: 117
Spring Valley Water Co.: 33, 47, 68 73-75, 96, 132, 148
Squatters: 15
Stagecoach lines: 55-56, 132
Stanford University: 33, 263
Stanford, Leland: 39
Stanger, Frank: 11, 21, 28, 209, 218, 221, 227, 248
Stauffer, John: 115
Steffens, Lincoln: 65
Stein, Emil: 198
Steiner, Ruth: 161
Stern, Mrs. Glen: 11
Stern, Sigmund: 116
Stettheimer, Walter: 161
Stockton & Shafter: 26
Stollery, David J.: 200
Stoner, A.L.: 248
Stoner, Harold: 183
Strahle, J.: 63
Strauss, Levi family: 116
Strong, Helen: 211
Sturge Cottage Church: 166
Sturge Presbyterian Church: 230
Sturge, Ernest A.: 164
Sugarloaf: 267-269
Sula, Pablo: 14
Sullivan, Charles: 225
Sullivan, Pauline: 130
Sullivan, W. Mark: 248
Sullivan's restaurant: 225
Sunnybrae School: 243
Sunset magazine: 113, 232
Sunshine Cottage: 239, 266
Sutro's Baths: 180
Swart, Franklin: 198
Swett, Jim: 218
Switzerland: 79

T

Tadeo: 15, 33
Taft and Garretson Co.: 55-56
Taggart, Harold: 209
Takahashi family: 222, 223
Takahashi store: 165
Takahashi, George: 220
Takahashi, Ishie: 230
Takahashi, Kamechiyo: 142
Takahashi, Kenge: 221, 222
Takahashi, M.: 220
Takahashi, Tokutaro: 141, 142
Tamura, Hidematsu: 164
Tanforan internment camp: 222
Tanouye, Sally: 220
Taver, Robert A.: 248
Taylor Estate: 41
Taylor family: 145
Taylor, Bayard: 16, 19, 35
Taylor, Edward: 28, 59, 145
Taylor, Evelyn: 232
Taylor, Fanny: 28
Telegraph: 131
Telephone: 75, 109, 125, 131, 195, 213
Temko, Allan: 245
Temple Beth El: 250
Templeton, Jane: 145
Teshmacher, F.H.: 15
Tevis, Will Jr.: 160
Thayer, Edwin: 149

Thayer, Herbert A.: 197
Thayer, Oscar: 209
Thiebaut, Paul: 193, 251
Third Avenue: 43, 46, 54, 58, 73, 77, 91, 118, 129, 170-174, 241, 255
Thompson, Robert: 100
Thorson, Pete: 109
Three Cities Chamber of Commerce: 175, 183, 187
Thurmond, Thomas: 204
Tibbetts, Ida: 120
Tilton: 81
Tilton Avenue: 52, 60
Tilton family: 52, 53, 120
Tilton house: 52
Tilton, Agnes: 52, 77, 81
Tilton, Etta M.: 52, 122, 124
Tilton, Howard: 91-92
Tilton, John Q. A.: 34, 49, 52
Tilton, Julia: 49
Tilton, Stephen: 49, 52, 59
Time magazine: 248
Times Gazette: 56, 75, 85
Toepke, William: 181, 200
Toll highways: 55
Tongans: 274
Topaz internment camp: 222-223, 229
Tormey, James: 203, 226-227
Tower Road: 49
Towns, Frank C.: 187
Townsend, L.R.: 78
Toyonaka, Japan: 230-231
Treasure Island Fair: 180, 200
Trinta, Manual: 206
Trolley: 132, 136
Trolley service: 125-126
"Tropic Lightning" Division: 252
Truett, Henry B.: 23
Truman, Pres. Harry S.: 236
Trustees: 101, 132, 135, 144, 146
Tucker, Mrs. Nion: 160
Turnbull School: 176, 259
Turnbull, William F.: 145, 176, 199
Turner, T.R.: 112

UV

U.S. Coast Guard Magazine: 227
U.S. Merchant Marine Academy: 227
Uchida, Bishop Koyo: 142
Union Hall: 53
Union Hotel: 73, 92, 135, 159
Union Saloon: 73
United Order of Workmen: 85, 92
United Railroads Co.: 125-127
USO canteens: 223, 225
USO dormitory: 222
Vallejo, Mariano: 26
Van Gorder, A.G.: 124
Van Gundy, Kenneth W.: 247, 253, 254
Van Trees, Frank S.: 120

Van Wyck, Mrs. S.M.: 81
Vancouver, George: 3, 9
Varney, Walter: 187
Vendome: 125
Vernon Terrace: 238
Victorian Days in the Park: 272, 276
Victory Gardens: 225-226
Vietnam War: 263-264
Villa Chartier Restaurant: 267
Villa Hotel: 231, 267
Volstead Act: 159
Voorsanger, Jacob: 118

W

Waggoner, Mrs. Norman: 11
Wahlstrom, Sandra: 256
Walker Hotel: 41, 75, 76, 83
Walker, E.H.: 67
Walker, Hannah Maria: 103
Walker, Mrs. Cyrus: 238
Wallace, George: 120
Walsh, Nick: 120
Wan, Nettie: 75
Wantland, Rae: 189
War bond campaigns: 225
Ward, Bud: 252
Ward, Carl: 263
Warnecke, John Carl: 247, 267
Warren Nellie: 62
Warren, Anna C.: 62
Warren, Earl R.: 62, 204
Warren, J.H.: 62
Warren, Mary F.: 21, 62
Warren, Mrs. J.H.: 31
Warren, Reverend J. H.: 59
Washington, Adm. Thomas G: 189
Waters, Basil: 253
Watkins, Reverend D.F.: 77
Watson, Rev. George Herbert: 64
Wayne, Hugh: 249, 252, 263
Wayne, Hugh A.: 238
Webb, Frank E.: 187
Weeks, W.H.: 172
Weill, Raphael: 102
Weissgerber, Oscar F.: 197-198
Weller, John P.: 102
Wells Fargo & Co.: 27
West Fifth Avenue: 47
Western Addition: 97-99, 109, 124
Western Flying Training Command: 218
Whipple, Josie: 62
Whipple, Mary: 62
Whipple, Sara: 62
Whipple, Stephen B.: 34, 41, 68, 92
Whistman, John: 19
Whitney family: 140
Whitney, Arthur L.: 115, 116
Whitney, C.E.: 115
Whitney, Leslie D.: 116
Widow Pension Law: 121

Wiesender, Julius: 102
Wilder, James: 65
Williams & Westell, arch.: 212
Williams, Andrew: 235
Williams, Barney: 169, 180
Williams, Doris L.: 213
Williams, John T.: 187
Williams, Les: 168-169
Williams, Noah: 166-169, 180
Williams, Robert: 167
Wilsey, E.P.: 160
Wilson, Ernest A.: 198
Wirostes tribelet: 13
Wisnom Building: 135
Wisnom family: 52, 53, 133, 141, 159
Wisnom Hall: 76, 84, 85
Wisnom Hardware:125, 131, 161, 178, 224
Wisnom House: 55
Wisnom, John: 178
Wisnom, Robert: 52-53, 73, 77, 95, 102, 125, 179
Wisnom, Sarah: 53
Wisnom, William: 125
Witch of the Wave: 29
Woman's Club: 204, 251
Women's Golf Tournament: 251
Women's Suffrage Club: 118
Woo Gan, General: 187
Wood, Freeman: 183
Wood, James: 246
Wood, Stanley: 111
Woodlake Apartments: 204, 238, 277
Woodward, Beatrice H.: 145
Wooley & Taft: 96
Wooley, Ruth: 192
World War I: 108, 146-150, 155
World War II: 217-232, 259
Wurster, Bernardi & Emmons Arch.: 238
Wyatt, Roscoe: 187, 209

XYZ

Yamada, Joe: 220
Yamamoto, Tomoko: 164
Yamanouchi family: 222, 230
Yamanouchi, Hasako: 223
Yamanouchi, Tetsuo: 140, 142, 164, 276
Yamanouchi, Yoshiko: 164, 275-276
Yano, Frank: 221
Yano, Warren: 221
YMCA: 233, 277
Yocalo, Evencio: 13, 33, 162
Yokohama Laundry: 140
Yoshida, Tomezo: 140
Young, William: 76
Younger, J. Arthur: 248
Yue, General Wong King: 187
Yuke, Chow: 162
Zelia, J.S.: 59
Zen Buddhism: 141
Zoning ordinance: 198

PREVIOUSLY PUBLISHED BY SCOTTWALL ASSOCIATES:

History of Petaluma, A California River Town
by Adair Lara Heig

Pictorial History of Tiburon, A California Railroad Town
by James Heig

Place Names of Marin
by Louise Teather

Both Sides of the Track
A Collection of Oral Histories from Tiburon and Belvedere
James Heig and Shirley Mitchell, Editors

Mount Tamalpais, A History
by Lincoln Fairley and James Heig

The San Francisco Fair: Treasure Island, 1939-1940
by Patricia Carpenter and Paul Totah

History of Palo Alto: The Early Years
by Pamela Gullard and Nancy Lund

Big Alma: San Francisco's Alma Spreckels
By Bernice Scharlach

Pioneers of California
True Stories of Early Settlers in the Golden State
By Donovan Lewis

California Heartland
A Pictorial History and Tour Guide of Eight Northern California Counties
By Sandra Shepherd

COMING IN 1994

San Mateo: A Centennial History
by Mitchel P. Postel

Hometown San Francisco
A journalist's account of the city from 1910 to 1950
by Jerry Flamm

Mitchell Postel attended San Mateo public schools and College of San Mateo. He received a B.A. degree from the University of California, Berkeley, and an M.A. from the University of California, Santa Barbara. He has served as director of the San Mateo County Historical Association for ten years, and is the author of a half dozen books on local history. He lives in San Bruno with his wife, Kristie, and his son, Conrad, age two.

SATURDAY
MAY 6th, 1922
AT 1:30 P. M.
UNDER A MAMMOTH TENT IN
HAYWARD PARK
CITY OF SAN MATEO

THERE WILL BE OFFERED TO YOU WITHOUT LIMIT OR RESERVE

AT AUCTION

170 BEAUTIFUL LARGE HOMESITES ON THE EASY PAYMENT PLAN OF **170**

$100 ONE HUNDRED DOLLARS DOWN and $10 a Month for an Inside Lot; Corners $150 Down & $15 a Month **$100**

GET FULL DESCRIPTIVE CATALOGUE FROM

BALDWIN & HOWELL　　　　**BARRY & AUSTIN**
318 KEARNY STREET　　SAN FRANCISCO　　409 Amer. Nat. Bank Bldg.

AUCTIONEERS

M. J. CONWAY, 2nd Ave. and B St., SAN MATEO